COMMUNITY IN THE BALANCE

WITHDRAWN
UTSA Libraries

COMMUNITY IN THE BALANCE

Morality and Social Change in an
Indonesian Society

James M. Hagen

Paradigm Publishers
Boulder • London

All rights reserved. No part of the publication may be transmitted or reproduced in any media or form, including electronic, mechanical, photocopy, recording, or informational storage and retrieval systems, without the express written consent of the publisher.

Copyright © 2006 Paradigm Publishers

Published in the United States by Paradigm Publishers, 3360 Mitchell Lane Suite E, Boulder, CO 80301 USA.

Paradigm Publishers is the trade name of Birkenkamp & Company, LLC, Dean Birkenkamp, President and Publisher.

Library of Congress Cataloging-in-Publication Data

Hagen, James M.
  Community in the balance : morality and social change in an Indonesian society / James M. Hagen.
    p. cm.
  Includes bibliographical references and index.
  ISBN 1-59451-078-4 (hc)   1. Manusela (Indonesian people)--Psychology. 2. Manusela (Indonesian people)—Kinship. 3. Manusela (Indonesian people)—Social conditions. 4. Community life—Indonesia—Ceram Island. 5. Social change—Indonesia—Ceram Island. 6. Ceram Island (Indonesia)—History. 7. Ceram Island (Indonesia)—Social conditions. I. Title.
  DS632.M289H34 2005
  306.8'09598'5—dc22

                                                          2005021858

ISBN 1-59451-078-4 (hc)
ISBN 978-1-59451-078-6 (hc)

Printed and bound in the United States of America on acid free paper that meets the standards of the American National Standard for Permanence of Paper for Printed Library Materials.

10 09 08 07 06   1 2 3 4 5

For my mother, Dorothy, and my late father, John

Contents

Preface	ix
Introduction: Community Matters	1
Chapter 1 Maneo History and Settlement	29
Chapter 2 Reckoning Kinship	51
Chapter 3 Espousal, Choice, and Desire	77
Chapter 4 Marriage, Gender, and the Conditions of Sociality	105
Chapter 5 The Good Behind the Gift	131
Chapter 6 Between Faith and Reason	149
Chapter 7 Community in the Visible Spectrum	173
Chapter 8 In the Crucible of Violence	195
Bibliography	213
Index	231
About the Author	237

Preface

Indonesia, the largest nation in Southeast Asia and the fourth largest in the world, covers an area of nearly two million square miles, much of it water, dotted by roughly 17,000 islands. The province of Maluku or the Moluccas, in the remote area of eastern Indonesia, where this study is set, is a microcosm of the nation being similarly dominated by the sea, with population concentrations, like Indonesia as whole, greatest in the coastal areas of the smaller islands.

The Maneo, who live in Maluku and are the focus of this book, reside in six small permanent villages, four inland and two coastal, and in the forests of central Seram, the largest island in the province, and are, thus, doubly distant from the centers of state power and wealth. I visited them first in 1989 and for 20 months between 1992 and 1994. My objective then was to examine Maneo kinship and marriage practices and explore, in a theoretically informed way, the day-to-day travails of living amongst relatives in close proximity: in short, doing the kind of ethnographic project that was common during the first fifty years of modern anthropology.

Alas, social organization does remain central to the book; however, in light of the communal violence between Muslims and Christians that swept through the region beginning as street fights in Ambon, the provincial capital, early in 1999, and continuing over the next two years and intermittently through the time this book has gone to press, I have been compelled to look at local social relations in broader terms. And not only because Maneo, specifically the two Maneo settlements on the south coast of Seram, reside in affected areas—a two-day journey by boat and bus from Ambon. The scope of violence raises important questions about how communities are created in more ordinary times because of the affinities kinship fosters and despite them. For as much as mutuality, a key dimension to community, is enhanced by being related, the day-to-day competing demands of dense, overlapping kin ties and kinship norms can generate conflict and can cause communities to fail—fail to grow like a sand pile sloughing off new grains (which may go unnoticed) or fail catastrophically.

When sectarian violence cut a swath through most of two provinces including Seram, which had been on the margins of most historic disputes of the last 400 years, the suddenness of the escalation stunned both the region's population and outside observers. Likely, those surprised included some of the instigators who helped spark it, perversely achieving what they could not have imagined—some 700,000 Muslims and Christians refugees and roughly 10,000 deaths by the end of the most intensive period of fighting. Although Indonesia as a whole is over 85 percent Muslim, Christians make up half the population of Central Maluku and that balance ensured no quick victory or a clear winner.

As I describe in the last chapter of the book, the rise and perpetuation of violence defies simple explanation. No Slobodan Milosevic stands behind the ethnic and religious antipathies, fueling them, orchestrating a Balkans-like collapse. Perpetrators there were, but on a smaller scale, and their machinations depended on mass frenzy and a mob to mobilize. The crowd's susceptibility to violence was induced by conditions undermining and distending relations with one another, including religious others; to understand this change in civil society, I focus on the concept of community. Admittedly, between Maneo and the opposing camps in the battle in Maluku, the circumstances of the groups' formations could not be more different. In some respects, the violence in Maluku represents the antithesis of the low-level divisiveness and strained amicability characterizing certain dimensions of Maneo social experience I write about here. For Maneo, so entangled in kinship they place little significance in being Maneo, blind to the community forest, so to speak, for all the kinship trees, community is relevant as a practical concern. A Maneo community is less an idea there than a site for a series of kinship interactions (and the deep memory of those interactions) in need of managing. Their relations are recurrent, dense, and overlapping; many can chart ties to neighbors in multiple ways. While they certainly would fight on behalf of kin, Maneo would sooner scatter than defend some collective representation. Conversely, for residents in and around Ambon where the fighting began and was most intense, religious affiliations have become the basis for defining boundaries. But within the opposing camps, affinities defined by a shared religious identity tend to be shallow and untested and the solidarity of 'members' merely assumed.

How could communal movements have become mobilized so destructively with so little warning? As several Indonesian scholars (notably Tamrin Tomagola and George Aditjondro) have reported, outside provocateurs, allies of former president Suharto's family in particular, sparked the fighting by training, arming, and financing combatants. When the fighting lulled, their agents fired off rounds and set fires to heighten tensions. Most ordinary citizens were simply bystanders caught in the crossfire. Even citizens quick to wield spears and machetes at the outset of the fighting likely did so, I believe, for the symbolic effect of the display. They had not necessarily intended to murder but to demonstrate solidarity, to be seen as fierce, and to convince themselves of the righteousness of the cause. By this account, crowds were pawns; even thugs like the Ambonese hired to protect Chinese gaming establishments in Jakarta, whose return coincided with the beginning of the fighting, were not soldiers—although the opposite is often claimed. Some militia members were coerced into fighting. A number of Butonese migrants in Ambon who had been forced to flee during the early phases of fighting to a distant homeland their parents or grandparents had left generations earlier were shamed into returning as militia members. Additionally, though the partisanship of the army (Muslim) and police (Christian) is well-documented, I also heard credible reports of soldiers abandoned by commanding officers without food or pay and thus forced to turn to locals for support, eventually taking their side in the combat. That they did so out of gratitude and not religious zealotry does not minimize their culpability, but it does demonstrate how processes beyond people's control propelled them into taking actions they would not otherwise choose to take.

I am more interested in how, among civilians, susceptiblity grew to the blandishments of extremists and in how residents developed a hypersensitivity to perceived and in some cases historically distant injustices, despite the long record of relatively amicable Muslim and Christian interactions, friendships, and marriage. Civilian attitudes were critical. Even after polarization began in the early months of 1999, the disentegration of civil society was not inevitable; the causal significance of religious difference could not be inferred from the violence done ostensibly in the name of religion. The shifts in religious affiliations centuries ago cited as one source of friction, the perceived regional political dominance of Christians, and the emergence of a more political Islam, gloss over more immediate cross-cutting ethnic, territorial, linguistic, and class differences. Indeed, there are countless examples of cooperation and inter-religious solidarity. Muslims and Christians have married back and forth, not always with the blessing of kin, but usually, in the end, adding to reserves of mutual understanding. Such marital disputes offered practice in ways to negotiate more serious enmities. Even if religious differences remained stark, they could be observed without incitement to action. Muslims and Christians in Maluku have shared much of their history, and many of their formal associations have included members of both faiths. For instance, Muslims struggled on behalf of the unsuccessful movement to create a separate nation for South (and Central) Maluku (Republik Maluku Selatan or RMS) in the early years of Independence (1949-53). This, despite the fact propagandists now contend it was entirely a Christian campaign, spreading the absurd notion that Christian attacks in the current fighting have been coordinated by RMS insurgents in Holland decades after its defeat. But ironically, as tension arose, sharing so much left only religious divisions to be exploited for the purpose of destabilizing the region—the result of which has been to make the fissure between Muslims and Christians seem more intractable and deeper.

At this point, to restore civility requires acknowledging that outside provocateurs did their work so effectively the situation on the ground, the loss of trust and mutual respect, has superseded what even a fully effective justice system (if one did exist in Indonesia) could possibly remedy. Some citizens have taken efforts to bridge religious divides, to maintain lines of communication, informally and through organizations in Jakarta and elsewhere, and to provide, in some instances, shelter for religious others at considerable risk to themselves and their families. In addition, beyond the cessation of hostilities, restoring peace demands understanding how ordinary people have become complicit in it and how everyday practice divided along religious lines works against reconciliation as the routineness of separation, though unavoidable in the short run, becomes habit. To say this is not to criticize or lay blame but to point out the fragility of civil life when risks entailed by doing well for others increase—risks otherwise ignored in more ordinary times.

The major thesis throughout the book is that civil collapse needs to be understood against the forbearance that kept disputes, disagreements, and fights from becoming riots in the past. Herewith, analysis of Maneo social life can shed light on the wider religious conflict that has swept the region. Comparison is instructive particularly insofar as the four isolated mountain settlements where my wife Jennie and I spent over half the twenty months of fieldwork lack effective institutions for adjudicating disputes and lie beyond the reach of the Indonesian state. In the mountains, the seemingly random movement of people who survive by hunting, foraging, and shifting agriculture and whose lives are thoroughly entangled in those of others, in fact, yields a kind of civility, a subtle balancing and adjusting of mutual expectations and understandings. A sense of civility imbues in people a practical awareness and sensitivity to the concerns of others around them. It emerges out of people's proximity and shared experiences. In the sense that Maneo relations with one another are relatively unmediated by the state, what happens between them offers a microcosm of everyday civil relations and practices within the larger and more urban community too minute to be subject to state interference or sanction. The reality (and key principle of civil life) is that no Maneo can order another to trust and cooperate. They have to persuade others, assuage any ill feelings, and manifest goodwill. The fact they can chart kin ties to so many others offers no guarantee of harmony; indeed, to some extent and in some relationships, tension is inevitable. For example, among brothers (real and categorical) far more passes between them than is mandated by the terms of siblingship. They are not told how generous to be, and they are under no obligation to reciprocate. Yet because of their proximity to one another, brothers—who tend to stay put—find themselves in the position of having to compete, head to head, over the resources they share. In a way, male sibling relations are paradigmatic of Maneo community relations more generally. The proximity that makes them vulnerable to each other also reflects their reliance and their understanding of the stakes if they do not manage to cooperate in certain areas of everyday life.

The tenor of relations ebb and flow; on one end of the continuum, community begins where understanding and empathy are tested and enhanced, where people's experiences with one another foster some tolerance. On the other end, community ceases at the point where such perspicuity is lost and the requisite sensitivity to difference—difference of opinion or difference in ethnicity or religion—is no longer sustainable. Or, to put the matter in more concrete terms, the terminus represents the point where community is transformed; it contracts in terms of the kinds of interactions and differences that can be accommodated—a paradoxical shrinking alongside numerical expansion—where difference comes to be perceived as an uncontrollable threat. I realize that to suggest that moral perspicuity represents another casualty of the conflict in central Maluku on par with the loss of life and property, and the accompanying physical and emotional suffering might seem an incongruous proposition. Does it not misconstrue the way sentimentality is appropriated in the service of power—specifically, in the service of those who have it and wish to preserve it? While such a possibility exists, skepticism risks conflating the objectification, representation, and codification of community responsiveness with the endowment that operates veiled, behind moral practice. Sentimentality may reflect some deeper concern over or empathy for the well-being of others. If this magnanimity, against more selfish desires and parochial interests, is never revealed entirely, it is because people are so often denied the chance to foster it. In the present context of civil life in Maluku, warfare has cut away at the hard-won ground of trust, tolerance, and civility. If, as I believe, Maneo preserve religious tolerance, though most are Christian, it is because they posit local origins for both Islam and Christianity. To deny this and contradict history would mean confronting others (Maneo and non-Maneo) as strangers; it would eliminate an effective way to foster civility among those who do not necessarily know each other or have reason to mistrust.

My perspective on this mutual understanding is Aristotelian. What drew me to Aristotle, first through his interlocutors (especially Alasdair MacIntyre and Martha Nussbaum), is the way he frames community as an ongoing project and not as principles or representations instantiated. He was interested in the polis (the city-state). But to say that a community (koinoneia) formed a polis was merely to recognize that its practices and organization had the overall coherence that qualified it as a political unit (Toulmin 1990:67), which could be variably defined. While Aristotle's observations regarding morality and politics were directed against Plato among others, they apply as well to Emile Durkheim's widely influential research on community. Durkheim theorized that people conjure representations of community from associations of minds—images that supersede those associations as totalities greater than the sums of their parts ([1915]1965). In arguing this, however, he assumes the efficaciousness of community symbols that move people to action—an influence that ought to be demonstrated. As Robert Belah (1973:xix) observes, Durkheim's quest to establish an empirical basis to Kantianism, led him to discover the equivalent of the metaphysical imperative in people's observance of obligations and norms. He believed people cooperated because they had to, and that the strength of people's ties was a function of rituals of affirmation or integration. That emphasis is misplaced; obligation describes only one dimension of people's commitment to one another, at most serving as a kind of salve on the vicissitudes of social life, offering limited perspective on the elusive domain of moral practice. People may have such obligations but have reason not to observe them. Social solidarity cannot be mandated; it is not a quality present or absent. Rather, it is engendered in the negotiation of differences in everyday practice, not from the apprehension of high-minded principles or axioms. The Maneo, lacking the institutional means for mediating the disputes, nonetheless manage to negotiate those disagreements most of the time. They understand that more unites them then divides them. Eventually, a similar realization may overcome the fear and hostility that besets a divided Moluccan society. Admittedly, my understanding of community emerges from the particulars of Maneo experience at a relatively peaceful and prosperous time for them in the mid-1990s. But much of Maneo moral life centers on instilling tolerance during times of crisis when it is really needed, and to hasten the return to civility. Having traveled throughout much of central Maluku, I am convinced this moral perspicuity and is widely held.

Notes on Methodology

I first traveled to west and central Seram in 1988 and again the following year looking for places to conduct research. In a sense, Maneo sort of selected me by being such wonderful hosts when I arrived in 1989 by trail from Manusela and Kabohari from the west. It was a joy to return there three years later in 1992 for 20 months research. Not only the people but the location appealed to me because it was so out of the way, east of Manusela National Park, a backwater within a backwater. Even the nineteenth-century scientist Alfred Wallace (Darwin's contemporary and cofounder of the theory of evolution), who traveled many places throughout his six-year sojourn in the region, never made it into the interior of Seram. What appealed, too, was that although remote, the Maneo did not constitute an enclave community. They seemed to embrace aspects of the outside; literally, they were moving to do so. Nearly 400 people, about half the known Maneo population, now live on the south coast, a two-day walk over rugged terrain from the mountain settlements from whence they came beginning some three generations earlier. In addition, most Maneo were Christian, their parents and grandparents having abandoned their animist beliefs and practices gradually over a period of decades the first half of the twentieth century. Christian Maneo and those living on the coast were certainly no less Maneo for converting and leaving; their subsistence, kinship, and marriage practices are little different from the mountains.

Jennie and I divided our time between the four mountain and two coastal settlements. For logistical reasons, we spent more time in the villages of Maneo Rendah in the mountains and Maneo Ratu on the coast, traveling every few weeks to other, neighboring settlements. While the data presented, particularly the stories and anecdotes, reflect our choice of residence, I do not believe different choices would have changed the conclusions reached. (Over the course of the field work, I did manage to spend at least a month in each of the settlements.) I collected several types of data. From approximately thirty sources, I compiled fairly comprehensive genealogies of most Maneo, at least those from the villages. Some Maneo live in the forest permanently and would flee at our approach; some of these individuals appeared in the genealogies, but, I suspect, many more did not. Jennie and I gathered basic census data on residents of the six villages, although this did prove difficult given the movement of people to the forest and to clove orchards near the coast for extended periods of time. In addition, we interviewed approximately seventy-five people regarding specific details of their marriages—that is, about choices of spouse, about the circumstances by which marriages came into being, about property exchanges that accompany and facilitate nearly all Maneo marriages, and about what happens afterwards in terms of where the couple lives and with whom. Because of the intricacies of Maneo kinship, answers to questions of relatedness were rarely simple, straightforward, or true to type. Finally, histories of two types were collected: oral histories of the lives of most Maneo elders (over fifty years of age) and the mythic, distant histories of Maneo origins. I learned as much of the latter as my teachers felt comfortable telling me.

Many of these interviews, particularly about kinship and marriage, were structured. Of course, much of what goes into a study of this sort comes from informal conversation, observation, and gossip. Initially, interviews and conversations were conducted in Ambonese-Malay, a regional variant of Indonesian as opposed to the local language; nearly everyone is bilingual. In fact, many of the young were more proficient speaking Ambonese-Malay than Upa'a (the local language), identified as Patakai-Manusela (Stokhof 1981). Church services and school (there was a sekolah dasar or elementary school in the mountains) were both conducted in more formal Indonesian, and students could be punished for speaking the local language. In addition, many parents spoke only Ambonese-Malay to their children. Being considered children of sorts ourselves, people often responded to us in the regional language even when we addressed them in Upa'a.

Ambon, the provincial capital of Maluku, lies two days travel from Maneo on the coast, two more from the mountain villages. We spent a fair amount of time there securing permission from government offices, meeting with sponsors at Universitas Pattimura, obtaining supplies, and so forth. We grew close to the family who owned the guesthouse in Tanah Tinggi; we knew people in the neighborhood; and we often met acquaintances from Seram who traveled and schooled there. It is something of a stereotype, but resident Ambonese, even immigrants, were quick to make friends as a statement of regional character (gaya Ambon) against the stereotypical reservedness of the nation's majority Javanese population. Because of this openness, even in the best of times, Ambon would never be confused for a harmonious place. Residents ascribed little virtue to the outward projection of calm. Since the riots, I have had to follow developments from afar, relying on reports from various Indonesian and English language newspapers, from several Web sites, and discussions with refugees and scholars in Jakarta and in the United States. Travel to the province was too dangerous when I last visited Indonesia in 2000. My own battle with muscular dystrophy, which was only diagnosed after my initial fieldwork, made travel to other places on the edge of the fighting too difficult to undertake.

Fieldwork (1992–94) was sponsored by LIPI (the Indonesian Institute of Science) and by Universitas Pattimura in Ambon and was made possible with support from the National Science Foundation (Award No. BNS-9113447), the Fulbright-Hays Doctoral Dissertation Abroad Program (Award No. P022A20004), the Wenner-Gren Foundation for Anthropological Research, and the L.S.B. Leakey Foundation. Support for earlier trips came from the Center for South and Southeast Asian Studies (CSSEAS) at the University of Michigan and from the Margaret Wray French Scholarship Fund. Later funding for travel, writing, and thinking came from a Taft Postdoctoral Fellowship at the University of Cincinnati and a Mellon Foundation Fellowship in anthropological demography at the Population Research Institute at Penn State University.

A large number of people contributed significantly to the project, not all of whom can be mentioned, and none of whom can be held responsible for the shortcomings contained herein. Ray Kelly, Robert Hagen, Tom Fricke, Nancy Florida, Skip Rappaport, Ken George, Chris Duncan, Sue Trainor, Scott Camazine, Peter Just, Alan Feinstein, Rob Valkenier, Kyle Latinis, Helen Stern, Ferry Nahusona, Dave Tatem, and Dave Akin have all helped the project at various stages and in various ways. Valerio Valeri and Roy Ellen, both of whom have conducted extensive research on Seram over a period of three decades, were also generous in their advice and encouragement; Jim Collins has been a friend as well as an advisor on all things Maluku. In Indonesia, I benefited from the kindness, and comments of Tamrin Tomagola and Iman Prasodjo who kept me alert to the broader and more recent context of religious and ethnic conflict. Chapter 2 is little changed from an article that appeared in Volume 26, No. 1, of the American Ethnologist ©1999 by The American Anthropological Association; it is reprinted here by permission of the University of California Press. Chapter 5 is reprinted from an essay that appeared in Volume 5, No. 3 of the Journal of the Royal Anthropological Institute ©1999. (The map of Ambon in chapter 8 is reprinted courtesy of the University of Texas Libraries, The University of Texas at Austin.) Arguments in these and other chapters have been strengthened from comments and question after lectures at the University of Cincinnati, Reed College, University of Oregon, University of Connecticut, Cornell University, Yale University, and Stanford University.

In Ambon, Jennie and I enjoyed the hospitality of Jan and Irene Hekkers, who made us feel like honored guests as well and members of their family. I also wish to thank Bishop Sol for graciously allowing us use of the library. Of course, I owe an enormous debt of gratitude to the people of Maneo for all the kindness, hospitality, and patience they showed us. Our research kept us on the move between the various Maneo settlements, so the thanks we owe to all the residents of these places who have helped us is too extensive to acknowledge on an individual basis and too profound to be expressed with mere words. In particular, though, I wish to thank a few of our teachers, hosts, and kin, Minggus Tamala, Feris Boiratan, Simpson Boiratan, Miram Ipapoto, Tomas Tamala, Tenchis Ipapoto, Pede Tamala, Miki Kohonusa, Lefe Boiratan, Marianus Ipapoto, Obed Boiratan, Alleta Halamuri, Josua Ipaana, Naomi Boiratan and Jafid Halamuri. Special thanks, too, to Guru Lukas Rehena and his family. Finally, Jennie Sternhagen and I were together in Maneo for about three-quarters of the period of field work (fifteen months). Over the course of the next decade, with the joyous distraction of Peter and Sam, I did the writing, but the work here is truly a collaborative effort. To the extent the various arguments and analyses succeed in making sense, it is a testament to her involvement in all aspects.

Preface xvii

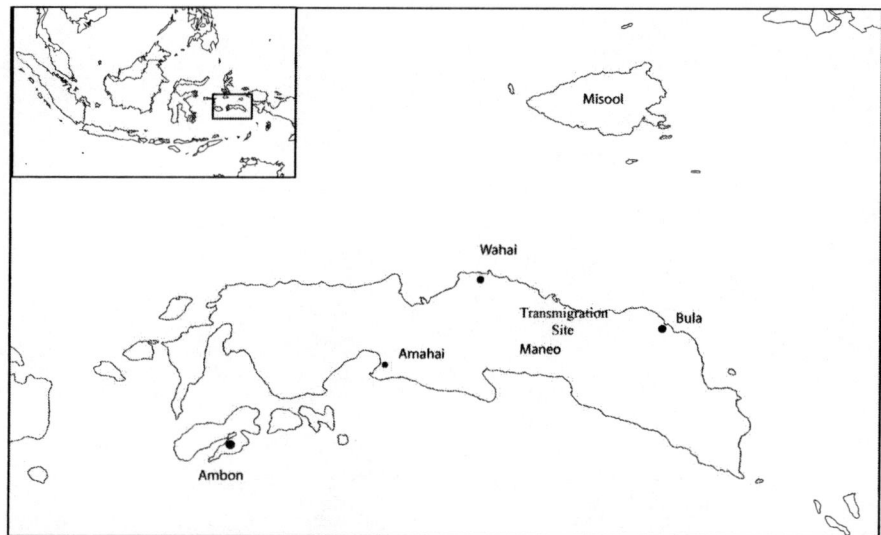
Figure 1. Seram and Southeast Asia

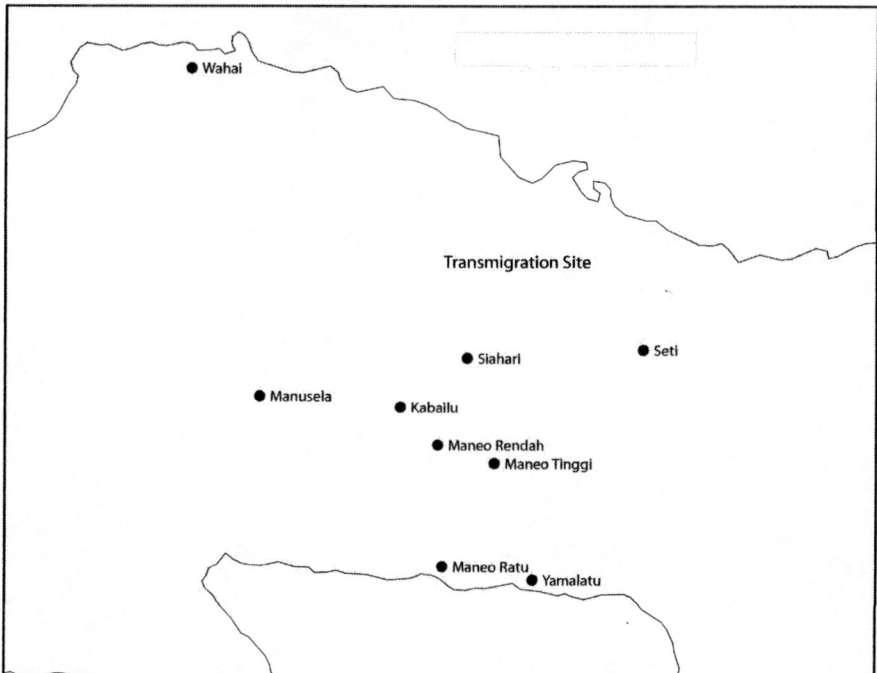
Figure 2. Central Seram

Introduction

Community Matters

In the modern world, moral authorities are proof of a society's inability to live a decent life." Lev Timofeyev in an interview with David Remnick in "Deep in the Woods: Solzhenitsyn, a new book, and the new Russia."

In June 1992, Jennie and I passed through the Transmigration site of Samal Baru on Seram's north central coast on our way to the village of Siahari, the northernmost Maneo settlement. We remained in Siahari for about two weeks before moving into the mountains. For reasons we could not immediately fathom, the place seemed odd. It contained ten houses, all but one of which seemed occupied at the time, and I counted some 30 residents. Only later, on subsequent visits, did we realize that the settlement is generally empty except on Saturdays and Sundays; the only house consistently occupied lay some 100 meters outside the village. People stayed when we were there because they were curious to see what we would do. When we departed for the mountains, much to their relief, I am sure, they left too, most of them returning to the Transmigration site we had recently passed through.

This was not an isolated occurrence. The disappearing act was repeated to varying degrees in the other three mountain Maneo settlements. We would arrive announced at a full village only to discover a virtual ghost village on unannounced return trips. The pattern of abandonment defied simple explanation. Siahari had a church, but then so did the Transmigration site where many lived during the week. Why did they not stay and celebrate services there? Elsewhere in the mountains, when people left for the forest, Sunday worship failed to bring them back. They remained apart for longer periods of time depending on the season. Many residents in the mountain villages left during the dry season, roughly May through September, and quite a few went to tend to and harvest cloves from orchards on the mountainside above the south coast of the island. But even in these settlements, dispersal did not follow economic interests entirely, nor was it necessitated by a subsistence regime dominated by hunting and foraging. If it did, and shifting settlements were the norm, mobility would leave unexplained the presence of permanent settlements and the fact that some Maneo tend to stay put. Maneo easily meet subsistence needs by processing the pith of sago palms, whether they live in permanent villages or not (Ellen 1978). What little amounts of cash they need to live in the mountains they can obtain in various ways that do not require prolonged absence. The Maneo have the flexibility to live anywhere, and they are capable of living with anyone, even by themselves. Yet without the experience of living together in villages they might have ceased to be, dispersed, or joined nearby groups (such as Kabohari and Manusela to the west and Seti to the east) and disappeared as a distinct people.

The question of Maneo residence exposes deeper issues of community. In its root form (Latin *communis* meaning common), the term refers to a group that holds things or principles in common, which may arise because of shared origins and de facto differences between different groups, or that occupy a common territory. Interaction, proximity, and intention are all central to the definition, but what accounts for community in the first instance?[1] If proximity is central, then, for a community of people to exist there should be some minimal level or frequency of coresidence—a certain number of nights spent nearby—below which it ceases. Either Siahari (the first Maneo village we stayed in) should not count as a community or, less satisfactorily, it might be considered a 'postcommunity' (Ortner 1997)—except for the fact that people continue to congregate there even if they do so for shorter periods and for different, ostensibly more religious reasons than in the past. Nor does language, custom or myth distinguish Maneo from neighboring groups; territories might have been divided differently and the communities of central Seram might have aggregated in other ways.

The contingency of Maneo community invites a novel approach: to see it as an effect of such facts as place of birth and descent that incline people to certain practices, delimiting realms of possibility, and as the objects of one's sympathies and attachments. As an object and consequence of choice, residential instability may indicate a weak sense of belonging. Indeed, Maneo, who include roughly 1,000 people (759 of whom reside in the six villages, with the remainder living permanently in the forest), offered few if any pronouncements of collective identity and hosted few celebrations where a local collective identity was asserted. Their identities, instead, are invested and embodied in kinship relations that cross village boundaries and span even linguistic and ethnic differences. At once expansive, kin relations are also highly particular and tend to mire people in complex, overlapping responsibilities that militate against common expressions of identity. Kinship does not negate community, however. There is no necessary tradeoff between the lived dyadic network of kin ties and a more diffuse communal solidarity or, rather, to the extent there is, it results from certain untested assumptions regarding people's orientations: that the existence of the image of the group as a whole and a sense of collective identity prefigures people's commitment to it.

To advance conceptual understanding of community it is necessary to examine the contexts in which it is talked about. For Maneo, community describes the site for interactions, typically freighted with certain kinship and affinal (in-law) obligations and entanglements. More social than geographic, people's encounters are situational; they meet, parry, and riposte on the uneven terrain of social relations. Community is a product of these encounters inasmuch as other tangential relations are brought into play and help set the stage for other interactions. It has a temporal dimension. But as Maneo, especially Maneo men, talk about it, living together poses endless dilemmas. The demands of sharing and the surveillance that comes from houses in close proximity with thin, porous walls, and children everywhere who serve as spies, makes the idea of life apart enormously appealing. Some complain of the general onerousness of community norms. Others refer to more personal animosities and express a desire to live apart from specific others. While there is a rough agreement between what people say and do in terms of residence, the constraints and compromises described would seem to provide strong disincentive to form permanent communities at all. The positives do not seem quite positive enough. Admittedly, they may come together to use others for their own ends, but communities composed of self-interested individuals would likely be short-lived, subject to constant shifting membership. Such groups may not even constitute communities, bearing more a resemblance to markets, where relations are temporary, anonymous, and agonistic. With the alternative of living apart so pleasant, and with so little apparently keeping people together, we have to ask why Maneo should even bother residing in villages.

In Eudemian Ethics, Aristotle raises this very issue: "the choice to live with others might seem, from a certain point of view silly" (1984:EE 12245a10–19). He suggests, as I do here, that the basic fact of association cannot be assumed. Somewhat unsatisfactorily, Aristotle speculates that people live together because of the pleasure they find in doing so, comparing cud chewing among cows in a herd to speech among people—speech which is as much part of our human endowment compelling us to seek others. Certainly, Maneo are not inured to the pleasures of company, and some talk (and not to themselves) of the tedium of living alone in the forest. Yet Maneo complaints about community, if we are to take them seriously, pose a more complex set of motives and influences: that in being thrown together, *Survivor*-like, the object is to avoid being voted off the island and to manage the best they can.[2] That is, they wish to associate and cannot help it. On the one hand, if being and belonging with others is a deeply ingrained disposition, talk about life apart is largely a fiction. On the other hand, wariness tempers the comfort people derive from others, for to live together and to ally with others poses a number of complex choices. The immediacy of these choices and the proximity of people to one another, Hannah Arendt observes (1959:182), gives social experience a certain perilousness.

Precisely because residence patterns cannot be explained by economic or political necessity or pleasure—Maneo have kin or affines in most villages and can survive on their own in the forest—decisions about where to live and with whom offer insight into the way trust and mutuality are fostered against uncertainty. As mere coresidence offers no guarantee of magnanimity, the persistence of community is partly determined by and reflects the tenor or quality of people's relations. In recognition, Maneo perceive the challenge of community life as minimizing (or at least not exacerbating) uncertainty, not with the aim of eliminating the dilemmas of social life altogether, which are everywhere, but managing them more successfully. Community, thus, for them is a proposition that depends on the highly variable success of strategies to facilitate amicability and contain the inevitable disputes. Comments on the possibility of living apart belie the fact that for them the almost Rousseauian idea of the solitary life of the forest dweller is largely imagined and creatively so as a comment on social life. Similarly, I suspect that those estimated 250 Maneo (or one quarter of the population) in the forest, in fact, live with others, though in perhaps smaller groups than in the villages. Even when villagers do live apart, which they might do for limited periods, they take with them the accumulated experiences of prior associations and expectations of future ones. Indeed, they really only confront choices between different forms of association—although outside the village they may reduce the number of chance interactions with specific others. Choosing where to live is really a choice of whom to live with. (In Maneo, where everyone is related, strangers do not really exist.) Such decisions invariably entangle persons in any number of relationship dilemmas that force them to balance competing demands, to choose whom to support and to what extent, and to weigh the inevitable consequences of slighting others. The cumulative effects of these day-to-day decisions determine overall levels of suspiciousness or magnanimity. In large part it is because of individual efforts to allay concerns and project confidence in one's neighbors and kin that voluntary societies like Maneo persist. The other option is to minimize encounters. For Maneo, living where they do, near broad expanses of sparsely populated mountainous terrain, the possibility of retreating to the forest in times of turmoil is crucial. I am convinced that choosing to scatter, as Maneo have at various times in the recent past, is more than a simple act of self-preservation. They do not flee to the forest because they fear losing if open conflict erupts, but rather because they recognize that when tensions abate they will go back to being neighbors. Scattering, as I will discuss in chapter 7, is part of a strategy to avoid misunderstanding.

Dispersal is evidence of a practical wisdom. Skill in discerning the possible consequences of seemingly innocuous and disconnected actions, to engage others or retreat from them as the situation warrants, enables the Maneo to foster a sense of community. The ability is exercised through certain rhetorical practices, in the stories they tell, and in conventions they observe. Of course, perspicuity is difficult to observe, as it is not easy to discern whether others are acting judiciously or selfishly, for instance, whether they flee from one another out of fear or understanding.[3] Moreover, the equanimity that helps fashion a sense of Maneo community is most apparent when it wanes. When perspicuity wanes, communities may atrophy; they may disappear, or, perhaps more ominously, they may mobilize. As communities mobilize, the nature of people's associations transform; their relations go from being sites of interaction and the focus of negotiation—communities "at rest," as Leo Strauss said (1964)—to being the reason for concerted and often violent communal action—communities "in motion." In this shift, and contributing to it, the moral ground of action becomes dangerously constricted. Of course, communities possess other ways of responding to challenges depending on political organization and leadership. Nor is mobilization per se in the defense of collective identity the root of social enmity. Communal hatreds can be inflamed in a variety of ways. What mobilization does, however, is help make such collective violence possible. Most communities, most of the time, do not ask much or, alternatively, lack the capacity to mobilize members in the kind of concerted action that would suspend or efface individual differences. In Maneo, mobilization is hindered by the difference and social distance manifest in kin interactions; the attention given to, and the constant maneuvering of persons in their relations with others impedes the emergence of a shared identity. As in countless other seemingly inert villages so far outside the fray of communal movements (though this zone is shrinking and only ever partial), mobilization may be resisted further because nothing urgent makes differences with outsiders consequential.[4] That is, tolerance may be cultivated as a part of a repertoire of practices that serve as the moral counterweight to the excesses and political machinations of would-be leaders. In this sense, Maneo political life can be observed as an expression of moral sensibilities, not (thwarted) competition over power.

More than a set of strong or weak orientations, community describes a continuum of movement. In extreme cases, differences are collapsed and expressions of individual preferences and personal liberties largely eliminated. Recall the political engineering debacle perpetrated by Khmer Rouge leaders in Cambodia who sought to instill solidarity through mass murder. Forcing children, as they did, to kill their parents was intended to eliminate contravening kinship-created difference. Plans drawn from failed modernist experiments and largely discarded blueprints of social possibility imbued Khmer Rouge leaders with confidence that if people could be united and differences crushed, then, broader transformations would follow (Scott 1998). Yet the means they employed—sowing terror and undermining trust—were the only lasting effects of the experiments. More recently, the luster of such nationalist schemes has faded, and smaller cult experiments remain perpetually short-lived and marginal. Yet in their stead, in the last two decades, xenophobia and ethnic antipathy have arisen out of the failed state policies and global market dependencies, and, in some cases, supplanted the high-minded state goals of inclusive citizenship (Anderson 1991 [1983]:7, 143–44). People have sought relief in communalism; and, in some cases, they have been led to it through deliberate incitement. During the latter half of his reign (1967–1998), Indonesia's former president, Suharto, cynically encouraged cultural expressions of ethnic and religious difference to prevent mobilization on other, more class-based grounds that were perceived as more threatening at the time (Kipp 1993). In the end, that strategy depleted reserves of civil tolerance and helped unleash a tide of communal violence, most disastrously in Maluku (Hefner 2000:70–80). Once the cycle of attack and revenge began, there was no ground for negotiation. Moral perspicuity shrank, public expressions of tolerance were driven underground, and random events and accidents were overblown or even fabricated and got lumped together as instances of concerted attack. As I describe in chapter 8, communalism emerged from the collapse of civil life, and its emergence, particularly as crowd movements, hastened it (Tambiah 1996). Yet settlement clusters of ethnically and religiously homogenous peoples are not perforce predisposed to mob violence, nor are communal movements fashioned whole cloth out of disconnected persons. Rather, the impetus is evinced in and, in part, derives from changes in people's relations—changes they may resist. It is with respect to this resistance wherein the significance of Maneo community lies.[5]

The Object

Most analyses approach community by exploring its representations, that is, how communities are perceived and imagined, and how the images bear on the identity and actions of members. Communities are perceived as embodied by their members and objectified by the boundaries around them that in turn make certain properties, such as territory, their own. People see communities as bounded and opposed. They possess communities (their own) because communities lay claim to them.[6] In this way, people become signs of their communities, socially distinct, named and categorized, and rendered the object of attachment, or the opposite. Communities like villages (*desa*) or neighborhoods (*kampung*) are codified and ascribed a place in political society to effect administrative control and study. Of course, people experience belonging differently and to varying degrees—a point I will consider below. Less ambiguously, people (outsiders) are perceived to emerge from their social milieus stamped indelibly by their associations; their identities become thoroughly suffused by the groups from which they come. Individuals are vessels of community, to the point that there are no disconnected aspects of identity, and even the most personal signifiers carry such collective traces. So deep is the community stamp that people's capacities are seen as determined entirely by them; that is, people are seen as innately generous or stingy, suspicious or trusting depending on their collective affiliations.

Yet people never belong entirely. From an individual's perspective, communities are composed of collections of others distinct from one's self whom those individuals necessarily see themselves similar to and apart from, as one among many. In reality, belonging to multiple communities, as nearly everyone does, further divides people's identities, orientations, and interests. In addition, at times, belonging can be emotionally fraught as people alternatively embrace, resist (usually futilely), and accede to the terms of collective membership. The sense of belonging that induces feelings of camaraderie among some may also fuel darker sentiments of redundancy, substitutability, and alienation.[7] Belonging presupposes a negotiation over terms that necessarily frames any description of the substance or quality of people's social ties. Membership, by itself, implies little about the trust and commitment people bring to others. Belonging may give confidence in others, but closeness is relative and relatives are not always close.

Representations of community reveal little of the substance of people's relations. Indeed, invoking a shared substance or form as a basis for community minimizes the give and take of social life and the calculations and determinations that comprise people's experience. Community is taken for granted when it is seen as arising from "ties of blood" (Durkheim 1973:73; cf. Schneider 1984:165–177; cf. Arendt 1959:25); that is, when community is presumed to be a feature of blood and a result of sharing it.[8] The assumption is that shared blood denotes sameness, and people who are the same or at least similar tend to get along. As a result, either conflicts are minimal or, more realistically, being connected to one another gives people resources to effectively manage any disputes among them. In this way, blood proxies for moral understanding. If they failed to negotiate disagreements, some would leave—an option that has some resonance in Maneo mythic history and contemporary life. The problem is that as a substance that people share to varying degrees, blood cannot also serve as a variable in people's orientations towards others since that explanation assumes precisely what it proposes to elucidate. As I will argue in chapter 2, that second cousins should not feel as close as first cousins cannot be explained with reference to blood (specifically to concentrations), for to do so confuses effect—the sentiment generated by such ties—for cause. What blood denotes, instead, is inextricably linked to its status as metaphor, or to what it connotes, closeness (Schneider 1984). For Maneo, invoking shared blood (*lasiae*), not something they do often, represents a strategy, an invitation to others to participate in some action implying, too, that the rejection of such a request means rejecting something more, a shared identity.

Once invoked, the communal or foundational aspect of shared blood becomes patent. It merely needs to be asserted for communities to begin to coalesce. In the fighting in Maluku, for instance, Christian combatants describe themselves as lambs bathing in the blood of Christ, whereas on Laskar Jihad Web sites Muslim militants post bloody images of fallen comrades. Partisans invoke shared blood to mobilize members. Or, conversely, they raise threats against blood's purity to call for collective defense of the group's integrity. And in Maluku, as elsewhere, threats to blood by contamination have served to justify religious and ethnic cleansing and the violent purging of members, typically women and minority subgroups seen as more susceptible (Das 1995). Again, blood comes to represent community, but only insofar as identity is conflated with it. Collapsing identity differences and totalizing them (against the other) in turn eliminates possibilities for extending oneself on behalf of others as others. Such assertions of collective identity de-legitimize difference so that even the expression of heterodox opinions risks indicating some deeper division or loss of conviction—a risk people may be reluctant to bear if their own affinities come into question. As difference is essentialized, the search for common ground is compromised; sameness comes to be defined in ever-narrower terms. People act morally, then, only out of likeness and to the extent they do, moral agency serves mere political ends, often without people being aware of it. Shifts may go unnoticed and levels of tolerance can erode over time. Nor does sameness offer any reprieve from potential conflict; conformity merely generates the appearance of order. In other words, communities reduced to sameness and uniformity, echoing Aristotle's criticism of Socrates's assertion, where order serves as an end in itself, are precarious, imperiled by ever-narrowing definitions of appropriate, identity-specific action and growing dependence on the identification and vilification of outsiders (Aristotle 1984: EE1261a17–25). Such a community's existence depends on movement and mobilization. Solidarity is foisted on members out of fear, and fear compromises the range and openness of people's interactions.

Imagining Solidarity

Even when blood is not invoked, scholars assume the end or telos of social life, particularly ritual, is the generation of solidarity.[9] Order is thought to presume the affinity of persons toward other members and contribute to it. It may be instantiated through a Rousseauian "contract"—an agreement over the terms of engagement—or, less rationally, order may be fostered, as Durkheim proposed, through other "sui generic" forces that transform private sentiments into social ones. Thus, community is evoked and made whole through its representation in ritual. The Durkheimian mechanism is elegantly chemical: the image of community distilled from the action and reaction of individual minds in a way analogous to the neural firings that generate individual perceptions. "In such a combination, with the mental alterations involved, [private sentiments] become ... a whole, exterior to the mind" (Durkheim 1953:24–26). Conjuring the whole induces an ecstatic condition that dissolves internal divisions allowing participants and observers to identify one another as one and the same (Turner 1969:104). The assumption is that without this transformation people would be cast adrift, and they would cease to be members.

As with "natural" communities, there are several reasons to question the efficacy and sufficiency of ritual as an explanation. Often, the collective component of ritual tends to be exaggerated (Valeri 1990a:72); moreover, the effects—the images of community generated—are not necessarily perceived. Some may fail to see the forest for all the trees. This is not to deny that ritual may instill a sense of solidarity at some level, for instance, by reversing social conventions that apply at other times. But it is indisputable, too, that ritual performances also chart differences in values and divisions among various participants, and between them and the spectators. More accurately, it could be said, divisions are not rejected in ritual so much as they are transcended in the evanescence of the moment. But as Durkheim himself acknowledged, even as ritual dissolves individual difference such feelings of camaraderie have to be sustained afterwards to have lasting effect. Camaraderie can be preserved through memory, as a "mental fact" (Durkheim 1953:14–15), or, and usually in conjunction with ritual, certain tenets are established that codify behaviors fostering the sanctity of the group otherwise manifest spontaneously in ritual. At most, such religious principles serve as guides; indeed, mandating conviviality and trust may have the opposite social repercussions if standards of conformance are set too high. And in Maneo, even if religion once worked that way, it does so no longer. Most consider themselves Christian, as are nearly all other interior peoples on the island of Seram. For them, ritual serves more expansive religious conceptions of community— the whole of the Protestant Church of Maluku (GPM). Traditional, pre-Christian rituals, such as divination and healing ceremonies (*sanafae*), have been driven out of the villages and into the forests where they are now only occasionally practiced; headhunting has completely ceased. And *husali* (a war dance) is limited to and largely encompassed by Christian holidays (Christmas and Christianized New Years), or performed on state occasions, such as the election of a *kepala desa* (village headman). In these contexts, performances of traditional dances celebrate a Maneo identity (though not solidarity) at the cost of the loss of practices (including local language use) that once distinguished them from neighbors, not just non-Christians (cf. Spyer 2000:250–60).

Are problems of integration of sufficient scope to warrant such ritually induced transcendence? Is solidarity a real problem or largely an effect of the model of community that presupposes it? It is only because community is assumed to be incomplete that individuals require some thoroughgoing transformation in orientations, something outside themselves, to bring it about. In effect, the model of community as representation or object presupposes a constant oscillation between moral collective life, implying mutual identification and subordination to authority, and amoral, self-centered life apart (Turner 1969:128–129; Valeri 1990a). As a result however, community and the individual become hypostasized, tensions appear greater than they are, and processes of negotiation, persuasion, and agreement, the vast middle ground of community civil life, disappears. In this view, people lack what William James called the wisdom of knowing what to overlook. My point is that Maneo do not live apart because of amoral proclivities, although they do impute these tendencies to people who live in the forest. Nor in ritual are people entirely disentangled from the dilemmas and concerns of day-to-day life, including choices about the extent of their participation in rituals and what it means. What ritual (along with myth) does, as Thomas Beidelman ([1986]1993) argues, is exercise people's moral imagination by encouraging them to adopt different perspectives on various supernatural dilemmas and great conundrums to gain insight on the more prosaic ones encountered in daily life.[10] Ritual offers ways to think creatively about conflict, common values, generosity, and conciliation.

The Ephemeral Community

When I traveled through the mountains of West Seram on my first visit to the island in 1988, and even on subsequent trips to central Seram in 1989 and to central and east Seram 1992–94, it was difficult to resist the idea that where there were concentrated signs of people, there would be a village—a village like others, a familiar and somewhat comfortable place. Walking through the apparently empty terrain of the forest (devoid of signs of people), then staggering through gardens, past temporary dwellings, and finally into the clearing of the village, I wanted to believe that all paths led there, even if I got lost. This equation of a place with a community is a difficult one to shake. In fact, paths near settlements traverse in all different directions; village communities are frequently dispersed. Maneo, as noted, often spend more time apart at somewhat isolated, ramshackle garden dwellings. Yet where they interact they form a community (see also Just 2001:96).

The indeterminateness of community is an important theme of Anna Tsing's (1993) remarkable analysis of people she calls the Meratus of Kalimantan, Indonesia—a people somewhat more peripatetic than Maneo. Tsing notes that the Indonesian state had sought to settle them, with mixed success, in permanent residences. Like the Maneo, their willy-nilly movement frustrated state plans to impose order in this remote backwater region of the nation. But the perceived wildness of these groups also offered the state a convenient justification for promoting Indonesia's Transmigration program, a massive resettlement campaign based, in part, on the proposition that if indigenous populations of the outer islands like the Meratus and the Maneo could not be trusted to embrace Indonesianess, then, the state would supplant them numerically with people whose affinities and identities appear more Indonesian.[11] Seram and Kalimantan both have large and numerous Transmigration settlements occupied by people from the more densely populated regions of Java and Sulawesi. Transmigration is seen by locals, justly, as part of a concerted program of internal colonization. Tsing's critique of traditional anthropological notions of community (as self-contained and relatively autonomous) is directed at the state's use of the concept in the creation of hierarchy of vertically-integrated places (with village communities on the bottom). The critique has resonances in Maneo, too. But there, since the demise of a separatist movement in the region in the 1950s and the consolidation of the New Order regime against mostly imagined enemies throughout the 1970s and '80s, bureaucrats in Ambon and Jakarta have paid less attention. A series of post-Suharto, democratically elected administrations, including the latest headed by Susilo Bambang Yudhoyono, have focused more on subduing secessionist threats at the ends of the country (in East Timor, Aceh, and West Papua) and at least calming ethnic and religious tensions.

But Maneo, like the Meratus, have an ambivalent view of the state; they see themselves as straddling the two worlds. While they recognize state officials are capricious and dangerous, they also benefit financially (if less so than in the past) from state largess and from the plethora of titles awarded, especially church office titles that number enough for nearly every adult to have one. Similarly, our own state-sanctioned presence was both welcomed and fraught. One Maneo official had a particular aversion to us: *pejabat* (his title translates as "official"), nominally the highest ranking Maneo representative at the time, was terrified that something would befall us for which he would be held responsible. To him, our presence was a sign of the thoroughly compromised nature of the local space of the settlements.[12] Though he was "in charge" in three of the mountain settlements, *pejabat* began to avoid them altogether and eventually moved to a small shelter 100 meters outside the village of Maneo Tinggi. Such trepidation was even more acute among Maneo who lived permanently in the forest (*masuanae*).[13] Occasionally, we caught glimpses of them fleeing from us on our trips to and from the different mountain settlements (usually along rivers where visibility was better). And no doubt on many more occasions they disappeared before we saw them, foiling nearly all attempts to meet them. They called us *walata* (a term for Dutch soldier) pointing to our clothes, especially our hats, though it had been nearly fifty years since the last Dutch soldier left the region. Their fear centered on the likelihood that any path we might chart to them might then be used by others, including missionaries, state agents, traders, and by village brethren—kin but potentially dangerous agents on the government payroll.

With people coming and going from the villages—and it should be noted, mostly going from the four mountain settlements—there appeared to be little order to village life, a discontinuous place of residence for otherwise disconnected persons. Adding to this perception was the fact that for two years, the mountain Maneo villages remained without a *kepala desa* (village headman) to represent them to the district Camat in Wahai, an impasse that resulted in *pejabat*'s de facto elevation, caused in part by his refusal to attend meetings to choose a successor. But is it reasonable to deduce that the mountain settlements in some sense represent failed communities? This would necessarily follow if we accepted Anna Tsing's definition of community as the "continually renegotiated and re-imagined constituencies of local leaders" (1993:65).[14] The problem with this approach is that it needlessly narrows the scope of community action to concerted action impelled by the political aspirations and acuity of leaders reaching out to distant sources of authority. In defining community as the constituencies created, Tsing turns the measure of community into the apparent motion or action generated by the group—that community only exists to the extent people are mobilized into followers (returning to the distinction between motion and stasis drawn earlier). Obviously, communities like Maneo do not exist in isolation. But reducing community to politics obscures the complex social dynamics created wherever lives become entangled in others. Communities at rest, as Leo Strauss observed, are not inert. The very balancing of relations and the division of loyalties that partly determines residence patterns also prevent communities from mobilizing.

The Peripatetic Community

Community is more than an amalgam of individuals arranged and rearranged among would-be leaders; it inheres in and grows out of people's interactions and experiences. Community is different from the place people reside. Likewise, it does not begin where persons end, as the source of rules or representations over and above them governing actions and determining orientations. Such assumptions fail to explain how communities become objects of devotion, struggle, or ambivalence in the first place, and how such sentiments are sustained and transformed. Better that community be seen through the formative experiences of living among others, for focusing on this domain of experience brings to light the less visible ways community, as the nexus of people's relations, pervades lives, envelopes people, intrudes on them, and shapes their dispositions and inclinations towards others.

Of course, such experiences with others vary; different communities give rise to different sorts of interactions, and even the same communities are lived, as it were, from different positions. Communities also overlap—a fact that tends to blur effects attributed to any one. And most if not all small ones, like Maneo, are nowadays nested within larger ones, defined by broader religious affiliation and by the state. People even in the remotest of areas can employ shifting reference points for their interactions, often indexed through language and style of dress (Spyer 2000:88–92, 284)—for example, the black frocks that Christian Maneo confirmed in the Protestant Church of Maluku (*Gerejah Protestan Maluku*) would wear to services to set themselves apart from those who have not been confirmed.[15] Conceiving community as interactions, and not reducing it to representation, shared identity, or the concertedness of action, reflects back the properties of particular relational milieus: how they differently enable people to maneuver through social entanglements or, alternatively, impede them from doing so. There are no guarantees. Community persists because of these maneuvers (and often despite them) and because people trust one another. Trust helps contain disputes just as its absence fuels them. When trust dissipates and suspicions spiral out of control, Maneo preserve a sense of community by dispersing and so avoid each other. Somewhat paradoxically, as much as trust, the presence of exit opportunities may actually preserve conviviality by reducing the possibility of confrontation and misunderstanding when tensions are high (Beidelman 1993[1986]:202). By the same token, though, to choose to live together becomes a sign of goodwill when it seems safer to disperse and the value of community is thereby enhanced. Unlike Aristotle's analogy of cows chewing the cud in company they may be barely aware of, company is the focus of much of Maneo awareness.

I have described briefly the casual remarks Maneo made regarding the challenges and occasional opprobriousness of living together. But their attitudes about fellow villagers present a more complicated picture. For all the difficulties various associations pose, there is also a promise. Maneo describe the first village in mythic history, *yamalia* (cave village), as the original home of the ancestors of all the races or nationalities of people of the world. Much of their history subsequent to *yamalia* details the mass emigration out of central Seram, and the specific paths the ancestors took, precipitated by endemic jealousies and rivalries. Because of that movement, they see themselves now as numerically small and relatively powerless in the world though still its center and source. As people left, they took with them their skills to build things, a fact they are reminded of when they see planes flying overhead—signs of the collective wealth and power they once possessed. But as the overall decline is visible from what little remains and the patent absence of material things, the actual movement of people, Maneo elders note, has been episodic and punctuated by glorious revivals that keep community both a possibility and a precondition to any reversal. They thus see community or *yamana* not only as the subject of nostalgic longing but as a project, and they steel themselves to preserve it against the threat of further loss despite any personal animosities they may harbor.

As a project, the Maneo idea of *yamana* bears some similarities to the Greek notion of *polis*, the city-state, in the sense that it is dependent upon the responsibilities assumed for it by its citizens and residents.[16] Like the polis, the Maneo *yamana*, describes a place of equals, or near equals—leaving aside the Greek's exclusion of noncitizens, women, and slaves, and the Maneo disempowerment of the young—and inasmuch as associations are voluntary (Arendt 1959:25–31). Maneo can move when relations deteriorate—perhaps more so than was possible in classical Greece. More importantly, Maneo can vary their contributions and intensity of their involvement in the relationships around them. Because they monitor the states of their various relations and understand that others are making similar assessments they feel some urgency to demonstrate their mutual goodwill through the willingness to temper demands and expectations, and through efforts to negotiate and not simply contest differences over the terms of specific relations. This is not to deny selfishness as a motive or ignore Maneo political aspirations, but, as a practical matter (if not explicit principle) they readily settle for less to find common ground. At the same time, the appearance of self-interested motives may be deceptive. The obstacles to civility, as Aristotle observes, mean that people hoping to do well often end up doing what is merely advantageous. The lesson from the polis is that success can never be taken for granted.

Such effort at accomodation may seem beside the point. After all, why do people not simply devise rules to ensure solidarity then follow them? Are not the problems encountered simply the result of such failures? In theory, a community predicated on rules does offer the possibility of shoring up social divisions (Rawls 1971). And as a model, the erosion or collapse of those norms may illuminate broader social dislocations and upheavals.[17] Yet the presumption, I contend, suffers from conflating rules with something more essential or foundational to community. Getting the rules right is no simple matter. Indeed, rules that mandate the redistribution of wealth may just as effectively legitimate differential access to power and prestige, and obscure how such rules have been used to promote the interests of privileged classes. They require interpretation to determine the appropriateness of the circumstances to which they are applied. Moreover, to be effective, rules have to be backed up with the threat of sanctions, entailing still more rules and procedures that are open to debate. Conflict resolution can never be imposed. In interpersonal matters, neither people's relationships nor the circumstances they find themselves in have discrete beginnings and ends, so that what might appear to be the just course of action to take in one context, becomes decidedly less clear when people reflect on the consequences actions will have foreclosing possibilities to do the right thing in subsequent contexts.[18] The shortcomings of this normative model of community become apparent in the context of kinship where the need to disentangle rules from notions of social justice is acute. There, some relations, particularly affinal ones, impose considerable obligations, including, in Maneo, the taboo prohibiting the mentioning of each other's names and the complex requirements of property exchange. These axioms are features of those particular relations and a consequence of how they are defined.[19] In fact, if the standards for appropriate action are set too high, as they often are, rules are likely to exacerbate tensions. As a model for analysis, narrowly defining community in terms of rules occludes from view the way moral deliberation and reflection inform choice of action to follow a particular one or not. As Owen Flanagan notes, justice theories on the whole tend to underestimate the possibility of a good community by obscuring how goodness is created or fostered in the first place (1991:124).

Moral Practice

More broadly, rules are better seen as guides for action and at most a point of departure for deliberation, not a substitute for it. People deliberate because the choices they face are numerous, and even when rules mandate exchange, for example, they often do not specify quality and quantity. These decisions involve other values and calculations. Maneo deliberate, too, because their choices differently affect others and often entail difficult social tradeoffs. Even if they did possess a set of principles that guided them to the best course of action, they would still have to deliberate over means to enact these principles and over what would constitute their realization (Nussbaum 1986:296–97; 1990:62). Alternatively, if rules did mandate specific levels of generosity, recipients would see giving as obedience to a rule rather than an indication of sentiment. Part of the meaning of the gesture, thus, would be negated, for there is no faster way to lose friends than to imply, by invoking a rule, that mutual benevolence is lacking (Taylor 1995:183). Morality inheres in social life as it emerges from people's interactions (Loraux 1986:102). It is social, John Dewey observes, "not because we ought to take into account the effect of our acts upon the welfare of others, but because of facts—others do take account of what we do, and they respond accordingly to our acts" (Dewey 1994:183; Levinas 1996:169). Morality receives different cultural expression. I found Maneo reluctant to speculate openly about moral motivations behind others' actions, though gossip was certainly common. They did not tell stories with Hamlet-like characters whose indecisiveness would exemplify and make more explicit the otherwise opaque processes that led to decision or paralyzed one into making none. I found no developed vocabulary or range of ideas that would locate the gravity of action in the decisions that precede it. Instead, Maneo talk about sitting (*ita ruwae*), a reference to how such deliberation is supposedly conducted. And they talk about knowing things (*manae*) but often in the negative, as when the motives of others lie outside the purview of their expertise: "*mana'aesi*" they would say ("don't know"), when asked to explain why someone suspected of lying or practicing sorcery would do so. In Maneo mythic narratives, too, the actions of heroes appeared unconsidered. Often, it simply was a vague desire (*kahana*) that animated them; the presence of taboos (*makahala*) checked their impulses (Valeri 2000). Of course, this elision of moral deliberation has less to do with reality than with the narrative convention. In casual conversation, the fact Maneo never admitted suffering from indecision likely reveals nothing more than an understandable aversion to expressing doubt or displaying any lack of confidence.

Of course, decisions are often difficult. I am convinced Maneo do deliberate over sharing food, over how much to ask for in negotiating marriage payments, even over choice of spouse. People deliberate over similar matters yet arrive at different decisions all the time. Deliberation merely describes the means by which people decide to commit themselves to actions consistent with what they feel to be right, whether articulated or not; it is "a search for a way to act" (Dewey 1994:141). This focus brings to the fore that aspect of agency that lies between and permeates what Anthony Giddens (1986) calls people's "durable dispositions," which are experienced as fixed, and the routines of everyday life. For people deliberate in ways that alternately affirm and challenge these dispositions; they do not act morally simply by acting against inclinations, nor left to instinct would people's natural goodness necessarily manifest itself. Instead, visions of the social good and people's specific desires to improve the tenor of community life and enhance levels of trust are tempered by the understanding that others retain their own, often conflicting views of circumstances, their own pressing obligations to meet, and their own grievances to honor. Thus, Maneo may agree on the nature of the social good yet believe with ample reason that their own acts of generosity may backfire. Good deeds may not only go unreciprocated, they may arouse antipathy.

When the most successful hunter in one Maneo village, a village where there was a shortage of meat at times, abandoned the practice, he did so, others said, because someone in the village became jealous of his hunting success, even though the jealous man shared in the spoils. Generally, raw deer or pig meat brought into the village is shared with everyone present; though smaller game, mostly marsupials, are not widely distributed. This particular hunter, therefore, may have ceased to hunt big game because he did not wish to contribute further to envy and the divisiveness it caused—exerting a downward effect on the frequency of such hunting. The other consideration that made continued hunting and the envy it aroused potentially dangerous to himself and his family concerned sorcery (discussed in chapter 7). Fear of sorcery is fueled by the possibility of directing mere feelings, such as envy, into a malevolent and virulent form of action; it projects private impulses outward and onto a social plane while usually disguising its source. Often these impulses are negative, though not always, as in the case of love magic or sorcery used defensively to counter the effects of suspected attacks. Overall, Maneo concerns about the ill-will of others and their own animosities—lest they be accused themselves—fosters reservedness. For instance, the Maneo neighbor who told me the story about the hunter only did so after the alleged jealous man moved away. Others are reluctant to name names for when they do they assume the risk that any criticisms revealed might rebound against them and jeopardize their own reputations or worse. Out of necessity, then, issues of fairness and justice, such as identifying culprits behind sorcery or other offenses yield to the more piecemeal management of grievances. Maneo strategies to contain disputes elevate comity and civility over probity or matters of personal integrity or honesty.

This is not a lesser kind of morality; being reasoned and informed by social circumstances, it is more realistic (Just 2001). For moral agency, as it informs people's deliberation, makes the innate facility to respond to and empathize with others—what Lawrence Blum sees as the root of morality (1987:310)—amenable to fine-tuned judgments about how to act and whom to trust. Skeptics may disagree with the necessity of calculation. After all, moral actions, at times, would seem to spring naturally without deliberation from other things, such as compassion or basic goodness that may or may not correspond to blood ties, kinship relations, or genealogical distance. Actions seemingly unthought, as when someone risks his or her own life to save another, may be conditioned responses. However, there are few opportunities to put such extreme instances of moral action to the test; better sites for assessing responsiveness are the intractable, more quotidian dilemmas of social life that require moral perspicuity and judgment precisely because they rarely ever offer a clear denouement or choice of right action. Because relations overlap, the resolution of one set of demands raises obstacles to meeting obligations toward others.

If deliberation is the means by which people act, moral perspicuity is evinced in the way actions entail responsiveness toward others not predicated on shared identity or the minimization of difference.[20] It reflects the capacity and willingness to perceive what simultaneously divides and unites persons: juxtaposing sameness and difference without losing sight of either. Where difference is collapsed, the basis of action shifts to one of shared identity; as a matter of practice, not entailing any risk or sacrifice, common identity narrows or restricts the latitude of agents to extend themselves beyond themselves (Nussbaum 1990:152). This is frequent in communal movements, and, to an extent, shared identity facilitates the mobilization of communities. When this begins, a sense of community, which includes recognition of difference, yields to a sense of common identity. While not moral per se, seeing others in terms of similarities and judging them accordingly, deprives agents of the capacity to act autonomously and to make a difference by their actions (Giddens 1984:14). Oversubscribing to collective identity suspends thinking through or beyond difference such that the only difference acknowledged is that which defines the excluded, those to whom tolerance and generosity are not extended. When the threats subside (and mobilization in defense is no longer necessary) or the dangers rise too high, such communities may collapse utterly. The idea that a sense of community is nurtured in the balance of difference and the presence of disagreements might seem a tenuous foundation for it, especially given other threats Maneo face—the onslaught of capital flows, logging, transmigration, and, since 1999, religious and ethnic strife. If equanimity is all there is, there seems little keeping community together or preventing it from becoming a mere emblem of shared identity under pressure of real or imagined threats. The ever-present challenges to moral perspicuity and difficulties of negotiating opposing points of view ensure that the facility is always exercised; without these challenges, ironically, the sense of community would suffer. Maneo have learned to endure conflict without overcoming it.

In analysis, the failure to recognize the endemic risks of social life is distorting. An example of such misrepresentation is Colin Turnbull's controversial study of the Ik of Uganda in *The Mountain People* (1972) based on fieldwork he conducted during a famine in the 1960s. Turnbull was criticized for a number of ethical lapses, such as naming names of persons accused of misdeeds and offering some ill-considered policy advice. Just as egregiously, he turns the Ik into a kind of parable of humanity lost. He asserts that they had abandoned all sense of community when he describes the ordinariness and nonchalance of the brutality he observed them inflict upon one another (1972:210, 230). Turnbull absolves the Ik of some responsibility for this, blaming governments for valuing animals over human life—a reference to a newly created nearby game preserve; and he adds that any group of people in the same circumstances would likely suffer the same ignominious fate. But Turnbull merely presumes to have fathomed their state of mind when he suggests laughter in the face of misfortune is unambiguously derisive and the absence of tears indicative of a moral emptiness (1972:211). Obviously, survival does depend on the goodwill of others, a goodwill noticeably missing from depictions of the Ik stealing food from each other. It is more than a fine point, though, to propose that famine in Uganda did not rob them of all moral sense, but, instead exacerbated dilemmas about how and whether to share, based on perceptions of what difference it might make. Conversely, when acts are not brutal or appear even kind, Turnbull describes them as inscrutable. He recounts the move of one Ik family, Nangoli's, away from the community in the search for food then back to their homeland during the height of the famine, a move that likely left them hungrier than when they lived away. At a loss for why they returned, he suggests they may have felt lonely and leaves the matter at that (1972:233). What might have been an interesting starting point for analysis—the dilemma between sociality and survival—becomes a dead end. Turnbull's approach only permits him to see morality and concern for others as a facility present or absence, not as a practice that compels people to do what they believe or feel is right with respect to others without any guarantees of success. This is not to deny that under pressure, inclinations can wane and communities can even dissolve or collapse. The point is, the Ik, for all their suffering, had not abandoned social life or been rejected by the wider society they were never much a part of. Turnbull robs them of the dignity of their struggle by conceding their defeat from the outset. Yet it is unnecessary to refer to such extremes of famine and deprivation to appreciate how the mere fact of living in association can pose dilemmas. Association can exacerbate tense relations, undermine confidence, and remind people of the grievances between them, just as the presence of someone who owes something reminds a giver of the debt.

Aware of this tension, Socrates observed that in certain circumstances moral action might mean minding one's own business (Strauss 1964:108)—a diffidence among the Ik that leads Turnbull to excoriate them.

But just as community cannot be explained by the political machinations of aspiring leaders, apparent selfishness is not anathema to it. Selfishness is not simply an individual survival strategy, for survival itself necessitates more magnanimous gestures. In short, a sense of community is not something that can be jettisoned as ballast in the pursuit of individual self-interest, even survival. Generally, and less dramatically, the daily challenges of social life revolve around more personal sorts of conflicts that do not directly threaten survival. These include adultery accusations, suspicions of hoarding, and the like; they are often longstanding. Rarely do these disputes take shape as clear violations of social norms. They do not occasion epiphanies of solidarity against violators; conflicts are multi-sided. They remain personal in a sense because reasonable people can disagree over events and over what constitutes proscribed behavior. Parties are positioned differently and conditioned to see controversies from perspectives embedded in particular relationship constellations. Ties are deep and enduring. For example, Maneo will ostrasize persons whose actions, such as incest, they find objectionable; they will even murder them on occasion, or so they say, the act is so repellent. But they have no means for disowning the perpetrators. Nor can alleged scoundrels be expelled to create communities free of fault. Persons may leave a village if they lack support, but they would deny ever being chased out. Having resigned themselves to the unavoidability of discord, Maneo recognize that trading in one set of relations for a new set offers no more reliability, no more ground for mutual trust, perhaps less. This uncertainty and endemic, if low level, conflict leads to two contradictory responses: on the one hand, because they lack effective institutions for dispute resolution, Maneo shrink from instability and uncertainty and so remain demographically small and residentially scattered. Certainly, sorcery fears play into this. At times, partly out of such fears, entire villages are abandoned. Yet because Maneo describe Seram as the origin place for all the peoples of the world, they acknowledge everyone who visits them as kin. Each arrival constitutes a return of sorts. They are thus remarkably open, even to the point of appearing naïve to the requests and claims of outside visitors. Before I arrived in 1989, Maneo donated a colonial era cannon barrel (*laela*) to someone claiming to be a representative from the Siwa-Lima provincial museum in Ambon, though such objects are highly valued in marriage payment exchanges. And over the years, they have allowed themselves to be deceived by a series of traders seeking valuable antique porcelain also necessary for meeting those affinal exchanges. They are not simply gullible, however. Maneo extend trust to everyone as a means to bring them within their moral orbit, prevailing on outsiders to see them as they do each other in specific relational contexts, not as a class or category, but as kin. Clearly, the strategy does not always work, but aware of being numerically small and relatively powerless, they may feel they have no choice.

The only real others for whom generosity is not extended are those people they call *masiae*, the suspected perpetrators of most sorcery attacks (see chapter 7). Maneo invoke this specter as a way to think metaphorically about their dependence on capricious neighbors and even kin; it is a reminder of the impossibility of fashioning a perfect world, and in more than simply a poetic sense. Sorcery (*mauna*), like other dangerous ideas, exacerbates uncertainty over the designs of others. Some may try to isolate themselves from specific allegations or threats and move to the forest where, some say, they feel less vulnerable. But sorcery exposes people's mutual dependence as it complicates it. The ability to mitigate uncertainty depends on the willingness to trust others, allay suspicions, and manifest goodwill.[21] Thus, paradoxically, though Maneo feel safer while alone or mostly alone, uncertainty increases when others are conspicuously absent. When only a few houses are occupied in a village, like Siahari and Kabailu, those remaining will often leave as well, when they would not otherwise, feeling too exposed and vulnerable in the open, once occupied space. Sorcery is corrosive to social relations, but it also focuses uncertainty in a form that makes it possible, in theory, to contain it—that is, by prevailing on people not to use it because it is so abhorrent. Maneo can bear some of the vicissitudes of social life by acting virtuously and foreswearing sorcery's use, by appearing to act with restraint without actually having to do anything.

They cannot simply assert their own virtuousness, for to the extent virtues elevate principles over relationships, they distend moral deliberation. Principled people are disconnected from a Maneo perspective. They harbor ambivalence about persons acting solely out of principle, like the *kapitan*, the warrior, who battles courageously but without regard for others, endangering enemies and kin alike, especially the women around him. An inversion of the sorcerer, the *kapitan*, as someone who stands apart from others, poses a danger because his power (only men become *kapitan*) is indiscriminate. He is anathema to community because he is incapable and unwilling to make the stop-gap compromises necessary for people to move through conflicts.

Simply put, the moral agent is not the paragon of virtue, and the end of action is not moral perfection. As a force that inheres between people, morality is manifest in the shifting alliances and recurrent tensions that inhibit the extension of one's self on behalf of others; it induces people to view situations from others' perspectives and to deliberate about choices of benefit to them, even when other considerations intercede and actions are not taken. The complexity of deliberation means that failure to follow through cannot be seen perforce as evidence of a lack of morality. Nor does amicability necessarily arise from it. People may act morally yet completely disagree. In fact, as I argue in chapter 5, beneficence may go unacknowledged. What is crucial to fostering sociality is how moral intent is perceived and how culpability is deflected. Some actions have to appear anonymous to help agents maneuver through the entanglements of relations, avoiding further offense by triangulating off of suspected inimical positions. In contexts where all parties are presumed to be interested parties, anonymous actions can help contain acrimony by publicly diverting its causes and symptoms, whatever personal animosities individuals harbor. Sometimes, anonymity affords the only path to common ground.

Volition

Morality does not disappear entirely behind discrete gestures and the mundane facts of sharing space, conversation, and a host of nonvalued material things. Sociality lies not only in what does not happen, fighting or village abandonment, when people disagree. In a sense, morality is too important not to communicate it. And the communication of moral intent is vital to Maneo understanding of particular social situations. They seek to determine the responsiveness of those around them and they are keenly aware that their own actions invite similar scrutiny of the intent behind them. Maneo endeavor to make responsiveness explicit in their choices. In the case of disagreements, they may not only act restrained, they manifest it so that restraint, then, becomes a sign of intent—that they chose it over other more impulsive and provocative responses. They recognize that choices have performative effects because of the imputed motivation. Accordingly, some decisions are celebrated that, in fact, follow fairly predictable courses of action or established routines. This does not mean, however, that perfunctory displays of generosity, where giving does not entail any sacrifice, are unimportant. Such apparent choices can be decisive when circumstances conspire to controvert expectations.

Choices bear crucially on the nature and quality of relationships, even in terms of the way relations are defined (see chapter 2). Indeed, in any and all relations, much of what goes on or is transferred between people is measured against a history of interaction and future expectations; the tenor of that particular connection is not determined by norms alone. For instance, someone in the position to share or exchange may be sensitive to the ideals of reciprocity without being entirely bound by them. And a potential recipient has some latitude in interpreting the intent behind an act of sharing or withholding, the results of which (if positive) incline them to suspend doubt and extend trust (Duranti 1993). For Aristotle, in his famous discussion of friendship, the volitional foundations of comity are so tenuous he retreats to the rare instance of true friendships—rare because they require tests, which, he readily concedes, many will fail (1984:EE1245b25). Any hypothetical community composed of perfect friends would be necessarily small. But scholars have questioned the very possibility of such perfection (Derrida 1997); and, turning the question around, we have to wonder whether it would be desirable for relations to be entirely predicated upon the accumulation of choices to be as magnanimous as possible. In other words, are not the civil friendships or partnerships, which are easier to negotiate, but which Aristotle describes as lesser friendships, of greater social importance (1984:EE1242a–13)? For one thing, the ideal of perfect friendship raises unrealizable expectations for cooperation from others. In turn, higher failure rates in meeting loftier standards may alienate potentially perfect friends and turn them into real enemies. In light of Maneo practice I would amend Aristotle's discussion of friendship this way: It may be wiser to seek to turn strangers or enemies into potential friends, with the understanding that untested friends may make better neighbors precisely for what they may remain hesitant to ask of others. Of course, this reservedness may not always be possible, certainly not for all relations. When people are forced to cooperate, they assume certain risks when they do. But Maneo enter into interactions with an understanding informed by the experience of participating on either side of exchanges, as givers and receivers, and from being at times decision-makers or subjects in other people's deliberations. Experience gives them the ability to empathize and inclines them (more than they would be otherwise) to extend themselves on behalf of others to temper expectations in the pursuit of a more diffuse and general kind of community well-being.

Aristotle's analysis raises another point for consideration: that moral choice entails some sort of sacrifice and practices are moral only to the extent people suffer for them. Suffering is important to communicate. I would note, however, that sacrifice can be created and acts can appear to involve it without actually risking much. Take the practice of living together in a Maneo settlement, the puzzle that began this discussion. I have argued that some form of community is a given, that individuals are never really alone; but that does not preclude the possibility and desirability of making village life a choice. Maneo often waxed about the ease of life apart in the forest where sharing and cooperation are unnecessary, usually not even an option, and where their actions are not so open to scrutiny. The sentiment is genuine. Although the enjoyment of it differs for men and women and from one family to the next, most claim to appreciate the respite from village life and live apart because they enjoy it, not because they need to. Just as they do not have to scatter in the forest to survive at certain times of the year, Maneo do not have to live together in villages. There is no imperative to do so; as I have maintained, the presence of settlements cannot be explained by the needs of persons for others. Nor are settlements the results of state policy to permanently locate Maneo at a single designated address; they were adamant about this. They do not see the choice as one between living where state officials want them to or living without community, even though this is how they describe forest Maneo who do not live in villages. In fact, social conventions apply and expectations are the same whenever, wherever, and whoever the parties happen to be.[22]

We observed the value of community life in 1992. Our arrival coincided with the planned moves of five families from one of the mountain Maneo villages to the Transmigration settlement we had passed through when we first came. The moves, the families assured everyone, were merely temporary; indeed, all but one kept their homes in the mountains and most returned frequently. Yet those who remained described feeling abandoned. They may have been reacting to the trajectory of mythic history marking the waning of Maneo power through population loss. But it is likely that people raised the stakes of departure in an effort to portray the moves as morally unacceptable. That is, they created a predicament deliberately to compel practice that conformed to what they saw as moral but, also, as in their interests—as morality and interest are perhaps more often conjoined than opposed. Framing the choice of leaving or staying as a moral one, they objectified through concrete practice less tangible desires and hopes: that is, the trust and mutual respect implied by living together in a village even if it is never fully realized. Implicitly, Maneo reject this when they leave. With so much uncertainty and so much at stake, moral purposes infuse and emerge from what remains unspecified or only implied by action (Calhoun 1995:143).

Again, morality inheres in people's interactions, not in the transcendence of them. While a sense of community certainly suffers from the presence of animosities, it also emerges from recognition of the divisions that animosities reflect.[23] By acknowledging difference, Maneo can make the choice to live together a virtue, one short of social mobilization and more conducive to "stasis," to preserving equanimity. This does not mean they have to stay put, but when they leave to enjoy the respite from village life, they do so under partly trumped up pretexts of economic necessity or something else. They might complain to me of social burdens they could not openly share with others since such complaints would likely be perceived as carping and fail to elicit much sympathy. Lacking a stage where such dilemmas and virtues can be aired, the village itself comes to resemble the Greek theater. And just like the actors there, they disappear sometimes in order to live together at other times.

Notes

1. A biological reef community's survival is partly a function of its size; if it is too small and the numbers of living coral and other interacting organisms reach some minimum level, the community dies. A human community similarly unaware of itself might consist entirely of a string of relations between persons connected only by two others, none of whom are the same. Such a hypothetical community would have to be small and end at some arbitrary point where the indirect influence of specific others could not be felt. Such a community would shift in composition from one person along the chain to the next. We typically do not think of serially connected people as constituting a community because of the human propensity to invest dyadic social relations with meanings that are embedded in broader systems of meaning, for example, as a parent-child relation forms part of family (even if there are no other members) or as neighbors relate to one another in the context of a neighborhood. That some networks of relations become culturally salient and objects of thinking, reflects among other things the reoccurrence and cooccurrence of interactions, the extent to which relations overlap and are intertwined, and the way those social experiences shape one's psychological constitution. No doubt, communities are more easily built on relations characterized by few, if any, degrees of separation. They appear less invented and command awareness, in a sense, because they are sites of recurrent, meaningful interaction. But such associations are invariably conflicted if they endure.

2. One popular reality-imitating TV program features contestants vying to survive each other on an island or some other isolated location. Strategizing goes alongside moral deliberation. Instead of correcting objectionable behavior (though such actions are pointed out), offenders are voted off. Participants are assigned to teams and subject to challenges which give them immunity if they win. Thus the cooperation necessary to avoid dismissal creates their vulnerability.

3. I am reminded of the scene from the film *The Wizard of Oz* when the Tin Man receives his long awaited heart, actually a commemorative clock—a testimonial—in the shape of a heart. To paraphrase the Wizard: some men sit around all day and do nothing but good deeds. In honor of your good deeds [the Wizard fumbles around for the word] I declare you "a good deed doer." In contrast to the Cowardly Lion's medal for conspicuous bravery and the Scarecrow's diploma for intelligence, moral sagacity is rather poorly marked and rewarded.

4. Leo Strauss was describing Sparta on the eve of the Peloponnesian War and its citizens' concerns for internal politics and administration. Being "at rest" there is little urgency to defend or fight for community, but far from being inert, the concept highlights the equanimity and the perspicuity—again, that faculty for seeing others—that characterizes a particular state of relations. Though little seems to happen, because there is little intensity or direction of political will (nothing to compel persons to deny or subordinate more individual pursuits) this represents a kind of moral work or project. My point is that communities at rest are communities nonetheless and do not cease being in the absence of mobilization.

5. For much of the last century, in reaction to the wild historical speculation of nineteenth-century evolutionism, anthropologists chose to assert the isolation and relative stasis of tribal communities to expedite the pursuit of more general principles—for example, explaining how domestic groups are integrated into larger polities. Of course, the assertions distorted both the influence of wider, dominant polities (Tsing 1993; Comaroff 1982) and the dynamism of local histories (Rosaldo 1980), indirectly contributing to colonial policies and designs. But just as questions of community, and of how communities persist, were being summarily dismissed as "Durkheimian" vestiges of outdated models, at the same time, political scientists (Anderson 1991) began to examine national communities in a sense not dissimilar to that described by Durkheim. Analysis, then, of the meaning of community in small-scale societies and of their composition still warrants attention (compare Das 1995). In some cases, the very survival of community has become an issue for the people themselves. But social consciousness does not just occur on the cusp of extinction or social transformation; it is a product of living among others. Social consciousness is the locus of morality.

6. In his widely cited book, *Imagined Communities*, Anderson proposed that the solitary act of reading early nineteenth-century newspapers instilled a sense of a nation. My emendation is that the sense of community developed out of the kinds of interactions and encounters reading may have led to; the central issue is how the dialogue took shape, between whom, relying on what contextual indices (Hagen 1997). The national community did not come into view through its representations but through the act of reading about it. The nation was read, as it were, from news reports of action, events, and the persons involved bounded in space and time. The implication, as others have pointed out, is that the nation is not a new community so much as a differently imagined one (Chatterjee 1993:230–34).

7. Community describes both a set of representations (variably cast) and the ongoing set of practices directed toward the negotiation and management of relationships. (These relationships are frequently the source of conflict, in part, traceable to structure or, more precisely, structural contradictions, although clearly not all conflict derives from structure). The relationship of community to kinship and structure is instructive. Historically, the focus of most studies of social organization has been the operation of structures: either how particular structures of descent, siblingship, and affinity generate stable social forms or, more realistically, how these structures generate contradictions that result in variable patterns of behavior (Kelly 1977; Comaroff 1980). In the scholarship on eastern Indonesia (much centered on islands to the south of Seram), a number of structural models have been proposed to account for observed variation in systems of descent and alliance, often downplaying practice (van Wouden 1968; Barnes 1980; Clamagirand 1980; Valeri 1975–76; van Dijk and de Jonge 1987; cf. Pannell 1990). Valeri's comment on the development of his own thinking about the Huaulu of Seram, from excessive formalism to appreciation of the nuances and "paradoxes" of practice could apply to much of the research in the region in reminding us that "actions are rarely complete, and thus they rarely coincide with their type" (1994b:2, 5). There are two problems. First, in terms of the "culture area" defined by societies to the south (van Wouden 1968; see also de Josselin de Jonge 1980), Maneo might appear less a variation on a common set of ideas and practices than a transformed (degenerated) society, a shadow of a former, more complete system. This sort of conclusion, though, would be quite misleading despite the changes they have experienced. Maneo seem to share a number of characteristics with societies in North Maluku (Baker 1988, 1994; Martodirdjo 1994; Duncan 1998; Visser 1989), generally considered part of a different cultural area (DepDikBud 1985; Andaya 1993). Second, expanding on Valeri's point (and so moving away from the categorization of "types" based on generalizations from patterns), the more interesting approach is to elucidate the interplay and articulation of principles of descent, siblingship, and alliance that simultaneously unite and divide people, not to abandon the concept of structure, but rather to apply a more analytically rigorous notion of it.

8. The significance of blood reflects its properties both as a substance that links persons and as a metaphor that stands for an emotional and psychic tie. This distinction is sometimes lost. For instance, just after commenting on the compellingness of consanguinity, or shared blood, Durkheim acknowledges that sentiment between consanguines is determined by the system of social organization (1973:133).

9. Donald Levine (1995) contends the social sciences emerged historically as part of an effort to explain society in the absence of gods (see also Nietzsche 1966:79)—that is, to identify on a social plane the equivalent of divinely inspired order. This view that the imperative of community is to integrate and that order is solidarity or at least contributes to it, informed much writing during the formative years of the history of the social sciences. Religion was believed to function to instill order; after all what other reason could explain the presence of ritual to an increasingly secular audience? And what more obvious and convenient explanation could be found by officials to account for the appearance of widespread social disintegration of tribal societies at a time when traditional practices and beliefs were being abandoned under colonial pressures and policies.

10. Myth and ritual occasion reflection on the values of social life and how honor, duty, and loyalties are assigned and under what conditions (Beidelman [1986]1993). They facilitate the moral imagination by creating situations faced by gods and ancestors that mirror various possibilities for dealing with more prosaic dilemmas. Maneo, along

with the ancient Greeks, keep spirits, sorcerers, and gods relatively close and on intimate terms, involved in daily affairs as culprits behind various accidents. At the same time, expectations of their participation in human affairs are circumscribed. Such spirits and ancestors (in Maneo) are in the community; they do not define community or stand above it; they do not necessarily enforce a community's moral order. Rather, their presence among the living offers a way to examine and imagine differently the terms of people's interactions (Tuzin 1997:98). That is, the traps that gods set to entangle people enable them also to think imaginatively about their predicaments with others, and not simply by serving up definitive answers to problems of suffering and meaning.

11. Colonial records discuss problems reconciling their expectations that leaders would have followers with facts on the ground and the strong ethos of egalitarianism and autonomy (Sachse 1922:139–40).

12. On my first visit to Maneo in 1989, *pejabat*, the assistant to the *kepala desa* (village headman)—the second highest ranking person, and the person "in charge" while the *kepala desa* was away—was so taken aback at my sudden arrival that he ordered my hosts in the village to turn me away the following day. To him, I was "government" (*pemerintah*) since I carried letters from the police and other government authorities in Ambon. And since *pejabat* was "government" too, he may have assumed I would have expected to stay with him. With his imminent departure for the forest, he may have hoped I would depart as well. Fortunately, my hosts did not share his apprehension and let me stay for several weeks hunting, roasting corn in the fields, and generally enjoying myself. When Jennie and I returned in 1992, having selected Maneo to study based on this earlier experience, *pejabat* again tried to raise fears that our presence portended disaster. In part, his concern turned on his presumed responsibility for our safety, which neither he nor anyone else could guarantee.

13. We learned about the forest Maneo, when we first arrived, from the son of a schoolteacher in Wahai who had spent some time with them and had supposedly earned their trust. Early on, we made some attempt to meet them, but our efforts through the teacher and various other intermediaries went nowhere. From what I gathered, except for being animist and having no contact with the state, there is little that actually distinguishes Maneo villagers from their forest dwelling kin. Both engage in the same subsistence practices, both have similar social structures; there is some intermarriage, and some move back and forth between the different territories.

14. The Meratus of Kalimantan, like Maneo, can avoid efforts at subjugation, in part, because of the remoteness of the mountains around them. From afar, they alternatively embrace and parody state symbols and nation-building practices and, like Maneo, imagine boundaries around them as more real (Tsing 1993:274). Both acknowledge the extent of state penetration, but the admission is calculated. By acknowledging encompassment Maneo reverse historic priority, transpose what is ostensibly outside inside, and therewith de-legitimize state power. But the move is oblique and largely hidden in esoteric stories of history.

15. Maneo also feel connected regionally through a radio program, *Berita Keluarga* (Family News), which announces illnesses and deaths of family members throughout central Maluku. (So and so "departed the earth" or is very ill at such and such hospital.) Though few Maneo travelled far away—only a small handful of students in Ambon or Masohi (the seat of government of the Regency of Central Maluku) and a few on church-related business—they listened because they knew the family names of almost all the people mentioned and felt some sense of empathy with their plight.

16. For Aristotle, community appears where kinship ends, where people's interactions turn on contexts other than their kin relations (that is, as citizens). But ignoring the kin dimension of civil life obscures how different domains of inside and outside, domestic and public interpenetrate. (Meyer Fortes understood that the "affective" domestic sphere of social life and the wider sphere of the lineage or clan interpenetrate; he proposed that the reciprocal influence could be explicated in terms of a society's "moral axioms" [1949:346; Firth 1951:186; cf. Evans-Pritchard 1951].) Maneo are certainly kin-oriented in the sense that relations among them are predicated on it. But within these smaller family or kin-based communities, in particular, people shift positions because of mobility or the movement and disappearance of others (replacement). Community emerges in the context of the tensions and challenges posed by succession and replacement. People are substituted into positions so as to maintain relationships. Much of experience takes place against these changes or their anticipation, the tensions they engender, and the rituals that mark them. Moreover, Maneo make kinship (siblingship, descent, and affinity) maximally inclusive, as all peoples of the world are believed to have emigrated from Seram or Nusa Ina (the Mother Island) in the mythical-historical past and remain connected by different ties. Kinship is not the source of morality; kin do not get along better than non-kin. Instead, it is one of any number of sites or contexts for deliberation and moral action. Kin can even choose to act in non-kin terms to reference membership in other, church- or regional-based communities, though at some risk of opprobrium.

17. In his influential study, *The Moral Economy of the Peasant* (1976), James Scott contends that the shift in early twentieth-century colonial policy towards the monetization of taxation undermined redistributive norms supporting historic Southeast Asian peasant communities. These norms had served as safety nets ensuring that there would be enough food for everyone in times of crisis or, that if they did starve, they would starve together. When the norms were tested during the Depression and found wanting, communities throughout the region erupted in violence.

18. Justice theories are predicated on the assessment of actions, leaving unexamined the questions for whom actions are just, who sets those standards, and how they are interpreted. And they fail to posit motivation.

19. The implication is that norms do not define morality, otherwise it would follow that other, relatively structured relations are somehow less moral, which must be demonstrated not assumed. What is moral may be expressed axiomatically, for example, "obey your parents" and "respect your in-laws," but not all that is moral is expressible in that form (Cook 1999:125; Valeri 2000:152). Nor do rules serve to stabilize relations that might otherwise suffer without them, and not only because people might become aware of the inequalities rules sometime mask—Nietzsche's point, echoed by Frederic Jameson, that "ethical thought projects as permanent features of human 'experience,' and thus as a kind of wisdom about personal life and interpersonal relations, what are in reality the historical and institutional specifics of a determinative type of group solidarity or class cohesion" (1981:59).

20. Identification with others has important psychosocial implications (see Hefner 1993:25–26; Blum 1987). Certainly, "relational identity" forms an important aspect of community (Spyer 2000:177). The question is, identity is relational to whom (not to mention how are relationships to be understood)? Competing orientations or valences pull some people apart as others are brought closer. This is not just a tension between indi-

viduals and collectives, but between different relationships. The locus of morality lies with the relationally constituted agent, but agency does not imply individual subjects.

21. People establish among themselves levels of trust and suspicions, and these accumulated interactions shape inclinations, perspectives, and expectations about others. Such orientation is manifest in the way people live through others, sharing experiences, if only vicariously, and in living for others, either to impress or dominate them or, more beneficently, to help them. The fear, loathing, love, and ambivalence people feel toward others also have profound social reverberations. Cumulatively, they imbue community members with confidence or not; they incline them to scrutinize others or not. In a sense, Freud captured this tension, but he transposed the contingencies of social life to effect a therapeutic strategy to allay anxiety within individuals. As has been pointed out (Ricoeur 1970), his emphasis is misplaced, though the uncertainties over relationships are real.

22. I learned this one day when I met a neighbor on the trail while I was returning from another settlement. He knew meat was in abundance there and he suspected, correctly, I was bringing some back. Although it was not obvious to me at the time, indirectly, he asked for some. I did not respond. We were all hungry and I am embarrassed to say my misunderstanding of his query may have been influenced by my stomach as much as cultural incompetence. He later sent his wife to secure some from my host, who no doubt apologized profusely for my stinginess. Community, thus, describes a site of moral practice, not its perfection; it is the locus for the development and exercise of moral capacities wherever and whenever people chance to meet.

23. Maneo do see communities as preserves from danger, particularly from such threats as state-sponsored headhunters seeking "donations" in severed heads for major construction projects on Seram's coast and agents like the *babinsa* (the local military police officer). Yet they also recognize that safety is illusory, so they address the conflict among them and assume some responsibility for it by weighing the possible effects of various actions on others.

1

Maneo History and Settlement

> The next moment the day became very bothering indeed, because Pooh was so busy not looking where he was going that he stepped on a piece of the Forest which had been left out by mistake. A. A. Milne, *The House at Pooh Corner*

Maneo are a product of many choices; choices about where to reside and with whom, and choices made socially consequential after the fact because of purported historical effects linked to them. Even the name Maneo might have been different but for a particular choice. Maneo comes from the name of a specific ancestor, actually, the first in a succession of ancestors, from one particular clan (*soa*), and not even the most prominent clan at that. By choice, the name became affixed to this group of some 1,000 people inhabiting the territory between the Samal and Kobi Rivers in the north, between the villages of Kabohari and Manusela to the west and Seti in the east, and extending to the south side of the central Seram mountain range. Any one of the other of the nine clans' apical ancestors might have descended to earth first and so had his name printed on the maps and associated with the people. It was something of an accident that Maneo came first and it was an accident in the sense that his descent literally resulted in one. Maneo jumped to the earth without first checking the landing spot which was gelatinous like cold, cooked sago (*ipapeta*), as was all the earth. Upon landing, he sank up to his head and was extricated only with the help of his brothers, the ancestors of two other clans who waited patiently for hard ground to form before they leapt.[1] As a name for a group of people, thus, Maneo represents a curious appellation; it is not a misnomer once accurate but no longer; it is not celebrated, but neither is it a slur—the term *alifuru* (used by Portuguese explorers and derived from the Ternate word *halefuru*) serves that distinction (Aragon 2000:52). They do not object to being called by that name; yet there is less to it than might be expected. Maneo fits incompletely, excluding most people only related collaterally to the original founding ancestor of the one clan, at the same time as it includes and unites members of all nine clans in opposition to neighboring groups. In a way, Maneo represents an emergent entity taking shape under outside pressure and evolving as a result of local initiatives: from raising and selling cloves and certain forest resources, and from the education of children (a few of whom have schooled in Ambon, the provincial capital).

Though Maneo describe their home in the mountains of central Seram in eastern Indonesia as the center of the world and the origin point of all peoples, they recognize that home is situated on the margins of the encroaching state. Most have schooled for a few years; most have converted to Christianity. They now find themselves spending more time than in the past obtaining things that they can sell in order to purchase other things made in other places that they find difficult to live without. The forested mountain boundaries that once insulated them somewhat from the direct effects of wider, regional and global events and processes has become more permeable. Much of the forest is still there; but although this boundary has always been traversed, the very distinctiveness of their way of life is being challenged further by the fact that many Maneo are presently moving from the "center" in the mountains to the coast. The sense of place so crucial to identity and community is blurring. A paradoxical result is that people are becoming more self-consciously Maneo in the context of becoming more Christian and Indonesian, just as what appears distinct about them disappears. Yet Maneo belong to multiple communities and in no simple sense is the local one dissolving into larger dispersed communities.

The Maneo challenge the universalizing ideology of the church that assimilates them into antecedent biblical genealogy (the descendants of Noah) and of the state that fosters citizenship by issuing individual identity cards using clan affiliation as proper names. They resist both by confounding efforts to meet expectations, for instance by failing to elect a village headman (*kepala desa*) to represent the Maneo mountain settlements in the District Office in Wahai. They obliged the New Order government of former President Suharto, who held elections merely as a showcase for the regime, by voting overwhelmingly every four years for Golkar (the government 'functional' party). But they were reluctant, to the point of resistance, to engage the state's local officials in a more continuous way. Dissent was partly procedural. The logic of campaigning was such that no one could openly claim they wanted the position or were the right candidate for it without violating political conventions and the expected comportment of *rajas*. Potential office-seekers laced speeches with self-deprecations ranging from professions of lack of experience or ability (*mampu'isi*) to lack of knowledge of formal Indonesian, necessary for meetings with the *camat* (the chief district officer). But gridlock, in fact, arose because this procedure was not observed after the last *kepala desa* resigned. Of the candidates whose names were advanced to replace him each disparaged of his own abilities except one—an exuberant speaker who had trouble stopping once he started talking, but who could neither read, write, nor speak Indonesian with any facility. By figuratively standing still while the others stepped back the man came to be selected as *pejabat* (official), much like the first ancestor who plunged to earth (though extricating *pejabat* proved to be more difficult). *Pejabat* had been born in a distant village and adopted by a childless Maneo family; he had few kin and no close brothers to check his aspirations (*ia mukai'isi*). Within a short time of being chosen, he moved out of the village to live in the forest, where he felt less obliged to share meat and performed his official duties sporadically over the years while collecting a small stipend.[2] In his absence, one of two official clan heads (although there are more than two clans in Maneo), assumed most of the responsibilities for communicating with the District Office.[3]

Maneo concede power to outside institutions like the state and the church, but they revise the terms so that what is outside becomes inside. They support the idea of a *kepala desa* as long as he acts a *raja*—a traditional leader; they would be loath to support a *kepala desa* who was simply a state functionary. This inversion is most apparent in the way Maneo elders represent history. Those elders who "know" history (*sejarah*) assert in whispers and behind closed doors that Maneo came first into the world; all the people, then, in fact, all that exists, people as well as inventions and ideas, originated with them. Figures including Jesus and Mohammed were all Maneo in the beginning. Specifically, they were the descendants of siblings (little brothers or sisters) of Maneo ancestors. Obliviousness to this fact does not undermine the belief in its truth since knowledge of origins is restricted to a few (Hagen 1995).[4] Maneo histories describe a series of journeys. These journeys do not merely occur within history, they create it. As with the first plunge to earth after which the earth was transformed, subsequent movement across the landscape left indelible traces of transformed earth as points along a journey. Indeed, historical movement created the landscape just as the initial miscalculated plummet formed the earth. And the world of hard places, in turn, belies their human creation; physical spaces become social places. Maneo recognize every mountain pass, water hole, stream, rock outcropping, and cave they pass on their hunting trips, travels to gardens, the coast, the Transmigration settlement, and every place has a name.[5] Once my principal teacher, Minggus, an extraordinary man, asked for the names of various places around the world, including a large river in North America. When I answered "did you mean the Mississippi River?" he responded with an emphatic "yes," though I doubt he had ever heard it before. For distant places, names confer prior ownership. Like the fanciful claims that Columbus "discovered" America, it is a way for Maneo to assert their prior status in the world. Places also need to have names so people can tell stories.[6] Recounting the names of familiar places—places visited or heard about in stories—can arouse powerful feelings as people are reminded of specific events that gave the land there its form (Tuzin 1997:104). A few spots, almost like geyser fields, remain volatile and susceptible to liquefaction if taboos such as speaking Indonesian there are violated. These and other moral lessons contained in the histories of places are ignored at great peril. Accordingly, when a young Englishman died in a fall on Gunung Binaya, the tallest mountain on Seram (3,027m), during the 1987 Operation Raleigh Expedition in Manusela National Park (to the west), Maneo experts interpreted the cause of his death as literally a misstep. They said the young man followed the wrong path, *"ia amalilu hala ama'a"* (literally "he forgot the path"), suggesting he would have been fine had he followed the right one, as the one taken by his ancestor, Queen Elizabeth, when she left Seram. Causality is, thus, linked to social terrain created in the first instance by the historical movement of people away from the center.

The fact that authorship of events translates into ownership of places helps explain one of the more puzzling features of Maneo land tenure practices. Whole territories are divided in a complex scheme of clan ownership. Even distant places have distinct boundaries. Most places have been owned from the beginning by specific clans, or even sub-clan groups; a few territories were acquired more recently on loan or in trades, the memory of which is preserved in the names of streams and other features. In fact, initially, our arrival raised fears that Jennie and I had come to Maneo to claim land our ancestors left. Knowledge of history and of ownership of places is fragmented; these fragments of knowledge mirror a richly diverse and worked landscape dialectically and contiguously linked to human activity and representations of that activity. Through their alleged effects, human acts are made consequential and physiography becomes a narrative. The zig-zagging paths (*hala*) that form Maneo histories order sequentially decisions and events in time (Parmentier 1987:133–134).

Subsistence, Gender, and the Parameters of Social Life

For Maneo, history is lived, and there is some urgency to heed it. They confront history in their travels, and the historic movement of people is retraced in the day-to-day activities of the living descendants of the original ancestors, particularly traveling through places on the way to gardens, hunting territories, and sago groves. The landscape is as varied as the activities on it and the movement and events that created it.[7] Maneo territory (nearly 700 square kilometers) includes grasslands (*imperata*), lowland and upland primary forest up to 1,700m in elevation (Edwards et al. 1992), swampy, and rocky areas, numerous streams and several good-sized rivers. Kabailu, Maneo Rendah, and Maneo Tinggi—the three most isolated settlements—lie at elevations of 400m; they are surrounded by gardens, and secondary and primary forest. To the north, Siahari, the smallest inland settlement, lies at 60m, nearer grasslands and the Transmigration sites. The two larger villages are on the relatively crowded south coast (Yamalatu and Maneo Ratu) offer different work opportunities and slightly different routines for residents. How Maneo move through these areas is linked to the division of labor, itself shaped by a gendered division of space and a repertoire of mostly subsistence-oriented economic activities. Just as male ancestors transformed the (female) world, it is primarily men who are considered more capable of now traversing it in the course of making a living (Atkinson 1990). Men, more or less exclusively, will venture into the forest (*aipunia*) alone to find food and other things the family needs. Except when traveling in the company of men, women generally restrict travel to the village and gardens, supposedly lacking the power and knowledge of how to travel in the forest.[8]

Travel determines hunting opportunities. Thus, hunting is generally the province of men because cuscus (*phalanger*), deer, wild pig, python, cassowary, fruit bat, and an assortment of large birds such as hornbills typically taken as food are found in the forest or the perimeters of gardens. Women will fish, as will men, and they will hunt small game opportunistically, much as men do—I even heard reports of some non-Maneo women hunting bigger game. But this is the exception. Some hunting is systematic (men will go to the forest for a period of time for that purpose); much of it is opportunistic. It is also restricted to specific clan-owned lands or to land owned by clan subsegments—ownership that confers rights to hunt on it and to limit the hunting activities of other members. When clan members feel that hunting pressures have been too great in particular areas or when, for other reasons, they wish to ensure a supply of game for future hunting, they may place markers (*sasi*), usually crossed sticks, designating an area off limits.

Hunting decisions reflect a number of considerations, the most important being proximity to markets and the opportunity to sell meat, especially deer. To take advantage of markets, some Maneo will move closer to coastal settlements or to the Transmigration site. They will also encourage the growth of grasslands and burn fields to attract deer to new shoots, especially along the northern hills and coastal plains close to Siahari and to the dry season residence of the people of Kabailu. Other big game (wild pig, cassowary, and python) seem to be more abundant at lower altitude than in the mountains, though whether this is due to hunting practices or to forest ecology is difficult to determine. Wild pigs, in particular, are attracted to gardens; where human populations are densest, on the coast and near the Transmigration unit, and around largely Muslim communities where pork consumption is prohibited, pig populations are high. The presence of big game affects efforts put into hunting, and success feeds on itself. Where there is a surfeit of game, everyone who can hunt does so. Where there is not, as around Maneo Rendah, effort tapers off at a threshold only partially determined by the apparent supply of game. Thus, around Maneo Rendah, sandwiched between Kabailu and Maneo Tinggi (about six kilometers in opposite directions), cuscus, a possum-sized, arboreal-dwelling marsupial, comprise the main source of protein; pig and deer are not widely hunted, though not simply because there is not enough big game nearby. If residents of Maneo Rendah hunted big game more often, they would burn grasslands to attract more. They do not hunt for it largely, I believe, because no one wants to be alone in always having to share (and never receive) or to be in the position of being criticized if game is not shared widely. Small game hunting represents a way to avoid these problems. Maneo do not share cuscus widely (it is simply too small); nor will they sell it to outsiders as kin from Kabailu and Siahari will larger game. They can also avoid the social (not to mention physical) perils of pig or deer hunting by not tending to their dogs; between 1992 and 1994, no dogs were being used in Maneo Rendah. Although traps for all game are common and people do climb trees for cuscus and python, hunting big game is facilitated considerably by dogs. Because dogs have to be specially trained, owners must determine in advance whether the effort will pay off, assessing, for example, whether others will be hunting large game and whether they can sell the meat.[9]

Photo 1.1 Processing sago in the forest.

While hunting and gardening activities are varied, sago (*metroxylon* sp.) represents the bedrock of food production and consumption. Sago is not domesticated, though new shoots are sometimes transplanted to more favorable locations and the vegetation around them is often cleared to enhance growth. Sago palms take usually ten to fifteen years to mature, though under ideal conditions as few as eight. When a sago palm (*ipia*) begins to flower, marking maturation, it is felled, peeled and pounded by men; women then press (*lamae*) the shavings (*aeha*) to extract the starch. Usually, husbands and wives undertake the work together—a division of labor that reflects nothing fundamental about the production process. Elsewhere, in western-central Seram, only men organize themselves into work groups for pounding and pressing sago (for example, among the Nuaulu [Ellen 1978] and Wemali [Grzimek 1991]). Although the state has encouraged the Maneo to change, citing the arduousness and adverse effects of starch extraction on women's health, no one expressed any intention to do so. (For an example of state intervention in the division of labor in Java see Brenner [1998:238].) This division of labor is socially consequential. The fact that Maneo husbands and wives take turns working together affects the duration of processing. It generally takes two or three weeks to process a single palm, as much as twice the time of the all-male work groups to the west. Once processing begins, a couple usually sees the process through till finished. A typical sago palm yields between ten and fifteen *lafana* (containers) each holding up to fifteen kilograms of raw starch. This amount is usually sufficient to feed a family of five for up to three months when supplemented with other starches including manioc, taro, yams, and sweet potato.

Roy Ellen (1988a) notes that sago starch extractors who practice little or no agriculture can still lead sedentary lifestyles, which is somewhat unusual for people who make their living hunting and foraging. But while reliance on sago may contribute to permanent settlements, at times in recent Maneo history, the causal direction has been reversed. Instead of leading to stability, sago has contributed to or facilitated increased mobility. First, as discussed, production helps keep households together since teams are independent and self-sufficient. When working sago, husbands and wives generally move to the groves (*dusun*) and live in makeshift shelters for two to four weeks, returning to the village on Saturday afternoons for church services that evening and the following day. Most families process sago three or four times a year, often synchronizing work around community projects, for instance, the construction of a new primary school in Maneo Rendah or work on the new cement church in Maneo Tinggi. If not for these community projects, I suspect, many might remain away from the village for most of the dry season as do residents of Kabailu and Siahari. Second, sago contributes to mobility because the processing itself is so productive. Sago constitutes roughly 50 percent of the Maneo diet. Yet in a sample of 1,322 person days of work (averaging 3-4 hours), processing comprises just 27 percent of the total work time. Preparing a tree requires just a short day, and raw sago can be stored for a long time (dried sago may last for years). The work is not seasonally restricted; it requires little labor investment. Maneo who lack a two or three week block of time may only process a little and leave the rest for grubs, which they will return to harvest. Finally, mobility is facilitated because throughout Maneo, *lafana* of sago are shared with kin or neighbors if they are ill or too busy with other work. The fact that they share, in turn, frees some to pursue other activities such as trapping birds, harvesting cloves, and undertaking community projects. Because there is enough—anyone who processes a palm almost always has a surplus—people can afford to be generous with it, though I observed that Maneo do keep track of whom they have helped in the past. In short, sago gives them options about how to live and with whom.

This flexibility has been essential at various times this century. For instance, during World War II, and especially at the end of the Japanese occupation in 1945 when Japanese and Allied planes crossed the sky overhead, Maneo felt safer processing sago under the forest canopy. Unlike gardens, sago *dusun* or groves are hidden; on the ground, footprints leading off from the main trails may be the only signs of production activity. Later, from 1951 to 1953, in the aftermath of the end of the South Maluku Republic separatist movement, sago production enabled the Maneo to effectively live on the run.[10] Like hunting, sago distribution varies over Maneo territory. Palms thrive in wet or swampy areas and around Maneo Rendah, Maneo Tinggi, and Kabailu (in the mountains). Where such conditions exist, there is more sago than can actually be consumed. Some men say they own hundreds of palms, far more than they could ever expect to consume in their lifetimes.[11] And in the largest groves, people are free to process any palm. In contrast, on the south coast, people from the larger non-Maneo villages own most of the sago and most of the land, Maneo having settled there only recently. Thus when residents of Maneo Ratu and Yamalatu process palms, they do so with the permission of owners with whom they share the raw starch.

Maneo also garden. Cassava or manioc, taro, yam, sweet potato, corn, and banana are planted in gardens slashed and sometimes burned from primary or secondary forest. They range from one square hectare (the largest) to just several square meters (house gardens), averaging just over half a hectare. Around the perimeter, especially around garden huts, they plant fruit trees—durian, jackfruit, mango, and oranges (Latinis 2000). Gardening practices vary considerably: there is great flexibility in terms of what is planted, who works (women or men) and in what phase (planting, tending, or harvesting), and in terms of the effort spent. Along the south coast, because much of the forest is now planted with cash crops (such as cloves, copra, nutmeg, and peanuts), land use for subsistence crops is more intensive (Ellen 1978). In the mountains, land for gardens is more widely available. There, men generally clear the gardens after a lengthy fallow (or from primary forest), sometimes with an ax, usually with a machete, and men and women share planting. Thereafter, women tend and harvest the gardens; men return to build and mend fences (although tobacco farming represents an exception to this pattern). Women will also clear trees if they are single and lack close resident male kin. As with hunting, Maneo prepare gardens on land owned by their clan (or spouse's clan); yet this rule is more relaxed in the mountains where ownership seems to count for very little. For instance, when several families moved to the south coast in 1953, they simply gave some of their land to families from other clans who remained. In the mountains, land use conflicts are few; people wishing to clear a particular plot simply announce their intention to do so prior to commencing, and any objections are usually then resolved. Hunting, in contrast, poses higher stakes since game is relatively scarce and meat is prized. Also, unlike animals and sago, which reproduce on their own, gardening requires effort to transform the land and plant crops—effort that is recognized as the primary source of all that is produced from it. This effort is reflected in the practice of naming individual fruit trees, such as mango or durian, for the persons who planted and tended them, regardless of the actual clan ownership of the land, even though, as a practical matter, ownership of fruit trees confers little. Only owners (including descendants of planters) may climb trees to obtain the unripe fruit; but in the mountains at least, anyone may collect fallen fruits and nuts. Naming trees, like the practice of naming places, serves as a mnemonic device for remembering the ancestors who planted them (Battaglia 1990), further inscribing the landscape with social and historical significance.

Like sago production, swidden-style gardening is highly productive. In all but the smallest gardens (less than a quarter hectare), harvests are generally greater than can be consumed by the immediate household that produced it. Unlike sago that can be stored and meat that can be dried and preserved, however, cassava, corn, and sweet potato do not keep and demand immediate distribution. (Taro is something of an exception.) The social relevance of this fact is that Maneo tend to plant a few large gardens rather than work numerous small gardens continuously. In the mountains, households tend to coordinate gardening activities with those of other households—either members of extended families or with neighbors and affines. They do not necessarily do this to economize. I found that mountain households with unmarried or newly married men not otherwise occupied with significant cash earning activities garden more than do other households. Parents may ask their sons and new sons-in-law to clear gardens; or those young men may simply seize the initiative on their own. In large part, they tend to drive agricultural production. By clearing land, which is arduous work, young men cultivate reputations for industriousness and mark their preparedness for assuming the full responsibilities of adulthood. To be sure, unmarried women face similar pressures to display industriousness. The difference is that women assume greater burdens less conspicuously and at an earlier age than men, such as tending younger siblings, cooking, cleaning, collecting firewood, and gardening. But as discussed in chapter 4, large gardens do enable women to contribute to community sociality as well as to each other's household diets (more than men's subsistence activities). This gives families, in turn, discretion over the allocation of time, even though the sharing of root crops is relatively undervalued. Households may have as many as four producing gardens or as few as two: a mature one (one year old) yielding bananas and taro (which does last), although no more cassava, and a new garden (three months old) producing corn but as yet nothing else. The production of surpluses means that between their own harvests, families are free to pursue other activities.

Gardening flourishes when people are able to stay in one place. Relatively large gardens, in turn, allow for increased sociality, especially in the mountains. When one of our neighbors observed that his ancestors gardened little, he was commenting on the fact that they were constantly moving. Others described the abundance of subsistence gardens since the 1960s, which coincided with an extended period of social stability. More recently, since the mid-1980s, the advent of cash cropping in Maneo has lured many families from the mountains to an area above the south coast for part of the year. In the mountains, if families foresee remaining in an area long enough, it makes sense to plant gardens and to augment staple root crops with beans and tomatoes. If they plan to leave them for any length of time, gardens have to be fenced to protect them from pigs—an onerous and rarely successful task. In the mountains, Maneo do not rely enough on swidden for soil ecology to affect settlement patterns. They may reach a point someday when sedentism and increased gardening do result in enough soil degradation to warrant a shift in village sites or dispersal, but within memory, the kind of population stability that would contribute to this has not been reached. On the south coast, where land is scarcer and residents more sedentary, they plant tree crops and tend to make up the difference by buying or borrowing starches (sago, cassava, or rice).

38   *Chapter 1*

Photo 1.2 Tamar harvesting fruit

Recent Maneo History

The conditions of sociality are also shaped by history. Around 1904, a Dutch-led patrol guided by a Maneo man from Kabailu came around the backside of the

Maneo stronghold described as a fortress (*benteng*), near the Aeya River, downstream from the present settlement of Maneo Rendah, taking them by surprise. At the time, Maneo were one of the last groups of interior Seram to be connected through a path known as the *Jalan Tutaruga* (Turtle Road). The betrayal that made the Dutch raid possible was one of a long series of betrayals; the people of Kobi betrayed the Maneo, as they later betrayed themselves. Throughout the region, the Dutch took advantage of local animosities to gain control. Contact, however, is not remembered as conquest. What Maneo recall is that Sainaka, then *raja*, extended his little finger to the Dutch officer, instead of his hand, and addressed him as "little sister" (*mulua anana*)—a term denoting the subordinate kin status of the Maneo ancestor of the Dutch officer. Indeed, the patrol soon left, or was dismissed, and contact thereafter, for perhaps for two decades, was sporadic.

Although Maneo reverse the terms of contact, they acknowledge certain watershed changes, the most important of which was the reconfiguration of settlements. Prior to contact, they describe their ancestors as living in smaller clusters on clan-owned lands. By the 1910s, at Dutch prompting, particularly by representatives of the Dutch Reformed Church, they began to settle in villages—though they did disperse for a time during the influenza epidemic of 1918—and they replaced elevated communal buildings housing several families with smaller ones with just one hearth and built on the ground. The houses were erected along neat clusters of rows kept clean of weeds, some planted with flowers, and separated from one another and from a wide path by a split bamboo fence. Yet there is perhaps less to the change than meets the eye. Extended families still manage to crowd in on top of one another in these single family dwellings. Half of the twenty-two dwellings in Maneo Rendah, for example, contain more than one couple, and half of these house three couples. When households do separate, couples frequently move close by and carry on the same communication and food sharing as before. Moreover, Maneo assertions to the contrary, there is no evidence to suggest that prior to the arrival of the Dutch, they formed more definite patrilineal groups, that patrilineality, as an organizational principle is in decline, or that Maneo did not live in villages.

Changes brought about by arrival of the Dutch did amplify the consequences of local conflict. The key event in the first half of the twentieth century was a pair of murders committed by Wara'a Ipapoto around the time of the 1918 influenza epidemic or shortly before. Settlements fragmented in the aftermath. First, Wara'a murdered his wife Kamsuni Salakatota in a fit of jealous rage or insanity (depending on who you ask). Pursued by her brothers, Wara'a fled to a large sago grove about thirty kilometers to the northeast. Eventually, the pursuers broke off the chase and the brothers then moved to the south coast (about forty kilometers away) where they established the settlement of Maneo Pantai (now Yamalatu). After Wara'a returned to the village, he killed Nunupao Tamala, supposedly because he believed Nunupao's brother was having an affair with his (Wara'a's) sister (a somewhat improbable motive unless he was insane). After the second murder, some of Nunupao's (Tamala) brothers also left

Photo 1.3 Maneo Tinggi

Yamalatu and married coastal women. Wara'a was then arrested by a police patrol and forced to labor for the Dutch for the next twenty years in southeast Maluku and what was then Dutch New Guinea until his release by the Japanese around 1942. Enmities surrounding the second murder were soon resolved, and new marriages were contracted between the clans; but this has yet to happen with Salakatota (the clan of the first victim). Seventy-five years later the murder still divides respective descendants: Salakatota elders insist that members of their clan cannot marry Ipapoto, a prohibition that is supposed to be in effect for five generations (the present being the fourth). In addition, Halamuri (the principal affines of Salakatota) have been reluctant to marry Ipapoto as well. Despite the real and enduring animosities created, it is not inconsistent to view the hostility as a convenient pretext for moving to the south coast to take advantage of easier opportunities there to sell damar (a tree resin) and other forest resources.

In the wake of the murders, and in the aftermath of the departures to the coast, those who remained in the old village of Wasoko (the first established after the Dutch patrols) moved higher up to a nearby mountain, perhaps for protection from each other. At this time too, in the 1920s, Christian missionizing and education began. The oldest Maneo recall learning to read and speak some Dutch; most Maneo assumed Christian names and were baptized, although some had not given up entirely on the practice of headhunting.[12] Maneo began to participate, if somewhat reluctantly, in state projects. Labor was conscripted to help build the Turtle Road completed around 1937, a path stretching from Wahai, the district capital on the north coast, through to the various mountain villages—a route still used in some sections and lined with wild pineapple. Once a year, throughout the 1920s and '30s, a Dutch officer came to Maneo to collect *belasting* (taxes). After the Japanese defeat of the Dutch in 1942, men were again conscripted to provide labor processing palm oil into soap; some less fortunate Maneo men were sent to Amahai and to Bula (the site of an important oil field) to work on and repair airfields—a dangerous job, and at least one Maneo man died when the Allies began to bomb the fields.

The postwar years, during the transition to Indonesian independence between 1945 and 1950, were quiet in central Seram. Maneo and others likely received little news (and would have shared little concern) about the Indonesian nationalist struggle against the Dutch. However, in Java, the Dutch were losing to the Indonesian army and leaders in Ambon were forced to decide whether to throw their lot in with this new and unfamiliar, Muslim-dominated, mostly Javanese government or declare an independent, largely Christian republic in South and Central Maluku. The decision to follow the latter course was based largely on a strategic miscalculation that the Dutch and the broader international community would support them (Chauvel 1990). That did not happen. The *Republik Maluku Selatan* or *RMS* army and government were quickly routed from their base in Ambon and forced to flee to Seram to continue their struggle. Despite some limited military success, the *RMS* were dislodged from positions near the coast at Amahai and Wahai and forced to retreat into the mountains in 1950. As the war for a separate republic in South and Central Maluku was winding down, though, the battles involving the Maneo and their neighbors were about to begin (see chapter 7). In 1953, as the Indonesian army gained control of the coastal regions of Seram, Maneo scattered to the forest, where a few families remained permanently. Many more (roughly fifteen households) linked by clan and affinal ties came out from hiding on the south coast. They appealed for land from a neighboring Muslim village in order to build a new coastal settlement, Maneo Ratu, about eight kilometers to the west of Maneo Pantai. Over the next two decades, twenty more households moved to the south coast, leaving only half the population in the village of Maneo Rendah that had been there in 1950—part of a widespread exodus from the mountains throughout Seram (Grzimek 1991). Some families were forced to move, and entire settlements were relocated; but many, too, were drawn by new social, economic, and educational opportunities. And, as in Maneo Pantai three decades earlier, the promise of political stability encouraged men in Maneo Ratu to marry into Christian families on the coast.

During the relative calm after the end of *RMS* military resistance in 1953, the church, formerly the Dutch Calvinist Church, now the independent *Gereja Protestan Maluku* or *GPM* introduced a new stream of Ambonese-trained ministers and consolidated gains made in the 1930s. If Maneo might have gone back to being animist or taken the route of the forest Maneo, attrition and a new wave of missionizing were making this impossible. By the 1960s, many from the generation of elders who had experienced life prior to Dutch "pacification" were gone. Most of their successors, including the *raja* (Gustov on the coast and Zakarius in the mountains) assumed Christian names and became involved in conversion by helping to suppress traditional ceremonies. Most Maneo had attended school, administered by the church, and learned how to read, many by practicing with the Bible. In 1964, Zakarius, the new *raja* of Maneo Rendah, founded the settlement of Siahari with the intent of attracting Maneo still living in the forest and converting them to Christianity. He succeeded in establishing a church and attracting a few families from the forest, but Zakarius's untimely death triggered sorcery allegations and reprisal against the newcomers from the forest. After his kin killed the suspected sorcerer, that man's relatives fled and Siahari was abandoned until a new group of families moved there from Maneo Rendah several years later. Since its founding, the settlement has grown and fallen in size; a school was built but never used. When Jennie and I arrived in 1992, occupancy was intermittent.

The situation in Siahari was influenced significantly by the creation of Transmigration units along Seram's north coast. In 1980, one was established about ten kilometers northeast of Siahari, swallowing the main Seti village to the northeast. Some ten years later, just before we arrived, another site was opened up just six kilometers to the north of the village, reaching into Maneo territory. Transmigration is a controversial government-sponsored, World Bank-financed program designed to relocate the landless poor living in overcrowded cities and villages of Java, Bali, south Sulawesi, (even Ambon) to the relatively sparsely populated outer islands—the largest planned migration scheme in the world. Throughout Indonesia, since the program's inception in 1970, approximately 7.2 million people have been relocated, including several thousand who have been moved into an area of roughly 40,000 square hectares along the north-central and northeastern coastal plain of Seram beginning in 1979 (Hayes et al. 1999). The program has also found political favor by combining considerable economic opportunities for companies in construction, logging, and various agribusinesses with nation building and the politically marketable campaign of helping to develop the "underdeveloped" outer islands (Tsing 1993). In this spirit, locals who elect to participate, or who have been forced to because their land has been taken, are encouraged to believe that the Javanese can teach them more efficient farming techniques, even though many Transmigrants never worked as farmers before enlisting. Participating families receive two hectares of land for farming, some tools, a house, and rice allotments for a year.

The greater farming efficiency touted by Transmigration officials has meant replacing sustainable land-extensive slash-and-burn agriculture with more intensive, continuous use of smaller plots, aided by fertilizers and pesticides. It has been a disaster on the northern coastal plane of Seram. Clear-cutting has exacerbated drought and flooding, and lateritic soils (heavily leached tropical soils with low nutrient and high clay content) have proved unsuitable for sustained agricultural use. Ten years after initiating Transmigration in northern Seram, most fields have been abandoned forming a 10-15 km swath of grasslands (*imperata*) suitable only for grazing—and not every family can afford livestock. In tacit recognition of the ecological precariousness of intensive agriculture where soil conditions do not support it, newer Transmigration projects in Indonesia's outer islands have sought to integrate population movements with labor needs in various state-run agro-forestry schemes. Many of the Transmigrants who came to northern Seram in the 1980s and '90s have moved back to Java or to new Transmigration sites, registering under names of different family members. Ironically, the most successful Transmigrants have been people indigenous to the area like the Maneo and Seti. From the perspective of Transmigration administrators, locals make fine recruits. They know how to make money selling meat and birds and can serve as middlemen to outsiders cutting select hardwoods and mining *geharu* (a sap used for incense). Locals are also less likely to abandon a site to move elsewhere, especially if they have nowhere else to go. Maneo (who can move back) told us they would return to mountain settlements after their children finish schooling. From their perspective, in addition to schooling, settling in a Transmigration area offers a way to expand opportunities to participate in the wider currents of state society and popular culture at little cost. For example, many watched TV there for the first time.

By moving, Maneo do not see themselves as relinquishing traditional land claims or losing their identity. In fact, they claim to be in better position to defend those rights from within the Trans, discouraging outsiders from entering the forest and encroaching on traditional lands. By 1994, nearly all Maneo from Siahari and half the households from Kabailu had "entered" the two nearby Trans sites. In Maneo Rendah, as discussed, while we were present, four families, out of twenty-two, took up residence in the newest Transmigration unit (known as Samal Baru). Maneo attach themselves to multiple places, although the state discourages people like them having more than one address. In the Transmigration site, some have successfully manipulated relations with non-Maneo Transmigrants, as Christians and as church leaders and local, cultural ambassadors. One rather entrepreneurial Maneo man, an "*RT*" in the unit (a term for neighborhood leader) designated himself a *raja* in order to extort money from his Javanese neighbors.

Transformation on the northern edge of Maneo territory, where Transmigration has simultaneously cut into and opened up people's horizons of opportunity, paralleled a different sort of development on the more hospitable south coast. For hundreds of years, Maneo may have been indirectly involved in copra, clove, and nutmeg cultivation following the cessation of Dutch efforts to eradicate and thereby monopolize spice production. Since moving to the south coast, Maneo have worked on the harvests of their Muslim and Christian neighbors. Beginning in the early 1970s, this work relationship changed and Maneo production dramatically expanded. Wilson, a young man born in Maneo Rendah but raised in the forest after the *RMS* debacle and recently widowed, moved to the mountains several kilometers behind the village of Laimu (between the two coastal Maneo settlements), where he cleared several hectares of forest to plant clove trees. Over the course of five years he planted a thousand trees on clan-owned ancestral mountainside above the narrow coastal plain. Wilson's initiative and success inspired others to carve out clove orchards from the forest and spend years tending young trees. For those living on the coast, it was possible to clear the gardens and nurture trees during the day without living full time in the forest. Others, like Wilson, who came from the mountains, lived more or less permanently in the new orchards until the clove trees were old enough to compete with other vegetation.

Throughout the 1980s until 1991, clove prices were high, as much as US$3 per kilogram. For an owner of an average-sized orchard of 100 fifteen-year-old trees, a yield of 150 kilograms could bring an enormous windfall, especially for persons accustomed to meeting subsistence needs by hunting and foraging. Much of the money was distributed throughout the community to workers who did not own trees but who climbed those owned by kin, and to affines as part of the complex system of marriage exchanges. Minggus, my teacher, even gave his affines an orchard he had cleared. In general, however, money or orchards used in this way are merely intended to augment the exchange of traditional valuables. No doubt, too, tax officials and Chinese and Bugis merchants siphoned off much of the money. From what remained, coastal Maneo used the cash windfall to build cement homes covered with corrugated metal roofs, and they acquired a taste for rice and fish. They also purchased new clothes; and cash from clove sales helped to fund advanced education for a number of Maneo children, several of whom attended universities in Ambon.

Within the 1990s, the expansion of clove orchards has largely ceased because of the creation (and enforcement) of Manusela National Park boundaries. Other barriers to expansion are the distances between new orchard land and the coast and a downturn in wholesale clove prices. The clove-fueled sense of affluence began to fade between 1989 (my first visit) and 1992–1994, creating a notable contrast. In 1991, Tommy Suharto, a son of the former president, established a clove agency (BPPC) to set prices paid to growers. The ostensible purpose was to stabilize prices and so spare the farmers the effects of fluctuation, but it was set at as little as one third of the actual market value (less than $1). When clove growing was still profitable, few Maneo bothered to diversify crops; in fact, some had even cut down nutmeg trees in order to plant more cloves. With incomes suddenly halved, people became desperate, and many parents had to pull children from schools in the early 1990s.

I suspect another change in practices of sharing was caused by the decline in income. Even Wilson, who may have grossed as much as US$4,000 a season, gave most of the money away. With little to spend money on, this would have been a reasonable activity consistent with the general ethos of generosity. Giving, however, is a complex matter, as I will discuss in chapter 5. Cash does not have any intrinsic value except as a token of exchange and convertibility; it is not distributed in the village like portions of butchered deer or pig. It has to be requested and requests follow the contours of particular relationships, generally affinal ones, where wife givers (*hahamana*) ask their wife takers (*hahapina*). Some exchanges are reciprocated; others are not and what is given in the case of cash is not counted. Requests can come from close or distant affinal relations; Wilson, for example, was approached by affines whose connections to his wife are so distant as to be untraceable even by genealogical experts. But as the value of money as a means to procure other things increases (because of a decrease in its availability and an increase in demand for it), affinal requests are becoming more insistent. In turn, people make up shortfalls, such as paying taxes on the coast and school fees for their children, by asking their affines for cash. Those being asked then pressure their own affines (wife-takers)—those who owe them. The presence of money (especially now that Maneo have experienced shortages) has begun to change the social landscape of Maneo, encouraging people to move to the coast where opportunities to earn it are greater. Cash has also influenced their interactions. It is difficult to say how much; harder still to predict what might happen in the future, whether, for example, cash will undermine social relations (Simmel 1950:335; Marx 1977:109–111, 179; cf. Bloch and Parry 1989; see Robbins and Akin 1999). But at present, social perturbations reflect not so much the presence and circulation of money as the abrupt decline in its supply.

Unlike neighbors on the coast, Maneo still enjoyed access to hundreds of kilometers of mostly primary forest. Whatever else happens to the price of cloves and, more dramatically, the ongoing civil unrest, they can still return to the forest and live off the land. However, new threats are emerging. In the north, new Transmigration units are encroaching into Maneo forests. In the south, in 1994, the company PT Djianti suddenly began construction on what was said to be the second largest cement factory in all of Southeast Asia (next to the Muslim village of Laimu and between the two coastal Maneo villages. The factory is to produce clinker, a raw material used for cement, from limestone. Limestone deposits cover much of the mountainside facing the south coast, just beyond the clove orchards (the vast area between the coastal and mountain Maneo settlements). The company has leased mining rights from the state for ninety-nine years and plans to level an entire mountain, no doubt clearing much of the forest around.

Contemporary Settlement Patterns

To return to the theme addressed at the outset of the chapter, the historic movement of people out of the mountains during the twentieth century recalls the mythic movement of people from the source. The movement is not unidirectional or new. There is reason to believe, however, that events over the past century have hastened the depopulation of the mountains. These ranged from pacification, the Dutch encouragement to resettle, the migration of other formerly inland peoples of Seram to the coast, to the specific incidents in Maneo history (beginning with the double homicide). Around 1950, the old village of Maneo Rendah encompassed as many as sixty households. Some fifteen left after the *RMS* disaster in 1953, and others followed to pursue new economic and educational opportunities offered on the coast or in the Transmigration site. There were twenty-two houses remaining when we first arrived in June 1992 (population 127); by February 1994, that number had dwindled to just eighteen—the last four houses were abandoned when families moved to the unit (although most claimed they would return). Maneo Tinggi (population 149) suffered a less precipitous population decline. There, only one family (out of twenty-five) moved to the Transmigration site, and their movement to the coast has slowed because the historic destination—Yamalatu rather than Maneo Ratu (where residents of Maneo Rendah tend to go)—is now somewhat overcrowded and suffering a shortage of land.[13] As for Siahari (population forty-three), the smallest settlement, most of the households have members who have entered the nearby Transmigration site (the old site, Surakarsa, established in the mid-1980s and the new one, Samal Baru, which began some six years later). Many of those people live in one or the other most of the time (particularly during the school year). The depopulation of Kabailu (with forty-six people in just nine households), which represents something of an exception, was set in motion decades earlier by illness, particularly the influenza epidemics of 1918 and 1957, more than emigration. Despite land limitations along the south coast, Yamalatu (population 203) and Maneo Ratu (population 178), have grown in population.

Maneo theories of history and demographic processes implicate largely internal social conflicts, as I will discuss in subsequent chapters. In general, patterns of movement are consistent with patterns of staying put: People tend either to move or remain with close siblings and affines (a theme in chapter 4). This is not to suggest that kinship considerations represent the most important motivations behind whether a family leaves or stays (although I heard several people say so), but that such considerations are crucial to the timing and determination of where people ought to move if they do. In these decisions, sibling relations are key, though certainly a person seeking to relocate who has close kin in all the villages will weigh other factors. Clansmen stick together. In each of the villages, the average number of male heads of household for each clan is 3.8; among the ten largest clans, the average rises to 4.4. Put differently, out of a total of thirty-five (male) heads of family throughout Maneo representing clan minorities (two or fewer heads in a village from a particular clan) twenty-one or a total of 60 percent either married in or were the first generation descendants of fathers who married in. Among the total population of male family heads (from majority and minority clans), only 23 percent (or thirty-seven out of 158) married in or are first generation descendants of fathers who married in. Likely, if they were not there because they were born there or have siblings there, the principal reason for their residence there is marriage. Except for their marriages, these male household heads would not have chosen to live apart from at least some siblings. They either leave when opportunities present themselves or through their children come to dominate a settlement. For married women, residence is generally determined by their husbands' circumstances—their natal villages (if different) and their distribution of marriage payments. I will explore the causes and effects of this pattern of clan distribution later. Here, I wish to make the point that ties to place, so important in terms of the Maneo mythical-historical narrative, articulates, at the same time, the significance of ties to people. For all the potential conflict between brothers—that is, living side by side in their natal village—they do not prefer to be alone (*kesa ia*) or without brothers. The disadvantages of living alone are realized in considerations of the support and cooperation someone can expect from close kin and, in some cases, protection from sorcery and allegations of its use. In fact, as a general trend, the few Maneo suspected of using sorcery and the larger number of believed victims all lacked close kin.[14] Close relatives close by represent a kind of insurance where no other such guarantees exist. The advantages of propinquity, both for sisters as well as brothers, are most apparent in light of the dangers Maneo might otherwise face in the absence of kin.

Notes

1. While not articulated as such by my informants, given the associations of maleness with the sky and femaleness with the earth described elsewhere in the region (McKinnon 1991; Valeri 1990b; Traube 1989:326), the sexuality of the encounter reveals rather obvious gendered tension between encompassing and encompassment.

2. Officially, Maneo comprise three villages, or *desa*—the two coastal villages of Maneo Ratu and Yamalatu in the district of Tehoru in south-central Seram, and one in the mountains in Wahai district to the north. In fact, there are four mountain settlements; Maneo Rendah is nominally the official village, with Maneo Tinggi, Kabailu, and Siahari being considered ancillary settlements (*anak desa*). Whereas there is just one headman (*kepala desa*) for the mountains, the two coastal settlements each have their own. A *kepala desa* is considered a *raja* (the colonial-era title of ruler that carried real authority only on the coast and in the larger settlements where the village headman may be the first to receive any portion of deer or pig brought into the village). The *raja* served as he wished and generally inherited the position. To campaign for office of *kepala desa*, therefore, would seem very un-*raja* like and likely discourage the support one hoped to attract. When I first arrived in 1989, the mountain settlements had a *kepala desa* who was residing in Wahai temporarily. He stepped down, after elders questioned his authority, and during the twenty months of fieldwork, 1992–1994, there was no *kepala desa* from any of the mountain villages. I believe residents fully expected to choose one. They convened several meetings to select a *kepala desa* along with a *pejabat* (official or assistant to the *kepala desa*)—to replace the reigning *pejabat*—and a *sekretaris* (secretary), *pisuruh* (messenger) along with two *kepala soa* (clan heads). Some of the lesser positions were eventually filled. But the selection of candidates for the top positions, *kepala desa* and *pejabat*, remained deadlocked. Until the current *pejabat* resigns, he cannot be replaced and since he does not attend meetings it has been impossible to obtain his consent for a new election for either position.

3. The value of elections centered on the distribution of titles and the connections they offered to other titleholders. It was less about power. Maneo seem to revel in titles; most adult males and a number of adult females have at least one. The appeal lies in locating them in a system of other title-holders: *pisuruh* is thus connected to *ketua LKMD* (the Public Works Coordinator) who happen to be neighbors. In turn, they imagine connections to their counterparts throughout the archipelago; and government titles overlap a

bevy of church titles (*pendeta*, *semas*, *penatua*, *tuagama*, and *koordinator*) superimposed on a kinship system that differentiates and militates against this more hierarchical, formal model of political integration.

4. Maneo history describes the aggregation and dissolution of community forms. The process is episodic. Even in the earliest mythic times, a period the Maneo call *Nusa Mutuania* (the old world), settlements formed, then later came undone under pressures induced by envy, animosity, and violence, only to re-form elsewhere on the landscape before succumbing again. Although the fragmentation of an original totality is the general trend, echoing a theme found elsewhere in eastern Indonesia (McKinnon 1991; Traube 1986) and Melanesia (Battaglia 1990), Maneo history does not describe this process as unidirectional nor as inevitable (see Valeri 1990a).

5. In June 1992, when we walked into the mountains of central Seram to begin field work, the emptiness of the forest was interrupted in just a few places by posters supporting the Government Party (Golkar) left from the recently concluded national election. To us, the signs were familiar, the forest and the sounds in it distinctly unfamiliar. Our perception of emptiness was a matter of habit to see the forest, as Thoreau had, as a place of solitude. Coming over a ridge and into a garden clearing we looked out across the valley to the village of Maneo Rendah on the other side. The view of the settlement offered a respite from the prior emptiness of the forest. Of course, after we had a chance to rest, eat, and clean up, the perception of familiarity with the settlement (even though I had been there before and people knew me) receded quickly in the face of new incomprehension.

6. One rather odd story describes the movement of three large boulders to their present locations on Seram. The moves just happened, as if the physical world was so pliable that objects could simply travel on their own accord or could be easily pushed. What the story speaks to is the belief that agency emanates from particular fields or systems of social relations inasmuch as the historic movements (of things and people) are described as being caused or driven by them (for example, envy among brothers or brothers' wives).

7. My account here is synoptic. Readers should refer to Roy Ellen's (1978) meticulous description of Nuaulu settlement and ecology for a full account of a production system similar in many respects to Maneo. The work that people pursue is varied; it is varied in terms of what people do, who they do it with, and how they distribute it. Routines hinge surprisingly little on seasonal change (from wet to dry), except for the availability of certain fruits and changes in hunting practices.

8. Women do possess extraordinary power, but of a more transformative and, men would add, destructive sort (see Valeri 1990b).

9. Hunting can be quite hazardous. In the canopy, the danger of falling is always present. As for big game, deer are certainly less dangerous than wild pigs, but when dogs are following a trail it is often difficult to determine at first whether the animal is a deer or pig. Pigs have been known to chase dogs back to their owners causing more than a few deaths and significant injuries. Hunting practices and differential hunting success and patterns of distribution all variously effect, and are affected by, the tenor of social relations.

10. Sago is notoriously devoid of nutritional value, but living in the forest processing sago likely encourages greater use of other forest fruits and vegetables that may offset nutritional deficiencies of a sago-dominated diet.

11. I calculated that to meet subsistence needs, the average family would need to own only sixty palms, given a fifteen-year growing period and no regrowth. This requirement is far less than the hundreds of palms some persons claim to own. In smaller groves, ownership does seem to matter more either because of proximity to villages or hunting territories, or because, being smaller, individual trees are simply singled out.

12. Perhaps, for a time, the motivation behind headhunting was redirected toward market "conquest," however fleeting: in effect, creating new enemies (albeit in a new context) since the old enemies were no longer enemies but, in some cases, fellow Christians (cf. George 1996:83–88).

13. On my first trip to Maneo a *kepala soa* from Maneo Tinggi told me that the government was seeking to relocate them. He vowed to move to the forest and hide rather than submit. The irony, three years later when I returned, was that families were moving out of the village entirely on their own, many to the government's new Transmigration site.

14. In the first incident, the victim, a young man, was killed when visiting a settlement on the north coast. He had kin in the village (not a Maneo settlement), but they were kin of his parents who had adopted him. Under circumstances that remain unclear, one of his own classificatory brothers killed him. In 1990, two brothers were killed in quick succession: the first, near Wahai, the second, near Kabailu. Both murders are generally attributed to land disputes; the brothers (both of whom were married) had no other close kin nearby.

2

Reckoning Kinship

> Yet see'st not in what misery thou art fallen, nor where thou dwellest nor with whom for mate. Dost know thy lineage? Nay, thou know'st it not, and all unwitting art a double foe to thine own kin, the living and the dead; aye and the dogging curse of mother and sire one day shall drive thee, like a two-edged sword, beyond our borders, and the eyes that now see clear shall henceforward endless night. Teiresias to Oedipus. Sophocles, *Oedipus the King*

In this chapter, intended as a general meditation on kinship pragmatics, I examine how the Maneo understand their identities and relations; specifically, I contrast Western views with local, largely pragmatic theories of knowledge by exploring the way Maneo use their knowledge of kinship in the course of conducting their lives. This focus on knowledge-use represents something of an accommodation on my part to the fact that while the Maneo orient their actions in terms of their relations and respective identities, they also improvise and manage the very knowledge on which kin-designations are based. Time and again, people would misidentify and relocate kin in the pantheon of their relations. Often the same kin were the subject of disagreement, but not always. The "mistakes" Jennie and I encountered belie more than mere confusion or calculation, which such improvisations would suggest. The inconsistencies raise two broader points concerning the ground against which claims are made. First, the anomalies only appear so from particular vantage points. It is this perspectival condition which made our efforts to compile genealogies perhaps more a liability than an asset to understanding how such knowledge is used (Barnes 1967; Zeitlyn 1993). Second, Maneo efforts to construct kinship, if not motivated by specific objectives, are nonetheless compelled by the actions of others in promoting their own interpretations of relationships. Situations in which such interpretations disagree or push the limits of what people know about relations can pose challenges that are interesting locally and ethnographically. Occasionally, the challenges can be quite dramatic, as when a stranger arrived one day and announced that he was the son of an ancestor. The event reveals the stakes behind such claims and the associated problems of assessing them. It also points to the extent to which knowledge is taken for granted in everyday interactions.

In August 1993, Maneo received word that Atan Boiratan, who had disappeared nearly fifty years before, was in fact alive and at that very moment making his way back home to the village of Maneo Rendah in the mountains where we had spent most of the previous fifteen months. This was stunning news.

When his family had last seen Atan as a young man in his twenties, he had just been conscripted into the Royal Netherlands East Indies Army (*Koninklijk Nederlandsch-Indisch Leger*, or *KNIL*)—the only Maneo to have ever served in the military—and was on his way to Java to help suppress the Indonesian independence movement just after World War II. The Dutch had long drawn conscripts from Seram and the surrounding islands. But for the majority of nonelites not invested in any way in the colonial system (including Atan and the rest of the Maneo population), modest support was based more on the lack of any perceived affinity with the Javanese-dominated nationalists than on the desire to retain the colonial system (Chauvel 1990). For Atan, conscription may have represented an opportunity to see the world. Furthermore, even in the 1940s, as now, it may have been perceived as a route to social mobility. Not long after his departure, though, news filtered back that he had been killed in a battle in East Java. There was no subsequent information to confirm or deny this through the intervening years until, unexpectedly, a young man appeared in the village claiming to be Atan's son and promising that his father and mother would return shortly, along with a cargo of rice, oil, sugar, a generator, and a soccer ball. Particularly among those few kin themselves, now elders, who had known Atan as children, the shock caused by the talk of this return reveals the extent to which attitudes toward and relations with the dead are predicated on their status as completely and consistently dead. Even ancestors are recognized by identifiable traces associated with them. Thus, the dead Atan's change in form evident in his return as a living person raised several troubling questions: Was this the same Atan people knew fifty years before? If it was, how would they recognize him?

There was an additional set of issues, too, that I will trace out toward the end of the chapter. Whether elders appreciated it or not they would have to be prepared, at some point, to reconcile what they knew of the history of kin relations with what Atan, a generation older, could recall. This would not be a matter of simply smoothing out differences about the facts, for efforts would have to be directed toward not only finding agreement about what each party knew, but also compensating for the difference in breadth of knowledge. With Atan's return, the process of forgetting would effectively be postponed a generation. Specifically, with his depth of knowledge he might call into question the "appropriateness" of new relations (particularly marriages) sanctioned by elders on the basis of their more limited understanding of relatedness. In sum, the sudden uncertainty of Atan's status caused by the announcement of his return, and the challenges his return raised, reveals pointedly the tension between the (sometimes ambivalent) desire and need to know how persons are related, on the one hand, and limits to knowing on the other.

Past approaches to kinship knowledge provide few clues for understand this tension. Much of the scholarship focuses on semantics (Hirschfeld 1986), on the meaning (Scheffler and Lounsbury 1971; Goodenough 1956) or translatability (Schneider 1984; Needham 1971) of local terms used to describe the different categories of relations. Recent studies, in an effort to move beyond this narrow focus, examine the broader context in which kin terms are actually employed and kin are classified (Zeitlyn 1993; see also Kipp 1984). In another direction, scholars expand and explicate the variable sources of kin ties (Carsten 1995a) in consideration of such issues as adoption, fosterage, and surrogacy (see Peletz 1995). For all the heat generated by debates over formalist and symbolist approaches, and over the biological and cultural dimensions of kinship (see Gellner 1987:164–165), however, there has been little light trained on the question posed above about how locals understand kinship. The elision, I suspect, may be an unintended result of efforts to describe the embeddedness of kinship in practical (Bourdieu 1977:5) and emotional life (Trawick 1990:118; Wikan 1990). Reducing knowledge to experience, in effect, bifurcates the subject matter between practice approaches and more formal cognitive models. But if the aim of the former is to bring to light this embeddedness, then people's awareness of their positions within a matrix of social relations has to be central to understanding how kinship and social identity are experienced. Michael Lambek's point (1993:84) that "being a person entails knowing things" (see also Herzfeld 1995:125), would suggest that in a society like Maneo, organized largely on the basis of kinship and marriage, what one knows of those relations determines, in some ways, who one is.

Knowledge of relatedness is crucial to the identities people construct and to kinship processes in general. Yet how that knowledge is assessed and used remains something of a given (see Bloch 1989:14). Moreover, the skills and acumen by which people acquire and retain knowledge of relations becomes an issue only when limits, or a lack of consistent information, undermine attempts by anthropologists and locals alike to objectify and manage (or diagram) those same relations. In light of these inconsistencies, Barnard and Good (1984:23–24), for instance, posit the existence of "subjective" genealogies that are based on informants' reckonings and contrast them to one "objective" or true genealogy. As measured against that standard, incompleteness or inaccuracy confirms the patently obvious, namely that some informants know less than others or that the facts they possess do not fit reality. Mistakes and dissimulation can be glossed over as impediments to the discovery of "real" kinship (e.g., Chagnon 1968:10–13), derived implicitly or explicitly from biology (Gellner 1987:164); however, any correspondence between local and Western theories of procreation and relatedness—one possible theme for discussion—obscures another logically prior one that concerns the contexts, and the differences in contexts, in which kin claims are made.

With this end in mind, my approach focuses on how kinship is experienced through the modalities of knowing. While it is true that mistakes in representation are sometimes just mistakes, and some people know more than others, the content of social knowledge, I propose, is inextricably linked to its use and to the context in which it is generated and circulated (Bloch 1989:121). This is not to suggest that there are no truths, but that, on the contrary, there are reasons to subscribe to multiple truths (Bowlin and Stromberg 1997:126–128) that are not entirely consistent. Accordingly, one can know too little as too much, as when relationship claims appear to contradict. For all these reasons, kinship knowledge is not an object that can be possessed in varying degrees and the constitution of that knowledge is bound up with the strategies for acquiring and managing it.

Questions of meaning in kinship are better framed as issues of process. So, to understand the way the Maneo conceive their web of social relations, we need to address several prior questions. How do people know their relatives? How is that knowledge constituted? And, what are the constraints or impediments to acquiring it? There are two points I wish to develop. The first is that awareness of someone's social landscape and, more specifically, her or his representation of it, cannot be interpreted as if it offers a transparent window onto a world of "objective" social relations. If this were the case then the accuracy of representation would be a sufficient condition for depicting such a world. But accuracy—for instance, that the biblical ancestor Japheth beget Gomer and not Cush—is not the only consideration, nor the most important. Accuracy describes a degree of correspondence; it is a condition of the statements about something rather than a characterization of the representation of the phenomenon (Rorty 1991:126–161; Bowlin and Stromberg 1997:126). Moreover, comprehensiveness—a correlate to the accuracy of knowledge—in Maneo, as I will discuss below, would lead to a bundling of contradictions. The second point is that extensiveness of, thoroughness, and limits to knowledge (its morphology, in short) is itself inextricably linked to the way people experience kinship.[1]

This discussion of awareness of social relations and identities follows a distinction Paul Ricoeur (1992:116–117) introduces between "sameness"—that person X with certain more or less unique characteristics, for example, a name, a face, even a social security number, is the same person from one situation to another—and "selfhood" that represents, at once, a relationally constituted, historically framed sense or awareness (see also Kelly 1993:459–460; Strathern 1988:13–15). Knowledge of sameness follows recognition of who a person is relative to previous points in time; whereas the sense of self, and by extension, the awareness of others, results from understanding how persons are connected or disconnected to those around them. These two ways of knowing and dimensions of being are intertwined. Specifically, they become intertwined in experience: people recognize others based on past experience and, reciprocally, the identification of others, along with the recollections that identification evokes, guides the tenor of the relations one keeps, if not the actual relationship designations themselves. Knowledge is a reflection of practice. This is habitus (Bourdieu 1977), but it has a particular ontological foundation. That is, kinship is mediated through and experienced in the stories people tell themselves and others; these narratives create continuities and these continuities, in turn, facilitate understanding and, critically, help frame expectations for future action. Establishing continuity is, thus, a compelling motive in its own right (Johnson 1993:152–154, 163–171). Yet, the narratives themselves are neither entirely coherent nor unbroken, given that the contingencies of experience demand constant adjustments. At times, continuities are disrupted—dramatically in cases of mistaken identities and in the discovery of deceptions and deliberate obfuscation—while more subtly, though frequently, when ties are forgotten as when ancestors disappear from memory. These dramatic discontinuities pose rare analytical opportunities; they also point to the fact that in day-to-day interactions the problem for analysis is generally opposite: the continuities created by sameness (that is, the identities of persons) divert attention from the other, historical dimensions of relatedness. In other words, identification and understanding become conflated and knowledge is reduced to that ability to recognize individuals who, it is assumed, occupy unambiguous, fixed status positions in relation to ego.

Doubts about Ancestors

Knowing is a manner of experiencing the world as well as a way of representing it (Valeri 1994a:199).[2] When we talk about knowing entities as elusive as ancestors the question arises, in what sense are they experienced? This is an important test of relevance; for representations to be compelling and to exercise some hold on imagination they have to be experienced. Yet one's experience with ancestors is of only their traces. These traces consist of the memories people have of the ancestors' names—which may be prohibited from being mentioned in some societies (see Chagnon 1968)—and of associated experiences. Alternatively, or in combination, traces are created by the transformations the ancestors undergo upon death and burial (Huntington and Metcalf 1980; Hoskins 1993:247–249), and by whatever continuing or new agency is ascribed to them as a presence in the world, even if that agency exists as a measure of the comparatively reduced agency of the living (Keane 1997a:95). In the special case of secondary burials, it is suggested that ancestors are empowered, but, at the same time, rendered amenable to control if only through the complicity of their descendants in dissolving their physical traces (Graeber 1995). Following Weber (1947:112–113), we might suppose, in general, that ancestors are subjects in ongoing social action to the extent they are capable of influencing the behaviors of others. The problem though, again, is that because ancestors, for the most part, are "beyond representation" except for those traces (Ricoeur 1992:354), to possess agency actions still have to be ascribed to them. A condition of agency in Maneo is recognition of an agent and recognition can proceed quite differently. But recognition is merely necessary and not sufficient to convince others of an ancestor's involvement. Different analytical solutions to this uncertainty are possible. Freud, for instance, perceived agency in the reactions ancestors instilled among the living, that is, the universal feelings of ambivalence which he intuited as evidence of resentment toward them that would have to be suppressed while they were alive (Freud 1950:60; cf. Opler [1936]1979). For Freud, it is the memories of ancestors that possess an ineluctable reality; the taboos they inspire—a mere "projection" of sentiments in his account—are signs of the force they presuppose. Traditionally, anthropologists have ascribed an existence to ancestors for different epistemological reasons: conceding the efficaciousness of local beliefs is believed to be necessary to fully render meaning from interpretation (Geertz 1973:93).

Yet we know that some locals are more skeptical than others and that the rituals which transform the dead into ancestors may, at times, fail to materialize or transpire as planned. Nor are all deceased persons who die uniformly mourned or their lives equally celebrated. In Maneo, memories of ancestors vary widely; for example, on occasion, siblings of the same parents would identify different maternal grandparents, or one could identify them while another could not. For some, ancestors obviously matter more than to others, and, to complicate things, some ancestors matter more than others. Variation in Maneo reflects perhaps the absence of elaborate mortuary rituals, including exchanges, feasting, or secondary burials found elsewhere that facilitate the movement of the formerly living into death or at least serve to register ancestors as a continuing presence (Graeber 1995). More significantly, variation in remembering suggests that the practice of forgetting here follows cumulative nonevents or displacements, as when elders die without passing on knowledge of the ancestors who preceded them or, of necessity, instilling in their children the value and relevance of preserving that knowledge (Battaglia 1992:14; Battaglia 1993; Carsten 1995b:331).

The situation in Maneo, no doubt, too, has been complicated over the last several decades by conversion to Christianity and by related changes. Even so, Maneo maintain that their ancestors, or their traces, have power and relevance in certain contexts—a fact that makes some identities too important to forget. For instance, uttering names in a sequence beginning with apical clan (*soa*) ancestors is considered a powerful and highly dangerous act; few people supposedly possess the knowledge, and the point of reciting it is only to perpetuate it. For the rest, an absent audience, it is sufficient to know simply that the information exists (cf. Valeri 1990c:180–185). Yet in another context, in re-telling myths, elders could utter the names of any of those same ancestors with impunity. Similarly, I encountered no obstacles to learning the names of at least some deceased kin in the process of compiling genealogies (cf. Opler [1936]1979), though I had been cautioned that this might be the case (Valerio Valeri, personal communication, May 1989). Finally, sorcery allegations that are leveled at specific ancestors in a nearby animist community (Ellen 1993)—a group with whom I would expect some commonalties—point for Maneo to nonancestral sources, "evil people" (*maisiae*), living in the forest to the east.[3] The fact is that the presence of ancestors is not a given, regardless of how informants might answer questions to imply that it is. Rather the presence of ancestors is a contingent proposition dependent upon a general readiness to accept the possibility as well as particular efforts to recognize and retain traces of them. Who are these ancestors? And how are they known? As ancestors are beyond representation, they not only have to be signified as an absent presence (Traube 1989:337–342), they also have to be acknowledged as subjects in social action. Again, their existence is dependent upon the vicissitudes and sociology of knowing.

If the contingency of recognition is obvious in the case of invisible ancestors, it is no less a problem, though less appreciated as such, in the context of knowing living and visible relatives. The complication here is that while living kin are more easily recognizable, they can also be misrecognized for that very reason. In contrast, misrecognition is rarely a consideration with ancestors given that they consist of mere traces or may be undifferentiated in some contexts, or that, in the absence of identifying signs, no one would necessarily know enough to know there had been a mistake. The susceptibility to misrecognition among the living, however, reflects the fully dialectical (and dialogic) basis of identity affirmation (Keane 1997a:15): the fact that agents can participate in their own dissimulation. The announcement of the impending visit of Atan Boiratan raises the issue of recognition—which is largely taken for granted in the more prosaic arena of everyday kin interactions—and how recognition bears on people's understanding of the terms of their kin relationships.

Before proceeding further there are a few details of the story to flesh out and some basic points about Maneo kinship to introduce. To be sure, there were doubts about Atan's status; indeed, either the rumor of his death or the promise of his return might have been wrong. There was circumstantial evidence to question Atan's death since no one the Maneo knew had actually witnessed it or had seen his corpse. This is an important point given that most people travel no further than the nearby Maneo villages and the closest non-Maneo communities. His disappearance, combined with the absence of any traces, may have yielded a modicum of hope for his survival. An additional fact that may have contributed to the suspicion that Atan was alive (and not returning from death) was that the Maneo knew that many native-born *KNIL* soldiers, approximately 3,250 persons, were sent to Holland in 1950 as part of the Hague Agreement negotiated with the victorious Indonesian government (Kahin 1961:453). For years these ex-soldiers and their families languished in political exile (Bartels 1986:29), and for much of this time, up until recently, it was difficult if not impossible for them to return to visit family remaining in Indonesia. Alternatively, there were reasons to be skeptical of the messenger's claims. If he had come from the Netherlands, several friends asked, why were his clothes so shabby, and why, they wondered, had he not brought photographs of his family and his home? So, it was with some incredulity that a meeting was convened by one of Atan's brothers' sons, Firiz Boiratan, a former village headman. In the course of the meeting, Firiz announced that if the story turned out to be true, members of his clan, Boiratan, must be prepared to meet him at the end of the road and accompany him and his wife on the two-day walk back to the village. Excitement rising, Firiz threatened to beat anyone of his kinsmen who refused; then, a moment later, slightly subdued, he pleaded with everyone present that "we" should all take part since, he said, "We are all descendants of Atan" (*"katong semua pun tatai par Atan"*).

There is a literal meaning as well as rhetorical weight to Firiz's comment.[4] Briefly, the Maneo orient themselves with respect to one another on the basis of relations of affinity, siblingship, and descent.[5] These orientations are largely determined at birth; thus, they appear to persons, and are represented by them as such, as ordered and invariant—a fact that inspires some confidence in the project of rendering ties diagramatically. Maneo "belong" (*rahae*) to one of nine patrilineally organized *soa* or clans, and marriages are mostly clan-exogamous and uni-directional, in accordance with the ideal of matrilateral cross-cousin marriage. Ties between persons are realized as, and metaphorically expressed in terms of blood (*lasiae*), which is contributed by both parents (see Visser 1989; cf. McKinnon 1991:110). Subsequently, kinship serves as a way for people to classify relations among them (Wagner 1977:624), principally as consanguines and affines. The pattern created, though, is deceptive; it is presumed rather than demonstrated and, more importantly, in the form of a system of ordered parts, the shape of the structure of social relations is unamenable to analysis of the processes which account for it (Bourdieu 1977). First, as we shall see in Maneo, there is considerable negotiation in interpretations of kin relations; the negotiations, specifically, surround issues of marriage, the exchange of marriage payments (*arata*), and the disposition or recruitment of children (see also Barnes 1980), and these determinations are invariably made amidst competing claims. A second reason order is deceptive is that persons are substitutable in some senses. In other words, the sameness established through recognition does not preclude, indeed it permits, interchangeability. In effect, the specific identity of, say, a deceased grandfather does not matter if he can be replaced by an equivalently situated person, a grandfather's sibling, for instance; thus, two lines of descent can be remerged and made closer, if they were divided at a previous point in time by representations of more proximate relations. And, of course, the opposite can occur as well.[6]

Maneo forge relations in the present with respect to an imagined or remembered past. For example, affinal relations are designated with respect to a history of marriages, such that one's affines may include the descendants of affines of ascending generations. The existence of alliances (*sesama*) take precedence such that even if the names of the persons are forgotten, the perdurance of obligations between parties continues to mark it. Elders caution their children not to break them ("*tepe riki sesama*"). By the same token, the reference point for determining affinity itself may be some kinsman other than ego. Maneo prefer (for men) matrilateral cross-cousin marriages—that is, with a mother's brother's daughter (*kaifini*)—or to someone who stands in that category. But patrilateral cross-cousins are also *kaifini*, and although such marriages are discouraged, for reasons that concern prestige and property transfers, they are discouraged only within five generations (see also Sherman 1990:57), roughly the span of time over which such ties are forgotten.[7] In sum, if persons are related both matrilaterally and patrilaterally and, say, a marriage is pending, genealogical proximity serves only partly to determine the appropriateness of one designation over another. The fact is that knowledge of genealogical distance, particularly beyond first cousins, is itself subject to the same vicissitudes that affect knowledge of identity. Claims of distance, in other words, are contingent on the contexts and conditions in which such knowledge is obtained and represented. Thus, in the absence of some definitive standard for evaluating and prioritizing claims in Maneo, a comprehensive history of marriages would mean simply that everyone, in theory, could refer to each other as affines.

Like affinity, sibling designations also infer a history of relations; the terms *hota'a* and *efa* for cross-sex and same-sex siblings respectively apply to true siblings (children raised by the same parents) as well as to all parallel cousins and persons with whom relations can be charted in such a way, that is, as father's brothers' children and mother's sisters' children. But whereas affinity and descent would delineate categories of persons based on more or less immediate connections—Valeri refers to these ties as syntagmatic (1990c:157)—siblingship in Maneo derives from a relationship of historical equivalence. The sibling connection, in other words, is analogic rather than contiguous. The tie is evinced and grounded in the Maneo origin myth (described below) in which the apical clan ancestors were themselves all siblings. As a result, and in reflection upon this, everyone in the present and within the same generation is, in certain contexts, a sibling as well. In general, as an organizing principle, siblingship encompasses people; it is opposed to descent and affinity as sameness presupposes differentiation.

Descent, the final principle of Maneo kinship, describes a pattern of alignment in which male ancestors are sequenced or with which a sequence of male ancestors is implied (*silsilah*). The sequence is realized and experienced in the patrilineal transfer of rights to territory and in the inheritance of certain physical and spiritual attributes associated with the patriline (though not exclusively so). That is, patrilineality takes on significance partly because only those ties (and not matrilineal ties) are remembered beyond a generation or two. This is not to suggest that people know the specific identities of their patrilineal ascendants; in fact, as discussed, most claim not to know; nevertheless, they believe that such knowledge exists and that it is held and preserved by other clan members. Finally, as has been remarked elsewhere, the historical order and alignment created by descent is inconsistent in terms of the actual practice of recruitment (Baker 1988:378; see also Sahlins 1965:106). Maneo children are recruited to particular patrilines and to an associated clan following the negotiation and exchange of marriage payments. Depending on what transpires, children can be recruited matrilaterally or patrilaterally, even to a third clan.

In sum, the categories of relations orient Maneo in different ways. First, for any two people, with the exception of true siblings, the relations between them can be charted in multiple and contradictory ways. Even if specific historical connections cannot be identified, they are presumed partly in an effort to shape a relevant context.[8] Secondly, the relatively small size of Maneo communities combined with the high rates of village endogamy increase the likelihood that two persons, prospective spouses for instance, are also related to one another (potentially) as siblings. This emerges from the fact that people's recollections of identities and relations vary and often contradict. What I am suggesting simply is that Maneo are aware that in designating someone as being in an "appropriate" category for marriage they are also eliding a history of contradictory ties.

Indeed, part of the intent behind particular claims of relatedness is to thwart other, competing interpretations. Stated differently and somewhat paradoxically, the "discovery" of relations proceeds only to the extent that these other truths are suppressed. The fact, then, that relative intelligibility does not cause more problems in social life reflects less what people know than what they are willing to assume, and even suppress, about the identities and relations around them.

Context of Remembrance

What place did Atan occupy in local imaginations of kinship? To be sure, it was not strategic. Despite his unprecedented military experience, few young people—Firiz's grandchildren and Atan's great grandchildren included—seemed to know his name. There are several reasons for this: the fact that he was only in his twenties when he left fifty years before, and that he was, or had been, unmarried and had no known children. Thus, while it was possible that he could have been remembered as part of a "pedigree"—that is, he could have been relocated and his relationships to the living revised—this had not occurred. Whether it would occur was unclear. More likely, I would have suspected, prior to the announcement of his return by the stranger, that in another generation, his military experience would have been transferred to a direct lineal ascendant, Firiz's father, for instance (instead of the father of one of Firiz's clan brothers). The odds that he would have been remembered were stacked against him. Atan's position, in this regard, was similar to that of Maneo women who are similarly lost from memory after two or three generations. Maneo women are lost because they generally leave their natal households upon marriage, or not long thereafter, and because their children generally follow (*lulu*) their husbands and join their clans. Even when children do follow their mothers—the result of insufficient property exchanged on their behalf—they actually belong to a woman's brother or her parents: accordingly, they are encouraged to refer to their mother's brother or mother's father as father (*amai*), and their mother's brother's wife or maternal grandmother as mother (*inai*). In the latter case, birth mothers may even be referred to as "older siblings." Even if children can recall who nursed them (usually their birth mothers), more often than not it is the revised designation of kin relations which is preserved and passed on to their offspring. In short, patrilineality in Maneo enables some men to become ancestors because they have descendants. By the same token, not all men, Atan included, are destined to have descendants because of the contingencies surrounding marriage, reproduction, and the transfer of marriage payments. Without descendants—that is, without the relations that make recognition imperative—the traces of ancestors are allowed to disappear.

The point I have been making is that knowledge shapes the world as well as reflects it; kinship knowledge is inextricably bound up with its use. As a practical matter, the central task is to acquire enough knowledge to become competent at identifying others, particularly close kin, and assigning them to the proper categories of relations. People build up competence through repetitive daily experience (Schieffelin 1990:18). Of course, competence in the use of kinship knowledge is a reasonable assumption given that without some modicum of it, it would be difficult to manage very basic social obligations, as it initially is for most anthropologists. Yet in light of the complexity of Maneo kinship, this would seem to be a low standard to aspire to: people can become competent at recognizing others, and so establish sameness. But in light of the array of relations that connect and disconnect persons from one another, expertise rather than competence offers a more relevant measure of the use of kinship knowledge. Maneo expertise in representing relations is partly a measure of memory—the command of the facts—as well as of judgment and authority. These capacities are combined such that the verity of a person's recollections must be backed up by her or his reputation, given that there is no written text and no ultimate authority to turn to. Furthermore, because there are multiple truths in terms of the way identities and relations can be represented, experts have to choose among them according to what they deem to be appropriate and achievable in particular contexts (Bourdieu 1977). Agreement about kin status thus reflects some consensus about the choice of truths to promote. Alternatively, relationship designations may be conceded because they are uncontested publicly. Simply, kinship is constituted by statements about it. These statements may be shaped as much by habit and indifference as by more tangible interests, for instance, the desire to cast relations in a more favorable light or to sow doubt about the appropriateness of someone else's claims. Just as language acquisition is, or can be, contested and impeded, kinship knowledge is similarly manipulated as part of ongoing political machinations. At stake in its control and dissimulation is nothing less than the terms and conditions by which people identify and interact with one another.

Recognition and Misrecognition

Paul Ricoeur asserts we know ourselves by our feelings—feelings that come from an intuitive understanding and familiarity—while we know others, not being able to fathom their experiences directly, through observation (Ricoeur 1992:38). When the others in question are ancestors, recognition, the process of making the other visible and familiar, is contingent on the identification of traces as subjects of emotional attachment or as causes behind some otherwise inexplicable events. Recognition thus follows the performances that establish the existence of the invisible. Yet even for visible, living relatives, recognition is constrained by the mode of representation, by the perception and interpretation of the physical signs to which they stand as referents and by the ground or agreement around such interpretations (see Keane 1997a). In fact, because of the very properties of those signs—the excess of their signifying content—they can be deceptive; the deception, in part, stems from the process of recognition itself, from the very feelings of certainty of an attribution or identification. For recognition describes a moment in inquiry when it is merely possible to make a determination; it represents an end point when observation and understanding are considered to be adequate (Rorty 1991:129–131). But if recognition permits misrecognition by foreclosing further inquiry, as I am suggesting, other than the confidence it reflects in people's powers of observation, what purpose does it serve? I do not wish to suggest that misrecognition is frequent in Maneo or elsewhere. Yet whatever its frequency, it is something to be avoided, and the stakes can be high if it happens. As discussed, recognition is essential to confirming sameness—for establishing a continuity of experience that a person with a particular face, a name, certain distinct habits, and who stands in a particular social relation is the same person from one encounter to another. That continuity is necessary to make sense of social relations and to enable people to behave appropriately and strategically. But recognition is not only necessary, establishing it is a matter of habit; it is a deeply ingrained propensity. Consider the fact that from day to day persons who constantly interact are often unaware of the changes or the dissemblances in them that are readily apparent to others in only intermittent contact. And, consider the remarkable case of visual agnosia that Oliver Sacks (1970) describes in a man unable to recognize faces—that is, to assemble the parts of faces into something unique and identifiable. The man compensates for his impairment by developing a facility to identify others visually by body shape or movement with the same verve as before but with far less accuracy. The malady, while uniquely visual, confirms the point that recognition represents only one facet of the process of understanding; by itself, it merely presumes a world of kin relations "out there." It is this fact, that recognition yields no basis for understanding identity beyond confirmation of sameness that makes misrecognition possible.

Consider the different understandings that inform concerns over incest. In the most famous instance in the West, Sophocles's protagonist Oedipus is led to misrecognize his mother because of his lack of understanding of relatedness. It is a remarkable oversight, yet it is precisely this aspect of the tragedy that has been elided from Freud's interpretation. Knowledge of relations, which is a condition of kinship, and is certainly central to the experience, is set aside for the sake of establishing something more ambitious: the purported universal impulses sifted from the unconscious mind (Ricoeur 1970:6; see also Arendt 1978:110).[9] Freud turns the contingent fact of Oedipus's ignorance that Jocasta, his wife, is also his birth mother into evidence of a monumental self-deception: what neither Oedipus, Freud himself, nor the (male) audience understand, what they suppress in fact, is their own desire for their mothers. Accordingly, Oedipus's fate follows as the result of a relatively small coincidence and not the monumental one I am suggesting that was made possible by gaps in knowledge. Freud's argument is that because of the ineluctability of desire, incest merely happened to have befallen him and not someone else.

Freud's discovery of (Freudian) psychology in this story represents something of a missed opportunity in the history of kinship studies to develop an understanding of the articulation of historical contingency and desire.[10] Perhaps he sought to banish chance and thought the coincidence too great to be of interest. In Maneo, where incest is also unusual, not to mention very unpropitious, the fact that it does not happen more often—though there is one such case they point to—is because they are vigilant against the possibility. They have to be vigilant because kin classification is relatively complex: regardless of distance, parallel cousins are considered siblings, their parents are parents too, and marriage between them is incest. Given the history of overlapping marriages and the expansiveness of purported kin ties, it is likely that many prospective couples may also be related as siblings, depending on people's knowledge and the circulation of that knowledge. Contracting the right marriage, hence, requires historical awareness. But it also requires that the persons involved promote the interpretation of the appropriate relations between the prospective couple and occlude any competing claims. This is never easy. As discussed in the next chapter, desire confounds the neat and "safe" ordering of relations. Sexual desire, evinced in the phrase "*mata koi hala kahana*" (what the eyes see the heart desires), can in fact drive out understanding; it is anathema to order. Desire, thus, is complicit in incest in Maneo as Freud would have it, but as an inchoate and undiscriminating force that precedes designation (Trawick 1990:144–148).

When I made an imprudent comment to a Maneo man that I had once observed his classificatory son, actually a distant relation, flirting with a clan sister, though an equally distant one, the older man responded angrily. His son, he said, would have to be taught (*ai kaiyare ia*); specifically, he would have to be made to understand who his siblings were and to recognize them as such. To the father, the sibling designation took precedence over other possible ways of identifying relations between the young man and woman. To the son, however, the father's designation may have appeared arbitrary; if he could have, I suspect, he would have promoted a different interpretation of his relationship with the woman. For elders, like this father, who wanted to avoid an unpropitious marriage for his son, relationships have to be good to think, to borrow a phrase from Lévi-Strauss (1963:89), to be safe to desire. The broader point is that however rare the instances of visual agnosia and misrecognition may be, Oedipus's fate would be far more common but for the understanding people have of how persons around them are related. By the same token, in Maneo, this knowledge is seen as incomplete, partly because it is beyond recollection—once known but now forgotten—and partly because people choose the relations between them and, in some cases, choose not to know. With an inkling of what he might have found, we have to wonder whether Oedipus, too, would have been more reluctant to seek the truth?

Impostors

I have discussed limits to the understanding of relatedness and the contingency of the signs by which persons are recognized, and I have suggested there is a difference in emphasis on importance granted to these two facets of knowing in the West and locally in Maneo society. In addition to the contingencies of signs, on occasion identities may also be misrepresented so as to facilitate misrecognition. This proved to be another feature of the story of Atan Boiratan's promised return. As I mentioned, the promise came from a young man who appeared in Maneo Rendah proclaiming to be his son. If his claim was true then Maneo were meeting for the first time a brother of Firiz (his father's brother's son) and a classificatory father to many others, yet a complete stranger in the sense that community members knew nothing of his past, had no recollection of him as a person, and certainly had no prior knowledge to prepare them for his sudden arrival. The recognition of Atan's son thus hung precariously on his assertions of the identity of his father and was confirmed to an extent only by the knowledge this presupposed: how else could the stranger have known about Atan? Yet if Atan did return to whom would he be recognizable after fifty years of absence, particularly given that those who had known him in his youth were all younger and their memories perhaps not so clear? And, in what sense would he be recognizable? There were no photographs of the young Atan against which people might measure physical changes and no photographs of the old by which that history of change might be reconstructed. If there were, certainly his family would endeavor to recognize his face—regardless of any other identities it might have—by superimposing the new image on the vaguely remembered old one, in effect, to make him whole, to join his face with their recollection of him. Perhaps, then, they would discover in his face a family resemblance, seeing in each other some previously undetected and imagined attribute (see Munn [1986]1992:142–43).

For the two weeks the young man lived in the village, Maneo elders sought to connect their recollections of Atan to these new and unfamiliar descriptions of his later life in Europe. Not for lack of trying, the attempts at reconciliation failed and the young man left the village as suddenly as he arrived. He was only heard about months later after having been arrested for theft on the south coast of Seram. When the deception came to light, Firiz Boiratan, Atan's nephew, laughed; others said the young man must have been crazy (*mumanu*). They may also have been relieved for reasons I will discuss below. What their Lévity may belie is a certain vulnerability created, on the one hand, by limits to their ability to assess the impostor's claim and, on the other, by both the desire to believe it was true and the fear that by rejecting it outright they might alienate the real Atan forever.

Details of the events remain frustratingly incomplete. I exchanged few words with the young man while he was in the village and never had the chance to talk to him after he left. Whatever his initial intentions, and however incomprehensible, they would be eclipsed by the overriding practical concern of doing what he thought necessary to perpetuate the deception, namely, to maintain Atan's kin's "mistaken" recognition of him. Like the famous case of Martin Guerre (set in a sixteenth-century village in the French Pyrenees), the incident raises the question: Why did the people not recognize an impostor?[11] First, as there was a desire among those closest to Martin to believe (Davis 1983:43), there was a similar readiness to accept the Maneo impostor's claim. Second, as Natalie Davis speculates, recognition itself proceeded differently in sixteenth-century France. Not only were their no photographs by which resemblance or dissemblance might be assessed, but the absence of mirrors in peasant households (as in Maneo) affected people's sense of appearance (1983:38–39); specifically, it meant that a different class of signs—less visual than aural and intuitive—were considered intrinsic and unique to persons. Mirrors altered people's self image and through that their recognition of others. Recognition, in other words, is still contingent, but the signs identity is contingent upon are embedded in, rather than separate from, other facts. The other facts together comprise an imagined continuity of narrative experience. From this perspective, what the eyewitnesses confirm is experience rather than some unmediated view of the other.[12]

The remaining question to consider is, how did the pretenders come to acquire knowledge of the histories of the persons they posed for? It was the locals' unwitting complicity as well as gaps in their knowledge of the other created by the disappearances that enabled the deceptions to proceed as far as they did. For instance, Arnaud du Tilh, the man who posed as Martin Guerre, found out much about Martin's life indirectly from Martin himself through some mutual acquaintances. With what he knew, he deftly negotiated his way through each encounter with Martin's family and friends, gleaning from them what he could in anticipation of the next, and thereby assembling a facsimile of the history and life experiences of the original. All the while, through each encounter, he altered people's recollections of their histories with him. Because of his success, Arnaud du Tilh was accused of bewitching those around him. Similarly, though less successfully, the false son of Atan obtained knowledge of him indirectly from Firiz, for Firiz I knew had been selling genealogical information to a non-Maneo man living on the coast. The impostor probably discovered Atan from the purchaser who had most likely sought Firiz's expertise in the first place to help him trace a genealogical connection to Seram (known locally as *Nusa Ina* or the Mother Land), that is, to gain access to certain powers (*ilmu gaib*) many people consider to reside there.[13] Whatever his original motives, the overriding concern for both impostors would have been the need to preserve the ruse, a fact Arnaud du Tilh forgot, perhaps because of his success, and something that became impossible rather quickly for the stranger in Maneo since he had pinned his claim of genealogical propinquity on the undeliverable promise of his dead father's return.

I have described sameness as occurring at the moment of recognition at the moment an image conforms as likeness to a previous image. At that instant, assessment is largely suspended and recognition is, thus, conceded even if it is subsequently controverted. In addition, I have tried to illuminate the contingency of recognition—to establish the possibility of misrecognition—and I have suggested that, as part of the knowledge of social relations, the discovery of sameness is less important than, or is properly subsumed in, contextual understanding: the understanding of the history of one's relations. The difference, and the necessity of the distinction between these two modes of knowing, is that unlike verity, which comes from recognition and is a measure of the adequacy as opposed to the accuracy of observation, the end point of understanding is graded; too much or too little and people become uncertain about how to define relations. In other words, ascertaining relatedness does not depend on, and cannot be attained through recognition alone; nor does recognition come any closer to understanding because of the number of people who affirm an identity or because of the sincerity of their claims.

The sincerity with which particular claims are promoted and embraced may not necessarily coincide with the consensus understanding of identity and relatedness. But it does raise an interesting point: what does sincerity in fact demonstrate? It is from such convictions, of course, that kin claims gain their compellingness and naturalness. To be precise, they come from the fact that the terms used to describe the relationships are consistent with people's experiences and confirmed by their understanding of their mediate connections. Depth of conviction does not change the fact that relationship designations largely precede and frame subsequent experience; nor does conviction mitigate the possibility (even probability) that designations may be differently defined. In fact, kinship terms may not be invoked in reference to genealogies or formal relationships at all (Zeitlyn 1993:201). Sincerity, then, is evidence not of truth per se but of the depth of commitment. Of course, not all Maneo claims about identities and relations are equally heartfelt; people have different stakes in those claims, and particular designations may be motivated. By the same token, not everyone is interested in the full pantheon of their relations, even less those of others. Thus, claims I heard, particularly about obscure ancestors—but claims, nonetheless, which confer some residual rights to, say, hunt on that particular *soa* territory—may have been issued in the interstices of public sentiment, where people are unaware of each other's claims and are largely indifferent (cf. Valeri 1990c:184). Indifference fairly describes the Maneo attitude to our queries about distant and even some close relations. But there is a catch: if a particular interpretation becomes "too public," that is, if the information is not disclosed properly, it risks inviting criticism. If claims or counterclaims subsequently appear false it is perhaps because they were not conceived in this context for the purpose of standing up to public scrutiny—a scrutiny, again, not based solely (or even most importantly) on accuracy but also on an appraisal of the context in which it is made. I am convinced that some claims I recorded were probably meant to be hidden (see also Noricks 1989:54), for instance, when a man asserted that his late father was not Maneo, a claim flatly denied by others we knew who knew better. In a sense, then, what people reveal publicly of their place in a web of social relations may not be what they feel sincerely but only what is necessary for them to disclose, based on calculations about a statement's reception, in order to interact effectively and to achieve the ends they seek.

The Performance of Kinship

Kinship constitutes performance and the world of identities and relations does not exist apart from their expression. Alternatively, expressions invest the representations of relations with an animating force sufficient, in some cases, to bring particular ties into being or, minimally, to raise the possibility of their existence. For instance, when someone claims to be a descendent of royalty, regardless of the improbability of the assertion, the statement affirms a category of ancestors and the hierarchical differentiation among them. In such a way, Maneo genealogical experts traced the ancestry of Jennie and myself back to Queen Elizabeth, who herself (along with Queen Juliana of Holland) was said to be a younger sister of the Maneo ancestors who remained in Seram. This claim reaffirms the belief that Seram and the Maneo, in particular, represent the geographic center and historical point of origin of the world. Of course, people can and do assert any manner of things, and the mere act of speaking, by itself, does not invest what is said with any intrinsic persuasiveness. The capacity of words to affect depends on the content and context of what is said and its consistency or correspondence with respect to previous statements and on the credibility of the speaker. Kinship knowledge is forged in the medium by which the Maneo construct their universe of kin relations, that is, by speaking about them and by allowing others—if only for being unable to prevent them—to interject their own interpretations. As a reflection of this, the content as well as the morphology of kinship knowledge varies.

Another point is that the uncertainty surrounding some relations is not a consequence or reflection of genealogical distance. For example, I talked to several men born out of wedlock who said they could not identify their genitors.[14] These men, already married, may have been reluctant to pursue the possibility that in uncovering the real identities of their fathers they might expose a prior sibling relationship to their spouses. Yet these are not instances of managing knowledge for the sake of expedience, as it is precisely this information I would expect they would wish to know, prior to a marriage, to avoid the stigma and the harmful, though vaguely articulated effects that follow. By not knowing they are not spared the effects.

As discussed above, Maneo express kinship ties metaphorically in terms of blood and because blood is the substance thought to connect persons. Implicitly, what matters are concentrations of blood; if they are high enough they exert a force thought to favorably dispose persons toward others who share it (particularly the less powerful to the more—a point of potential advantage should the need for political support arise). For example, one of my key informants, a grandfather and the mother's father of a child born out of wedlock, sought to hide the identity of the child's genitor. He had adopted this child as his own, and he was concerned that recognition would awaken a desire in the child to follow his biological father, particularly in any disputes that might divide the child from his mother's kin. He would not attempt to limit his movement, nor would he prevent him from ever seeing his father, only from knowing his immediate relation to him. By preventing his son from knowing, he felt that the attraction might remain vague and undefined. Alternatively, I heard genitors—or persons claiming that status—discretely brag about fathering various children born out of wedlock (*anak luar*). The utterances, out of the range of their girlfriends' kin, create possibilities, regardless of their validity, that alternative interpretations of identities and relations may be promoted in the future.

The opposite situation can occur as well, as when a younger brother in one of the houses we lived in was identified (falsely, he maintained) by a woman's kin as being the father of the woman's child.[15] Her kin likely used the claim to try to force a marriage. In this respect, knowledge becomes a way for people to shape the world while, at the same time, claiming merely to represent it (Valeri 1990c:181). Finally, Maneo attempt to fashion the world of possibilities by drawing distinctions that are, again, covered up in other contexts. I noticed, for example, that parents readily distinguish between children borne by them (*uhuna tunia*) and adopted children (*anak angkat* or *uhuna arata*) (Carsten 1995a:236; Peletz 1995:348) when referring to their own who are being raised in other families. Yet the same distinction is not drawn when parents refer to children of their own households. Knowledge of relatedness is crucial in these instances, for it shifts the locus of action from contracting, for instance, a "safe" marriage, to representing the categories of relations of the parties as appropriate. In sum, the terrain of kinship is actively shaped and contested. The inconsistencies in representations reveal the political negotiations that form part of the experience of kinship, and the lacunae reflect, at times, simply what people do not wish to know.

The Moral Context of Changes

It is largely taken for granted that behavior does not affect kinship status, that even bad fathers are no less fathers (Goodenough 1951:115–118). Similarly, it is assumed that "kinship organizes affect" (Trawick 1990:152) and not the reverse. The point I will develop here, however, is that regardless of the improbability that behavior will change status or that affect will organize kinship, affect is not always nor entirely contained and constrained by the particular mores governing and animating specific types of relations. Kinship statuses in Maneo can change; the problem is that change may be difficult to detect because it is piecemeal, sometimes unilateral, and protracted. Consensus about changes in a relationship may never even be achieved fully; unanimity is not determinative. The aim of revision, I suggest, is to make right and therefore to make sense of a history of interactions. There is no inherent reason why interests and interpretations should agree. Although revision in the terms of relations is likely the exception and not the norm, the frame of reference for making such determinations is the personal history and historical context within which relations and identities become important.[16] As Richard Rorty suggests, "principles wait patiently for the outcome and then the crucial terms which they contain are redefined to accord with that outcome" (Rorty 1989:194-195 n.6).

For example, Maneo negotiate and transfer property as a way of determining their relationships with their children, that is, whether their children will address them and ultimately remember them as parents, grandparents, or even siblings. There is considerable deliberation and a history of deliberation extending back for generations that precedes birth and filiation, and such deliberations may never be fully resolved. In the midst of these negotiations, adults are quite aware that their efforts will determine, in effect, who their children are—that is, whose children they are. Nothing else is quite so important. Yet despite the awareness of their efforts in determining the relatedness of others or, rather, precisely because of what depends on it, Maneo generally perceive their own ties to parents and their parents' siblings and affines as inviolate. The most inviolate of these relations are ones that connect men with their male ancestors (cf. Valeri 1990c:174). But ties between male ascendants and descendants appear inviolate only because the contingency of such ties—the fact that they are dependent upon the negotiation and transfer of property—is obscured. Moreover, Maneo recognize certain ancestors without questioning the possibility that they may not be who they seem, or that their relationships to them may be defined differently. Again, an imposter like Arnaud du Tilh may, under certain circumstances, stand in for another if no one is in a position to know any better, or a collateral, like Atan Boiratan, may be relocated as a direct lineal ascendant.

The assumption that kin terms do not change is predicated on a dubious analytical separation between actions and sentiment and the designation of relationship categories. Designations are usually announced by adults on behalf of children; occasionally, however, the terms of relations are revised posthumously (though it is difficult to know this). I also knew of two living adults who revised, or were in the process of revising, their own statuses. In both instances, changes followed events that compelled persons to reflect on the moral circumstances of their relationships. In one, a man revised his relationships after a fight in which he killed his brother-in-law. He changed status, becoming a member of his mother's clan, he said, because his former siblings refused to support him. The second, more complicated case involved a young unmarried mother, Johana, and her brother, Niko, both of whom had affiliated to their mother's clan because the property transferred upon their father's marriage to their mother some twenty-five years before had not been sufficient. As in roughly half the cases of matrifiliation, the two had actually been adopted into the family of their mother's kin—one headed by their mother's father's brother, a man whom they addressed as father. On different occasions, Niko and Johana recounted a history of childhood neglect that culminated in an incident Niko described in which their foster father pushed Johana onto the rocks in a river bed, cutting her head. The relevance of the event in the context of ongoing kinship negotiations became apparent only later. In effect, the blood-letting aspect of the story was highlighted to negate the parental contribution of *lasiae* (blood) and to give testimony to the extent of moral indifference, likewise contradicting the normal solicitude of a parent toward a child. Sometime later the children were separated and sent to live with other kin, Niko with his mother's father's sister, while Johana returned to her true father and mother.

Niko's clan affiliation was never in question; he had remained affiliated with his mother's kin. Johana's status, though, was indeterminate. When I asked her outright she dodged the question and, instead, listed the various contributions of food and money for school and clothing she had received from her biological father—contributions, along with blood, that are determinative of kinship (Durkheim 1965:378). When I asked her father, in turn, he deferred to her, an admission calculated to foster ambiguity and to preempt, I believe, any possible objections from his affines and her former siblings. I never asked the affines and, for their part, they never volunteered anything to me. They may not have even known or they may have been indifferent. Of course, had I raised the issue with them directly it might have taken on a public significance that it did not (yet) have and in light of which they could not have afforded to ignore it. Significantly, the stakes in this revision included not only Johana's immediate relationships but those of her young son whom her biological father (the child's true grandfather) intended to adopt. When the adoption occurs, as I believe it will, it will resolve, if tacitly, Johana's own status. That is, her relations, eventually recalled by her descendants, will be determined not by the prior ties with her parents, but by her son's relationship with her father and mother. Through their silence, in effect, Johana and her parents have helped create conditions that will determine, in turn, whether she becomes, and is ultimately remembered as, her own child's sister.[17]

Forgetting

As discussed, continuity is imperative to organizing social life, and it is an inevitable consequence of it. But while kin are recognized, continuity is created in spite of the absence of complete information which would guarantee that persons will not be exposed in the future as impostors or that the terms of their relations will not be controverted or redefined in light of new knowledge. In fact, and perhaps as a consequence of imperfect information (the improbability of acquiring a definitive understanding of relations and identity), Maneo suppress some kinship knowledge or its possibility. Suppression is tacit in that defining relationships in a certain way eclipses, at least for the moment, other representations. Alternatively, and more actively, people simply endeavor not to know or, at least, not communicate what they suspect to be the case. It was the fear that this silence would be interrupted that helps explain some of the anxiety the Maneo may have felt upon hearing news of Atan's return; for given his depth of knowledge and his status as an elder, he might legitimately question the appropriateness of some present relations.

This brings up some broader questions about memory in the context of kinship knowledge. While its importance has long been observed, it is as a footnote in most studies. In one article in which the subject is addressed explicitly, Hildred and Clifford Geertz (1964) propose that the widespread use of teknonyms in Bali (names derived from descendants as "mother-of" and "grandmother-of") precipitates the forgetting of knowledge of the specific identities of ancestors that would otherwise be retained if their unique birth names could be recalled. One of their conclusions is that this "genealogical amnesia," far from being a cultural liability, effectively enables the Balinese to maintain group cohesiveness centered on a temple complex (Geertz and Geertz 1964:105–106). This occurs because the Balinese avoid the potentially divisive identification that would result from having different ancestors. In a similar vein, Janet Carsten proposes that shallow genealogical knowledge in Langkawi, Malaysia, facilitates immigration and assimilation by occluding the history of residents' disparate origins (1995b:318).[18] But what is actually lost when genealogies are forgotten? I have argued that kinship knowledge is predicated upon recognition that establishes identity through time and upon the understanding of how oneself and others are relationally situated. What teknonyms mask are not the relations but the identities of specific ancestors. For instance, persons who are recognized can also be misrecognized and occasionally substituted; likewise, generations, as discussed, can be collapsed without anyone being the wiser. Effects—that is, the loss of ancestors—are confused for causes. The point is that specific identities of ancestors only matter in a relational context; whether they are remembered or not depends on their value in organizing relations. In a broader sense, what is relevant then is not what people can remember but what they cannot afford to forget. Genealogical amnesia in Langkawi and Bali reflects the fact that ancestors do not serve as points of structural differentiation or aggregation; they are largely unimportant in terms of organizing fields of social relations. This does not mean—and here I depart from Carsten—that the differentiation that comes from descent and affinity is a hindrance to migration and assimilation. Outsiders in Maneo are assimilated through marriage and through the revision of genealogies after a generation or two, and assimilation is facilitated, too, by the belief that the ancestors of all the peoples on earth came originally from Seram.[19] Kinship not only creates identities through ties to people and place (Carsten 1995b:329), it creates different persons depending on how persons trace their connections and disconnections to others (Strathern 1987:275).

Like the Ilongot of the Philippines (Rosaldo 1980:16) and the Belauan of Micronesia (Parmentier 1987), Maneo conceptualize social history in spatial terms. The connections and disconnections (ties of affinity) are referred to as paths in the forest and across the landscape. The framework gives the history of relations a particular reality consistent with the general belief, just mentioned, that Seram represents the center of the earth. As new paths are followed, however, the old do not simply disappear; they become overgrown, continuing to have meaning as traces (Traube 1989:339). And, the paths the traces indicate are believed to be recoverable. All knowledge, kinship knowledge included, is, in this sense, immanent.

Maneo refer to the beginning of history as the "old world" (*Nusa Mutuania*) as a time when everyone was related to one another as siblings. In the old world, reproduction, such that it was, constituted asexual replacement. A person (male or female) gave birth by slicing open the calf of his or her leg, then died. Birthing changed, in fact, the whole world changed, when a brother and sister had intercourse. The birth that followed was no longer fatal to the mother, but other amenities (the food, clothing, shelter once available for the asking) suddenly and forever after, had to be procured through persons' own efforts. Copulation was a moment of fundamental transformation. Once Maneo began to reproduce sexually, the population grew in numbers, but the long life they had once enjoyed came to an end. What sex did, then, in the first instance, was introduce differentiation between genders and between siblings and affines that became manifest in subsequent generations. And once the process of differentiation was set in motion, it had a certain inexorability; it had to be perpetuated to avoid incest and maintain the various lines of marriages to affines. This imperative helped make awareness of the paths recoverable. By the same token, what prevents people from remembering all the distant paths is not merely ability, it is also the unwillingness to pursue them. The problem is that too many paths means that relations become crisscrossed and confused; conversely, if there is too little knowledge, ties in the present become as undifferentiated as they were in the distant past (Wagner 1977). From this perspective, when people do assert relations, they may be doing so preemptively in order to prevent others from interjecting their own interpretations or, perhaps, to sow doubt about the appropriateness of someone else's ties.

Conclusion

Awareness in kinship refers to the ability to recognize others and to orient them in relation to one's self and others. Particularly where distinctions are drawn and it is necessary to determine how persons are related (as siblings or as parents and children) and unrelated (as affines), it is important to be able both to represent the social field of persons and positions and to shape it in appropriate fashion. People do not simply lie about kinship or represent it as accurately and unambiguously as they can, for the world of kinship is shaped, too, by suppressing certain information. That is, because of the surfeit of potential ties between persons, public disclosure merely singles out certain relations from others. Sometimes those other relations are suggested privately in reaction to what Jennie and I reported others had asserted. In both public and private contexts the intent of the speakers informs the content of what they say about kinship and there is no inherent contradiction in this.

I have discussed the contingencies of signs by which persons recognize and situate others. A final point I wish to consider is that knowledge plays a part in people's relational designs—of marrying the "right" person and having important ancestors—because, and not merely despite, the very limits to knowing. I have already discussed the inability of persons to discriminate consistently between relations beyond a distance of, say, first cousins—assuming that relative distance would even be a criterion for selecting certain ties over others if people had this information. But the fact that they do not, not only makes the issue moot, it calls further attention to the fact that there has to be some other means of arbitration, a situation that opens the way, in turn, for persons to interject their own preferences. Indeed, if they do not, others certainly will on their behalf. By the same token, persons avoid pursuing relations and identities that if known and passed on may foreclose some of their options or call into question the appropriateness of some relations. As a class, the identities and marriages of the siblings of ancestors tend to be the ones suppressed, and it is evidence of this suppression that Maneo genealogies appear unbranched at the upper ends of kinship diagrams. Maneo genuinely believe that their past was less populated than the present: With fewer collaterals of lineal ancestors, there are fewer ways to trace relations between persons. However, there remain enough ways to do so—again a function of small population size and relatively high rates of village endogamy—so that at least some alternative relations and identities are openly asserted.

The very process of perceiving and recognizing others also involves the construction and creative use of constraints. Perceptual cues might be either insufficient or, in some cases, too abundant to be conclusive. Occasionally, people are misrecognized; however, misrecognition is a consequence of the fact that identification serves the primary purpose of establishing continuity of experience in which it is only necessary to know enough rather than know definitively. Most Maneo, particularly in the mountains, do not carry "positive" forms of identification. And although some on the coast do have Indonesian Residency Cards (*Kartu Tanda Penduduk*), it never occurs to anyone to check someone else's; no one ever asked to see the *KTP* of the impostor son of Atan Boiratan, for instance. The inconvenience of misrecognizing living kin is perhaps mitigated by the relative certainty that one's own ancestors cannot be misidentified or, at any rate, that mistakes will not come to light. In sum, the predicament posed by needing to know, on the one hand, and the problem of knowing too much, on the other, is held in check by simply knowing enough to be able to use knowledge effectively.

Notes

1. Following Charles Taylor (1989:130–131), I focus on the dimension of experience rather than the "thing" experienced, that is, kinship. Thus experience represents the object of attention. Of course, Taylor adds, people's experience and awareness differ; access is asymmetrical. While this fact makes it difficult to generalize about Maneo kinship experience, difference in awareness is crucial to bear in mind in efforts to push understanding of the processes by which people apprehend and construct kinship.

2. How do people come to understand and recognize the relations around them, the majority of which are determined by the circumstances of birth? These are relations of siblingship, descent, and marriage; and it is the relations, as opposed to the groups they constitute, that occupy a privileged position in Maneo identity formation. Relations are prior in the sense that attachment to groups—also a source of identity—are simultaneously undermined by diverging ties within the various groups (at the clan and subclan levels). The divisions are manifest further in that there is only a vaguely articulated pan-Maneo identity per se—a fact that reflects their relative historic isolation and their all-encompassing origin mythology. But identities are relationally rather than oppositionally defined or, to be more precise, opposition is a feature of only some relationship designations, for example, affines as opposed to siblings. How kin are recognized and how identities are framed depend on how relationships are differentiated, which requires that individuals be just that, distinct but consistent from one context to another, and situated in a particular field of relationships.

3. The relevance of this difference is that ancestors are distinguished among themselves; they have names, whereas the "evil people," though they may act at the behest of known (or suspected) members of the community, are undifferentiated and anonymous. The fact that most Maneo have converted to Christianity may partly explain the neglect, particularly, of unbaptized ancestors. Furthermore, it may contribute to a rhetoric of modernization, part of the move to jettison and transform their perceived outward status in the world as backward.

4. Firiz's exhortation that we should all meet Atan and his wife at the trail head because "he is our grandfather" takes him as an explicit reference point in urging collective action. It also takes advantage of a common kin designation that persons separated by two or more generations call each other "*tataï*" regardless of clan affiliation.

5. Kinship is generally analyzed in terms of structures; I reserve the term *structure* to refer to the analytical construct deduced from the network of relationships between specific people. For example, a conjugal relationship forms part of a structure of alliance in reference both to the wider set of relationships created among and between the siblings of the spouses, and to the history of previous marriages. The structure of descent, in contrast, refers to the specific relationship between, say, parent and child, in light of the wider set of relationships between ascendants and descendants. Structures are virtual (Sewell 1992); they are not true or false, and they may or may not correspond to local understandings. We can talk about a structure of descent traced entirely through the matriline (through a line of mothers), but such a structure (an abstraction) has no cultural salience in Maneo.

6. Siblingship, conveys not contiguity but analogy, that is, an analogous series of siblings modeled on a prototype sibling relationship that purportedly unites all apical Maneo ancestors. But because blood ties are eclipsed, siblingship implies difference as well as unity (Kelly 1977; Peletz 1988; Smith 1981; Pauwels 1994).

7. I teased one bachelor about his prospects for finding a spouse in a neighbor's house with several unmarried daughters. He said he could not look there because his father knew of a patrilineal connection, though he could no longer recall the specific relationship. While the son was willing to follow his father's wishes (not long thereafter he married someone from another house) I suspect that when his father dies his utterance on the subject will be forgotten when, in the future, it comes time for his own sons to marry.

8. Incest refers to sibling marriages and to marriages between generations; thus, it depends on the prior identification of relations between persons as sibling (*hota'a*) or as

parent or child. Incest arises from the classification of that relation rather than from a principle of clan exogamy per se. In fact, there have been several endogamous marriages in Maneo, none of which were (or are presently) considered incestuous.

9. Freud discovered this idea by turning his considerable powers of observation inward. He describes his epiphany in a letter to William Fleiss: "I have found love of the mother and jealousy of the father in my own case too, and now believe it to be a general phenomena of early childhood.... If that is the case, the gripping power of Oedipus Rex becomes intelligible.... The Greek myth seizes on a compulsion which everyone recognizes because he has felt traces of it in himself. Every member of the audience was once a budding Oedipus in phantasy" (quoted from Ricoeur 1970:189–190 n.14).

10. In a provocative essay, Meyer Fortes claims to have discovered Oedipus in West African society. The discovery, he says, lies in the belief in a similar notion of destiny (Fortes [1959]1983:19–20, 33). The Maneo, I imagine, would tell the story differently to emphasize the more obvious tension between desire (*kahana*) and knowing—specifically, the limits to knowing that permit misrecognition.

11. The deception was perpetrated by one Arnaud du Tilh in the village of Artigat in the 1550s. As Davis (1983) describes the story, Arnaud du Tilh succeeded in substituting himself for Martin Guerre eight years after the latter's disappearance and to no less close a set of kin than Martin's wife, an uncle, two sisters, and various other relatives. The deception continued for nearly four years and only unraveled after the impostor sought—inappropriately for the people in that region—to sell land, an act that outraged his uncle and initiated the lawsuit against him that reached its apogee when the original Martin appeared to testify against Arnaud du Tilh.

12. Davis suggests that any deception of this scale would likely fail because of irreconcilable moral contradictions. Inevitably, impostors would be drawn into situations in which they would be compelled to make choices; in those choices, they would sooner abandon their disguises than sacrifice their "real" interests for adopted causes they could not thoroughly embrace (Davis 1983:59–60). Certainly causes are central to a person's sense of self (Taylor 1989), but Davis's notion of in what this sense of self consists—the locus of such causes—is more problematic. To be sure, there is no empirical evidence to directly support or refute her argument since only those deceptions that are exposed become public knowledge. What I would suggest instead, however, is that not all deceptions are so blatant or great; for deceptions of the scale she proposes, where contradictions would be irreconcilable, the sense of self has to be presumed to be invariant. As I have been discussing here, identities can change as the narratives within which they fit evolve. Thus, outright deception, morally reprehensible from the point of view of the deceived, may be subjectively experienced as mere revision. Martin Guerre is not Piltdown Man.

13. Knowledge is object-like, even exchangeable. The value of genealogical knowledge (partly a function of exchange) in the wider sphere of Central Maluku derives from the widespread belief that the original inhabitants of the mountains of Seram, like the Maneo, possess knowledge of magic and that the knowledge, furthermore, can be accessed through the identification of contiguous genealogical ties. Specifically, based on those ties, persons may claim rights to that knowledge.

14. In the United States, a recent study of questionable paternity, based on the random sampling and comparison of the DNA of children and their purported fathers, found that in roughly 10 percent of the cases there is no connection. The relevant fact here is that the fathers did not know—or at least claimed not to know—and, of course, were never informed of the discrepancy by the scientists.

15. On the whole, Maneo parents do not seem to mind when their daughters have babies out of wedlock, except when having babies interferes with schooling (more a problem on the coast). Indeed, parents call such out of wedlock children a *berkat* (blessing). Children or grandchildren are valued in part because they are perceived as extensions of the self in addition to the other benefits that accrue from having descendants.

16. An elder told me he broke off an arranged marriage for which property had been exchanged to a woman he recalls as having been like a sister to him. Whatever other reasons he may have had, he cited the fact that she used to carry and clean him as an infant. The prospect of marrying her, he said, made him feel embarrassed (*mukai*).

17. Our neighbor's precocious three-year old daughter, who was adopted by her maternal grandparents, refers to them as parents and calls her mother "sister." She claims she was not born (*ailaikana'isi*), but, rather, appeared on a rock in the river. At the risk of making too much of the story—not knowing, too, whether she had been told this by her grandmother—I simply point out the obvious, that the meaning of motherhood is redefined perhaps with the intent to advance some different declaration of belonging.

18. Carsten proposes that siblingship, the dominant principle of Langkawi kinship, is future-oriented (1995b:319). Other than its opposite, a past-orientation, it is not clear what this means. If idioms of siblingship predominate as part of people's self-conscious attempts to forge ties and build community among a people with different histories (Carsten 1995b:326), then, must we conclude that descent is conducive to just the opposite—social divisiveness? Disparate histories and different lines of descent are separate issues that can only be adequately addressed in the context of controlled comparison. Carsten's observations raise the (unintended) possibility that patterns of kin relations arise from their ostensible effects. To remedy this confusion there needs to be some account of the motives, and not only causes, behind Langkawi patterns of kin use and behavior (Carsten 1995b:324–325). The search for motives necessarily implicates the values instilled in a particular system of social organization (Firth 1964:64–66, 84–86) and calls attention to the contexts in which expressions of relatedness emerge. Such values and interests, though, are rarely uniform and consonant. Finally, if we define kinship principally in terms of the creation of identities, in what sense does kinship generate or explain community—as merely a "collective construction of identity" (Carsten 1995b:331)?

19. The sibling ties that Carsten describes of Langkawi are not always conducive to cooperation (see Bourdieu 1990:170); and the normative force of such designations can only partly explain (and contain) actual sentiment and behavior.

3
Espousal, Choice, and Desire

Habitude fostereth love; for whatso is struck by repeated blows, be they ever so light, is in time's long course overcome and totters. And seest thou not therewithal how, falling on stones, do droplets of water in time's long course bore holes through the boulders? Lucretius, *On the Nature of Things*, (Book IV 1255–1287).

[Marriage] is the triumph of hope over experience. James Boswell, *The Life of Samuel Johnson LL.D*

When Maneo marry (*husawa*) nearly every phase in the process is contested, in some cases the process is protracted, and the results are consequential to a marriage's outcome. The outcomes vary; in hindsight some marriages are seen to begin auspiciously, others are not. Though much of what happens later to a couple are contingent events—a young spouse dies, the husband's side succeeds or fails to mobilize sufficient marriage payments (*arata*), the couple have children or not—Maneo are quick to draw causal connections to earlier decisions, chiefly to choice of spouse. They see marriage as a kind of narrative just as they do the nexus of kin relations. The scenario described by marriage narrates a sequence of events initiated by espousal, followed by a gradual shift in orientations and practices that can extend over a lifetime. Marrying turns into being married, the state Lucretius describes above; a couple becomes a family. This understanding of marriage, as a sequence of events makes possible theories of causation and the assignment of actions to agents, and it opens space to ascribe motives to them. It renders marriage a domain of shared experience and a subject for conversation and speculation.

The experience of marriage poses enormous social challenges. How competing desires are managed affirms basic community values, even as tensions linger. There is rich potential for analysis, yet with few exceptions anthropologists have shied away from the "lived experience"—the modalities through which desire, even boredom, induce habits and dispositions (although see Trawick 1990; Wikan 1990; Borneman 1996:220–221; Carsten 1997:194–219). As a consequence, espousal, the chance moment where desire is most acute, is given short shrift. For historic reasons, the profession has tended to focus either on the antecedent processes making any particular union possible or on the structural consequences that follow marriage choice—the new set of relationships betrothal initiates. My concern is not just that choice is overlooked; it is that choice is made inconsequential through abstraction and generalization. To ignore how espousal is perceived and undertaken leads analysis to oversubscribe to the structural determination of the processes bringing a particular marriage into being, as if the specific effects of one choice are un-replicable by any other, except those deemed (structurally) equivalent. Yet no one, not even Maneo elders seeking to arrange a marriage for a child, see a prospective spouse as if he or she was interchangeable. Persons select persons who, by that very process, are unique. Relatedness specifies who one is not supposed to marry, that is, those whose relations categorically exclude them, which is a potentially wide category.[1] Even among the prohibited categories, siblings and persons of adjacent generations, there are exceptions; conversely, not all marriages to *kaifini* (cross cousins) are equally good matches. Recognizing the myriad choices in marriage emphasizes the contingent and variable dimensions of community life more generally.

In theory, Maneo enjoy considerable latitude in choice of spouse, and many different pairings are possible. But the challenge to marrying well is acute because, in reality, options in spouses are often limited.[2] Availability is constrained by residential contingencies, changing demographics, and the continual ebb and flow of enmities and desires, a fact that leads me to believe scarcity is a problem and source of tension in many marriage markets (Goody 1990:371, 380–82; cf. Lévi-Strauss 1969:xxx). In addition, choice matters because the opinions of elders and kin of the couple. Their receptivity to choice of spouse largely determines whether the couple will encounter subsequent difficulties.

Why should public opinion matter beyond mere well- or ill-wishing that any such spectacle might occasion? One reason, elders caution, is that espousal ought to follow rules; rules objectify people's sensibilities (Bourdieu 1977), most forcefully when they appear to be transgressed. For instance, Maneo recoil in disgust at the possibility of incest; and they decry marrying obliquely or between adjacent generations, though less intensely. These feelings are genuine, but the rules that inspire them have cogency because people choose to apply and interpret them in certain ways. Whether particular matches come to be seen as propitious or not depends on the identities of the persons involved, including the personal histories of the whole range of prospective in-laws (Carsten 1997:235). The misdeeds of ancestors leave few descendants untainted.

Once espousal is announced, Maneo line up as kin or affines and marriage becomes an alliance, contingent matches become structural events. But people sometimes remain on the fence when their participation would otherwise seem warranted and uncomplicated, genealogically-speaking. Kin can support a choice or subvert it; if they deem a particular match to be inappropriate, they may withhold support to minimize the prestige it might otherwise accrue. Conversely, their support represents their acknowledgement that a particular match is right (*o'hoa*). Rodney Needham (1962) missed the point when he asserted that marriages are too important in so-called simple societies for elders to permit the desire of the couple to influence espousal.[3] Precisely because everyone's desires (the attraction of the prospective couple included) infuse choice and render that choice the object of one's desire, marriage becomes a point of conflict. Elders fear that random marriage (*husawa puta puta*), which may or may not be on the rise and certainly can be interpreted otherwise, will unleash other chaotic forces. "*Nusa piluwa*" Maneo say of a world turned upside down by passion run amok. Meanwhile, the young face uncertain prospects in finding and attracting a mate (*jodoh*).

Choice of spouse also matters insofar as it transcends what differently positioned individuals may hope to gain from it. Espousal represents a real juncture in the way social relations (and fortunes) are differently reproduced. That decisions might be different occasions commentary about social values a particular choice is seen to reflect (Firth 1964:221; Borneman 1996).[4] While Maneo seek to contract appropriate matches and generally hope others' marriages will be as well, appropriateness looks different for those being paired in arranged marriages (*sa'ae mulua*) and those choosing each other (*suka dengan suka*) in so-called "love marriages." It varies both for young and old, and for men and women. Moreover, perspectives may change over time and opposition may soften or harden depending on what happens to the couple.

At first glance, different marriage scenarios might be interpreted as representing alternative outcomes in a contest of wills between young and old. Indeed, Maneo commentary lends support to such interpretation. However, the difference between marriages arranged by elders and love marriages is largely superficial and obscures a more important one: that is, the extent to which people use marriage to promote narrow, parochial aims where interests seem competitive, or accord a marriage greater status by being seen to subsume individual interests. Paradoxically, because more recent marriages cannot aspire to the latter goal, more may be regarded as appropriate than in the past as problematic ones are overlooked and criticisms that might have been voiced are not.

To Find a Spouse

The social entailments of initial marriage choices in Maneo and elsewhere can be understood in a multiplicity of ways: in terms of what will become or what had preceded it, or in terms of its social consequences or its emotional and attitudinal ones. Historically, most studies in anthropology have tended to restrict analysis to the broader social patterns reflected in and set in motion by espousal (Needham 1962). From this perspective, choice of spouse is constrained by the structure of group relations as the structure of those relations are reproduced by (constrained) choice. The structure is mediated through the posited operation of underlying principles—a set of marriage rules (Lévi-Strauss 1969)—or, in more recent feminist approaches, through systems of inequality and hierarchy (Ortner and Rosaldo 1980; Collier 1988). Such approaches have been useful in illuminating how marriage shapes society. The problem is that the matter of choice, which focuses on the identities of persons as well as their structural position, is largely ignored or subsumed into the teleology of the system. When this happens, the temporal process is collapsed into an event, eclipsing the way interests and desires are shaped. Overlooking choice, in other words, closes off analysis to the factors that would account for the way decisions leading to events might have been different (Borneman 1996:229).

Espousal is difficult to study because the winnowing of the field is completed prior to a proposal becoming public. Maneo young keep plans secret. One young man in Maneo Rendah, whose love interests were the subject of much discussion, went so far as to invent a girlfriend from a distant village where he had traveled on church business. His real fiancée turned out to be a local girl just finishing school. Even suitors are sometimes duped. Several older men told me of rejected proposals, something, I suspect, that is fairly common. They laughed as they recalled gifts they had given in courtship only to discover their love interests themselves had other clandestine interests that became apparent after the gifts ceased. Discretion was sometimes carried to such an extreme that lovers barely had the opportunity to communicate with one another prior to a marriage proposal. A note containing a verse (*panton*), and serving as a de facto proposal, might be the only direct communication. In one case, a female intermediary refused to deliver the note and in the end married the man who sent it. Opacity contributes to the urgency of missed signals and hidden designs. Of course, this is not unique to Maneo. In Shakespeare's Romeo and Juliet, but for a chance request that led Romeo to attend a masquerade ball sponsored by his family's enemies, the Capulets, he would never have beheld Juliet. In part, furtive marriage proposals, intercepted messages, gift giving and elaborate wooing reflect perceived scarcity in local marriage markets.

The Maneo population of potential spouses is quite small since communities themselves are small and dispersed. Even if they have not met, most know everyone else indirectly by reputation, which tends to emphasize the negatives (the prurient and embarrassing). Chance meetings with eligible strangers are highly unlikely in the mountains.[5] On the coast, the option to marry out is somewhat greater, but even there, limits to the size of the marriage pool make choices more contingent on the place and timing of a marriage offer than would be the case if options were greater.

Readers familiar with Bourdieu's approach to kinship will see that my own analysis of betrothal owes much to his discussion of "practical" kinship (1977:34)—the rewriting of relationships to make choice of spouse appear to conform to social norms or ideals. However, on the matter of choice, he, as others, says very little. "Officializing," or making marriages meet high standards, begins only after a prospective spouse has been identified. Bourdieu emphasizes the strategizing that goes into contracting an auspicious marriage, one that reflects as it projects a family's reputation. But the ends of such strategizing are largely presumed, as though nothing less important than honor could be allowed to influence choice (Keane 1997a:228–229). Putative motives to explain choice of spouse can no more be deduced from observable actions or strategies than practices can be seen to follow from cultural rules.[6] Doing so merely reverses the argument about monolithic culture that Bourdieu himself criticizes. By failing to account for how marriages might have been different, he inverts the properties of the model of culture that he sets out to replace: that is, the assumption of the consciousness, coherence, and immutability of the system (de Certeau 1984:56–60).

While I will have more to say about motivation and about the tension between elders and young below and in the next chapter, for the present I wish to make two points. First, actions, including espousal, are determined with respect to a complex set of sensibilities, understandings, and interests not reducible to strategy narrowly defined. Desire interrupts calculation. Moreover, the importance people attach to marriage cannot be measured only in terms of the prestige it may confer on a couple and their families. For one thing, any overt quest for prestige in an egalitarian society like Maneo would likely discourage the support of others needed to insure the success of such a match in the first place. Nor for that matter can a marriage that fails to garner public attention be considered inauspicious.

Second, Maneo are quick to react to prospects of conflicting desires, passions, as well as self-interests getting out of hand. They recognize their mutual dependence in marriage and that so much of what happens to their community subsequently is attributable to the goodness of the match. Dependence, though, also contains within it threat from the passions of others and the possibility of betrayal (Nussbaum 1994:206).

The Good Marriage

Maneo claim that good marriages, in general, follow a matrilateral cross-cousin pattern, that is, a marriage between a man and his mother's brother's daughter (MBD), an anthropological ideal as well. Maneo elders assert this ideal in a refrain they pass on to the young *"tepe riki sesame"* (do not sever an alliance). Of course, if all Maneo men married their mother's brother's daughter—if such marriages were prescriptive—the concern would be unwarranted, and the wife-giving, wife-taking relations (*hahamana-hahapina*) that constitute alliance could not be reversed.[7] But in Maneo, marriages to patrilateral cross-cousins (which do reverse wife-giving/wife-taking relations) are not prohibited, and many marriages join persons for whom no ties between them can be traced. Such a random distribution in relations between partners might lead to the erroneous interpretation that a certain percent of marriages represent deviations from the norm or are unpreferred.[8] Instead, as I will argue, the appearance of randomness is largely a function of conditions affecting the availability of potential spouses, and that once availability is considered certain patterns emerge. Why should availability matter? I do not wish to imply that authority is breaking down and leading to a kind of marriage scramble and free market in prospective spouses. Maneo elders did claim the past was more ordered. Yet when I sought to apply that explanation to the rash of "bad" marriages in one settlement, Kabailu, the same elders were quick to dismiss the argument.[9]

These elders (from different Maneo villages) explained Kabailu's current spate of wife-stealing, divorce, odd marriages, as well as a relatively large population decline (from roughly twenty households to less than ten) in terms of the alleged murder in the 1920s of a minister by ancestors of some of the present residents of the village. Accordingly, they were being punished for the sin (*dosa*) committed decades earlier, whereas I had been quick to attribute sexual license there to weak authority, as if desire were an autonomous force to be checked by authority, Maneo observers accounted for apparent deviance in terms of a different desire, one tinged with antireligious, immoral sentiment. Thus one manifestation of desire explains another; in this case, rampant sexual desire fed on murderous desire set in motion decades before.

The apparent randomness of marriages in Kabailu and elsewhere holds only to the extent marriages are arranged with respect to prior genealogical knowledge or knowledge of alliance relations. This specification changes the argument; it shifts analysis from the way the history of prior marriages are conceived (as alliances) to how persons can be made "safe" for marriage by choosing how best to define relations between spouses (cf. Needham 1962:76, 110). Many circumstances permit marriage by one reckoning and not by another. There may be agreement or not. However, it is not the case that knowledge uncontested reflects shared interests (cf. Bourdieu 1977:39) or that genealogical determinations lend themselves to free expression of what is merely convenient and useful to know. Maneo want to know the truth: They need to fashion consensus precisely to avoid or prevent unpropitious marriages, or ones that come to appear so after the fact. Any contradiction between the quest for truth and shaping consensus dissolves in light of the fact that the object of knowledge, here Maneo social relations, may be overdetermined by genealogical reckoning in one instance, while underdetermined in another. Again, knowledge is directed toward resolution rather than discovery. Accordingly, acquisition proceeds only to a point where knowledge is adequate to make a determination of the status between prospective couples.

Differentiation

The effort of generating favorable kinship consensus is disguised. Relations between persons appear as a natural consequence of the history of relations even though generations can be collapsed, branches can be recalled or forgotten or merged into a lineal line of ascent in order to structure other events. In marriage, specifically, the key principle is differentiation, that is, persons hoping to marry must appear to come together across an affinal divide, for it is in bridging the divide that marriage assumes much of its social value (Valeri 1994b). At base, differentiation is categorical; affinity is defined by its opposite. The status of a prospective spouse is established by virtue of the person being made the offspring of cross-sex siblings or by tracing possible marriages to past marriages. A relation of sameness is defined as a relation among parallel cousins or the offspring of same-sex siblings, which is the default relation in Maneo history. In the beginning, all relations were based on sameness (Wagner 1977:624); all Maneo were siblings (*efa*)—the paradigmatic community relation. The original nine clans' ancestors reproduced asexually; that is, reproduction consisted of mere replacement and differences in gender were muted (Valeri 2000:318).

The Old World (*Nusa Mutuania*) ended and relations between persons changed when a brother and sister (*hota'a*) had intercourse, an act interpreted as incest.[10] The New World (*Nusa Holuwa*) initiated the current era of sexual reproduction, population growth, and increased mortality; and it set social differentiation in motion, thus becoming a criterion for marriage. With each succeeding generation, differentiation is recreated as the children of cross-sex siblings become cross-cousins (*kaifini*), a process that transforms kin into affine. But with the imposition of difference as a condition for marriage, potential ambiguity emerges in representing it. First, inconsistency arises in the way ties are remembered and forgotten (Bourdieu 1977:33). Maneo can recall some marriages of their ancestors. But the memory of such marriages hardly constitutes a record. Nor is that knowledge the province of any group or lineage per se as I discuss below (cf. Valeri 1980:181; McKinnon 1991:104). Second, ambiguity is fostered by the incongruence between the conditions for maintaining alliance (i.e., mother's brother's daughter or MBD marriages) and the terminology system. Specifically, all cross-cousins, whether patrilateral or matrilateral, are *kaifini*, and marriage is permitted between them. In a sample of seventy-five marriages, 28 percent were between spouses with known matrilateral ties (that is, the bride was related to the groom through his mother's kin), 11 percent had patrilineal ties, 3 percent had both, 50 percent had no known connections, and 7 percent of marriages were contracted outside Maneo clans.[11]

Lévi-Strauss proposed that a kin system that permits bilateral marriage (matri- and patrilateral cross-cousin marriage) deviates from the ideal, generalized exchange model predicated on the one-way movement of brides that supposedly weaves together and stabilizes relations among multiple clans (1969:440–449). Over generations, the contrasting pattern of father sister daughter (FZD) marriages create potentially unstable dyadic exchange networks, with shortened and severed alliances.[12] Maneo elders do promote MBD marriage, but not because it represents a necessary condition for reproducing alliances. Their objection to marriages (for men) with patrilateral cross-cousins turns on the fact that the transfer of property that accompanies marriage resembles sister exchange.[13] That is, if men exchange sisters in marriage, *arata* has to be immediately returned to the giver. This violates an aesthetic sensibility rather than a moral one. Commenting on one such case of sister exchange, several married men insisted their wives transfer the objects without any ceremony. Such marriages are considered inauspicious in part because men lose the opportunity to realize or continue wider (or longer) exchange networks when *arata* circles back on itself in alternating generations. In effect, transfers between patrilateral cross-cousins are unmemorable. The movement through time joining different exogamous groups and marked by the movement of *arata* is collapsed as the back and forth trajectories balance each other out.

The Pattern of Espousal

Such unremarkable patrilateral marriages can hardly be prevented given the limited availability of potential spouses. Certainly, there is no inherent reason that genealogical proximity should matter, even if scarcity were not an issue. Maneo stand to gain little by marrying close, for instance, as a strategy for preserving family wealth since there is little wealth to begin with and little wealth disparity among families (cf. Goody 1990). Marriages between persons for whom no ties can be recalled, more common than not, may in fact still follow known alliances. For example, in Minggus's first marriage (described below), his mother identified a prior affinal tie that even Minggus, the expert on Maneo genealogies, could not trace.[14] When I compiled data on the distribution of marriages among clans (*soa*) from all collected genealogies, nearly a comprehensive account, going back three generations and, in some cases, five, the absence of any clear pattern confirms the impression that Maneo contract marriages largely without respect to the clan status of the partners. I should add, too, that within this five-generation span, there does not appear to be any shift in marriage directions from one generation to another. No pattern is being masked that might emerge by focusing on fewer generations.

This is not to suggest that a pattern is absent. For instance, men of the Tamala clan obtain most of their wives from Boiratan families (24 percent) who find a high percentage of wives from Ipapoto (35 percent) who, in turn, complete the circle by obtaining wives from the Tamala clan (30 percent). This pattern, however, does not obtain for the other clans. The percentages of wife-giving and wife-taking between clans yields a ratio that is relatively balanced, with one exception. In that case, apparent marriage asymmetry between Tumio clan (wife-givers) and Tamala family (wife-takers) emerges from just two marriages, a number too small to confirm a pattern. In general, at the clan level, alliances tend to balance. Marriages in one direction are reversed later, even within the same generation (cf. Clamagirand 1980:145)—a situation that implies that even if groups are contracting alliances, that group is not the clan even though clan members do own territory in common and act in concert in some contexts. (It may very well be that a categorical matrilateral cross-cousin, a wife who falls into such a category, may come from a clan different from a genealogical MBD, perhaps the clan of patrilateral cross-cousin. However, in none of the twelve known matrilateral cross-cousin marriages from the sample of seventy-five could such a tie be traced.)[15] Scholars elsewhere have argued that alliances are established between groups instead of individuals (Lounsbury's point [1962] and also Needham's) so that what happens to individuals, strictly speaking, is irrelevant to what groups do. For groups, one marriage may be as good as ten. But such explanation invites other problems: for instance, how are groups to be defined? In what sense are they meaningful? And even if alliances are contracted between groups, there is so much intermarriage that there must be some criteria for ascribing one marriage greater value. To assume that the marriage with the greatest value is the one that continues an alliance, conforming to the MBD pattern, assumes what ought to be explained: the motives a person has for marrying a particular person and not someone else. An important clue, and perhaps a concession to scarcity, is the absence among Maneo of an injunction, noted for other populations in the region, that would prevent groups of brothers from marrying groups of sisters (McKinnon 1991:24; Valeri 1975–76:92). Elsewhere, this arranged difference in marriage trajectories among siblings forms the basis for the hierarchical differentiation of groups, as brothers must marry women from differently ranked houses (see also Boon 1977; cf. Goody 1990:303). Hierarchy is reproduced through constraints on marriage choices. Even if they wanted to, Maneo elders lack the means to coordinate all but a few espousals.

There is a tendency in analysis to infer the substance or quality of social ties from the degree of cohesiveness of the system of kinship, from the extent to which extant patterns correspond to the norm. When Minggus, my key informant on such matters, unites all the members of his clan through connections to a pair of half brothers (information that might be construed as evidence of the corporateness of the clan), he is really commenting on the alleged superior status of his clan. The presumed unity of the clan is thus primarily an artifact of his genealogical construction; but, as I have said, clan members (his siblings and their descendants included) do not act in concert with respect to marriage or, for that matter, most other practices. Even with clan ownership of land, Maneo recognize important subclan divisions. Only Minggus possessed such detailed knowledge of genealogy, and it is his stature, ultimately, that is enhanced by displays of erudition, more than the status of his clan.

From the perspective of a posited system, Maneo marriage exchanges remain dyadic and disconnected, inconsistent from the perspective of any group. Moreover, espousal cannot constitute those groups since the coordination of marriages among brothers (or sons) presumes the existence of an institutional authority for doing just that. I do not think it is the case that the Maneo once had such institutions or that marriage payments functioned that way.

For elders, the key issue in espousal is which alliance to promote. The phrase "*tepe riki sesame*" (do not sever an alliance) presupposes the existence of multiple alliances—alliances, moreover, that may persist when marriages skip generations and that may be conceived from different points of reference (a brother or an uncle perhaps). Various alliances form around and follow specific relations (Trawick 1990:131). The value of alliance per se thus affords no means of discriminating among them. Alliances are remembered through known marriages and through perdurable obligations that allow wife-givers to ask favors of their wife-takers for a period of up to three generations after a marriage. It is the continuation of the obligations that wife-takers owe their wife-givers that signifies the continued existence of alliance, as though the obligations to historical wife-givers presupposes the affinal relationship, not the other way around (cf. Needham 1962:43). When elders caution against severing an alliance, they may be expressing the concern that certain obligations risk no longer being honored. But this is inevitable; to honor some alliances means foregoing others. Alliances dissolve and re-emerge within and across generations. The ephemeralness of the alliance system is tolerated, in part, because it cannot be avoided given the way affinity is understood, as extending alliances over time and outward over social space. It is tolerated, too, because of a history of cross-cutting marriages, owing to various demographic exigencies and the multiplicity of ties between peoples.

To pursue this point further, I broke down the distribution of marriages by subclan (and largely co-residential) sibling groups. Among two subclan groups, Ipapoto (with forty-seven marriages) and Boiratan (with forty-six), where brothers tend to co-reside, most unions are with women from the same clan, that is, with women who are themselves clan sisters. For instance, Jon's siblings (Ipapoto) in Maneo Rendah have more Boiratan and fewer Tamala women to choose from. By contrast, in Maneo Ratu on the coast, where Abner Ipapoto and most of his group reside, the situation is reversed. I should add the same tendency toward village endogamy applies to women as well, because sisters choose to stick together. Though women usually do not initiate proposals, in choosing among suitors sisters do consider the benefits of residing together. More so than for men, coresidence for them is an explicit motivation.

While Maneo do not prohibit parallel marriages, they do claim it is better for brothers to avoid marrying sisters. The reasons are practical. Chief of these is the desire to avoid owing too much in the way of marriage payments to the same wife-givers. Wife-givers set demands for *arata*; these can vary, and there are no limits to the quantity and kinds of *arata* sought. But even though demands are usually tempered by what wife-givers can reasonably hope to receive for their daughters (chapter 5), wife-takers are disadvantaged. This is because marrying sons to the same family limits the wife-takers' recourse to certain delaying strategies in the event those particular wife-givers' demands turn out to be not so reasonable. They cannot play demands off against different affines. With obligations to the same family effectively multiplied, they have fewer ways to check them. In turn, wife-givers or affines will feel greater pressure to ascertain the extensiveness of a household's *arata* resources. And they will likely suspect prevarication when wife-takers come to them empty-handed. They may accuse parents of their sons-in-law, who control the allocation of *arata*, of conflating obligations, thus, making two marriages matter less than they might be separately if affines were different. Whether this occurs, the perception would tend to harden the resolve of wife-givers not to reduce *arata* demands when finding payments proves difficult.

Avoiding Incest

These property (*arata*) strategies remain secondary considerations, however. They are the concerns of parents and kin as well as grooms but follow the choice and timing of espousal rather than precede it. The crucial determinants are those limiting choice of spouse (Goody 1990:338). It may be that such limits reflect a tendency to be attracted to persons around them (coresidents); although too much intimacy at an early age, as Westermark proposed, may diminish desire. I collected several accounts of men journeying to find wives (as well as several accounts of women traveling, though not as explicitly in search of husbands). Men traveled to look for potential wives as they had journeyed in the past when they also hunted heads (cf. Needham 1962:80). Nearly all such efforts failed. The men then returned to contract easier but somewhat more problematic marriages at home, where brothers might be in competition, where relations between prospective spouses might be defined as siblings, or where relations appear to span generations in oblique marriage—a lesser evil. One oblique marriage was roundly denounced by kin, while another, with no less obvious intergenerational connection was not. Foremost, Maneo strive to avoid incest; they make very nuanced discriminations in prohibiting and condemning particular marriages which inspire deep feelings of anger (*palalamu*) and shame (*mukai*). But the reasons behind those feelings are not entirely consistent. Couples may arouse the ire of kin for any number of reasons related (or not) to marriage choice. Even so, rarely, I think, does this lead kin to abandon them since there are almost always other ways to interpret relations. Condemnation builds as the consensus of incest does; the fact that few are construed as such reflects some tolerance of ambiguity and what they would describe as the vigilance of persons guarding against it. Ignoring it when others do take note publicly may expose oneself to moral condemnation and jeopardize other relations.

I recorded three clan-endogamous marriages; none were proscribed, none led to any significant controversy, even though they were open to such interpretation given the presumption of some common male sibling connection between the couples.[16] For each of these apparently endogamous unions, close kin I interviewed cited some precedence, a previous endogamous marriage or some other way of mapping relations between them, for instance, through adoptions and half siblings. I should add that state and religious authorities, in contrast, display little ability to discriminate in their interpretation of such relations despite rote professions of desire to follow local custom. Sometimes these misperceptions can be problematic. For instance, with Maneo being forced to register with the state for everything from schooling, baptism, moving to the Transmigration site or between mountains and the coast, owning clove trees, etc., their written names—given name first, clan affiliation last—assume the appearance of, and are iconic of, complete and discrete persons. These outside perceptions matter because part of the definition of good marriage includes licensing by the state (at a cost of up to US$25) and approval by the church as a prerequisite to participation in communion and to achieving full status in all other church-related activities. The atomized and self-contained individual, a view promoted by state and religious authorities, may not be new, but rather increasingly important as interaction in these wider spheres of practice become more frequent (Fricke 1995:23). When incest accusations arise, condemnation follows because agents (the couple themselves and various others) permitted a marriage between persons whose relations could be defined that way. In contrast, when non-Maneo church leaders and government officials see common *soa* names on marriage certificates, they simply assume incest. Maneo are not oblivious to such suspicions; they know what others say about them and, at times, they seemed to apologize for that misperception, particularly since the church and state have on occasion used such misunderstandings as a pretense for moral condemnation. Ironically, the one marriage Maneo agreed constituted incest—a marriage between offspring of two true sisters or parallel first cousins—united siblings who were members of different clans. The church and state were unaware; lacking the facility and any interest in making such discriminations, they had no reason to condemn it.[17] Moreover, the couple lived in Wahai, the district (*kecamatan*) capital on the north central coast of Seram and, from the Maneo perspective, close to the centers of state and church power. Had the couple lived closer to Maneo kin, a relative told me, they would have been "shot" (*tembak*).

Maneo cannot presume incest will not happen merely because the clan affiliation of spouses differ, nor because of the value given to non-incestuous marriages in perpetuating alliances. It takes effort to prevent the sometimes multiple, overlapping ties between persons marrying from being defined as incest. Contracting favorable marriages depends on managing kinship knowledge after the fact, again delineating and foregrounding appropriate ties when these are multiple. It also depends on forgetting ties or construing them differently (which is easier when key relations are between half siblings rather than full siblings). Furthermore, and perhaps foremost, avoiding incest depends on preventing public (mis-) recognition, where the perceptions of others can lead to condemnation of a marriage despite the way some (including anthropologists) perceive the tie. Maneo may do this by retreating to the forest and affecting a transformation on their return, for example, by returning pregnant and becoming parents.

This strategy for transformation is not foolproof, and failure can be instructive. While we were in the field two brothers-in-law (their wives were sisters) began sleeping with their stepdaughters—daughters of their wives from previous marriages. The arrangement began when the families were hunting and processing sago in the forest; it became more permanent after they moved to the forest above the south coast where Jennie and I would see them on occasion in our travels back and forth from the mountains. When I asked them, delicately, about the appropriateness of the relationships, both men insisted that their stepdaughters were co-wives by virtue of the fact they had "paid" (*sa'ae*) for them. One stated this directly: that the mother and daughter represented a "package" purchased through marriage payments; the other man intimated that his stepdaughter was his because he raised her, giving him the prerogative, as he said, to "reap the field he sowed" (*karia wokana*). More typically, and under different circumstances, raising a stepdaughter generates feelings of parenthood and protectiveness. Men in the village dismissed their justifications; they said the two men were simply bored with their old wives. By contending their stepdaughters were second wives or *liwata* (spouse's same sex sibling) they sought to collapse the mother-daughter relationship. Nearly everyone said the relationships were *"ohoasi"* (no good); some raised concerns about the daughters. But only after one of the stepdaughters fled did Maneo state any willingness to intervene, and this was merely to press *arata* demands. If they were to yield, the demand would have had to come from the daughters' deceased real father and his brothers. In addition, condemnation did not follow because sex had already blurred understanding of the prior relationship between stepdaughter and father.[18] Sex had confounded existing ambiguity, generally more ambiguous the older the stepchild is. One of the stepdaughters bore a child, possibly the stepfather's (although there was some encouraged doubt about this). My suspicion is that over time the child's relationship with her grandmother will effectively redefine the one between grandmother and daughter so that they will be remembered as siblings.[18]

One interesting aspect of these cases was the difference in the way Maneo men and women talked about them. Women were appalled. By contrast, although men I surveyed condemned their actions, several spoke almost longingly of the prospect of sleeping with stepdaughters—a desire they noted that was thwarted by the constraints of village life. By construing incest in the abstract as a pleasure (real incest would be too dangerous), indeed as one of many pleasures available in the forest, Maneo men framed village life as a sacrifice. Thus, the desire Lévi-Strauss considers at the end of *The Elementary Structures of Kinship*—to keep to oneself by keeping for oneself (1969:497)—has currency in Maneo rhetorical practices precisely so men can forego it.

In the case just cited, the relationships failed to draw the condemnation that might otherwise be expected (not to exclude the possibility it might someday). In other instances, however, and for different transgressions, objections and reprisals are fiercer. The goodness or opprobriousness of a prospective marriage depends on people's judgments of the qualities of prospective partners, and not merely of their qualities, but also of their kin. A prospective son-, daughter-, brother-, or sister-in-law, hence, is often seen to embody the qualities of their "bad" relatives (to the exclusion of more benign characteristics).

As described in chapter 1, after Wara'a Ipapoto murdered his wife Kamsuni Salakatota some time during the second decade of the twentieth century, her kin swore an oath (*seti*) prohibiting any marriage between their respective descendents (all clan members) for five generations. Later, Wara'a later murdered Nunupau Tamala after the Nunupau's brother was discovered to be sleeping with Wara'a's sister.[19] The murders dramatically affected subsequent settlement patterns: Many Salakatota moved to the south coast (Maneo Pantai), and some Tamala later followed. After the murder, Halamuri, many of whom were married to Kamsuni's kin, founded the separate mountain hamlet of Sirwai where most of their descendents live today. Tamala clan leaders never proscribed marriages with Ipapoto, although when the next marriage occurred between them a great deal of *arata* was demanded by Tamala wife-givers. But for the Salakatota elders, the murders permitted them to act on behalf of the clan to prohibit marriage in the memory of a clan sister. When Ipapoto and Salakatota do eventually marry—this is the fourth generation—the marriage will be presented as formally ending the enmity. While Salakatota elders describe the prohibition and its eventual termination as instances of concerted clan action, in fact, however, the absence of any marriage between members of the two clans represents a low standard for measuring concertedness. Similarly, the few marriages between Halamuri and Ipapoto are largely a function of availability and proximity. Because of the murders, the respective descendents of Kamsuni and Wara'a left to establish separate villages, which made it possible for Salakatota elders to assert their authority with little risk it would actually be tested. In other words, the oath may have only made official a pattern that a history of separate residence has largely sustained.

Desire

The genealogical models for understanding marriage in anthropological contexts might be usefully augmented by one drawn from the Personals advertised in many newspapers. In the Personal Ads section, at least as they appear in U.S. newspapers and increasingly online, choices are framed with respect to the purported qualities and attributes unique to these otherwise anonymous persons. In short, choice foregrounds identity—what is known or just imagined.[20] Of course, people's opinions about identities are shaped by a history of interactions, and deeply held affinities and antipathies. Maneo seem to feel it is important to have opinions about others; even if they are not heartfelt, they may become so because of people's particular allegiances.

For those directly involved, the anticipation of choice kindles desire. Desire (*kahana*) is driven by its object, specifically, by what is perceived as attributes of the object, whether person or thing (Nussbaum 1994:169). The Maneo expression "*mata koi, hali kahana*" (what the eyes see, the heart desires) makes explicit the link between perceptions and feelings.[21] The irony, not lost on them, is that as desire comes from seeing in a particular way, love blinds those in it to the basis of the relationship between them. Because of this, the young have to be taught (*ai kaiyare*) to discern sibling (*hota'a*) from cross-cousin (*kaifini*); and discrimination has to be practiced. Arguably, this is successful most of the time so that desire that appears contingent, in fact, drives practice in fairly predictable ways. Those desired generally fall into the category of persons not excluded or who are safe to desire, even though choices are not entirely contained within the list of the socially approved. Desire tends to push boundaries and this moral perilousness makes marriage decisions a proper subject for control. The uncertainty also contributes to the value of marriage in Maneo. The chaos unleashed by desire helps frame some of the contingent aspects of Maneo social life pointing to the way, in theory, desire may be domesticated and channeled in socially productive ways: in a sense, to hold as many people together as possible (Augustine 1958:351; see also Nussbaum 1994:274).

General theories of kinship and marriage tend to ignore sex entirely or else bracket it off from consideration (exceptions include Trawick 1990; Borneman 1996). Where it is discussed it is done so as biology, thus, something outside culture to be "organized" by it (Fox 1967:75). However, recognizing sex as a culturally salient motivation and not as biological drives or disembodied representation sheds light not only on the question of what sex does to social relations, but also implicates other nonsexual motivations or desires that control and direct mating in socially meaningful ways. I do not believe this misinterprets Maneo understanding of the matter.

The discovery of sex in mythic history is credited as having brought an end to the Old World (*Nusa Mutuania*), and with it, an end to long life, big bodies, even fair skin. At different historic junctures, the rain (*roha*), a metaphor for semen, wrought destruction. It transformed the undifferentiated landscape just as the undifferentiated social one was altered by desire. Although the Old World was sparsely furnished, nothing much existed there (the creation of things awaited movement of people through the world), it was nonetheless complete in the sense that people had what they needed. Desire, however, changed everything; by desiring, things formerly available simply for the asking, like food and shelter, became hard to obtain. Such simple needs suddenly required effort. This original transformation occasioned a social awakening. The desire that brought death and changed the world also became essential for survival in it. Death made desire a source of value, the animating condition for social values to be realized (Nussbaum 1994:192–238).

In other contexts, desire is depicted as part of a person's gendered identity, a force of varying intensity and manifestation due to different capacities to channel or resist it. It serves as a convenient foil for ascertaining claims of superiority (Brenner 1998:150). Alternatively, desire is seen as emanating from or out of specific relationships before becoming manifest as a propensity discursively configured, but only to a point. In other contexts, the construction of desire is used to predict marriage choices. For instance, a young man's close relation with his brother supposedly engenders an attraction to his mother's brother's daughter (Radcliffe-Brown 1952:27–28; Homans and Schneider 1955; cf. Needham 1962:30–40). Freud described the son's desire for his mother. Others have identified the sibling relation as the key. But here, instead of being "extended," desire is inverted and becomes repulsion—the core of Westermark's thesis (Goody 1990:128)—or even "displaced" onto the nearest equivalent (Trawick 1990:152). But whether, as Trawick contends, affectionate sibling relations explain close cross-cousin marriage, or whether the tendency to marry close kin follows patterns of bilateral devolution, as in south India, is harder to demonstrate (Goody 1990:259–261).[22] Putative, correlation between desire and observed marriage patterns does not imply causation.

Maneo invoke recognition of desire in mythic narratives as a causal force shaping history as well as more recent events. If desire is not entirely contained by theories that give it shape, it serves as a trope for the compulsions it describes.[23] Confronting desire is a first step in making its dangerousness potentially amenable, turning wild coveting into domesticated responsiveness (Nussbaum 1994:188–191, 274). Desire helps make sense of, or renders others' motives transparent. For example, when I asked people about the murder of Kamsuni and Nunupao early this century by Wara'a (Wara'a was Kamsuni's husband and the murders split the village), most explanations centered on sexual relations and on feelings of jealousy and honor. Which feelings were foremost in the various histories I collected depended on whether the informant was a descendent of Wara'a or of Kamsuni's brothers. The motives continue to have relevance because the Salakatota elders, especially, make forgetting impossible. In contrast, Wara'a's descendents, on the whole, feigned lack of interest and knowledge of his state of mind except one person, the only adult male direct descendent of Wara'a's subsequent wives. He argued that the marriage had merely been one of convenience, implying that it was a loveless marriage. In both the accusation and the vindication of the act, desire was cited as a principal cause, for example, Wara'a was insanely jealous or that he had to kill Kamsuni because she had committed adultery and incest at the same time. Different interpretations call attention to the assorted dangers desire can animate. The force it generates moves people to action, whether as rage or as wanting. It propels people to action with little regard to the possibilities of satisfaction; desire transports the motivation behind actions beyond individual agency and onto the object acting on the person, at times leading to tragic ends (for example, see the Friar scene in Romeo and Juliet).[24] Alternatively, madness (*mumanu*) is thought to derive from unfulfilled desire or personal loss. Thus, in bringing about some measure of its fulfillment as it redirects it, marriage curbs the chaotic and destructive impulses of desire. Appropriate marriage does not alLéviate tension, however. In the course of collecting fifty marriage histories, the fact that others often object to choice of spouse creates new tensions and points to something central in the meaning of betrothal.

Arranging Marriages

In arranged marriages, *sa'ae mulua* (to purchase a woman) or *masuk minta* (in Indonesian, to enter and ask), the desire and interests of the couple are ostensibly redirected by parents toward broader, more inclusive ends. This includes, but is not limited to, extending previous marriage ties. When Maneo arrange marriages, the parents of the groom initiate the process by sending word of a visit. Rather than entering through the front of the house (*haha*) as befitting other formal visits, they come through the back of the house into the kitchen (*ipahata*). They sit on the floor, chew betel nut, and engage in small talk until long after the main point of the visit is clear. The subject of marriage may be broached by inquiring into the ripeness of a particular fruit. There are risks involved in attempting to arrange a marriage, including rejection by the parents and the couple themselves. Arranged marriages also elicit greater property demands from wife-givers, which registers the prestige of the match. In fact, just six marriages in the sample of seventy-five qualify as arranged, the last in 1980; and elders doubted there would be any more. The reasons for the decline are complex and reflect not only changes in the wider context of alliance—the fact that the state has largely succeeded in imposing alternative means for establishing peace—but also factors internal to Maneo marriage itself, most notably, a reduction in quantities of *arata* (the valuables exchanged in marriage).

If the goals of parents in arranged marriage seem relatively transparent, to perpetuate an alliance and arrange a prestigious marriage, these are not necessarily antithetical to the desires of children. Most elders want their sons and daughters to marry people with whom they are compatible. A few marriages in the past were said to be arranged *roi kalu* (from behind); that is, after the prospective spouses agree to marry, the parents of the groom approach the parents of the bride to arrange the marriage. The story Minggus told of his own arranged marriage in 1956 is instructive and echoes some common themes, though it was unique event in other ways. And it was his story, too; had his wife (now deceased) described the events, the narrative would differ as it would if I had solicited the story from either set of parents.

> In 1955, my mother arranged a marriage for me with a woman, Faranzina, from Kabohari [a non-Maneo village about ten km to the west]. Some property was distributed. But I did not know who had been arranged to marry me. Later, my mother said she selected Faranzina because she thought she was intelligent and hard working and that we would make a good match. She wanted to continue an alliance, following the marriage of an ancestor from my mother's clan. But she also wanted to prevent me from marrying Batsebah. In fact, Batsebah and I had just had a child together. Mother was incensed. "You act like you're rain falling indiscriminately," she said, "but you're not; you're human and I gave birth to you, so you must obey me." Father said nothing. He thought I might poison myself if forced to marry a woman other than the mother of my child. Mother insisted, however. She even slashed my leg with a knife. At this time, I knew only that a match had been arranged; I did not know whom I was supposed to marry. On my way back from Wahai, I passed through Faranzina's village and was invited to eat at her parent's house. A seat was left open next to her. Her parents said, "don't run, here she is." I spent one night there and returned home the next day saying I would be right back. Instead, Batsebah and I fled to the forest. In the meantime, my mother, father, and sister's husband went to Faranzina's village and returned with her to Maneo Rendah. Realizing there was no alternative—that I would be denied the *arata* I would need to marry Batsebah—I gave up and moved back in with my parents and new wife.

An important feature of this story is that it is mothers, and not fathers, who take the lead in arranging Maneo marriages. Of the six arranged marriages in the sample, five were initiated by mothers. Men may talk about marriages generically as a means to mark enmities between groups or, if marriages are allowed, to mark the formal cessation of hostilities. But the meaning of alliance cannot be disassociated from the persons most responsible for perpetuating them (Carsten 1997:198). Minggus describes his father as being completely absent from negotiations and as having been more concerned about Minggus's well-being than about his choice of spouse. Specifically, his father fretted that as he, Minggus, had just fathered a child with Batsebah, he would be "pulled" by that child, regardless of the fact that the child would likely follow a different clan. Forced from this child (rather than the child's mother), the father thought his son might attempt suicide. According to Minggus, paternity (not descent) mattered more to his father than concerns over alliance. Minggus's mother, by contrast, went to the length of spilling her son's blood in order to compel him to accede to her demands. The loss of blood signaled her willingness to sacrifice her son for the sake of alliance. Though she was unlikely to follow through, the threat provides a vivid commentary of (for her) the value of alliance. When women take the lead in arranging marriages on behalf of sons thus, they cannot be said to be representing the *soa*—not to deny that their actions may appear that way or be construed that way—for they are excluded from them (cf. Trawick 1990:139). The reasons are complex. Both women and men tend to forget the memories of clan sisters (fathers' sisters and fathers' fathers' sisters); even mothers (including mothers' mothers and fathers' mothers tend to disappear from the memories of male and female descendents). It may be that Maneo mothers forget less and thus know more of the alliance histories of their own natal kin than their husbands. Of the six arranged marriages, only one was to a true mother's brother's daughter (MBD); one was to a mother's father's mother's brother's son's son's daughter, two other spouses were classificatory MBD (wives were members of the mother's clan), and two marriages were with wives whose genealogical connections to husbands were unknown, including Minggus's. These ties may be generic. In other words, as past marriages give meaning to present ones, present marriages valorize particular alliances and not others. But the key point illustrated by this contest of wills between Minggus and his mother is that it is through sons that women, as mothers, become powerful.

Most young people are not as accommodating as Minggus; other mothers may not be as determined. His mother's insistence, he hints, helped him frame the choice he faced: to reduce a competing set of values, the personal love and affection he felt toward his girlfriend and his new child, to raw, unvalued desire as a way to resolve the dilemma. It was, too, an especially prestigious marriage in that considerable property was mobilized and distributed. When I asked Minggus whether he would seek to arrange a marriage for any of his young sons, he said he doubted it, better that they should *"cari jalan sendiri"* (find their own way). Again, whether that happens depends less on Minggus than on the sentiments of his new wife. Finally, I should add, interest in extending a particular alliance does not preclude other motives. Minggus's mother was also intent upon severing her son's relationship with his girlfriend, Batsebah. She is one of Wara'a Ipapoto's granddaughters (the murderer of Kamsuni Salakatota and Nunupao Tamala), though this fact did not prevent another of Minggus's clan siblings from marrying her shortly thereafter.

Opposition and Acquiescence

Several Maneo elders complained that marriages nowadays are mostly random pairings (*husawa puta puta*), not continuing any alliances and not serving as occasions for group mobilization. But, I think, it is just as likely that marriages in the present have always been random in comparison to marriages recalled from the past.[25] For such statements of change and degeneration reflect a theory of history as more integrated, coherent, and ordered than the present; they may also convey a nostalgia for a time when the amount of *arata* transferred was greater, when the young supposedly respected the authority of elders. Many of the reasons cited for parental opposition to marriage choices nowadays are relatively new. Maneo youth imported the idea of romantic love, *cinta*, in Indonesian (there is no cognate in *Upa'a*) from boom boxes, *kaset* (cassettes), love songs, posters, and stickers as part of Maneo "youth" identity. They, more than their elders, travel outside to the Transmigration site, to Wahai and to the south coast where representations of *cinta* are seen and heard. With many life choices still ahead of them, the young use these images to illuminate their own experiences to help frame important decisions. Finally, these images embody what the young may perceive as alternative values, in apparent opposition to parents' interests. With chalky stones on well worn river rocks, two young poets scratched out their yearnings (that many of their parents could not read), signing their missives "Roi van Mental, Anak Derita" (Roy the Insane, the Suffering Child) and faded pop rapper "Ais Vanilli" (Vanilla Ice). Through these messages, the young articulate opposition to parental authority and so, perhaps, come to see themselves in a different light. Yet the opposition, perhaps more implied than real, is fostered in order to overcome it. In a sense, whatever recent changes have occurred (the data are inconclusive), elders have been complicit in it. Young people seek out potential mates under the gaze of parents, kin, and neighbors, all eager to report on the slightest hint of activity. And signs of activity abound. Between barking dogs, creaky doors, and the intense surveillance in the village, late night trysts are not secret. Unless the relationship is unambiguously inappropriate, observation generally does not lead to cessation of liaisons. When relationships threaten to become public, when betrothal becomes marriage, then objections do arise, when it is usually too late to intervene.

When we first arrived, we became close to one young man, Jon, who was in the process of marrying. He and his girlfriend, Tamar, spent nights together at her house but before dawn each morning out of respect for her kin he would return home. The relationship was common knowledge; Jon had given a piece of *arata* (an *afala'a*). When the relationship threatened to progress, however, Tamar's mother, Alleta, objected, and the young couple fled to the Transmigration site. The marriage, I should note, did not controvert any marriage rules; it did reverse a *hahamana-hahapina* tie, but that reversal itself followed a previous reversal a generation before. However, if alliance were an issue, it would have been for Jon's kin, particularly his mother, and she said very little. For a time Tamar's mother remained steadfast in her opposition; she even tried to send a brother's son to the Trans to try to retrieve her daughter. Alleta may have believed that the death of her oldest daughter was due to marrying someone she had also opposed, and she may have feared a similar fate awaited Tamar. What had happened with her first daughter certainly gave her no confidence in her younger daughter's ability to choose wisely. It may also be the case that Alleta suspected Jon had inherited the "bad" character of his great grandfather, Wara'a, suspicions confirmed when his temper flared on several occasions. I should add not all of Wara'a's numerous descendents remind others of him, just as for many younger Maneo his murderous rampages were mere stories. But the identification here had enough resonance for others to see in Jon his grandfather, Wara'a's, personality traits. Jon was partly Wara'a and Wara'a had murdered his wife and another man. Eventually however, after nearly six months of opposition, realizing that her daughter would not give in and not wishing to drive her away permanently, Alleta conceded.[26] In 1994, the couple moved into Alleta's house and joined her husband, the widower son-in-law formerly married to the older daughter, their four children (who belong to the deceased wife's clan), the widower son-in-law's new wife (her children from a previous marriage), and several other agnatically related kin.

There is a sense in which resistance to the marriage choices of sons and daughters is a tension added for dramatic effect. Nearly every couple we interviewed recounted some conflict that required a period of flight (*pete hini aipunia*)—a flight to the forest literally, but as likely a flight to another village, the Trans, or Wahai. They perceived some danger of being apprehended and separated by angry brothers and parents of the bride, sometimes with the tacit support of the husband's kin. When we asked parents about those same marriages, however, opposition was downplayed or never mentioned. While resistance creates suspense for the couple and is recalled to demonstrate their resolve, for elders, the drama they helped set in motion is seen as more routine. Maneo do not recognize a separate category of elopement since it is the exchange of *arata* that confirms the marriage, which is only delayed by flight. In addition, in allowing, perhaps even compelling the young to flee, elders absolve themselves of the responsibility for the choice of spouse of sons and daughters and allows them to accede with dignity to any broader social pressure to allow the couple to marry (Fortes 1962:7). If the couple who run off hope to return pregnant to try to present marriage as a fait accompli, the parents hope and expect the new son-in-law to return with *arata*. While I will have more to say on the importance of *arata* and the dispositions of affines in chapter 5, here, I merely wish to point out that the opposition by parents of the bride is stoked as a way to command deference and, critically, to compel husbands to distribute property. Hostility, whatever real sentiment might lay behind it, is made demonstrable as part of a strategy to obtain *arata* as arata mollifies the anger of wife-givers (*hahamana*) for the loss of a daughter or sister. Anger may also be employed by wife-takers (*hahapina*), though with more discreteness, to elicit sympathy and to bring to bear community pressure on affines to lessen *arata* demands.

While conflict serves the performance of marrying and making affines, at the same time, it is important not to lose sight of the fact that much of it is real. Maneo inflict hardships and suffer scars from opposing the wishes of parents and siblings or children with an intensity that cannot be explained solely by its dramatic effects or as a strategy for attracting *arata*. What constitutes the "real" terms of the struggle though is seen differently. Parental objections may be reinforced by claims that a marriage violates social norms. In cases where incest or intergenerational ties between prospective spouses are not obvious, however, objections arise more because of perceived shortcomings of the person. In a sense, Maneo young suffer the interference because of too much familiarity with the persons involved and because of the long memory of their elders where the insults of ancestors are concerned. Elders can find fault with almost any prospective son- or daughter-in-law and not only because of the readiness to hold them responsible for the collective transgressions of ancestors and kin. There is genuine concern that a marriage choice that is not perfect will lead to tragedy. Again, betrothal seems to focus this concern; and because of this, the appraisal of choice, for good or ill, and efforts to sway it, can affect what follows. Despite the opposition, I think there is widespread agreement between parents and children over what constitutes a good marriage. It is one that joins the proper category of persons or follows previous marriages and renews an alliance relationship. A good marriage is completed with *arata* and the appropriate displays of mutual respect—all attesting to the compatibility of the husband and wife. But elders have the luxury of taking a relatively dispassionate, long-term view of choice. Less concerned about the availability of spouses, they can afford to compare and imagine differently who might make a better choice. Unless elders are prepared to go to extraordinary lengths, however, their objections probably have little chance of ending a relationship, much less bringing about another, to them, more favorable one. For them, making a marriage of a son or daughter auspicious means extricating it from the contingent causes of spousal attraction that lead to random couplings. They do this by infusing choice of spouse with a social and moral gravity that makes the occasion momentous.

Conclusion

I have addressed the single-mindedness desire induces; but desire is not madness. It only seems to make choice of spouse inevitable by creating a powerful set of expectations that can only be realized by that choice. Desire, again, makes the object of it appear unique. Yet as the young are caught up in the pull of desire and the way representations of it (as love or *cinta*) give sense and direction to actions, there are other motivations that help direct it. The idea of romantic love in the West, as in Romeo and Juliet, is propelled by the youthfulness of the protagonists as if youth and reason are antithetical. In that story, neither protagonist is presented with options. My point is that desire follows choice as much as leads it. First, the young are acutely aware of the constraints of time and the contingencies of place. They may be fond of co-residents, but they recognize a local prospect is easier to woo. Not acting and fueling desire may mean losing a prospective spouse to a sibling. The explicitness of this concern in second marriages, evinced in the gift-giving discussed above, reveals the calculation that desire, as it is talked about, obscures in the first. A second factor in the selectiveness of desire is its mimetic quality. Marriage, especially a first marriage, marks the transition to adulthood. For the young, selecting a spouse represents perhaps the first major life decision. The authority that comes from being married has to be earned by challenging the authority of others and demonstrating one's worthiness. However, the autonomy and respect that eventually accrues to a man from heading a household is very often preceded by an extended period of dependency in the household of his wife's kin where a new husband, in particular, enjoys less independence than he would have had were he living with his parents. Desire to marry is instantiated further by the wish to follow one's peers (see George 1996:131, 138–141)—to begin the process based on quite clear expectations (despite the changes in Maneo society) to separate from their natal households and establish their own. Younger men and women observing their older peers see their actions not only as desirable but also as right. The data are inconclusive given the difficulty of pinpointing dates and ages, but elders suggest that with less parental involvement, marriages are occurring at younger ages. The communal project of making marriage is perhaps subject more and more to personal, individual projects.

Notes

1. This observation, that relatedness delimits a pool of potential spouses, contradicts one of Lévi-Strauss's central propositions in his tome *The Elementary Structures of Kinship*, that marriage systems that operate by excluding certain kin from being considered prospective spouses fall into the category of complex systems (1969:i). Yet by all other criteria Maneo would qualify as an elementary system.

2. Similar marriage systems have been used to help define an ethnographic region including Seram encompassing much of eastern Indonesia, that is, where difference describes mere variation (van Wouden 1967; Fox 1980). Such regional comparisons can be overdrawn. Maneo seem to share more in common with populations in North Maluku historically associated with the kingdoms of Ternate and Tidore (Visser 1989; Baker 1989) than with the Lesser Sunda islands in the south where van Wouden's famous study focused. They straddle two different culture areas. To the south especially, systems of production and consumption facilitate more stable and larger settlements along with more pronounced status differences than in Maneo. As Goody (1990) observed in general, roughly similar patterns of marriage (as in the Lesser Sunda) may reflect specific strate-

gies aimed at acquiring and preserving wealth and status—strategic concerns not in play in Maneo where relations are more egalitarian.

3. Rodney Needham asserts, incorrectly, that marriage choice is too important to be resolved by sentiment (1962:43). Rather, I think, the challenge is to understand the ways in which sentiment, broadly defined, is consequential.

4. The importance ascribed is accurate in only some Maneo marriages: not all merit celebration. Marriages invite public scrutiny because they are understood to mirror community, to reveal what the community is to become, including how well elders maintain social order. Marriages become meaningful in this broader social context. But in this broader context, a match becomes meaningful differently.

5. Espousal was fodder in the debate in British social anthropology between Leach and Fortes over whether marriage helps reproduce descent groups or the alliances between them, one being seen as an effect of, and so less real than the other. And the neglect was never remedied in critical appraisals of traditional kinship studies which, in the case of feminist arguments, merely substituted systems of descent and alliance for ones predicated on gender, that is, on the premise of the universal exchange of women (Rubin 1975; cf. Strathern 1984; cf. Peletz 1988).

6. Bourdieu describes the practice of entrusting the "least qualified" (and most marginal person in a family) to tender a marriage offer, since their efforts can easily be disavowed without sullying the family's reputation should it be rejected (1977:34).

7. Marriage divides categories of wife-givers (*hahamana*) from wife-takers (*hahapina*). According to Valeri, the meanings of the categories (which happen to be the same in Huaulu) "reflects the complex interplay of affinity and consanguinity and the retranslation of the latter into the former" (1980:185). The affix "*haha*" refers to verandah—as in verandah of the house—"*mana*" and "*pina*" denote male and female respectively. The house or rather part of it stands as a metaphor for the affinal relationship. I do not believe the reverse could be said: namely that the terms for wife-giver and wife-taker are metaphors for discrete social units. That wife-givers (*hahamana*) are masculine and wife-takers (*hahapina*) feminine derives from the affinal opposition between the children of the brother and children of the sister: a reference to the fact (or ideal) that sons of the sister (*hahapina*) marry daughters of the brother (*hahamana*). Since sons, in contrast to daughters, "stay put" (they remain in the same house), from the brother's perspective, wife-givers—represented by the house—are male. It is a complex matter; the important fact to note is that the *hahamana-hahapina* relationship, in effect, constitutes and indexes the alliance.

8. Scholars have argued that systems of marriage effect the tenor of community life differently. MBD marriages foster "stable" alliances between corporate groups (Lévi-Strauss 1969:441) even while contributing to "unstable" status differences (Leach 1965; cf. McKinnon 1991). Patrilateral cross-cousin marriages, in contrast, create discontinuities between out-marrying groups (Needham 1962). If the tenor of community relations could be so easily inferred from the purported effects of such marriages the entire study of Maneo community life could end here. Obviously, I do not think it can.

9. The "bad" marriages in Kabailu included one in which a man (one of the only elder men of the village) left his first wife then "stole" a neighbor's wife whose son from a previous marriage had already married this man's own daughter. He had stolen a woman married to a classificatory son. In fact, I was warned by friends in the other villages to be very careful lest someone there use magic to steal Jennie. They exaggerated the disorder in Kabailu to cast aspersion on the residents there. Conversely, Kabailu vil-

lagers accused some of the people of Maneo Rendah of using sorcery capriciously for no reason other than to cause suffering.

10. Since marriage among true siblings is proscribed, at a minimum, the true sibling relationship referred to is the tie between a set of parents. In reality, though, (and I would have to add usually) the true sibling relationship lies further back than one generation.

11. The seventy-five marriages in the sample were contracted between 1945 and 1994. At the time of the interviews, I did not solicit any information the couple may have had of a prior genealogical relation between them since asking for this may have occasioned some contrivance in their responses and given a false degree of specificity. Instead, I mapped relations through genealogical records collected earlier. These records do contain a few inconsistencies surrounding ambiguities in the clan status of persons— particularly the children transferred between clans or "property children" (*uhuna arata*). And inconsistencies were greater following periods of demographic instability. For example, increased rates of mortality and adoption as a result of the 1918 and 1957 influenza epidemics created some confusion about the identities and specific relations to proximate kin. Another caveat comes from the fact that genealogical knowledge is unevenly distributed. One informant, Minggus, contributed much of the data. While I used his recollections, which were extremely accurate, to verify what others had reported, his information frequently superseded what these others knew of their own ancestors. Accordingly, the record of connections I could trace through his clan, Tamala, is greater than for those relationships charted for other clans. The uneven distribution of this knowledge thus raises the possibility that fewer persons were actually aware of the specific connections between them—though their elders may have been—than is implied here. In other words, the data may overstate the importance of specifying genealogical relationships between persons contracting marriages.

12. Valeri asserts that alliances are contracted between "real" groups (1980:184) and that these groups correspond to lineages. But group boundaries can be drawn in any one of a number of ways that confirm the pattern. There is reason to believe that persons act on behalf of collectivities in some contexts and as individuals in others, and that the boundaries of the group vary. But the existence of the group—an effect of the group orientation of individuals—is an empirical question, just as alliance represents an empirical phenomenon and not an epiphenomenon with respect to marriage. Needham assumes that the authorities, elder men, determine marriage choices (Needham 1962:43). Even if, as a group, one strategic espousal is as important as ten in perpetuating an alliance, it is not clear why that marriage should be valued above the others. Another problem with the structural models is that even when unilateral cross cousin marriage is the norm, it is not always practiced. Again, relations and alliances, which are relations between relations, cut multiple ways. To remedy this incongruity (created by the model) between the conflicting structural entailments that follow choice of spouse, Needham introduced the distinction between prescriptive and preferential systems (1962:2–3). He did not think it likely that such important consequences could hinge on an otherwise arbitrary choice of spouse; the "systems" had to be distinguished (Needham 1962:76 n.4). But if the integrity of the system of relations were at stake, it turns out the actual preferred might, in fact, have a higher percentage of actual MBD (mother's brother's daughter) marriage than those groups that meet Needham's criteria for having a prescriptive system (Lounsbury 1962:1308).

13. Ideally, marriage (to a woman) who stands as the descendent of a man's patrilineally related male ancestors is proscribed for five generations (to a parallel cousin), so that the direction of alliances (of the flow of wives) is not reversed within that genera-

tional span. But this knowledge of affinity is fragmented, and, I think, it must be apprehended by informants as fragmented too (see Trawick 1990:131), given Maneo awareness of forgetting.

14. There is considerable discrepancy between the numbers of marriages of sisters, including father's sisters (FZ) and father's father's sisters (FFZ) versus brothers, father's brothers (FB) and father's father's brother (FFB), most notably among Tamala. Polygamy, which occurs infrequently, explains little; rather, the discrepancy evinces the tendency to forget clan sisters more readily than brothers. In other words, more often than the reverse, brothers married women for whom there are no genealogical traces. That the marriage totals for clans other than Tamala are more balanced (or show higher wife-giver totals) reflects the enormous discrepancy for Tamala, since I compiled many of the marriages of sisters from other clans from their genealogies.

15. From the sample seventy-five marriages analyzed, only twelve couples had traceable genealogical connections; only two were related as matrilateral cross-cousins. Two other marriages out of the twelve were generationally oblique (between generations) in violation of stated rules against incest, though only one was actually condemned.

16. The appearance that these marriages are somehow anomalous belies an analytical conceit: the reverse of the strategy de Certeau observes that people employ in the process of marking out boundaries—instead, using the concept of boundaries to mark out the discrete genealogical space of the clan (1984:122; see also Bourdieu 1977:33–34).

17. As in the origin myth in which sexual intercourse had to have been incest given the sibling relation between all same-generation persons, the real danger of sexual desire lies in its power to blur distinctions, to turn kin into lover. Sex is a powerful sign and a powerfully transformative act. It can be subversive; it can also support existing social institutions. The extent to which it is subversive depends on lack of institutionalized tolerance (Borneman 1996:229).

18. I did see one of the men in a film I was asked to review. He was living with clan brothers in the forest along with his first wife and a child (his wife's granddaughter and possibly his own daughter). The desire that led to this bad arrangement threatens to confound, and not just transform, the social landscape. I should add that in two similar cases, older men tried to marry the widows of their deceased sons. One case occurred two generations ago: the effort succeeded and nothing disparaging was said about the relationship. Indeed, most knew nothing about it. The other attempt, however, did not; the daughter-in-law fled and her kin subsequently accused the father-in-law, who is still alive, of practicing sorcery. Such stories and concerns are not limited to Maneo and other remote places. A January 1996 writer using the sobriquet "Mortified" wrote to Abigail Van Buren (Dear Abby) about her mother who recently began a sexual relationship with her son-in-law (the writer's half brother). Abby responded that although that behavior might "raise eyebrows" it is legal in thirty-five states in the United States and that it is essentially their business. Maneo would probably agree, recognizing of course that in the cases just described one of the daughters objected and did flee. Yet other people's business is always a popular subject of conversation both for Dear Abby readers and Maneo.

19. According to Wara'a's descendents, he had been recruited to marry Kamsuni after her intended husband, the man for whom the marriage had originally been arranged, died attempting to ford a flooded stream. It was an inauspicious beginning; after several children had been born, Wara'a murdered her. In discussing the reasons, his descendents emphasized the mitigating circumstances of alleged infidelity and a loveless marriage, although that explanation does not help explain why he later killed Nunupao Tamala, the brother of a man Wara'a suspected of sleeping with his (Wara'a's) sister. In that incident,

he killed Nunupao after discovering his sister's apparently lifeless body. In fact, she had merely feigned suicide by dabbing fish poison on her lips and lying perfectly still after being told she could not marry Nunupao's older brother. Wara'a only killed Nunupao after Nunupao's brother fled. Despite the differences in interpretation, and the allocation of blame, members of both clans cite the incident when they wish to point out the potential problems of arranged marriages. Kamsuni had been betrothed to someone else who had died attempting to cross a flooded stream and Wara'a himself had been planning to marry another person when they were compelled to wed. Peace was restored between Ipapoto and Tamala after the second murder through the exchange of *arata* (property used in marriage presentations), followed in quick succession by a number of actual marriages.

20. Needham's argument that alliance is too important to be "determined by sentiments" 1962:43) raises two problems. First, he contends there is a wide availability of potential spouses in theory (Needham 1962:84). But the theoretical abundance of possible spouses does not necessarily describe the situation in Maneo or elsewhere. Men may have to journey far to find a suitable partner; not for the love of a mother's brother do they travel (Needham 1962:80). Second, just as alliance there is less a jural institution as Needham's description would lead one to think, so too motivation is more complex. Though the authority of elders and the sentiment of the young often clash over choice of spouse, such a generalization risks confusing appearance for reality.

21. Seeing animates desire, that is, seeing in particular ways. The lover thinks of his or her desire as being aroused by the sight of the beloved, Lucretius tells us. Desire also shapes perception of its objects. "Out of the many visual effluences, or simulacra, that are at any one time present in the air around us, we single out for perceiving those that correspond to our antecedent desires and concerns" (Nussbaum 1994:165).

22. Quite differently, Trawick proposes that cross-cousin marriage persists in Tamil society because of the "longings" (for siblings) that can never be fulfilled (1990:152). This observation allows her to "show continuity between abstract patterns ... and the lived reality of actual people on the ground" (1990:118). My criticism is that by subsuming value into sentiment she fails to grasp how such values are experienced. This leads to a fatal conceptual leap: from her well-founded observation that kinship organizes affect, Trawick asserts that affect organizes and can explain a system of marriage—a statistical effect, I contend, generated more by conditions of availability.

23. At base, desire remains an inchoate and volatile force in Maneo that shifts between forms or manifestations. It is a force to be harnessed. Desire is not sexual desire per se but undifferentiated desire; sexuality is a powerful manifestation of that desire but it is not the source. When men *husali* (a war dance)—now only performed for Christmas or New Years or a change in political office—the frenzy is sometimes uncontainable. Dancers "see red" (the color of the *kasupai* or red headband men wear) and occasionally they have to be restrained. Something outside the person is thought to animate the desire. Thus after a brawl started during a *husali* dance, a man smashed the drums because, as he said, it was the drums that were making people crazy (*mumanu*).

24. Freud, by contrast, sought refuge in the scientific certainty that drives hidden in the subconscious give rise (unidirectionally) to imagination, to the dreams and fantasies revealed in the narratives of his patients. Analysis of imagination, thus, serves to confirm the existence and force of the drives. But Freud's approach, for all its insight, is backwards in the sense that it obscures the way that imagination animates desire and directs it. It is not sex (or instinct) but the imaginative force of inchoate desire that splits the world between old and new and that opens discursive space for reflection, motivation, as well as

explanation. In stories Maneo tell of their neighbors and their mythic heroic ancestors, desire is a profoundly disruptive and creative power that defies simple explanation.

25. Just as marriages can appear similar even though dynamics responsible for their coming into being are completely different (Bourdieu 1977:48), the reverse is also true: similar tensions and desires bring about formally different appearing marriages.

26. This seems to be a general pattern for contested marriages; except for the few arranged marriages, daughters, rather than sons, are usually the ones pressured to break off a relationship. But unlike Minggus, in the case study above, daughters suffer no lack of resolve when standing up to their mothers. Although just before I left the field another man threatened his parents that he would hang himself if they did not allow him to marry his patrilineally-related girlfriend.

4

Marriage, Gender, and the Conditions of Sociality

Sir, it is so far from being natural for a man and woman to live in a state of marriage, that we find all the motives which they have for remaining in that connection, and the restraints which civilized society imposes to prevent separation, are hardly sufficient to keep them together. Samuel Johnson to General Paoli, James Boswell, *The Life of Samuel Johnson LL.D*

Mother, how frightful is the strife of kindred, and reconciling hard to bring about! Polynices to Jocasta, Euripides, *The Phoenician Women*

Marriage is a defining moment. Maneo face no other choice that is quite as explicit and as consequential to social life and community well-being. For once selection has been made and a marriage initiated, husbands and wives begin to become situated within new fields of social relations, to each other most notably, but more importantly with respect to their affines as well as siblings and parents. This repositioning, in turn, subtly shifts relations between other connected persons. But even as the circumstances of marriage have changed over the last century as Maneo have moved out of the forest and despite increased love marriages and the need felt by many to seek approval from the church and licenses from the state (at a cost of US$25), the practice continues to precipitate a split within the natal household and resituate persons in interlocking webs of relations. Moreover, since the cessation of headhunting over two generations ago, marriage now serves as the only public occasion that marks a man's transition to adulthood; it has always been the only juncture to adulthood for women, though muted. Thus, it may be more important than ever in preserving for Maneo a sense of cultural continuity, even as the elements of practice and its meanings have changed.

As described, the process requires the approbation of others (particularly those to be replaced in succession) who may contest a marriage, and not only because of choice of spouse. Opposition may arise because of timing. Parents and brothers of wives may prolong the *kapia* phase—the probationary period of marriage when husbands live with their wives' families—to increase pressure on husbands to distribute *arata*. But if the aim of the delay is to increase amounts exchanged, that would neither explain the means of *arata* circulation, nor the reason why husbands and kin may hold it back for a time, which they do. The different phases and their duration map the protracted process of succession and the complex intersection and collision of interests.[1] Succession is pulled, on one end, by the aging and death of parents—the death of one or more parent by the time a child marries is common; those responsibilities must be fulfilled. Succession is pushed, on the other, by the birth and growth of the couple's own children.

This chapter focuses on the way one set of relations, among same-sex siblings, become consequential through marriage and, in some respects, determinative of the tenor of community relations more generally. To this end, I employ a distinction, observed by Borgatti and Everett (1992), between relations that are structurally equivalent, for example, relations among siblings connected to each other through the same parents, and relations that are structurally isomorphic, where relations are identical but persons, for example, siblings' children, are different by virtue of having different parents. This distinction parallels the distinction addressed in chapter 2 between identity and relatedness, between persons occupying identical positions, where one identity may be substituted for another, and persons in similar positions categorically alike. Marriage outcomes differently mark structural transitions from equivalent to isomorphic sets of relations. No persons are identical, but it is in marrying wherein differences most matter. For instance, depending on the outcome of marriage payment exchanges, offspring are assigned parents who, in fact, may not be their progenitors. The tension that surrounds marriage derives from redundancy. Among brothers, marriage choices tend to crowd out their siblings' possibilities; and, as I will discuss below, they (categorical brothers) frequently accuse one another of adultery. In contrast, sisters' marriages avoid these tensions because they move away upon marriage. Not directly participating in natal household succession and avoiding redundancy enables them to participate differently in community relations.

Divisions among otherwise close brothers arise because, or in anticipation, of their establishing new relations with wives, affines, and especially children. Interactions with their "alters"—brothers in equivalent structural relations—become superseded by respective relations with their children (relations that are isomorphic but not equivalent).[2] In other words, a man's relation with his children changes relations with his siblings; it changes his orientations. The shift may occasion conflict, inviting feelings of competition and redundancy, which may be overcome or exacerbated depending on an array of factors including the number and ratio of brothers to sisters, one's place in the birth order, and their history of interactions. Of course, conflict per se does not define the experience of sibling relations. For communities composed largely of brothers, attenuating ties to siblings represents a problem exacerbated by the underspecification of the terms of their relations. The undifferentiation and structural equivalence of brothers engenders experiences and expectations of close cooperation when young that may go unfulfilled when they are older and confronting diverging paths, entangled in different relations (Bourdieu 1990:170).[3] Partly because they share so much, brothers are inclined to see situations, particularly disputes, quite differently (see Padgett and Ansell 1993:1,263). Untangled from the reciprocal obligations that help anchor the interactions among affines, disagreements among brothers can easily become magnified. Significantly, the situation is different for sisters, who disperse socially if not physically. Patterns of dispersal and residential convergence, shared interests, and the potential for conflict reflect the more general observation: that marriage, kinship, and the complex network of relations they create do not simply make community, but rather, establish the uneven conditions and obstacles to its realization.

Marriage and the Movement of Women

Marriage situates men and women differently. The biological difference necessary for reproduction is reinforced by the Maneo division of labor. The presence of at least one man and a woman is necessary to maintain any household. Usually, coresident men and women are married, but I visited households consisting of unmarried brothers and sisters or a single parent and a married child and spouse, and joint households with different combinations of adult men and women. More importantly, marriage orients husbands and wives differently with respect to kin, affines, friends, and neighbors in the wider community. It is a consequence of the fact that Maneo women move upon marriage whereas men typically do not. Once marriage payments have been completed, women should never return to the households in which they were raised. If men moved at marriage, for instance, daughters rather than sons might be entrusted with knowledge of genealogical origins.[4] My teacher, Minggus, said as much when he told me he was taught Maneo myth and history instead of his sister because of the expectation that she would move away and that her children, to whom she might pass that knowledge on, would devolve to her husband's clan. Moreover, if men moved, male ancestors might be lost from memory and descent, in theory, might become matrilineal.

The "mobility" of women in marriage is reinforced by the division of labor (women generally do not hunt) and by the division of space that restricts their subsequent movement. Physical immobility, evinced in restrictions in women's movement in the forest or back to their natal households, indirectly supports the logic of their transactability—that men must move them in marriage. And women's detachability from their families has other ramifications. On Seram's south coast, a midwife will charge Rp10,000 (US$5) for delivering a baby girl and just Rp5,000 (US$2.50) for a boy. Girls are harder to deliver, one midwife told us, because of the grief they bring to their mothers when they marry and move away. The reasoning is perfectly circular. To say that Maneo women marry out, however, implies a specific understanding of "out" since, in fact, there is no norm of patrilocal residence; instead, they are separated from their natal kin. More precisely, upon completion of *arata* payments, or when payments are at least sufficient, the couple can choose their place of residence and may move anywhere.

In the cultural scheme of marriage, separation entails movement or some representation of movement as a way to bring it about. The physical separation of women from their natal household is necessary because marriage is defined as a transaction involving women. Wives are said to be purchased *"sa'ae mulua,"* though they are not sold (see Valeri 1994b)—a rhetorical move that makes brides transactable only against the flow of property. The exchange turns women into tokens of something else (measurable by quantities of *arata*) in order that subsequent restriction in residence mobility can register the transition as complete (Strathern 1984, 1988). Marriage, though, does affect women's proximity and interactions with natal kin. The impracticality of returning property once given makes it difficult for a woman to return home (*ia lae'umusi*) in the event she should wish to. No similar prohibition restricts brothers from visiting married sisters.

It turns out, however, that not all those who move are women.[5] Failure to marry with *arata* means that husbands move; subsequently and formally their status as husband goes unrecognized. Gender roles are not reversed, but husbands become de facto brothers or sons and the generation between them and their offspring may be collapsed. I should add here that insufficiency of payments, though, is not only an indication of failure to meet *arata* demands. Wife-givers may raise demands to register objections over choice of husband, but they can also adjust them to bring about different residential and relational outcomes. For example, a woman's parents can decline property to prevent a daughter from leaving her natal home (Goody 1990). One Maneo Tinggi couple insisted that whoever marries their daughter will move into their household (with the children following them), in effect, reversing the usual "gendered" movement of men and women in marriage in order, they said, to have descendents to look after them *"ai sopo ami."* In addition to seeking old age insurance, the father, Jafid, also wished to be remembered: to be remembered (*hisinai*), as he remembers his own ancestors, requires grandchildren.

The physical separation of a married woman from her natal household is mitigated by the Maneo propensity to marry locally. There are several reasons for contracting local marriages. People find it easier, and women, in particular, see certain advantages in choosing husbands whom they know and whose families are familiar. Although mothers claim they discourage sons from marrying sisters from the same family for fear of being too indebted to one set of affines, that appears not to be a concern regarding daughters. Though no one ever said as much, good marriages for daughters may be different from good marriages for sons. The observed clustering of marriages between sets of brothers and sets of sisters evinces a desire of women to be close to sisters and fathers' sisters. From the seventy-five marriages studied, which were contracted between 1945 and 1994—a period of considerable dispersal after a second coastal and fourth mountain village was established—a total of forty, or 53 percent, of the spouses came from the same village. Furthermore, in seven out of the thirty-five marriages between persons from other villages, the husbands had lived for at least a year prior to marriage in their wives' village, raising the actual percentage of endogamous marriages to 63 percent or nearly two-thirds of all marriages. Even where some physical distance was crossed, as in the remaining twenty-eight village exogamous marriages, women moved to their husbands' village in only fifteen instances. To be sure, this symmetry in the movement of husbands and wives reflects the timing or phase of the marriage, since choice of residence can only be made after sufficient distribution of marriage payments. Even so, upon completion of *arata* exchanges, I expect that only four recently married couples residing uxorilocally in the wives' settlement (out of the twenty-eight "distant" marriages) will eventually move to the village of the husbands' kin. The point is, while the husband's natal village is initially a factor in determining where to live, reflecting ties to kin and ties to place, it is not the only one. Now, upon completing payments, couples may weigh various economic considerations and the better educational opportunities available for children on the coast or in the Transmigration site. The trend since 1953 is that men from the mountains who marry on the coast settle more or less permanently there.[6]

This trend has contributed to the perception that the mountains are being abandoned. It was exacerbated around the time of our arrival in 1991 when several established families moved to the new Transmigration settlement of Samal Baru. The people moving often portrayed their actions as temporary and justified the move in order to avail themselves of opportunities that do not exist in the mountains. But for those remaining, migration to Samal Baru, combined with the exodus of married couples to the south coast, has fueled fears of a more permanent loss. As Maneo see it, a settlement is lost without people; and without a presence in the mountains there is really nothing to distinguish Maneo from other groups who have abandoned the mountains. As I described earlier, the appearance of change also gives Maneo elders in the mountains occasion to speak out on behalf of the community and rail against the erosion of tradition and to imply that alternatives to patrilocal residence are a contravention of social norms (when it is not clear it ever was a norm).

In fact, Maneo marriage bears only indirectly on the matter of residence, since what is specified is only the separation of sisters and daughters from their natal kin. Again, once marriage payments have been completed, regardless of where a married woman lives, whether next to her parents or in another village, she should never return to her family's hearth. This restriction constricts women's options. Although brothers may visit, which they do when they need *arata*, the injunction appears to curtail women's ability to manage relations, as we witnessed on several occasions.[7] When one fifty-year-old woman, whose husband had recently left her, returned to her natal village to visit, both her brothers sent her away. Soon afterwards, she moved to the Transmigration site with her youngest children. Similarly, when a twice widowed, presently unmarried woman came to her natal village to see her son, who was adopted by her brother, she avoided her brother's house entirely; the brother described the avoidance as a matter of honor for the two of them.[8] When another woman abandoned both her first and second husbands and ran off to her natal village to live with her daughter, her brother's son vowed that if he caught her he would beat her naked in front of the whole village. His anger left no doubt that the honor and respect owed his affines mattered more than any sympathies he might have harbored for her.

To be more precise, in terms of the movement of women upon marriage, the exchange of property merely indexes the degree of separation from their male siblings and parents. In the three cases, from the sample of seventy-five marriage histories collected, where little or no property was transferred, two of the women eventually left their husbands. Their stories, recounted to me, detailing what was not exchanged, raise some doubt as to whether, in fact, they were married, whether the women or men saw their relationship that way. The two women who left their relationships implied they had not married. Their attitudes confirm the more general point that the greater the quantity and kinds of objects exchanged (in a relative sense), the greater the investment in the relationship as a spousal one, not only by the couple, but also by their respective kin (especially brothers) (Valeri 1994b:4; cf. Leach 1971:120).

Maneo women, too, have a vested interest in the transactions; they want payments exchanged on their behalf. One woman, Manda, claimed to have been beaten by a clan brother after her first marriage when little or no property was distributed; and she complained of her second husband's failure to distribute any property. She may have feared her brother's anger, though that was not our impression, since her brother, a distant relation, was now an old man with two daughters and little need for *arata*. Rather, for her, I believe, the exchange her husband should have made was a matter of honor.

While women may enjoy greater latitude to divorce husbands and return home should they wish to when little or no property is exchanged, it would be wrong to assume they would, especially if children reside with them. In other words, the practice of marriage exchange does not juxtapose a wife's interests to the interests of her husband even though she has to move because of those payments. She suffers from a husband's inability to meet payment obligations, just as he does; and it is her children, as much as his, who are lost when they are adopted by parents or brothers. Though women suffer differently than men in marrying without *arata* they have much to lose by marrying poorly.

The fate of women who are widowed, divorced, or remarried is revealing for what does not happen. Including Manda, there are thirteen such women in the three mountain settlements of Maneo Rendah, Maneo Tinggi, and Kabailu who are no longer married to their first husbands. Eight of them initially married outside their natal village and moved to their husband's communities; the other five married locally. Of these thirteen women, ten subsequently remarried—the other three, all in their fifties, may not have felt the need or had the opportunity to do so.[9] At any rate, nine of the ten women who did remarry found second husbands in the villages where they had first married. The one exception, a woman who married a second husband in a village different from the one she married in, moved to the community where her oldest married daughter happened to live. Thus, the mother's marriage followed her daughter's. But when her second marriage ended in divorce, she moved back to the village of her first husband rather than her natal village because, as she told us, she wanted to be closer to her married sons and grandchildren who live there.

Furthermore, it turns out that only four of ten women who remarried married brothers of first husbands, that is, leveritic marriages to persons classified as *liwata*. So while marriage payments separate sisters and daughters from their natal households, those exchanges do not determine subsequent remarriages. It reaffirms the observation that wives are not "owned" (*rahae*) by their husbands' clans, and marriage payments cannot be said to represent a "purchase" in any unambiguous sense (Valeri 1994b). When affinal claims are asserted to a brother's wife, those claims are to tokens of persons. That is, if a widowed or divorced woman remarries a husband from a different clan, her new husband may have to transfer *arata* to kin (usually brothers) of the first husband. Whether this happens, however, varies depending on the presence of kin and their willingness or interest to press for compensation. Moreover, because of their own relational positions, including the affinal obligations of sons, these men—the brothers of widows' husbands—may or may not wish to do so. Continuing obligations from first marriages do not perforce constrain subsequent marital choices. Instead, the tendency for a woman to stay where she first married—eleven of the thirteen widowed or divorced women live presently in the villages into which they first married—reflects a fundamental shift in her orientations. As a woman moves in marriage, so, too, do her interests and expectations. Over time, with the birth of children and grandchildren, a woman's closest relationships shift from her parents and siblings to her descendants. Indeed, all widowed or divorced women in the mountain Maneo settlements presently live in proximity to one or more of their children. In a way, women can accommodate the putative norm of patrilocality without much actual compromise or sacrifice.

To be sure, as the shift in orientations occurs only gradually, once payments are sufficient, generally once two objects have been given with the expectation of more, changes initiated by the move can be dramatic. If a woman moves to a village different from the one in which she grew up she may be regarded as a relative stranger, except by any sisters and fathers' sisters whose marriage moves to that settlement may have preceded hers. Cut off from siblings and kin, a woman in a new village may find herself alone (*kesia ia*). She may be resented by sisters-in-law (husband's sisters) who married locally or who have yet to marry; and her ability to forge new cooperative relations may be restricted (Trawick 1990; Carsten 1997:230). She may be resented because her sisters-in-law are, in a sense, replaced by her in their natal household; literally, a married woman who has recently moved to her husband's village will often live for a time with her husband's parents and his siblings. The consequences range from the mundane—a woman without close kin relationships may have no one with whom to sit and gossip and groom—to the life threatening. This was Nadi's predicament. She had grown up in one of the coastal villages and moved to the mountains when she married in 1980. From the start, her parents opposed her choice of husband, one of Wara'a's numerous grandchildren. They may also have been troubled that her marriage followed no immediate precedent and that she had moved to a settlement where she had no close kin, no sisters or paternal aunts. After the birth of her eighth child, Nadi produced little breast milk and her infant was suffering. Though wet nursing is common and even though seven other women in the village were lactating at the time—and three of these were in-laws (her husband's sisters)—none offered to help her. One sister-in-law we approached responded tersely that Nadi never asked for help. Nadi herself may have been reluctant to ask (see Carsten 1997:109–112). Whether she did ask or not, or was refused, the lack of cooperation here evinces and contributes to a level of mutual distrust not found in other affinal relationships.

If the need for cooperation was somewhat unusual in this instance, the resistance to offering it was not. In proposing that the cause is structural, that resentment derives from a woman's replacement by her brother's wife, I need to be explicit about what the argument does not entail. Observing a similar tension among sisters-in-law residing in the same Tamil household, Trawick (1990) speculates that the sister's resentment of her brother's wife is fueled by the sister-in-law's intrusion into the formerly exclusive relationship the sister enjoyed with her brother. Trawick's argument, more psychological than structural, is predicated on a specific condition: a latently sexual, mutual attraction between brother and sister (1990:170–186; cf. Boon 1990). In contrast, in Maneo, the tension between brothers' wives and husbands' sisters hinges, more generally, on the anticipation of separation the latter experiences and the specter of her replacement in the natal family. The degree of tension can vary; it may be nonexistent if sisters-in-law reside in different places. But Maneo women are not only replaced by their sisters-in-law in terms of their relationships with brothers (Trawick's thesis), they are also replaced in terms of their relationship with their parents. From parents' perspectives, as daughters-in-law, sons' wives replace daughters lost upon marriage as mothers of their grandchildren. Thus rivalry may be predicated on succession within the household and shaped by the conditions for household reproduction rather than by replacement for the brother's affection. Once ensconsed in a new settlement, Maneo women acquire power and influence through children and, as their children age, through negotiations surrounding their offspring's marriage choices and *arata* demands.

The tension between sisters-in-law, I think, becomes particularly acute in the context of adoption. As mentioned, a husband's inability to meet affinal obligations means that one or more child affiliates matrilaterally. In roughly half the cases, matrilaterally recruited children are actually adopted by maternal uncles and their wives, or by maternal grandparents if they are still alive. If children are adopted, true mothers are effectively replaced as mothers by sisters-in-law (as true fathers may be replaced by brothers-in-law); and true mothers may become sisters depending on the circumstances of the adoption. Adoption is a rich vein to mine for stories and opinions. We were repeatedly told of the difficulties children (*uhuna ana arata* or property children) experienced who were sent off to live with maternal kin, particularly uncles.[10] One neighbor, Dina, whose daughter was to be sent to live with her brother on the coast, confided that her brother was cruel and might mistreat her; she also expected no sympathy from her sister-in-law. As odd as it sounds, though, I cannot be sure that

Dina, in fact, wanted her daughter to be treated as well as her brother's own children. Being treated differently from true children (*uhuna ana tunia*) will help ensure that her daughter will remember Dina as her real mother. If Dina's fears of neglect are realized, it will not only be because of the alleged cruelty of her brother. More likely, it will occur when her child is older, when she is able to take advantage of her more ambiguous relationship positions. The daughter may be slighted compared to true children when she needs money, perhaps the scarcest resource, for such things as school fees. It is a dilemma for parents, too; in fact, one father who had his own children told me he would not adopt any from his sister because of the perceived expense of raising them. If slighted, adopted children may seek assistance from birth parents and other kin. Such actions, in turn, may look like betrayal to the foster parents who raised them and who, for various reasons, are inclined to interpret such solicitations as acts of disloyalty. The implication is that if relations are more complicated for adopted children it is because true offspring cannot split loyalties so easily. That the nuclear family thus corresponds to a Maneo ideal is only because relationships among members cannot be any closer.

If the potential for rivalry and tension among sisters-in-law is great, it is not systemic. First, sisters of husbands themselves marry out, so except for those usually younger unmarried sisters, sisters-in-law are not forced to share a hearth. Nor, unlike husbands, do they share a patrimony—rights to clan names and knowledge, even access to land for their children. Second, rivalry among sisters and, more importantly, sisters-in-law are mitigated by the routines of everyday life. Nadi may not have a wet nurse for her child, but she was not without friends and colleagues in less intimate activities. Women's cooperation follows from the division of labor that places them in charge of most domestic chores, such as tending to children, cooking, collecting firewood, and cleaning, and gives them primary responsibility for gardening once men have cleared the land.[11] Often Maneo men do garden and occasionally women will hunt opportunistically and clear gardens.[12] Put simply, the division reflects no innate requirements for performing the various tasks, aside from breastfeeding, that could readily be accomplished in the course of undertaking other tasks. But the division of labor does give greater opportunity for women to socialize and to mobilize informally in support for issues of community concern that men in some ways lack, even if women's activities are undervalued by men (see Brenner 1998:166–167). When families are in the village and not in the forest processing sago or hunting, women's activities keep them in close proximity to one another; being around the public space of the village provides women greater opportunities for socializing. Much of this socializing revolves around and through children; women tend to their own children and they watch out for neighbors' children. The fact that women generally cook, too, makes it possible for them to share food.

Even gardening offers an important venue for women to socialize. Manioc, the most important root crop, covers about 40 percent of the average garden (cf. Ellen 1978:163). When it is ready for harvest, the yield invariably exceeds the needs of the immediate family of the garden owner. A family of six would require at least thirty-two days to consume the manioc from a typical quarter-hectare garden (assuming an average consumption rate of 300 to 500 grams per person per day). So, women invite sisters, affines, and neighbors to join them in the harvest. If women did not share, gardens would have to be smaller to avoid spoilage—manioc turns bitter if left in the ground too long—and gardens would have to be planted more often.[13] And the consideration given to sharing is evinced by another fact: Maneo plant smaller "convenience" gardens around the periphery of the village, which often produce enough manioc to meet immediate household needs. Men generally clear gardens, but large gardens are planted, generally by women, because harvests enable women to share company and food.[14] By the same token, the sharing of harvest crops among women, while appreciated, does not match the value that men assign to the sharing of meat—their primary contribution to meals. In contrast to meat, there is little accounting for or recognition of the produce shared. The lower value of garden produce deprecates the public significance of sharing it. This does not mean that sharing manioc is unimportant, but as Aristotle observes, one cannot be generous—or be seen to be generous—if being generous involves no sacrifice.

In sum, although women's trajectories in marriage divide them from sisters and kin, the division of labor and everyday activities brings them together. This collaboration and communication provides women opportunities, if undervalued by men, to contribute to and foster a sense of community. With fewer opportunities than men to distinguish themselves—from the acquisition of formal leadership positions or through the demonstration of hunting prowess—there is less to divide them. It is not necessary to presume the existence of any innate gender difference in moral sensibilities (cf. Gilligan 1984); more reasonably, women's generosity is simply not tested in the same way. Of course, women's proximity in daily activities also means they have more opportunities to insult each other and to put each other in the position of being targets of disputes. Sometimes confrontations are staged. On one occasion, Margi, with whom Jennie and I were living at the time, began yelling loudly at a sister who had abandoned her sick husband and had begun to live openly with another man. But it was her father, feeling Margi was the appropriate messenger, who had asked her to shame her sister. On another occasion, a neighbor woman, who beat her philandering husband for having an affair with her clan sister, said she held that sister responsible. These incidents are not exceptions. Proximity makes it harder to hide enmities when one has been insulted.

But while women exercise considerable influence in shaping social life and sometimes take positions that pit them against other women, rivalries among them are not endemic in the sense that they are among men. Because they marry out and because they are denied certain opportunities, women are less often put in the position of competing with one another. We observed this lack of

Photo 4.1 The women of Kabailu cleaning the village

competition and nascent cooperation in women's early socialization. In Maneo Rendah, among the three large agnatically related households where we spent most of our time socializing, the disputes that erupted daily among the children (twenty under ten years old) ended with the older sisters intervening, comforting the wounded, and meting out the appropriate punishments. Only occasionally would older brothers get involved in these "peace-keeping" activities. Finally, we noticed, too, that whereas girls would carry their younger brothers and sisters, generally the boys in the house would only carry their infant sisters. This is not to imply brothers would never carry little brothers, but that sisters were more likely asked to do so. This difference reflects specific values and expectations inculcated in boys and girls that are carried over to adult interactions.

Marriage and Men

As women move in marriage, men stay put. More precisely, eventually they can stay put once *arata* payments have been deemed sufficient, though not necessarily complete. Once sufficient, then, men can return (*lae'u*) to the villages from which they came. Staying put also means that men's offspring usually join their clans. While their children are still siblings with maternal parallel cousins—their mother's sisters' children from a different clan—their ancestry is reckoned differently. Marriage situates men differently in relation to kin and affines, differently from all except brothers.[15] The fact that brothers stay put poses a number of dilemmas that render relationships among them more complex than would be the case if men married and moved. What contributes to this complexity is the value of having brothers nearby.

Early on in our field work Jennie and I attempted to help Depe seek medical attention for a severely infected leg that had left him unable to walk and stranded in the mountains. Depe had been very helpful on my visit in 1989 when he alerted me to the whole matter of property children. At that time, he was still able to move around with a crutch. In June 1992, Jennie and I began to talk with villagers about how we might get him to Ambon, the provincial capital of Maluku. We planned to escort him as far as Wahai, then, put him on the boat to take him the rest of the way with a relative and the necessary funds. In retrospect, it was naïve of us to think that simply offering to pay for the trip and the likely operation he would need would somehow make it happen. Depe faced some difficult choices and grim prospects apart from the operation. He had never been to Ambon, only a few Maneo had, and other than the one relative to be sent with him, he must have wondered who would look after him and, more importantly, whether he would fare any better if, as was likely, his leg had to be amputated. Our own motives were not entirely selfless. We were eager to enhance our standing at the beginning of our field work by showing everyone our concern by helping Depe the one way we could, financially. Perhaps, had we met Depe later in our work we may have been less motivated to take action. As it was, if we had thought more about the various complications he faced, we might never have suggested the trip and the operation in the first place and, so, raised his hopes. Of course, we could not decipher Depe's own feelings; nor, perhaps, was he entirely sure how he felt himself, even though he had approached us about a cure and had agreed to go along with the plan. He had survived already for over a decade with this infection. This was perhaps the only certainty he knew. Despite the fact that the infection was progressing, the symptoms would sometimes abate slightly, though usually after nearly killing him. He may have harbored some hope that life could continue in predictable fashion without the intervention.

After announcing our intentions, a party was assembled to carry him piggyback down to the Transmigration site, a distance of about 25 kilometers. The party consisted of a clan sibling, a brother-in-law, and two neighbors (who were also affines), along with Jennie and myself. Before getting very far, however, the pain in Depe's leg became too great in the position he was being held and we were forced to turn around. To proceed any further, we would need to carry him on a kind of stretcher, which meant another delay as we would need a few more people to carry it. We were told these people had to be kin so as to avoid any suspicions in case Depe died on the way. But while siblings might be quick to avenge a wrongful death, they were slow to help keep him alive. The group never did come together. Over the course of the next eighteen months we heard from Depe's kin about how they had at times offered to help but had been refused. Initially, I had thought they were simply making excuses and that, in local parlance, their "voices were fat" (*hurumina*) or that they were being duplicitous (*mukuhaha*). But their attitudes reveal something about Depe's relational position. Even assuming he had been committed to seeking treatment, he simply did not have enough close brothers to help. He had been a property child to a couple who had no other children and who themselves had only one other sibling between them. His one true brother, who devolved to his father's clan, lived some distance away in the forest. Depe's isolation was a given. If he had closer siblings than those distant kin we interviewed, he might have avoided the sorcery that likely caused his plight in the first place. The attacker, whoever it was, might have been deterred by the increased possibility of discovery and certain retribution.

His infirmity exacerbated his social isolation by making that isolation more apparent. He was, quite literally, less visible in the community. Depe's case illustrates the more general problem the relative equivalence of brothers and their proximity generates. Precisely because the structure of relations does not specify them, a range of feelings can emerge between brothers, from closeness on the one hand to deep ambivalence, even suspicion, on the other. Brothers are substitutable and too many in close proximity crowd each other out (Smith 1981:236); stated differently, in having everything in common brothers have to compete for everything (Kelly 1977). Redundancy creates incentives for brothers to differentiate themselves. And in a way different for men than for women, men's agency—how agency is mapped as social standing—is predicated on individual achievement. Thus for Depe, not being a competitor in a sense robbed him of a social presence. With his social demise, Maneo may have prefigured his physical one.

If social distance among affinally related women is bridged to some extent by the tasks they engage in, either jointly or in close physical proximity, men's activities preclude easy socializing. Men spend less time around the village; less time cooking and caring for infants, and less time in large groups. In fact, their mobility may constrain forms of cooperation: away from the village, they often work alone clearing gardens and hunting on their clan territories. Even when men hunt with brothers or their affines, it is usually in pairs only. At the end of the day, men of Maneo Rendah would often sit outside and call to each other from their porches. Tomas would call to Simpson, Kalbus would call to Jahaiya. But although they could talk briefly in this fashion—it is not easy to hold a conversation from twenty yards apart—the men were reticent to visit one another. They might shuffle down the village's central path without committing themselves to a destination. The slow jaunt would give prospective hosts an opportunity to find tobacco or hide it, or to make themselves scarce before their disappearance could be considered an insult.

In this respect, our presence was highly disruptive because we always had tobacco. After working on our own garden or checking fish traps, we would often sit outside to write field notes on the porch. Inadvertently then, and not because the guests always enjoyed our company, we facilitated men's socializing by furnishing tobacco and making it available for redistribution. Again, the contrast with women's visits is telling. Although many Maneo women smoke, tobacco does not give rise to the same expectations and constraints if it is unavailable or in short supply. Betel nut is always available and for women it alone is considered sufficient fare for guests. In addition, whereas men generally approach from the visible central path, where their progress can easily be monitored, women move more discretely and freely behind houses. They enter each other's houses through the kitchen, and it is there, out of view, where they remain.

Despite the fact that men travel widely, visiting different villages and entering primary forest, which women seldom do, men's movement, paradoxically, is circumscribed. When men travel in the forest, they merely pass through, if at all, other clans' lands to reach their own territory. Traversing through another clans' land can be dangerous. Doing so may raise suspicions that they are hunting there—a violation likened to adultery (*pahazina*). They also expose themselves to the danger of unfamiliar places that may be *makahala* (taboo sites), where urinating or even saying certain, usually Indonesian, phrases can cause illness or death. Men can be sure of the location of dangerous *makahala* sites only in their own territories. Even the notion of clan ownership is ambiguous and contentious. Maneo clan lands, ostensibly owned by all members, are divided further and used exclusively by specific clan subgroups, as Benno Grzimek (1991) observed for western Seram. Thus, in practice, the Tumio of the village of Maneo Rendah do not know and cannot hunt willy-nilly on Tumio land in Kabailu. In fact, several murders just before we arrived were believed to have occurred because of competing land claims; the land in question lay close to the Transmigration site north of the mountain settlements and had resources with some market value.

Maneo men are constantly reminded of the divisions that exist between them. Even the sharing of meat poses complications. In theory, as I will discuss in the next chapter, deer or wild pig are shared among all households in the village. Yet in practice such expectations generate suspicions and conflict when they are not realized (cf. Turner 1979:155). Again, the contrast with the sharing among women of root crops, like manioc and taro, is revealing. These crops are abundant and there are few expectations regarding sharing; if people need some they may simply ask without any systematic reckoning of who gave what to whom. Although Maneo would deny they keep track of distributions of game, in fact, they do and are quick to feel slighted when their generosity is not reciprocated (Bercovitch 1994).

I have suggested that the respective relations among brothers foster a certain disinclination to cooperate, and that the sentiment between them may be unstable and highly variable because of the relative absence of obligations and mutual interests that largely define and frame orientations in other sets of relations. This instability, I maintain, is not a given; the tenor of relations is not unstable merely because of the lack of norms. Feelings for one another reflect the structural positions that brothers occupy in their overlapping network of relations. The case of two families, described below, illustrates the complications of sibling equivalence and isomorphism. The problems are not unique to sets of brothers, though they are more acutely experienced among them than among sisters; nor are the specific conflicts depicted inevitable. The first case describes the problem of redundancy; that is, effects of demographic crowding caused by too many brothers. In the second case examined, redundancy is reversed. Nonetheless, the family became divided over an incident that exposes the full implications of sibling substitutability: the un-differentiation and equivalence of brothers that facilitates their displacement and replacement.

Tinus

Tinus Ipapoto and his wife Lepe, both in their fifties, raised fourteen children—including one who died in a fall from a tree and another, the oldest, who was adopted (*anak harta*) by Lepe's brother. That family, including grandchildren, represents a significant presence in the village of Maneo Rendah, about 17 percent of the total population of 127. Yet they are now much less a presence than a generation or roughly twenty-five years ago, and it is this decline that is most interesting.[16] Until 1970, Tinus and his four brothers lived together with their own rapidly expanding families. The oldest brother moved to the coast just after he married and all his sisters had married out. Since many other families had, by then, moved to the coast, the relative concentration of Ipapoto clan members was increasing. I have discussed the Maneo tendency and advantages of living together; at this point, though, the brothers were looking for a reason to disperse. Crowding was skewing marriage prospects, especially for the growing number of next generation Ipapoto sons. The pretext came in around 1970 when one of the sisters "ran off to the forest" (*poho humai ia pete roi aipunia*) with Tinus's own brother-in-law, Romi, and the brother-in-law of another Ipapoto brother—the two of them having married true sisters. The event, a sister-exchange marriage, might just as easily have been ignored given that it violates no marriage rules and is seen simply as unpropitious. The two brothers were embarrassed, but that sentiment did not divide them since they shared little responsibility for what had happened. Other than them, no one took offense. Tinus married his wife, his brother-in-law's sister, ten years before that brother-in-law's marriage to Tinus's sister. In fact, the specific cause of dispersal was not the marriage but what happened afterwards. The couple had eloped and had been living in the forest for nearly a month when Tinus brought them back to the village, citing his "affection for his sister" (*ai sayangi ia*). Only then did the two Ipapoto brothers, unconnected by marriage to this brother-in-law (*mamai'a*), move away with their families. The brothers' dispersal points to other, structural conditions.[17]

By 1970, Tinus and his brothers' young children—all of whom are parallel cousins, hence, clan siblings—were taking over the village, demographically speaking. (All but one of their sisters had married and moved away.) If the sister exchange was something of an accident the brothers could not prevent, the dispersal that followed was not. In a way, this concentration of brothers combined with the dispersal of sisters, whose children would have been cross-cousins, was conspiring to make a "bad" marriage inevitable by narrowing choices for available spouses and increasing the likelihood of less valued "sister exchanges" or, worse, incestuous parallel cousin marriage.[18] The sister-exchange marriage precipitated emigration because the brothers were prescient enough to interpret it as a warning of problems that might beset their children if they did not disperse.

Firiz and Dobe

The case of Firiz and Dobe illustrates the social dynamics between brothers when children are few. Firiz and Tenche, his wife, had no biological children. But Firiz had shared property (*arata*) with his brother, Dobe, at the time Dobe married some forty years ago. As is sometimes done, after Dobe's first and, as it transpired, only son, Teli, was born, Firiz and Tenche adopted him. Later, they adopted one of Dobe's daughters. Since the brothers lived next door, in effect, they more or less shared these two children. How intertwined Firiz and Dobe's interests were, beyond whatever personal qualities and idiosyncrasies that might have made them close, was made clear after an incident in 1994. Firiz had another son, Rino, whom Firiz and Tenche adopted from another clan sibling. Rino had married Ami and lived next door in the *kapia* phase of marriage—the probationary period of uxorilocal residence—with Ami's widowed father and their two children, both of whom were property children and affiliated matrilaterally. Anud was one of Dobe's property children, a son from a classificatory sister whose husband failed to distribute sufficient *arata*. Rino and Anud, offspring of different siblings, were not shared between the two households.

The conflict was precipitated by an allegation that Ami had committed adultery with Anud. Rino told me he discovered his wife's infidelity while at church. During prayer, while his eyes were closed, he said he saw a note float down from the ceiling and land on the Bible lying between him and his wife. When he opened his eyes and the Bible, the note slipped out. It was from Ami, addressed to Anud, arranging a rendezvous. When Rino confronted his wife after church she cursed him loud enough so that much of the village could hear. Anud immediately fled to the Transmigration Site.

Firiz wanted Ami and Anud taken to the police in the district office in Wahai where, he expected, they would be beaten. While police are sometimes asked to intervene in domestic disputes as part of their work, Firiz's suggestion was unusual given that adultery accusations in Maneo have a standard method of redress that involves the exchange of *arata*. Firiz also refused to talk with his brother. His reaction lacked proportion to the offense. Clearly, he was frustrated. But his decision to stop talking with Dobe, despite the pain it caused them both, was motivated by more than the adultery offense. During our conversations, Firiz never indicated he held Dobe in any way responsible for Anud's transgression. Indeed, according to Firiz, Anud stayed infrequently with Dobe. He had been in school in Wahai for much of the time we were there. Thus Anud was not "*tunia*" (a true son) as Teli and Rino had demonstrated themselves to be.

I think Firiz deliberately escalated the dispute, including the threat to involve the police, in order to make clear his position on other injustices centered on his son's treatment by Ami and her father: the continued uxorilocal residence and the matrifiliation of Rino and Ami's two children. Firiz dragged his brother into the dispute to register and give public measure to the shame he felt on his son's behalf so that Dobe, too, might be made to experience some of his anguish. In drawing his brother into the matter, Firiz hoped to force a resolution that would, if things worked out, free Rino from Ami's father's house and bring about the "return" of at least one of his grandchildren. Neither Firiz or Dobe wanted to exacerbate problems within their extended family. Firiz even told me that Anud could marry Ami if that was what was necessary to restore amicability. No doubt, he would have been glad to see his son extricated from a relationship with a father-in-law who set unreasonable *arata* demands and wanted to free him from a wife who would curse him in public, saying "*uti kalana*" (his penis smelled). Firiz, though, could not speak for his son who was not so conciliatory and less likely to consider the long-term amity of the extended family.

Eventually, Firiz and Dobe settled the differences between them thanks to the mediation efforts of their joint son, Teli. During the week after the incident, Teli moved between the two households and communicated the feelings of the respective parties, primarily assuaging Firiz by reporting on Dobe's contrition. Firiz responded by telling Teli of the sadness he felt missing his brother's companionship. In a way, Teli's efforts were made easier given what little actually divided them; he had very little to do.[19] And Teli, being the son of both families, was well-positioned to shore up the fissure—a fissure that might have divided the descendants of the two brothers under different circumstances and were he not the bridge between them. Of course, a permanent rift was not something Firiz was willing to risk since it would force Teli, in effect, to choose between his fathers. Given the relations that united them, resolution was inevitable. The divisiveness or disorientation embodied in the persons of their separate sons, Rino and Anud, was mitigated, in effect, by a common son close to both (cf. Carsten 1997:235–255). The brothers' relation to Teli thus reversed, for a generation, the fissioning process whereby close brothers and their descendents become distant.[20] That is, as son of the two brothers, Teli replicated his fathers' relationships with their own father—a recombination of orientations that may be fairly common with joint-parentage and high rates of infant mortality.

I suggest that the alleged infidelity of his daughter-in-law, Ami, was for Firiz merely the final insult in a long line of insults he had had to endure on behalf of his son Rino. Rino, though, likely viewed the situation differently. For him, adultery was the central issue. But formal redress was unlikely. Adultery compensation consists of a fine (*biari pina'lalesa*) paid to the husband and his kin as compensation for being displaced in marriage. But if the perpetrator is a brother, fines may be omitted since the givers and recipients may be one and the same persons. Inasmuch as the brothers occupy equivalent positions in their network of relations, intrasibling tensions do not threaten any broader (interclan) rifts. Embarrassed by what had happened, Rino felt vulnerable and, as far as his wife was concerned, substitutable.[21]

Rino's case was one of nine adultery cases we knew about. Five of these involved clan siblings, that is, one of the perpetrators was a sibling of one of the victims; in one case, antagonists were sisters. These confirmed incidents are less revealing than the distribution of suspected adultery. Though less easy to document, many of these involve brothers. In one incident, in the coastal village of Maneo Ratu, a young man caught an unmarried clan brother, Juni, in the kitchen of his house "seeking food" (*cari makanan*) from his wife. Seeking food is a euphemism for sex; but it is an open-ended quest that engages a lot of young men Juni's age. Venturing into a married brother's kitchen is also sometimes just directed at finding a meal. In order to deny emphatically it was anything more, Juni ran home, grabbed his machete, then destroyed his brother's fence. The case illustrates one reason brothers often suspect one another: It is because brothers are expected to be hospitable with one another. It is fully expected that bachelors like Juni and Anud will enter their married brothers' houses in search of food. Brothers travel in the same space and they are, structurally speaking, substitutable as husbands, affines, sons, and even fathers. The voicing of suspicions, thus, serves to assert boundaries and limits to sharing that are otherwise absent. On a trip to the mountains, Tomae told me about how he had been the object of suspicion by a man newly married he called father. He laughed about how suspicious this husband and wife were of each other, so much so that one never left the house without the other. Because of sibling familiarity and substitutability, when fears of adultery are floating around, brothers, though not necessarily close ones, are likely suspects. Suspiciousness contributes to instability, even precariousness in the way brothers relate to one another. Their interactions can suffer because of the absence of definitive expectations and normative obligations, which are a consequence of relational equivalence and redundancy.

A Note on Hierarchy

Brothers in Maneo share much. They are often in close proximity, so the tenor of their relations can determine the general quality of community life. When men take center stage on the occasion of formal meetings or state- or church-sponsored rituals (including Christian holidays, New Years, and National Independence Day, August 17), they do so as representatives of the community, but also, frequently, as brothers. To transcend the bounded and entangled ties of kin, men go to some length to assert their agency in shaping the world. Through inclusive speech forms, they present their activities, in contrast to women's, as more public and high-minded, even though women's activities afford greater opportunity to contribute, if less formally, to community life. Demonstrating agency requires that brothers differentiate themselves. But displays of autonomy fuel perceptions that when individuals act on behalf of the community they are, in fact, pursuing narrower ambitions of promoting themselves above others.

In the gridlock around elections, in the jealousy over someone else's hunting success, and, most palpably, in adultery suspicions, the tensions among even close kin would seem to raise questions about the precariousness of Maneo social life. While I do not wish to deny the potential for instability, it is possible to overstate or misunderstand the problem.[22] Part of the misunderstanding, as Joel Robbins points out, comes from the undertheorization of equality, specifically, from an overly enthusiastic and uncritical acceptance of Dumont's idea that hierarchical differentiation is necessary for constructing social wholes (Robbins 1994). Maneo do have a system of ranking. This ranking, however, does not reduce complications of sibling equivalence and redundancy so much as it exacerbates them. In fact, public expressions of hierarchy in Maneo were few. As far as I could tell most people did not give inequality much thought (see Valeri 1990:62). Once, just after we arrived in Maneo, the former *kepala soa*, and former resident of the hamlet of Siahari (now an *RT*—a kind of block supervisor—in the Transmigration site), told us he married the daughter of a *raja*. Other Maneo scoffed at his claims and, I think, saw his self-promotion for what it was.

Where hierarchy is most often expressed is in reference to age differences or birth order among siblings, specifically brothers; claims concern who came first (*tai ki*) (cf. Valeri 1975–76:96). This notion of precedence is a useful metaphor that helps shape the past (Lambek 1998), as it justifies a certain social order in the present. Yet the fact that it can be recast or even ignored makes hierarchy, what birth order ostensibly denotes, also unstable. After their own birth, age position among brothers can change retroactively based on the order of birth of their own children, so that a younger brother can become an older brother (*kakak*) or older father (*bapak tua*) to his brother's children. This is not an exception. Precedence in the distant past is similarly reversed. The *raja*, up until Indonesian independence were, and "should be," some would say, members of one particular clan, Tamala. Clan members base this privilege on the order in which the apical ancestors, themselves all brothers, descended to earth at the beginning of time. However, the first brother to descend was the founding ancestor of a different clan, not Tamala, a "commoner" whose name, Maneo, became the sobriquet for the whole community. Because of Maneo's overhastiness, the hierarchy established by precedence was overturned and trumped by ability (*mampu*). And since *mampu*—perceptiveness, intelligence—varies, the notion of ranking in Maneo tends to fuel competition rather than resolve it.[22] To integrate people effectively, ranking has to articulate interests commensurate with a particular status. In other words, interests have to be channeled, expectations and imaginations circumscribed, so that order is preserved or, at least, not contradicted. And this ordering is only partially realized, if ever. In Maneo, the idea of inequality is patently more important for those at the top than for those at the bottom. Openly, men merely strive only to be equal (Carsten 1997:104; Robbins 1994).

Conclusion

I have described how marriage situates people in social space, and how it creates new relations and gives those relations immediacy. Affinity entails obligations and siblingship becomes consequential through affinity. Inevitably, a person's orientations change with marriage; interactions with siblings and parents are displaced by those with affines and children. Much of this shift is anticipated in socialization practices and in conventional meanings ascribed to particular categories of relations. For instance, daughters "cost" parents more when they are born because contact is expected to be curtailed upon marriage. Women move against the flow of property (*arata*). Without the valorization that *arata* confers, conjugal relations are prevented from becoming or extending alliances; in terms of conventional kin designations, a son-in-law or brother-in-law is recast as son or brother. The expectation that women will move also spares daughters the sibling competition that brothers experience in their interactions. As daughters or sisters marry out, eventually their place is taken by sisters- or daughters-in-law. Depending on how they marry, locally or in the "direction" of sisters or aunts, wives may be cut off from natal kin and estranged from the women they effectively replace. But whatever tensions exist can be overcome, first, by the division of labor that keeps women in relatively close proximity and, second, by the birth and growth of children, in short, by the accompanying shift in orientations from natal kin to new family. Despite the fact that Maneo women are largely excluded from formal public activities and, indeed, partly because of it, their work affords them greater opportunity for cooperation and consensus building on issues of importance to them.

Men, in contrast, stay put. Staying put, in theory, means that brothers remain together. But the concentration of brothers, while valued, is complicated by structural conflict generated by the fact that sons (multiple sons) succeed their fathers in fields of social relationships; male sibling relations are complicated further by the fact they are interchangeable and redundant. The equivalence of brothers may limit marriage options for sons, particularly if sons are numerous. Moreover, the familiarity and hospitality expected of brothers can fuel suspicions of adultery as a way to assert boundaries that are otherwise denied. The effort men put into differentiating themselves contributes to their arrogation of political authority and to the valorization of men's activities. That is, men assign value to those capacities that serve to differentiate themselves. But while ostensibly representing the community, men cannot avoid suspicions that they are promoting their own, narrower interests, a contradiction that women, situated on the margins, are uniquely positioned to observe.

Notes

1. When marriages are arranged (*sa'ae mulua*) the process of succession is accelerated or at least not delayed. Upon the distribution of *arata* (during the *hahapina* ceremony), the couple moves to the husband's natal household. Nowadays, as described, this is a rare occasion, perhaps never to be experienced in Maneo again. At the same time, when arranged marriages were common, the couples marrying were older, informants said. Delays in succession were experienced at the front end of marriage and regulated by elders.

2. In advocating a more processual approach in anthropology, Rosaldo, at times, seems to conflate structure with stasis or static social forms (1989:93–107; see also Bercovitch 1994). My point throughout this analysis is that structure refers to relationships between specific relationships, not to any particular institution. The existence of a corresponding social form to the structure being studied is a matter for empirical analysis. In other words, implying nothing about stasis, structure need not be limited to, or conform to, existing social institutions in order to be employed usefully as an analytical construct (Lévi-Strauss 1960:52; see also Kelly 1977:279).

3. The relations of siblings are equivalent and undifferentiated with respect to the parents or ancestors they hold in common. Orientations begin to diverge because of their newly established affinal relations, since it is through wife-takers (one's sisters-in-law), and ties to individual brothers-in-law, men are able to marry. (For an interesting early discussion of the development cycle of the family see Freeman 1961, 1962.)

4. Women are usually prevented from acquiring powerful ancestral knowledge mostly out of fear that they will transmit that knowledge to their own children who are typically recruited patrilaterally to their father's clan. Put another way, because women travel in marriage and men stay put, in theory, though not always in practice, men keep clan knowledge to themselves. This movement may also partly explain why men become ancestors rather than women; if women were invested with ancestral knowledge they would be associated more centrally with the clan (this knowledge being one of the important indices of the clan). Depending on the conditions of transmission—mother to daughter or mother-in-law to daughter-in-law—the content of the knowledge would likely shift, that is, patrilineal descent might become matrilineal descent and women might become clan ancestors. In fact, as Minggus suggested, the actual practice and necessity of transmitting ancestral knowledge belies other considerations that have less to do with gender, namely, who can be trusted, who has the ability to learn, and, perhaps, who is the most deserving.

5. Generally, there is a period of uxorilocal residence, the *kapia* phase of a marriage, of one to two years on average. While *kapia* is described, euphemistically, as a time parents can observe the couple and lend advice, the duration of it largely depends on the timing of the distribution of *arata*, which, in turn, may be delayed by a man's kin until children are born. If the marriage fails to produce children, *arata* expectations on both sides may be lowered.

6. In only one instance did a woman from the coast marry a man from Maneo Rendah in the mountains. Conversely, the two men from the coast who recently married women from the mountain settlements live there only because they have yet to complete

marriage payments. In fact, one of the couples, without approval, had already moved back to the husband's natal village.

7. The logic is framed as indebtedness. The ideal matters because enacting it is invested with the honor of various participants. The honor, for men, reflects their indebtedness to wife-takers in exchange. Josua told us of his acute embarrassment (*mukai*) that he had so far been unable to help mobilize *arata* for his son's marriage. As with the movement of women in the forest, men who remain in the *kapia* phase of marriage become defined as less than male. The idea of movement more accurately denotes affinity than encompassment. It emphasizes the impossibility of return should a woman wish to leave her husband, even after he dies.

8. Elsewhere, Goody (1990) cites the occasional return of married sisters in China as evidence of the enduring strength of sibling ties: that wives are not alienated from their natal families as is often depicted. As well as evincing continuing cohesiveness, such visits can also be a source of domestic tension. Among the Tamang of Nepal, for instance, Fricke et al. (1993) observed a correlation between marriage instability and the frequency of married women's natal visits. The prohibition against natal visits in Maneo would not explain relatively low divorce; death is a more frequent cause of separation. Rather, divorce is more highly correlated with the absence of children and is greater before marriage payments have been completed when the couple is still residing with the wife's kin (see also Carsten 1997:57).

9. In three out of the six recent cases where wives left their husbands and returned home temporarily, none of the women were beaten. In the 1970s, a woman fled her new husband after property was distributed. Supposedly, she fled to the forest to live with (and marry) a clan sibling and the two of them were pursued by the abandoned husband's brothers who, it was said, intended to kill them. In another case, one woman, who abandoned her second "provisional" husband for failing to distribute property, found a third husband in the same village. When she and her new husband returned to her natal village to the west, they were turned away.

10. Some adopted children, now adults, recall suffering and neglect in their adopted households, particularly if they had to compete with other (true) children roughly the same age or younger. In some, though not all, life histories of "property children" (*anak harta*), suffering is an important theme. Yet the example of Hero raises the question, had she not been adopted and had it not been a foster father who had "tossed her on the rocks," would the event have been singled out (as her brother had) and recalled as evidence of systematic neglect?

11. Maneo women enter into marriage for similar reasons and with the same enthusiasm as men. In fact, there may be no specific age where the prospect is undesirable. Elders complain that their children nowadays marry at younger ages than they did—an observation I have no way of confirming given the uncertainty surrounding ages and dates. If elders have sought to prevent this, they have not succeeded. During the *kapia* phase of marriage, women keep the company of their families, while enjoying the new status and respect of peers. They are relieved that some of the burden young unmarried women of a similar age face once they finish school. For unmarried women assume much of the daily responsibilities of their mothers, whereas young wives in their mothers' households are expected to tend first to their husbands even though all the tasks of members of the household are pooled.

12. Unmarried men, by contrast, are relatively free to travel to seek income trapping birds; finding gaharu (the eaglewood tree, some of which contain a valuable resin used for incense); selling meat, durian, or canary nuts; or even to *"nanggur aja"* (to wander).

13. I assume a density of 2.8 manioc plants per square meter with a yield of 350 grams per plant. Garden sizes vary considerably depending on who cleared them; some were greater than a hectare in size, the average is roughly .25 hectare. Of course, the contents vary as well. I estimated 40 percent of the average garden is comprised of manioc. By comparison, Ellen found in one Nuaulu garden that manioc constituted only 7 percent of the crops (1978:163–167), while it made up over one-third of the total grams of domesticated plant resources in the Nuaulu diet (between 300 and 500 grams a day)—a discrepancy explained by sharing. Most Maneo households tend multiple gardens and they easily produce more than they can consume. In fact, it would take between 196 and 329 days for an individual (or between thirty-two and fifty-five days for a family) to consume the estimated 98,000 grams harvested from an average garden—too long a time to avoid some spoilage and long enough for some of the roots to turn bitter in the ground. Alternatively, a harvest shared among the entire village would be sufficient to feed everyone for several days and considerably more than that for the largest gardens.

14. Women sometimes invite sisters, neighbors and affines to share a harvest, especially prior to special feasts. (On these occasions, women will eat together as a group after the men.) Sharing among women is no doubt appreciated, but the lesser value of the harvested food, in comparison to meat, depreciates the public significance of the act, or at least one would think so. In Wilhelmina's kitchen one afternoon, she offered us smoked deer her husband had been saving. It may be that for women meat has less value because of the problems it sometimes causes. Often it causes problems for women because as wives they assume responsibility for distributing the spoils of the hunt in the village, thus alleviating men of some of the burden and responsibility for "misallocation."

15. In contrast to brothers, affinally related men *(kaisau* and *momoi)* tend to cooperate. Male affinal relationships are less complex than those sibling relations in part because they are highly structured in terms of obligations and deference. The tension among brothers arises from their equivalency in relation to their parents and ancestors—and the tendency to coreside (see Smith 1981:236). The relative equivalence of brothers generates, precisely because it does not specify, a range of feelings between them, from closeness on the one hand to deep ambivalence, even suspicion, on the other.

16. Tinus and his true siblings were eleven, six brothers and five sisters. In the generation preceding his, Tinus's father was one of nine children (although six of those were half siblings). The direct descendants of Tinus's father (including sisters and brothers) alone number roughly 140, over 100 of whom are still alive (a total of nearly 10 percent of the entire Maneo population). Twenty years ago, nearly all of these descendants were born and raised in Maneo Rendah—a pattern consistent with the tendency for brothers to stick together. Many have since scattered. Dispersal has followed the general emigration from Maneo Rendah since Indonesian Independence and the end of the *RMS* campaign. But although consistent with the general trend, the factors responsible for dispersal contradicts the general settlement patterns of brothers coresiding.

17. As the Ipapoto men were becoming a dominant presence, further complicating their marriage prospects was the fact that they were prohibited from marrying members of the Ipaana clan owing to a putative sibling relationship between clans (although one such marriage exists). More importantly, Ipapoto were prohibited from marrying Salakatota because Wara'a (Marianus's grandfather) had murdered Kamsuni (a Salakatota)

early this century. And because Salakatota and Halamuri marry—members refer to each other as *hahamana* and *hahapina*—Halamuri, too, have contracted few marriages with Ipapoto. This leaves Ipapoto free to contract marriages with just three Maneo clans, two of which are underrepresented in the mountains, foreclosing a number of marriage possibilities.

18. Among the entire group of Wara'a's descendants, there has been just one MBD marriage, primarily, I believe, because of the fact that sisters of Ipapoto men have married out and followed husbands to the south coast, that is, three of Marianus's five sisters. Not to discount entirely the possibility that the near absence of MBD marriage reflects some deliberate strategy, the fact the sisters married out reduces the likelihood of subsequent marriage between the descendants of brothers and sisters. With brothers concentrated in one area, the choice of wives for sons of subsequent generations is limited.

19. Doing little here is an instance of "robust agency" (Padgett and Ansell 1993:1,310), in the sense that it is possible to see in Teli's actions meanings that the two brothers wished to see.

20. In Maneo Rendah, out of a total of nineteen male-headed households an average of 6.1 (or nearly one-third) are related through ties of siblingship or descent. The mean, however, is ten with Boiratan now replacing Ipapoto as the numerically dominant clan. I suspect given that what happened to Ipapoto in the past may happen in the future to Boiratan, namely that brothers on their own accord will move their families to other villages or perhaps to the Transmigration site.

21. The presence of brothers, particularly true brothers, poses a contradiction between the indivisibility of patrimony—in a sense, only one son can succeed to his father's place in a line of ascending ancestors—and its divisibility in terms of recruitment, that is, the recruitment of multiple and equivalent persons. If not manifest among true brothers, who generally do cooperate, it nonetheless emerges among, and in reference to, the descendants of siblings (cf. Kelly 1977:246). Conflict cannot be attributable solely to personalities. In fact, we might reasonably argue just the opposite, that the division of labor, the culture of local politics, even the distribution of game, facilitates cooperation among close brothers at the expense of more distant relationships (sibling or affinal). Indeed, residence patterns seem to bear this out, along with various statements from informants testifying to the importance of having brothers nearby, as with Depe. But the conditions of cooperation insist on sibling equality which Depe, ill as he was, simply could not meet. Concerns about marriage (for children) and about adultery describes some of the adverse consequences of having brothers in the same community, just as lacking them may compromise one's survival. The fact that brothers tend to stick together, thus, exposes the presence of factors, some particular, others general, that divide distant kin and that serve to make otherwise close kin distant. The real issue perhaps then is not whether it is better to have brothers but the effects of having brothers in the same community.

22. In general, the first brother ostensibly is the one to whom the others defer (this is confirmed in observations of children). But Maneo do not embrace primogeniture; there is little in the way of divisible property, and the valuables men need for marriage payments come from the sisters with whom they are paired. Older brothers only enjoy marginally greater access to *arata*. As for prestige, it follows from ability, and ability does not correlate with birth order at all. In fact, birth order might negatively correlate with perceptions of certain kinds of ability. *Raja*, for example, are not necessarily the first born, and clan historians (like Minggus) are selected on the basis of memory and aptitude. The oldest are likely to be impetuous (as in the story of Maneo's descent to earth);

nowadays, they are likely to be *anak harta* and belong to their mother's clans. Age differences significant in children disappear as they age behind the ethos of sibling equality. The local sibling terms, *efa* and *hota'a*, distinguish gender ordinally, or in terms of the speaker, that is, same sex or cross sex, but do not distinguish age. Indonesian or Ambonese Malay does distinguish older from younger siblings (*kakak* and *adik*). Occasionally, the oldest brother of a father would be called *bapak tua* (old father).

5

The Good Behind the Gift

> Scientific understanding proceeds by way of constructing and analyzing "models" of the segments or aspects of reality under study. The purpose of these models is not to give a mirror image of reality, not to include all its elements in their exact proportions, but rather to single out and make available for intensive investigation those elements which are decisive. We abstract from nonessentials, we blot out the unimportant to get an unobstructed view of the important, we magnify in order to improve the range and accuracy of our observation. A model is, and must be, unrealistic in the sense in which the word is most commonly used. Nevertheless, and in a sense paradoxically, if it is a good model it provides the key to understanding reality. Paul A. Baran and Paul M. Sweezy, *Monopoly Capital: An Essay on the American Economic and Social Order*

The Maneo reside within a region in eastern Indonesia famous for its complex exchange practices, and exchange features prominently in social life (see van Wouden 1968; Fox 1980; Hoskins 1993). Particularly in marriage, the objects (*arata*) which circulate as payments are highly coveted, sharing them is valued, and giving is both necessary and confers certain benefits. Nevertheless, exchange often does not occur, and when gifts are not given local expectations suffer, but less than would be inferred from the anthropological models which, like Marcel Mauss's (1967), treats exchange as obligatory. Recent scholarship has begun to identify broader shortcomings in Mauss's model regarding the agency and contingency of practice (Bourdieu 1990; Bercovitch 1994; Weiner 1992).[1] My contention is that these critics go too far in abandoning Mauss's project to explore the relation between exchange and social solidarity—turning Mauss on his head, in effect, by reducing deliberation about whether to give to dispositions "which do not allow for the possibility of behaving differently" (Bourdieu 1997:233)—or that they do not go far enough in questioning his moral ontology, that exchange is necessarily obligatory. Instead, in this chapter, I will argue that sociality, what Max Weber calls "mutual orientations" (1947:118–123), is intrinsic to deliberation and not merely an effect of exchange, and that the contingencies of social life (for example, the scarcity of objects) impinge on persons' abilities without affecting their desires to give.

This Aristotelian idea that most people wishing to do well end up merely doing what is advantageous (1984:NE 1162b35) points to a concept of morality more useful than Mauss's, one that is better suited to understanding the stakes and motivations of Maneo exchange. Briefly, Aristotle's view of morality focuses on the way people arrive at decisions, including their perceptions and dispositions that precede action. Hence, morality may be reasoned without being rational (1984:NE1142a31-b10; Nussbaum 1986); it may also be informed without being determined by local conceptions of the good.[2] That is, although dispositions and notions of the good dispose persons toward certain actions, they do not determine them. For Aristotle, what is at stake and what is specifically moral in action is the responsiveness of agents toward others (Blum 1987:310). This view obviates the need to assume that agency is intersubjective or individual.[3] Rather, responsiveness varies as persons' orientations vary, and orientations, in turn, are shaped by one's understanding of context. Moreover, being oriented toward others, responsiveness is freighted with social consequence inasmuch as actions invite interpretation of the ostensible moral content of one's decisions (Aristotle 1984:EE 1241a12–14; Derrida 1997:256).[4]

I became interested in applying Aristotelian morality to analysis reflecting upon a specific conversation with a neighbor, Epe, in his garden one afternoon in August 1993. Epe complained to me about Martin, his classificatory brother and a member of the same *soa*, who was unwilling to share *arata* which he, Epe, needed to help meet his marriage payment obligations. Epe suspected Martin had some; moreover, he railed against the fact that his own father had given *arata* to Martin to help him meet his marriage payment obligations in the early 1960s. Why had property not been forthcoming here? Other approaches tend to explain away the question. For instance, it would provide scant consolation to Epe to categorize the nonexchange in terms of "generalized reciprocity" (Sahlins 1972) in which repayment is open-ended or, in some sense, unnecessary because there is "no book-keeping among relatives" (Valeri 1994b:6).[5] More importantly, the approach would do little to illuminate the moral deliberation behind giving and receiving and obscure the ways Martin and Epe understand their situation. As I intend to show, Maneo invoke no moral principles that would mandate sharing. Such an absence, however, implies neither a facile moral relativism nor an absence of morality altogether. Rather, moral sensibilities inform efforts to shape perceptions of actions and events precisely as a way to induce responsiveness and to mitigate the appearance of unresponsiveness.

Maneo Marriage Exchanges: An Overview

The system of marriage payment exchange (*ai putulu arata*) describes an amalgam of practices with several structural entailments (Comaroff 1980; Barnes 1980). First, through these transfers, Maneo recruit descendants.[6] Usually, clan recruitment is patrilineal, through ties to a child's father; but, to be precise, the pattern is generated by the quantities and kinds of payments transferred. And usually when exchanges are incomplete or insufficient, at least one child joins her mother's *soa*, and in half the cases, she is more or less adopted by the mother's parents or by the mother's brother. This does not mean, however, that matrifiliation represents the default route of *soa* recruitment in the absence of payment, since both parents are believed to contribute substance to the child

(Visser 1989).[7] Despite some matrilateral recruitment, Maneo nonetheless conceive descent looking up, as it were, almost exclusively in terms of a line of male ancestors (Baker 1988). The revision preserves the idea of patrilineality as an important kinship trope through which history is organized. As both cause and consequence, female ancestors and their kin tend to be forgotten more quickly.

A second entailment is that the transfer of *arata* structures relations between affines and among kin. Ideally, men marry their matrilateral cross-cousins or *kaifini*—the term for patrilateral cross-cousins, too. Accordingly, *arata* is expected to flow unidirectionally over generations and generally it does, at least in most people's recollections of object movements. Yet sometimes marriages are contracted in which property circulates on itself in the same generation, as when sisters are exchanged, or *arata* circulates on itself in alternating generations, a pattern which denotes patrilateral cross-cousin marriage. Although, sister exchange and patrilateral cross-cousin marriages do not constitute incest, neither are they desirable. In practice, the problem is that shortened exchange circuits preclude people from assuming that marriages correspond to the desired pattern, precisely because by being shortened the back and forth biographies of specific objects can usually be recalled.[8] Conversely, when *arata* follows the desired paths, these paths mark and help reproduce discrete alliances between wife-givers (*hahamana*) and wife-takers (*hahapina*). This is important given that the combination of small settlement sizes and high rates of village endogamy in Maneo enable prospective couples (or people around them) to identify multiple, sometimes contradictory ties between them. Thus exchange helps disambiguate relations when there is a surfeit of knowledge, or helps constitute such relations in the absence of other information thereby facilitating the nongenealogical expression of relatedness.

The Objects and Their Movement

The objects used in marriage exchanges affect how they are acquired and distributed, and they are responsible in part, too, for a growing crisis over supply. *Arata* consists of porcelain plates (*afala'a*) of different sizes and patterns (mostly sixteenth- and seventeenth-century pieces of Chinese and mainland southeast Asian origin), bronze gongs (*kafiata*) from Java, and colonial-era iron gun barrels (*laela*). Most of these objects are at once unique enough to be traceable, to serve the purpose of delineating relations based on recollections of their particular pathways. But they are also sufficiently convertible, as particular gongs belong to a class of gongs, to permit certain objects to stand for others, most notably, to facilitate the movement of people against them.[9] Convertibility includes, too, their sale for cash, and conversely, though more rarely, it allows their purchase (with cash). As discussed in the last chapter, *arata* are also transferred in feud resolutions and for the payment of fines, such as for adultery or for reneging on marriage promises.

Photo 5.1 Minggus, his family, and *arata potoa*

The objects exchanged in Maneo possess distinctive semiotic properties determinative of the categories into which they fall (Kopytoff 1986:68).[10] In Maneo, there are two broad kinds of objects: *arata*, which count (*hitung*), and *arata*, which merely accompany (*lulu*). Among the roughly twenty varieties of porcelain plates, only five (along with the gun barrels) constitute *arata potoa* (big property) that can be counted against affinal demands; the rest are not: gongs, smaller plates, including nonantique dinner plates, and items such as radios. The problem is that while gongs are still being produced, *laela* are not, nor are porcelain, although I suspect some fakes have been imported from antique dealers in Ambon in recent years. Moreover, quantities of *arata potoa* (hereafter *arata*) especially porcelain, have declined precipitously within the last two decades as objects have been sold to meet new demands for cash and because of the narrowness of the criteria defining appropriate *arata* itself. With few exceptions, Maneo profess a reluctance to substitute other items, such as clove orchards or lump sums of cash.

Entanglements, Disentanglements, and Changing Exchange Practices

Since the 1950s the quantities of *arata* exchanged have declined from nearly thirty per marriage to an average of just two since 1990. Before disentangling causes from consequences, it is necessary to describe the practice, the changes in it, and the strategies of participants.

Briefly, Maneo marriage exchange comprises two types: the distribution of *arata* between affines that marks the marriage payment itself, and the mobilization or pooling among nonaffinal kin that precedes it. In theory, affines may move property entirely between them depending on the temporal coincidence of those distributions—that affinal transfers occur all at once—and on the sufficiency of the quantities distributed. In practice, however, coordinating these exchanges requires complex planning on the part of parents, including storing *arata* left over from marriages in previous generations, pairing sons with daughters, even identifying classificatory daughters whose property from future marriages may be earmarked for sons lacking sisters. Success demands no small amount of luck. Men hoping to marry have to be fortunate enough to have more sisters than brothers, to have those sisters marry with property, and to have affines whose *arata* demands are reasonable.

As is widely noted elsewhere, gift exchanges help generate inequalities by making it more or less easy for people to move through important social transitions (e.g., Thomas 1991:14–15). These inequalities are central to the meaning and function of the practice. Couples need *arata* to marry and to gain children. Once they succeed, they can issue their own demands. Parents of sons, for instance, can withhold *arata* to influence the marriage choices of their children, although with shortages their authority seems to be eroding. Parents of brides wield authority by demanding *arata*. While they press their demands can fairly

Photo 5.2 Firiz and *laela*

directly, I found that demands between brothers-in-law have to be tendered more discretely because deference is especially crucial to preserve among same-generation affines. If *arata* is not forthcoming, brothers may try to elicit it by cajoling and even threatening to beat their sisters but not their affines.

For all parties, in fact, some respect has to be preserved in order to prevent escalation of a "staged" hostility (Valeri 1994b) into something more dangerous. If gifts are not forthcoming, or if new husbands and their kin come to feel mistreated because of excessive *arata* demands, people may come to perceive the actions of others as malicious. I was told, for example, that a neighbor would have been killed in the past for his cruelty toward one of his sons-in-law. That the man had been able to press *arata* demands so harshly, I believe, is a measure of the son's-in-law social isolation, specifically the absence of any close kin who might issue and help make credible a threat of reprisal. The dilemma for wife-givers is that although requests may be negotiated and broadly scaled to availability, they can never be reduced for hardship in particular cases, for instance, if a groom happens to be the youngest son in a family of five boys. This is because reducing demands unilaterally would decrease the effort on the part of husbands to pull property to them. Doing so would concede the outcome of the exchange performance before fully exhausting the possibilities of dislodging more *arata* from those who should make it available.

If authority accounts for some part of the effort Maneo expend to obtain *arata*, participants are also motivated by a sense of vulnerability. Specifically, Maneo enter into marriage exchange with the understanding that much of what happens is beyond their control and that the stakes, mostly of failure, are enormous. These stakes include the couple's residence and the clan status of their offspring, whether they follow their father or mother's ancestors. If a prospective husband fails to give enough, he risks never being able to participate in the full range of social relations; he risks not being recognized more widely as an affine; and he may be forgotten or his relational position revised by his own descendants. In extreme cases of nonexchange, called *falahusu* (to carry the bow), a husband is assimilated into his wife's family, described as a kind of slave (*hukumania*), and his children are encouraged to refer to him and his wife (the biological mother of the children) as brother and sister. This situation can arise either because a couple's genealogical connections are believed to violate explicit rules against incest and intergenerational marriage, or marriages turn "bad" precisely because they fail to attract *arata*, even if the relation between parties follows the preferred matrilateral cross-cousin pattern. Thus, failure may be contingent or the capricious design of others.

But if the increasing scarcity of *arata* is raising the risk of failure, at the same time there are changes that seem to be weakening some of the personal and structural effects of marriage exchange. For example, the *Gereja Protestan Maluku* (the Protestant Church of Maluku) or *GPM* along with the Indonesian government is encouraging the removal of marriage from the province of custom (*adat*). With the complicity of the elders who maintain *adat*, they are insisting on church and state recognition of marriage, a condition of which is the patrilineal reckoning of the couple's offspring. To the extent that this pressure is effective, it removes one of the threats Maneo wife-givers have at their disposal to attract *arata*. Similarly, with the spread of cash and the growth of its importance, there is now a perceived cost in having extra children adopted from one's wife-takers. Some Maneo parents, in fact, feel they have enough children and have no wish to adopt more because of the expense of clothing and schooling them. With less incentive to distribute *arata*, in turn, Maneo may put less effort into keeping objects in circulation. In addition, the changing venue of marriage payment transactions may also be reducing incentives to exchange. Prior to 1975, 36 percent of marriages were celebrated in a ceremony called *hahapina* in which wife-takers distributed *arata* openly and en masse while being feted by wife-givers. Since 1975, however, that number has fallen to just 9 percent with the last such celebration occurring in 1984. Under the weight of these changes, and in light of the discontinuation of *arata* transfers among non-Maneo on the south coast of Seram, there is some possibility of marriage payment exchanges ceasing altogether. The practice persists (and the reasons are complex), but the presence of hidden exchange counters any suggestion that the practice continues as some nostalgic reenactment. Maneo are not trafficking in simulacra of *arata* as the ritual and performative context has changed, not the objects themselves (see George 1996:190–92).

Preliminary Analysis: The Force of Exchange

Incentives to exchange in Maneo, I suggest, include a desire to be generous, a moral concern irreducible to any exigencies and effects of practice. But if morality inspires giving, would not the decline in rates of it register some attenuation in the nature and strength of ties in Maneo society? In fact, could such a decline be the source of Epe's criticism of his brother's stinginess discussed above? If so, one might conclude that *arata* is becoming more commoditylike and more likely to be sold or hoarded by relationless individuals (Gregory 1982; Thomas 1991). But this explanation raises a prior question: Of what would morality consist for social bonds to be so soluble?

Mauss's analysis of exchange is instructive in terms of the way he avoids the issue. As discussed, he never considered the question why gifts are given in some circumstances and not in others, nor how traditional exchange practices could persist alongside marketlike transactions (Gregory 1982). He simply may not have foreseen the possibility of different systems co-occurring, nor been very interested by the prospect. But more importantly, I think, he was precluded from considering moral responsiveness, a key measure of the quality and strength of social ties, because of a central assumption in his model, that in the absence of these exchanges (and in the absence of formal systems of governance) the social collectivities would necessarily fall apart. Individuals would find themselves mired in struggle against one another in a Hobbesian war of all against all (Sahlins 1972:168–183). In his famous exegesis of the Maori concept of *hau*, Mauss discovered the force of obligation that supposedly prevents this fragmentation (1967:3).[11] Yet the idea that the *hau* pushes people to action against their natural propensities is perhaps less a Maori conception of morality than a European one presupposing opposing desires which neatly mark the very divisions between persons that exchange (the animating condition of sociality) thus resolves (Bellah 1973:xix; Johnson 1993:15–16).[12] The logic of the model is circular; critically, self-interest is opposed to a moral force rather than combined more usefully as a moral sensibility. This opposition leads to two problems. First, it obscures the fact that the social tensions exchange bridges are, in some respects, anticipated in the very practices themselves. That is, the tensions reflect the performance, the agonistic displays which are central to the meaning of affinity (Keane 1997a; Valeri 1994b). Second, as a motive, obligation is inadequately grounded in practice in light of its status as a kind of rule and its concomitant lack of specificity. In fact, there may be many ways to meet obligations, as there may be any number of mitigating factors that would compromise their uniform implementation. Not only would timing affect the meaning of exchange (Bourdieu 1990; Sahlins 1972); in addition, in certain contexts, one may honor the spirit of giving (and not the gift) without actually ever transferring *arata*, but by fostering the impression that a return is forthcoming by saying or doing nothing to preclude it. In sum, obligation is hardly the social force to induce conformance to norms; nor, for that matter, could the decline in exchange be used to reveal evidence of the waning of obligation.[13] Furthermore, obligation affords no explanation for why persons would exchange in one context and in one set of relationships and not in others. There is no basis for comparing Epe's and Martin's respective perceptions of their bond, nor any basis on which to compare their tie with the one between Epe's father and Martin.[14]

Sources

It has been noted that the way exchanges are conducted are determinative of what they mean (Bourdieu 1990:126). With respect to the changes in Maneo marriage exchanges discussed above, one might argue that hiddenness along with declining quantities of valuables has led to social fragmentation. If it has, however, the causal relation has not been direct. For wife-takers to avoid the matrifiliation of children depends on meeting the quantities of *arata* demanded. Wife-givers have been the ones deciding to hide exchanges because, I believe, this enabled them to avoid public scrutiny. Critically, Maneo cannot ask for objects randomly (*pasua puta puta*) without accurate knowledge of the type and whereabouts of the items being sought. Hiddenness, thus, provides recipients with a plausible way to deny having *arata* when they are approached for it; not knowing may make people reluctant to ask, which potentially changes the trajectories of gifts (cf. Appadurai 1986; Kopytoff 1986).

Despite the likelihood of dissimulation that hiddenness has probably increased, there are some useful points to be gleaned from analysis of the data on exchange. As reported in Table 5.1, sisters and fathers represent the largest two categories of contributors of *arata*. It is a pattern that confirms the point, argued above, that successful exchange rests on the coordination of prior affinal distributions in which fathers and sisters serve as conduits. For them, generosity is relatively easy, as, typically, they have no personal need for *arata* that would require a sacrifice for parting with it. In other words, their choice is not whether to give, but rather to whom and when.

The more interesting statistics reflect the percentages of contributions from brothers and fathers' brothers. Like sisters and fathers, these kin generally re-

Table 5.1. Sources and quantities of marriage payments

Years	Case	Z	F	M	B	FB	FZ	Other
1990-94	12	7 (28%)	6 (24%)	1 (1%)	0	2 (8%)	0	9 (36%)[a]
1985-89	15	31 (47%)	17 (26%)	8 (12%)	5 (8%)	0	3 (5%)	2 (2%)[b]
1980-84	9	29 (52%)	16 (29%)	0	1 (1%)	2 (4%)	1 (2%)	7 (13%)[c]
1975-79	7	29 (38%)	32 (42%)	2 (3%)	6 (8%)	1 (1%)	5 (7%)	1 (1%)[d]
1970-74	9	41 (58%)	21 (30%)	0	6 (8%)	1 (1%)	2 (3%)	0
1960-69	8	23 (30%)	42 (55%)	0	0	7 (9%)	3 (4%)	2 (3%)[e]
1950-59	5	105 (71%)	25 (17%)	0	7 (5%)	10 (7%)	0	0
1940-49	2	95 (89%)	10 (9%)	0	0	0	2 (2%)	0

D=daughter, S=son, F=father, M=mother, B=brother, Z=sister, H=husband, W=wife
[a] 4 DH, 4 FF, 1 unknown; [b] 1 FZM, 1 MMBDS; [c] 2 FF, 4 DH, 1 unknown; [d] 1 FZS; [e] 1 FF, 1 unknown.

ceive little or no compensation for sharing.[15] Yet unlike them, when brothers and paternal uncles share, they risk giving away *arata* they may need for their own marriages, or, at the very least, they may foreclose options to give to others standing in closer relation.[16]

There are different ways to interpret the data on male kin sharing. First, brothers and fathers' brothers represent relatively ungenerous sources of *arata*, given the large numbers of kin who fall into these two categories. They are, at best, an underutilized potential source of *arata*, a point of "inefficiency" in the exchange system.[17] Furthermore, their lack of generosity may hinder sisters sharing more widely. Brothers and uncles are no doubt aware that even if they are presently married, many will eventually remarry and face new affinal demands. In one Maneo village, for example, the fourteen men over the age of forty married a total of twenty-five times between them (an average of 1.7 marriages per person). Multiple marriages over one's lifetime require multiple *arata* distributions. For this reason, increasing scarcity may be raising the cost of sharing. Furthermore, men may be disinclined to be generous in the absence of any upper limits to what may be distributed in marriage. Finally, nothing enjoins parents and brothers from holding *arata* indefinitely (compare McKinnon 1991:191), just as turning a porcelain plate into a wall decoration—as one informant said he hoped to do—violates no explicit norms. But if Maneo exercise considerable latitude in the way they dispose of *arata*, that latitude does not give license to people, particularly brothers, to do as they wish. Rather, precisely because of moral considerations, discretion poses profound dilemmas about sharing. If the dilemmas did not exist and moral deliberation were not directed toward arbitrating among competing desires, one would expect an increase in hoarding as quantities of *arata* have declined in recent decades; with less property in circulation, each transaction assumes proportionally greater value, and any failure to meet specific demands poses greater risk.

An alternative interpretation, I suggest, highlights the apparent absence of hoarding. That is, as a percentage of total contributions, brothers' and fathers' brothers' gifts have remained relatively steady in recent history. Indeed, given the overall decline in quantities of *arata*, the full measure of male kin generosity may be understated.

Scrutiny and Scrutablity

To be precise, the social effects of exchange depend on the motives ascribed to agents, particularly when inaction defies expectations.[18] Such assessments vary to the extent the contingencies of exchange are recognized and appreciated. For example, during interviews several men claimed it is prudent to withhold *arata* just after marriage in case the relationship ends, one or the other is infertile, or if the wife dies in childbirth. Such delays may be vigorously contested by the wife's kin, but are not considered unreasonable, and are not especially divisive as long as the pursuit of personal advantage is disavowed. Such understanding, however, is fragile. In the case described in chapter 4, the young man I have called Rino may have offended his affines by withholding property. He had already given some *arata* and he felt he was unjustly kept (*kapia*)—the euphemistically described probationary period of a marriage—by his in-laws who had also retained his two children. His affines knew he was withholding an object; he may even have flaunted it. And because of the disrespect they perceived, they refused to pursue the "reasonable" course of action of returning at least one child to him and ending the *kapia* phase of his marriage. In 1994, the conflict escalated with the accusation of adultery. While there is no evidence of any direct causal link, the mutual disrespect, I believe, made it less likely that either party would take the steps necessary to arrive at some mutually satisfactory resolution.

In another ongoing dispute, a neighbor, Helena, complained about her daughter's prospective husband, who had just returned empty handed from a journey to his natal village to seek *arata*. Unmoved by his excuses, Helena suggested the young man schemed to steal her daughter. She made the point by angrily denying that her daughter was like a bunch of bananas ("*ia wahai fitamusi*"), a reference to the disrespect the absence of a gift denotes. That is, she perceived his inaction as intentional; and she held him responsible for the consequence: her interpretation of his intent. Helena invoked bananas in our conversation, I think, not to draw a comparison with her daughter, but because the market in them serves as a cogent metaphor for a particular kind of asocialty (Thomas 1991). It is a reference that makes sense in light of the pervasive Maneo experience of feeling cheated in commercial exchanges (see Peterson 1984; Gudeman 1992:285–287). Her primary objective thus was to bring public pressure on her son-in-law and to test him by making a gift the measure of respect.

Respect is crucial to affinity. But if objects move between affines because of the meaning of the relation, why do they not move when they should? Is the reason as transparent as Helena's prospective son-in-law told Jennie and me: because he cannot, because there are too few objects to go around? I contend that scarcity does represent a growing hazard to exchange in Maneo both by increasing prospects that couples will suffer the real consequences which follow nonexchange and by the chance that the inability to give will be read as purposeful disrespect. But scarcity describes less a cause of failures to give than a consequence of decisions to give.

Scarcity

Obviously, scarcity complicates the efforts of persons to get some or all of what they want or need. It also poses dilemmas for givers insofar as sharing with one often means not being able to share with another. Because of this, as Eytan Bercovitch (1994) proposes, people resort to hidden exchanges. However, scarcity may be less acute and less a cause of hidden exchange or of the failure to give than symptomatic of a prior lack of generosity. First, despite increasing scarcity, there is no real evidence to conclude that Maneo affinal relations have become more strained in the last few decades, or that increasing hidden exchange and nonexchange is fostering social strife (Miller 1995). For one thing, demands by wife-givers have diminished somewhat, if not proportionately, along with the abilities of wife-takers to transfer *arata*. (Reduction in demand has been triggered in part by scarcity, but it reflects, more importantly, other factors, including the role of the church, its emphasis on patrifiliation, and reappraisal of the expense of raising adopted "property children.") Thus, even as scarcity may be making individual *arata* dearer, changes in what they are necessary for may be making Maneo less inclined to pursue them, at least with the purpose of giving them away. The onus of non-exchange does not lie unambiguously with the would-be giver.

Second, I have argued that scarcity is not so much a cause of nongiving as it is a consequence of it and of the divisibility of objects. Divisibility partly depends on the physical properties of objects (Peterson 1984). In practice, though, the distribution of things divisible is subject to moral deliberation. Inevitably, actions arising from such deliberation invite close scrutiny. Consider the way Maneo distinguish the divisibility of big and small game. Some species, like the cuscus (*Phalanger orientalis* and *Spilocuscus maculatus*) are small and shared on a limited basis, whereas larger game, such as pig, can be big or small and vary in the extent to which portions may be distributed. At stake is more than a meal. In one typical dispute, Markus told us he had recently shared a pig with the entire village. Yet when Demian, his neighbor, killed one not long afterwards, Markus complained he received nothing. Demian responded that the pig was too small to distribute widely and that he had only been able to give portions to his closest kin. This did nothing to appease Markus. For him, any dilemma Demian's household may have experienced when allocating the meat in no way mitigated the insult he felt. If his neighbor had intended to convey his respect he could have easily done so by making portions slightly smaller. Significantly, the complaint centered on a perceived offense that Demian was willing to risk by keeping more for his family. He was not censured for violating any explicit principles. Of course, consumables like meat impose certain constraints on sharing which differ from those governing more durable and less divisible objects such as Maneo *arata*. In fact, the durability of *arata* makes scarcity even less a cause of unavailability, I contend, than an effect of prior exchange decisions which otherwise keep objects in circulation.

Sociality and Exchange

The relevance of exchange to sociality reflects what it reveals about the intentions and concerns conveyed, themselves shaped by the way relations are understood (Carrier 1995:31–36). Specifically, wife-takers must give *arata* as a condition of affinity; wife-givers, in turn, must be prepared to issue a rebuke if it is not forthcoming. Because exchange is mandated in this context, the relationship in some respects actually militates against the possibility of spontaneous generosity between them. In other words, real cooperation is sacrificed in order to convey the gulf that formal exchanges are supposed to bridge (Valeri 1994b). But if the meanings specific to relations are central to moral practice, not everything hinges on them. When Maneo negotiate over *arata* and withhold it out of prudence or, more rarely, in an effort to undermine the interests of others, they do so largely without intending to implicate the basic terms of their relations. That is, while exchange among affines is compelled partly out of respect for representations, deliberation about giving is not entirely determined by these conditions. Likewise, goodwill is not adequately expressed by merely confirming that category of relation; affines seek other evidence of respect.

In contrast, the terms of consanguinity pose a different, more acute moral predicament. Particularly for brothers, deliberation about whether to share *arata* is influenced less by conditions for representing the relation than by other, largely underarticulated considerations. In fact, little actually hinges on transfers among kin that would facilitate the pooling of *arata* for those in need. Kin are not mandated by explicit norms, and nonexchange does not carry the overt social consequences of the sort that would follow from nonexchange with affines. Brothers remain brothers if they do not share, whereas affines may be redefined as brothers or sons in the event of nonpayment. As mentioned in chapter 2, the one case of a brother changing his clan status stands as a notable exception. The change followed a murder of the man's brother-in-law; in the aftermath, the killer's siblings—some of whom shared an affinal relation with the victim—felt that their sibling relations with the killer compromised the respect and deference they owed their affines. Unusually, then, the different relations became entangled and it became necessary to change the one to salvage the others.

The absence of overt representational implications attached to giving among (male) siblings puts the puzzle of nongiving with which I introduced this chapter into sharper relief: Why do brothers sometimes cooperate and share *arata*, while at other times and among other sets of siblings they do not. Analysis points to two related causes. First, the absence of conditions mandating sharing among brothers adversely affects the overall supply of property by limiting the speed at which objects circulate. (This is crucial since supply is a function of both the rate of exchange and the quantities of property available.) Essentially, by not being more generous, siblings reduce the chance that others will obtain sufficient *arata*. Of course, the reverse is also true, and were exchange to become more frequent among male kin, supply would increase (cf. Nettle and Dunbar 1997). While more frequent exchanges would not guarantee the evenness of distribution, I contend, it would contribute to that likelihood precisely because of it and contribute to an ethos of greater beneficence (compare Bourdieu 1997:n.3, 241), and so disincline brothers to hide it from one another. Of course, the apparent decline in exchange is raising the obstacles to acting generously. Even so, sharing continues, the particular case of Epe and Martin notwithstanding.

A second cause points to the particularities of how requests are actually made and answered. My impression is that Epe probably never actually asked his brother, Martin, for help. Instead, Epe's complaints to me may have been based on the perception, to which Martin may have contributed, that even had he asked, *arata* would not be forthcoming. Martin simply would have denied having any. Both Epe and Martin's strategies foster some desired ambiguity. For his silence, Martin maintains the possibility of generosity in the future while fending off requests in the present. Not pressing his demands, Epe effectively retains his options to make his request more overt at a later date. Yet if Epe's expectations of a gift were low to begin with, his criticism may have been motivated by a more attainable end: to use the nonevent as a pretext to undermine Martin's reputation or, at least, to register his frustration with his brother's lack of cooperation. His frustration, I should emphasize, was genuine. Epe cast his complaint in historical terms of an unacknowledged claim based on the prior contribution that his father had made to Martin's marriage some thirty years before. Failure to recognize this earlier generosity likely undermines any desire Epe may have had to assist his brother if the need were to arise. Yet Martin, for his part, may have had little recollection of this gift, which was only one fairly small part of a large *hahapina* ceremony. When *arata* was given, Epe's father's contribution may never have touched Martin's hands, a fact which may have relieved him, to some extent, of the necessity of recollecting it. Not only may there be no unacknowledged debt, there may be no memory of generosity, since there would be no specific person to whom an act of it may be ascribed. As in this case, giving may always be remembered more often than receiving. Yet, as I have argued, not all acts of generosity are unrecognized, nor is recognition of generosity itself a condition of sharing. Significantly, some Maneo brothers continue to share even with scarcity and hiding on the rise.

Conclusion

Most studies of exchange address the consequences of actions, including the prestige accorded participation, the way giving differentiates people, and the contribution it makes to community life. However, seeing the social value only in the performance and in the results which follow, while ignoring the way it enacts a desire to meet expectations, will elide the complex and irreducible moral dimension to exchange. The value of giving is evinced in part in the thought and regard for others which frames deliberation.

In deliberation, Maneo face a number of complications in their efforts to keep exchanging. Quantities of objects have declined, making it harder for persons to meet expectations; hidden exchanges, while perhaps slowing down rates of circulation of specific objects, occlude outward manifestations of the commitment of persons to the social relations that exchange countenances. While people know the extent of their contribution to the marriages of others, discrete property exchanges raise obstacles to knowing the extent of support in one's own. This change may be undermining the foundations of community life which, as Arendt notes in general, are predicated in part on the visibility of activities which allows for the expression of collective virtues (1959:176–178). With exchanges only partially public, there is little witnessing of explicit commitments; hiddenness is creating gaps or interstices in how Maneo appear to others and others appear to them. But this change, to the extent it is new, cannot be read as evidence or cause of a degeneration of past solidarity (see also Keane 1997a:230). A reasonable case could be made that, were it not for sharing among siblings at present, the practice of marriage payment exchanges might actually cease. Alternatively, if it does end in a few years, the reason may be, at least indirectly, sibling stinginess. The irony is that because of growing difficulties in representing relations, and thus conveying the respect affines expect, marriage exchange may be exacerbating real conflicts between affines as well as fostering unresponsiveness among kin. But if the practice does cease, I expect not a breakdown in sociality but a shift in expressions of goodwill and respect to other sites.

Notes

1. For instance, Eytan Bercovitch (1994), observes that people hide exchanges precisely to avoid sharing more widely, thus undermining the sociality the practice is said to otherwise generate. Going further, Annette Weiner (1992:63–65) says that the real motive for exchange is to acquire and hold on to powerful objects, the effect of which is not to forge community from otherwise disparate individuals but to make manifest political struggle over status.

2. The good behind the gift is a good relative to the contingent conditions of a certain way of life (Aristotle 1984:EE 1228a1–4). The good exists not as ends or means exclusively, but as Nussbaum notes, as means "pertain" to ends (1986:294–297). Collapsing this means-ends distinction, I believe, draws needed attention to the way persons perceive the values toward which actions are directed and to how persons perceive themselves through those actions (Nussbaum 1986:306). Alasdair MacIntyre makes a similar point in distinguishing "internal goods," in which means and ends are mutually shaping and, in some sense, removed from specific outcomes, from "external goods," directed towards specific, tangible results affecting one's position in relation to others, not the quality of relations themselves (MacIntyre 1984:190).

3. Signe Howell (1989:434) proposes that action assumes collective dimensions through people's identification with the objects in circulation; that is, the objects serve as icons of the ancestors who simultaneously stand over the group and for it. While she makes a strong argument against Weiner's overinstrumental and individualistic analysis of gift exchange, she errs by conflating morality with collective identification, leaving no room in participation for deliberation and virtue.

4. Part of the aim of interpretation is to establish and confirm some basis for trust. Unlike honor, which Bourdieu notes can be secured through the practical mastery of principles (1990:100), no similar recipe exists for fostering trust because capricious self

interest in Maneo is seen as anathema to it. People build trust gradually through regular interaction (cf. Fortes 1969:249). Loss of it, in contrast, is usually more precipitous.

5. Mobility affects the Maneo sense of locality and sociality in two broad ways: it makes it possible to opt out of daily interactions, and it allows people to pursue relations over an extended range of settlements. Thus, mobility does not compromise possibilities for creating community so much as it alters conditions for doing so.

6. In a sense, the flow of *arata* registers outwardly what Maneo recognize as an inner and largely invisible movement of blood. I do not wish to imply, however, that blood (*lasiae*) constitutes the unambiguous ground of kinship. Although the term usefully proxies for kinship in some contexts, blood contains other meanings not subsumed under it.

7. There is a corresponding aesthetic and moral sensibility to these transfers which complements the structural logic (Hoskins 1993; Valeri 1980:190–92; McKinnon 1991:251). Maneo men said they would be embarrassed by the immediate and reciprocal exchange of *arata* between wife-takers and wife-givers. They offered their opinions in reference to two neighbors who had married each other's sisters. The marriages violated no prohibitions; however, the men insisted that the sisters, not their husbands, ought to transfer the *arata*, as the exchange perpetuated no alliance (*sesama*) nor accrued any wider significance to which participants might wish to stake their reputations.

8. Individual objects possess a nostalgic value. In interviews several fathers of daughters pined for particular porcelain they had given away in their own marriages. In yearning for the return of those objects, they were making explicit and heartfelt their present *arata* demands against daughters' husbands while revisiting a valued and idealized past, replete with property and an abundance of power and knowledge now lost (Keane 1997a; Traube 1989). Similarly, married women wax nostalgic about the objects transferred on their behalf. In one case, a woman even complained about the dearth of *arata* exchanged in her recent marriage. Rather than perceiving themselves objects in exchange, Maneo women may recount them as a way of expressing their participation in history.

9. Maneo complain about those who have sold *arata*, though many have done so in the past. Nowadays, because of the scarcity, selling objects secretly would be virtually impossible.

10. Headhunting and the search for marriage payments represent similar pursuits. In earlier times, when a Maneo man ventured to a distant village in search of *arata* and was insulted by his hosts (he was given mouse meat) his quest veered into a murderous one for heads.

11. Words or other semiotic media must accompany the movement of property through intended channels of interpretation (Keane 1997a; MacIntyre 1984:161). Meanings can change, however; in Maneo, scarcity is contributing to reinterpretation so that persons feel less pressure to transfer *arata*. That is, elders recount the patterns of *arata* picturing the fauna that had first transacted them and who, subsequent to that exchange, assumed human form. The objects are invested with value (and given agency) by virtue of their journeys between people. Conversely, participation in exchange helps transform persons from who they had been before (Munn [1986]1992:129; Howell 1989:421). Nowadays, as objects are being hidden, there are fewer occasions to remind people of the traditional associations between the patterns and giving, and between giving and humanness.

12. When Minggus had his daughter draw up a list of his affinal distributions and contributions to sibling marriages, then hang the sheet of paper on an otherwise bare wall

of his house, he was reminding visitors of his capacity to shape his own marriage future and, by implication, the marriages of those to whom he contributed *arata*. While the medium here perhaps was unprecedented, the sentiment was not. Tellingly, he had no similar list of the contributors of the objects he had given away for his own three marriages that would remind visitors of his dependence on others. Score-keeping makes manifest the value of particular marriages within a range of possible outcomes (Valeri 1994b:175). That is, the differences in marriage exchange outcomes are made different against the constellation of values they reproduce.

13. In his own exegesis of the *hau*, Marshall Sahlins interprets it as a kind of debt (1972:157–168; cf. Weiner 1992). But if it is a debt, for that debt to be felt it has to be recognized. The complication is that persons may forget the sources of *arata*, which would likely compromise debt's force in compelling reciprocation.

14. As Mauss's model has been applied, obligation serves as the force which enables persons (primarily chiefs) to use gifts competitively to humble recipients. Receiving gifts is not an option and being a recipient beholdens one to the giver. The analytical edifice linking exchange to social forms, however, presumes the obligation to give. The assumption makes obligation appear to sustain social consensus rather than to follow from it, though the focus on obligation is not entirely misplaced. For example, Lorraine Aragon (1996) describes how obligation enabled the colonial government (and the Church) of the Dutch East Indies to use gifts to subjugate previously isolated populations early in the twentieth century. Similarly, Richard Smith (1995) notes that in the context of ongoing postcolonial development projects in Amazonia, largess is inducing indebtedness and a looming sense of subordination among target groups. The caveat is that it may not only be obligation but awe over disparities in wealth and power which generates the described effects.

15. If this tension is what makes persons moral (Mauss 1967; Parry 1989), of what does morality consist? Valeri seems to concur with Mauss in privileging moral obligation. Referring to agnatic exchanges, he says, one gives "because of feelings which are nothing but obligations turned into sentiment" (1994b:6).

16. When Maneo brothers share *arata* they sometimes reciprocate with a child, particularly if the brother giving the property happens to be married and childless. However, just as *arata* will often be given without any return, children will also be given without any property contribution. Significantly, they will be given to brothers who are unmarried and who would, thus, likely probably need *arata* more than any children for the success of their own future marriages.

17. The term *inefficiency* is relative to the condition Pareto Optimal, the ideal, in which it is not possible to make others better off by circulating goods more rapidly.

18. In a coastal Maneo village one afternoon, a man showed me a porcelain plate that he said he hoped to turn into a wall hanging. In the interview, he made no mention of the object's historic movement nor of how he obtained it and from whom. He merely stated his desire to use the plate as a decoration as people in Ambon, the provincial capital are known to do; his objective, I think, was to use it to stake a claim to membership in the wider world of Central Maluku. It was a sentiment we heard echoed by a few others on different occasions. His neighbors' reactions were muted. No explicit norms were being violated; everyone agreed he could do as he wished.

6

Between Faith and Reason

[My neglect of religion] was not the result of argument, but mere absence of thought. James Boswell, *The Life of Samuel Johnson LL.D*

Discussion, so far, has focused on agency and the choices that Maneo exercise in the course of living their lives, managing kin and exchange relations. Nearly all decisions require consideration of their effects on and interpretation by others. As they maneuver through various social encounters, Maneo try to ascertain and influence how their intentions will be perceived. Interpretations of agency reciprocally influence their evaluations of interactions more broadly and affect how suspicious or magnanimous they will be in the company of others. The tenor, even composition of community may be at stake. In privileging the experience of face-to-face interactions as the locus of community, I do not mean to dismiss the profound effects of Maneo involvement in the wider cross-currents of colonial and postcolonial Indonesian history. Charting involvement with the wider world, as I do in this chapter, to examine possibilities for local, everyday interactions goes beyond mere description of the impact of outside events. The impact exceeds simply undermining local stability or bringing change to an otherwise unchanging traditional society (Viswanathan 1998:42).

I begin by pointing out that Maneo stand at some remove from outside agents. As is the case with similar small-scale, upland communities elsewhere in Indonesia and Southeast Asia (e.g., Li 1999; Tsing 1993; George 1996; Rosaldo 1980; Atkinson 1989), local culture in the central highlands and on the south coast of Seram arises from the dialectic between everyday practices and the encompassing historical and political context. Distant from centers of power, Maneo are marginal to them. They are relatively powerless, except for the fact they retain considerable mobility. Being marginal they are aware of, and possess certain ideas about what they are marginal to (Keane 1997b:38)—ideas that give them some recourse to overwhelming power disparities. For them, distance from state centers makes it possible to invert the terms of power relations and to construe alternative, hidden agencies. It facilitates imagining personal relations with state officials, filtering out the complications of those officials' duties and responsibilities, and situating them in the nexus of local kin relations as a tactic to bring them into negotiations. Personalizing relations is fraught, however (and likely never as successful as hoped). Interactions with officials expose Maneo to their indifference and malevolence. Moreover, as the wider world is localized, alternative possibilities for conceiving and managing local relations open up, along with the recognition of other ends and moral understandings. Among other dangers, the importation of supralocal, nonkin forms of interaction risks supplanting the terms of the local and traditional ones to which people are accustomed. Participation in the wider world yields the possibility of retreating from local obligations.

The Maneo occupy a place on the distant periphery of historic and contemporary centers of power in Southeast Asia. Central Maluku has been, until recently, relatively sparsely populated, especially the central mountain range of Seram. In part, remoteness follows from their own efforts to avoid the more immediate impact of arbitrary state controls and claims. A few Maneo did move to the coast in the 1920s under their own initiative following the murders described in chapter 1. Just as they were not forced to the coast by the Dutch, they have not had the experience of being backed into a remote enclave by ethnically distinct, politically dominant lowland neighbors, as upland peoples have elsewhere in the Indonesian archipelago (e.g., George 1996; Tsing 1993). Historically, Maneo have sought to preserve forested space around them as a buffer to manage their relations with outsiders and, when necessary, to serve as a refuge from them. Living in the forest also enables them to take advantage of opportunities to trade in forest resources. At the same time, the choice to remain in the mountains deprives them of the possibility of occupying a less marginal position in state and global systems. Maneo know that living in the mountains places them at a disadvantage. By living there they risk being labeled *alifuru*, a derogatory term meaning hick or hillbilly, despite the economic windfall some have derived from their clove orchards. In recent times, too, they have seen the state annex the land of their neighbors for the massive state Transmigration project on the northern half of central Seram. And they have witnessed the spread of forest clear cutting by the timber industry. In 1989, one clan head (*kepala soa*) vowed that if the government tried to resettle them out of the mountains, he and his family would flee further into the forest (*pete roi aaipunia*) as the *suku terasing* and other Maneo families have in response to threats in the past, although three years later, that fear had been replaced by one of kin moving to the Transmigration site under their own volition. Certainly, there is nothing so distinct about their way of life and language that would prevent them from living nearer political, administrative centers. If they move to the coast or the Transmigration site they can take advantage of better trade and educational opportunities. Many of the moves may be temporary; some Maneo keep multiple addresses much to the dismay of state officials who want to assign them a single fixed place of residence (*alamat tetap*). The ease and frequency of movement keeps the subject of residence and the reasons for living together at the forefront of many conversations.

In a way, Maneo are both connected to the wider world of Maluku and Indonesia and removed from it. But if they have been relatively successful in keeping various outside authorities at bay as their own continued mobility attests, the eagerness of some to voluntarily join the army or work for the Japanese in Bula during World War II belies a more complex attitude regarding outside engagement. Indeed, it raises questions of whether or in what sense an outside exists beyond the boundaries of dense forests, mountain passes, and rivers. Certainly, the Maneo have benefited from a menacing reputation toward uninvited outsiders, and their isolation has given them some latitude to rework on more intimate terms the history of their relations and encounters with non-Maneo. They embrace outsiders as long lost kin; and, for similar reasons, most accepted Christianity, specifically, the *Gereja Protestan Maluku* or *GPM*. This openness has instilled and contributed to a sense of inclusiveness and of common membership that contrasts with the attitude of "exclusiveness" pervasive among animist groups (Maneo call them *orang Hindu* in reference to their polytheism) elsewhere in the region (cf. Valeri 1990a; Ellen 1988b). They have not had distinctiveness forced upon them (although they do feel unique in other ways); they do not endeavor to uphold traditional religious beliefs and struggle, as some groups have, to get their beliefs "recognized" by the Indonesian government (George 1996:259–60)—the consequence of a policy that demands that all citizens subscribe to one of five dominant religions. Yet it is not the case, or it at least cannot be assumed, that a sense of local community is dissipating. Although Maneo do not profess a strong sense of local identity, preserving community remains a vital concern. They recognize they could be swallowed up by their neighbors or disperse and lose their language and traditions. It is a concern expressed most by elders, some of whom have also sent their children to school elsewhere and have kept hidden from them much of their mythic past. The secrecy surrounding their origins, while necessary in certain respects, makes this knowledge increasingly irrelevant and dispensable and has contributed, more generally, to the loss of distinctiveness.

The History of the Church in Maneo

Churches are ubiquitous in Christian villages throughout Central Maluku, just as mosques occupy prominent places in Muslim ones. Until the recent spate of ethnic and religious violence, they often shared space in villages. These physical structures are signs that the village (or some portion of it) had "entered" religion (*masuk agama*). The term *masuk* denotes a joining. As a conversion metaphor, it derives from the physical fact of entering a church (or mosque) and is as much a sign of commitment to a world religion as it implies a rejection of the traditional beliefs left behind. In turn, the community of believers that enter together forms part of a larger religious body. As I discuss below, "entering" leaves unanswered questions raised when one "becomes," that is, the extent of the change initiated or even the direction in which change is effected. In this respect, entering Christianity represents just a beginning. And these first tentative steps could be variously interpreted. For Maneo, entering was not a concession; and they are adamant when saying that conversion came from local impetus, that the Church is their church built by their sweat and toil.

This sense of ownership contrasts with state claims of sovereignty over Maneo and similar small, out-of-the-way communities. On a two-month exploratory trip through eastern Seram in 1993, Jennie and I saw billboards in nearly every village proclaiming "*ABRI Masuk Desa*" (The Armed Forces of Indonesia have Entered the Village). As part of the *ABRI Masuk Desa* program, small military units were assigned to work on public projects, for example, rehabilitating a village mosque, and of course erecting the large sign in a prominent place on the settlement's outskirts. The way *ABRI*'s "entering" is perceived differs from the religious meaning of the term, but the comparison is instructive. After *ABRI* enters the village, they leave. Their work serves as much a reminder as a threat that the military will return if state authority is openly challenged. In contrast, for the church (or the mosque), entering was more voluntary and consensual; threats (of apostasy) came only later. Thus, unlike state claims of ownership of its citizens, Christianity was not so obviously imposed in Maneo. The faith was soft-peddled by Dutch-trained catechists from Ambon and the surrounding islands just after pacification, in the second decade of the 1900s. At the time, missionizing constituted part of an effort to tie up loose ends in the empire (Keane 1997c). The Dutch Reformed Church, which became the Protestant Church of Maluku in 1935, sent several of these catechists to Maneo to teach the gospel along with Dutch, mathematics, and history. Although many Maneo adopted Christian names and some were baptized during the 1920s and '30s, this early phase in the encounter effected no deep transformation. Ambonese missionaries lived in the mountains intermittently. Their teaching was interrupted entirely from the 1940s until the late 1950s by the Second World War and the *Repubilik Maluku Selatan* (Republic of South Maluku, or *RMS*) insurrection (described in the next chapter). Only after this twenty-year interlude did Maneo begin to embrace the faith and identify themselves as Christians.

The reasons conversion was protracted are several. Christian unity was called for by the retreating Republic of South Maluku soldiers and officials, between 1950 and 1953, as a desperate move to obtain local support. They invoked the threat of the creation of an Islamic state. But the decision to convert was not a consequence of political identification, because Maneo were abused by the *RMS* troops and well received by the Indonesian army, many of whose soldiers were Muslim. Indeed, just a decade earlier the Japanese had been hostile to any professions of Christian faith. The Maneo had time to consider their choices; and it may have helped that they lacked strict guidance during the 1940s and 1950s. They did not convert (*ai pakashi'aiya*) under duress as occurred elsewhere and later in the region (Duncan 1998, 2003), or under pressure from state policies that equate indigenous belief and ritual practice with atheism (Weinstock 1987; Atkinson 1987). Conversion in Maneo long preceded the anti-Communist pogroms of the New Order regime that associated animism with Communism during the Suharto dictatorship, 1965–1998. Nor did the process mirror the Maneo realization of the power behind colonialism and the institutional reach of a world religion, though for some, no doubt, conversion to Christianity did serve as a source of prestige.

Understanding conversion requires recognizing Maneo agency in "entering" Christianity, seeing it, not as capitulation to outside forces, but as a pragmatic move.[1] In part, conversion represented an attempt by them to exert some control over what they were being taught and how they were represented to the outside world. Maneo in the mountains were perhaps more isolated than all other known non-Christian communities on Seram. The case could be made that entering the church enhanced their prospects for remaining where they were: answering the desire to connect across the expanse of forest and sea to a wider community without surrendering their position in the world. In turn, relative isolation and local supervision of religious instruction gave them latitude to negotiate the terms of their conversion. This is not to say they converted to remain in the mountains, because many have moved nearer or to the coast. Rather, the organization and resources of the church offered a bridge across the distance that separated them from the outside.[2] It also offered a way to maneuver through the local relational predicaments by introducing alternative notions of moral personhood.

This emphasis on the pragmatic aspect of conversion emphasizes the choices by which Maneo committed to Christianity. It highlights the terms on which they converted and which they use to justify the decision long after the alternative—reverting back to animism—ceased to be an option. They saw the choices leading to Christianity as reasonable. In the sense that reason is "that faculty in virtue of which we commit ourselves to a view of the way things are" (Nussbaum 1994:375), aspects of the faith gradually began to infuse the Maneo worldview. Maneo became Christian through a series of small, mostly incremental decisions that altered people's habits. It was acceded to, in part, because it had become routine and ordinary. Acceptance did not hinge on the "greater rationality" of Christianity or on the persuasiveness of its agents, but conversion did facilitate the negotiation between what Maneo saw as discrepant worldviews (Viswanathan 1998:176). Acceptance of some practices helped preserve the Maneo place at the center of the world. Rather than disputing the facts of biblical history, local experts subsumed them into their own antecedent origins. Initially, conversion required few concessions, especially in the absence of strict oversight. Maneo were never forced to concede their identity, as they had not staked their identity on their beliefs about God or the ancestors and various spirits around them. Indeed, conversion gave them an enhanced "modern" sense of being and purpose. Only gradually, over the decades of the mid-1900s, did changes begin to bring them down the path and into the fold so to speak, distancing them from traditional beliefs and practices and occluding options they would have once entertained. In the course of this transition, traditional practices became defined as distinct and bracketed off as heathen from the ever-expanding sphere of explicitly Christian practices.

Colonialism

Christian missionizing represented a formidable and concerted campaign in the Dutch colonizing project. In outlying areas throughout the archipelago, the church served as the main instrument for Dutch expansion, though not without fomenting divisions between colonial secular and religious authorities (Kipp 1990). Maneo, as noted, were spared many of the direct effects. While they accepted certain elements of the faith through Ambonese intermediaries without much objection, Maneo steadfastly refused to agree to the intermittent Dutch demands that they relocate from the remote mountains of central Seram to the coast. Indeed, their remoteness gave them considerable latitude for action. They could appear to be compliant with government policies without having to follow through; and they could appropriate various cultural ideas and influences as their own. Relative isolation and the sparseness of population allowed them to avoid, for instance, corvee or forced labor. The one exception was work on the *Jalan Tutaruga* or Turtle Road in the 1920s that connected Maneo to Wahai. The transition to Dutch rule was eased, too, by the fact that Maneo only drew notice relatively late in the colonial project during the time of the Ethical Policy when modernizing and "civilizing" were becoming explicit concerns.[3] By then, Dutch administrators' intentions were, if not entirely benevolent, certainly less commercial than in other places in the archipelago and at earlier times.

At times, Maneo were willing partners. Religious conversion availed them of educational opportunities; through it, they developed a facility with Indonesian or Ambonese-Malay, the language of the Bible and instruction, that, in turn, helped them manage relations with outsiders. Local schools, which taught basic reading, math, and Dutch in the regional dialect, were administered through the church even after Indonesian independence. Hoping for success in school, Maneo parents even now insist on addressing their children in the regional dialect rather than the local language (*Upa'a*). Christianity was also seen as a route to certain esoteric powers, and Maneo participated to acquire these, but only after appropriating the source as their own. Thus they turned the encounter on its head. Local histories recount how outside agents came to propitiate their support and acknowledge their authority, then left.

No doubt Maneo decisions to abandon some practices were difficult. Yet it is likely, too, with some decisions that they did not feel they conceded much. For example, they would not have seen baptism (*permandian*), one of the most important events from the church's perspective, as a spiritual down payment. Nor would they have thought the adoption of Christian names would supplant the use of traditional ones, which they call *lalana Hindu* (animist names).[4] They still give Hindu names to their children, but the names, in contrast to their Christian names, are rarely ever uttered. Like many of his peers, Minggus's father decided to baptize him after an illness nearly took his life following the failure of traditional healing practices. Other changes, including the adoption of Christian burial practices which required moving corpses to the ground (the Christian way) from the above-ground platforms where they had been suspended, did not significantly alter what happened to the deceased. Spirits (*topoyea*) continued to feed on the bodies as they had in the past. As Maneo converted, conversion created a hybrid Christianity and more heterodox views of community (Hefner 1993).[5] In turn, people's responses to changes under way hastened further change (Viswanathan 1998:41).

By the 1990s, all but the oldest Maneo villagers were Christian from birth. Increasingly, the church forms part of their identity and constitutes a part of their past. But Christianity serves as a variable source of identity. Rather than resolving and consolidating issues of being, acceptance of the faith added to the repertoire of possible ways of being. Christianity provides another layer of identity that can be adopted to mitigate the relational demands and perspectival implications of Maneo kinship. Between the two ways of self-presentation—the Christian way being more fixed and hierarchical—was space for critical reflection, negotiation, and deliberation, particularly for skeptics (Keane 1997a:163 n.7; 1997b:39). I do not mean to deny that some see in Christianity their salvation, but many more likely find coherent religious meanings elusive. For them, Christian doctrine is subsumed by the exigencies of daily life, of finding food, shelter, or even love. At the same time, having no route to return to the pre-Christian past, they seem almost resigned to the faith, becoming more Christian in a sense by becoming more like other Christian communities (though not necessarily followers of more evangelical traditions).

This assimilation of diverse local traditions within Christianity had been foreseen. In the 1960s, the Reverend Frank Cooley, a trained anthropologist, saw that throughout Maluku local traditions (*adat*) were being subsumed under standardized *GPM* rituals and liturgical practices. Once acquiescence began, he thought the supra-local authority of the church would make negotiation by local leaders on behalf of nonreligious and traditional interests more difficult (Cooley 1966). Church authorities could force changes and prohibitions by inviting invidious comparison, by holding the local communities up to allegedly more devout ones. Local values could be construed as doctrinally suspect; to delay adopting Christian strictures would be to prevaricate. In the end, to opt out once the process began would require making a break far more definitive and dramatic than the actions that brought Maneo to Christianity in the first place. Moreover, church officials might not even accept such a break. Non-Christian Maneo are merely said to be "nonactive" (*nonaktif*). They are long past the point of remaining pagan and there is little likelihood now of large-scale apostasy, because Christianity has become thoroughly infused into the fabric of their past and their possibilities of being. But if they come to feel abandoned, if Maneo feel their efforts on behalf of *GPM* are unreciprocated, they reserve the option of abandoning the church, though not Christianity per se, by joining a new sect. One persistent rumor we heard, no doubt entertained partly for this effect, concerned possible inroads of the Seventh Day Adventists and their alleged plans to erect a church in one of the smaller Maneo villages.

Counting Christians

To a significant extent, *GPM* missionary work has given way to administration, especially as the pool of potential new converts (*orang yang belum beragama*) has nearly disappeared. (The elusive *Suku Terasing* to the east of Maneo are perhaps the only remaining candidates for conversion in this region of central Seram.) Administration has meant keeping Christians in the flock. Church leaders count all Maneo village residents as specific congregation (*jemaat*) members, even persons living in the forest who attend services sporadically and go by non-Christian names. Counting removes ambiguities that might arise surrounding people's real beliefs and convictions, such as those villagers who never attend church. By virtue of living in the village or having kin who do their names appear on the *jemaat* list. Counting also puts pressure on individuals who do go to church to keep up attendance and to tithe each week to pay for church maintenance and trips by local officials to the *Classis* (the regional church assemblies). Local religious authorities certainly want to avoid the perception of any member of the congregation opting out; and to some extent, conviction blinds them to the possibility anyone would.

Church administration is territorial. Via the assertion of spiritual claims, the *GPM* claims stewardship over the entire mountain region of central and western Seram. Conceiving communities as Christian and *GPM*, specifically, makes them bulwarks of the faith against outside threats. Officials are mindful of the inroads of other denominations. Against such threats, they have sought to consolidate and shore up community boundaries, allowing religiosity to be fostered within explicitly Christian spaces, just as shared faith connects distant Christian communities. (A few Maneo, in fact, have traveled across parts of the broader *GPM* world through the *Classis* at the district level, traveling to conferences and retreats; they are aware, too, of connections to the Indonesian Council of Churches and the World Council of Churches (Cooley 1966:148).[6] To cultivate the faith from within, the church has defined an ever larger cluster of traditional practices as anti-Christian and has displaced them to heathen sites outside the community. For many Maneo, it was not even safe to discuss these practices. The *sanafa* drums, for example, which we heard in the forest, were only explained as a divination ritual after we returned from a trip to eastern Seram where we participated in one. For the church, what was heathen in the *sanafa* was the practice of bringing spirits onto the plane of human experience and making them amenable partners (not oppositional elements) in the affairs of the living. Reciprocally, accusing recidivists of engaging with spirits served as a way to define other traditional practices as heathen. Evil spirits can be believed—for example, the spirits known as *setan*—they just cannot be propitiated. In Protestantism, only God and Jesus enjoy that privilege.

The church's ascendancy in Maneo is partly due to success in scheduling. In addition to attending Sunday services, residents were encouraged to participate in Bible study sessions conducted at various times of the week. These weekly services and warm-ups have displaced other subsistence or trade pursuits to "times in between," to "spare time" that served to diminish the collective value of such activities. Often there was little time for anything other than church. Even sleep was surrendered around the Christmas and New Year's holiday, and those who could not resist and did try to sleep were fined. During the dry season (April through September), when families in mountains scattered to process sago and hunt, residents returned just for religious services. When collective work was being planned to work on the school or clean the village, time set aside for "individual" subsistence was time that had to be granted. Too much time devoted to subsistence or income-generating activities could be construed as vaguely sinful. Even if returning to attend church was really done to alleviate the boredom of being apart from others in the forest, as one Maneo neighbor commented, the lack of alternative entertainment venues worked to enhance the importance of these weekly religious gatherings.

And the secular was subsumed within the religious in another way. After the conclusion of services, the preacher (*pendeta*) addressed issues of concern to the community. In the absence of other matters, what was usually discussed was church-related business. One week it may be matters relating to church offices, the next week, the need to replace the thatch on the church roof or, more ambitiously, a proposal to construct a new cement church. The village of Manusela some 30 km to the east had just finished a new church a year or two before I visited in 1989. Maneo Tinggi began a similar project around 1991 that will take years to complete and, in the process, displace most other village activity, require hundreds of dollars and hundreds of trips to the coast to carry bags of cement and sheet metal roofing.[7] Construction was interrupted for much of the time during the period of fieldwork; residents complained that some are not doing their share and success seemed far from certain. Limits to local leadership and the absence of the *pendeta* (who left in early 1993) had complicated efforts to sustain the enthusiasm. For the proponents, what is at stake in the project is the very Christian foundation of community, adopting norms and standards of comportment that are doctrinally consistent. Indeed, the church has worked to promote the view that Christianity, in fact, makes community possible, that it would be impossible without it (cf. Viswanathan 1998:95).

The Maneo turned to their ministers for guidance (*pembinaan*) and the ministers, in turn, have sought to establish the ascendancy of the church in political and social matters. With the assistance of local leaders, *pinatua* and the *majelis*, they have helped trumpet notions of Christian agency, while diminishing Maneo capacity to engage the world without the church. For example, after service one Sunday, the preacher, a young man from South Maluku, discussed the decision of some families to move to the Transmigration site, even though residential decisions largely revolve around other considerations, including better schooling and economic opportunities not obviously connected to religion. Tackling the subject served as a rhetorical strategy to empower him to opine about it.[8] He also took it upon himself to advise the congregation about state political matters by encouraging Maneo to vote *PDI* (the New Order political party most amenable

Photo 6.1 The new church under construction in Maneo Tinggi

to Christianity) in the 1992 election. Marriage was another ongoing concern. All marriages had to be sanctioned by the church, for which the couple had to pay. Church sanction was a condition for participation by married adults in all communion rites (*ikut perjumuan*), including the privilege to wear black frocks to Bible study sessions and Sunday services. The *pendeta* also condemned the practice of polygamy (though very few marriages were polygamous) and used the failure to "pay for" the church's approval to exemplify the threat of moral turpitude, backsliding, and foundering. The complex moral deliberations and exchanges that serve to legitimate traditional *adat* marriages he construed as amoral concession to mere custom (Kipp 1990:220).

But moralizing from the pulpit can be risky, as he himself discovered. In 1992, the *pendeta* spoke of the need to "*disciplin*" and curtail ("*dinonaktifkan*") the ministerial work of a local *majelis* member involved in an adulterous relationship. Adultery, as noted in chapter 4, is usually resolved through the payment of fines. Yet he never enforced the decision and the young man continued to preach on occasion. The reason, I suspect, had to do with rumors of the *pendeta*'s own ongoing adulterous relationship. He had recently married a non-Maneo woman on the north coast. When his affair eventually become public, with the pregnancy of his mistress, he fled. One of the many complications he faced was that he had obtained *arata* for his wife's kin from the very same persons to whom he would now owe fines, as kin of his mistress.

The Dialogue

Aside from adultery, the perceived arrogance of outside ministers is viewed as a more endemic problem. Maneo realize the dialogue with Christianity has been unequal (see Comaroff and Comaroff 1991:245). Christian leaders typically speak past Maneo experience, even those Maneo in positions of church leadership. Yet no side fully commands the terms of discourse and there is considerable room for misunderstanding and ambiguity (Rafael 1987). Invariably, the practical realities of conversion have exceeded church leaders' abilities to impose explicitly religious meanings on what people, individually and collectively, have gone through. Even as Christianity has offered a more encompassing language for connecting experiences (Hefner 1993), for instance, relating suffering to God's will and introducing problems of theodicy, everyday practices in Maneo have entangled Christianity in operations that have exceeded the limits of what can be put into words (Keane 1997a:160).

Church officials (both local and non-Maneo) possess their authority by virtue of their titles and appointed tasks during Sunday services; they also manifest authority through displays of superior devotion, by being seen as having embraced the faith more completely than others. As leaders, they must weigh in on the beliefs and practices of parishioners, usually adopting stock pronouncements or scripted responses. The peril they face, consistent with the dilemma of Maneo political life more generally, is that of appearing arrogant (*kaewel*). Maneo parishioners are very alert to it. The preacher from Damar in South Maluku had crossed this line; likewise Semas, the Maneo church leader in Siahari, was widely condemned for his stinginess with meat, which he sold to the residents of the Transmigration site. With the proceeds he bought a suit. Wearing the suit as he did every Sunday reminded parishioners, I think, less of the glory of the occasion and his industriousness, which he prided himself on, than of his greed (*kilihau*). In his stinginess, residents saw the church's apparent indifference to the specifics of exchange and kinship, and to the dyadic ties that particularize relations between persons. The church's indifference may have been intended to foster equality and sameness among congregation members as a category apart from the privileged church officials who enjoyed the status of parents (e.g., *bapak pendeta*). Indeed, Semas himself had rejected kin ties and reinvented his own paternity, claiming to us that his father was an *RMS* soldier from Ambon—an outsider and someone of power. Though his assertion may have represented a naïve attempt to stake some claim to a broader, regional identity, others saw in this fabrication and his unwillingness to share meat a much narrower and selfish set of aims. "*Seng tahu diri*" (he doesn't know who he is), neighbors said. It was also evidence that the church sought to use kinship idioms, particularly between parent and child, without the requitedness and emotional affinity that mediates "real" relations between kin.

In church, this inequality was particularly apparent during the litany, the part of the service when the minister calls for a scripted response or affirmation from the congregation, oftentimes from a standing position. On one memorable occasion, several men in the Kabailu congregation parodied this practice by standing up when they should have been seated and repeating the church official's every word, not just what the script called for. Moreover, they did so wearing blouses and skirts. Later I had a chance to talk to one of the protesters who said he resented being addressed as an undifferentiated junior by a person (a local assistant minister) who was also an affine (a wife-taker). What he did not have to say was that he and his friends objected to the fact that the preacher that day had come from the village of Maneo Rendah, with whom relations were strained. Kabailu church services had been interrupted for some several years after one of the residents was accused of murder by people from the preacher's village (Maneo Rendah). The accused was reported to the police and he spent several months in jail in Wahai before being released for lack of evidence. The protesters understood and sought to subvert the use of displays of religious piety to denote superiority. They suspected, rightly, that some Maneo from other villages would use the claim to be better Christians as a rhetorical weapon. Just as the spate of church building from Manusela to Maneo Tinggi was motivated, in part, by the desire to "keep up" with other villages, criticizing others' apparent lack of devotion represented a way to revel in one's own outward signs of superior faith. Yet despite all the resentment and the infrequency of services there, Kabailu residents nonetheless kept their sago-walled church maintained.[9] Perhaps they understood, too, that the appearance of backsliding, evinced by the actions of the cross-dressing parodists, would make the revanchists in the church elsewhere see residents of Kabailu in need of redoubled proselytizing.

Expressions of the faith permitted and contributed much to local political maneuvering. But Christian meanings were also altered in the process. Consider the idea of evil. In Christianity, it represents a chronic and embodied state of sin (*dosa*); in Maneo, being tainted by sin had a different meaning and it was invoked in narrower, more limited contexts, akin to taboo violations as a cause of inexplicable accidents and infirmities. One woman, for example, attributed her infertility to the sin an ancestor must have committed, not knowing or at least not disclosing what that might have been or who that ancestor was. Similarly, difficult childbirth, which is not uncommon, is believed to result from undisclosed acts of adultery and requires confession to ensure the survival of the mother and baby. In theory, this connection permits the tracing of symptoms to amenable root causes; in practice, it also allows responsibility to be deflected and redirected. A perpetrator's personal culpability is mitigated because the cause of the malady is shifted, in part, to the rule that has been violated. But when Maneo (or Christians elsewhere) do want to assign responsibility, particularly for sorcery, they can. They say such people are evil (*masinaha*) and that the source of that evil resides in people's hearts—an idea similar to what some evangelical Christians in Ambon told me about certain people who have "black hearts." In Maneo, really evil people, those who practice sorcery, are said to possess two hearts (*hali hua*): a good heart behind which the evil one works. Evil represents duplicity that operates, inexorably, to twist the designs of agents, whatever their stated intent.

In the search for causes, certain events may have straightforward explanation, for instance, murder out of passion, such as the case of Wara'a Ipapoto (whose enemies never accused him of having two hearts). But the possibility of a second evil heart opens new vistas for interpretation of people's hidden designs. This belief in a second heart flourishes in the absence of open discord, cautioning people not to be too trusting. Of course, no one would claim to have two hearts, nor would they necessarily know if they did. But though the more mainstream Christian notion of sin is more volitional and temptations to it, which everyone shares, can be resisted, there is some similarity between sin and the Maneo concept of evil. Neither can be predicted with any assurance. Thus Augustine begs forgiveness in advance of the wickedness he is sure to commit (1963:49), failing to follow what he knows is right because the *good* will "has what the other lacks" (1963:177).

Sorcery beliefs flourish alongside Christianity, in part, because Augustine's magnanimity—the ability of people to transcend their more selfish desires—is not easily achieved. The threat also persists in the perceived need to root sorcery out; community well-being is at stake. Even as church authorities have banned certain practices designed to identify sorcerers (though not belief in them), Maneo found other ways to discover the identity of the perpetrators. One case stood out. It involved the alleged sorcery murder of the church leader and former *kepala desa* in the late 1960s, Zakarius Boiratan, who helped found the village of Siahari a few years earlier. Supposedly, he had seen his own death, a premonition he shared with his brother that pointed to his would-be killer, a man named Amo who had recently moved to the village from the forest. When Zakarius died his brother was quick to take revenge. In the pre-Christian past, Maneo would have conducted a divination ceremony (*sanafa*) to ascertain the identity of the sorcerer. However, receiving a premonition, which was religiously acceptable, accomplished the same end. It merely inverted traditional divination practices by substituting the reported speech of the victim for the ancestral voice summoned in the *sanafa* ceremony. After the fact, both sources possess the authority of the presently dead—the premonition having been reported after the church leader died. Neither procedure offers specific reasons for the attack, and motives are never sought. Like pagan divination, the linguistic postconversion delivers results.

The Word

Christianity poses some linguistic challenges. Being imported, the faith is predicated on acceptance of a more self-referencing language with fewer correlates to immediate or everyday Maneo experience. Christian concepts are expanding the Maneo worldview, and increasingly, I think, do make sense. However, the gulf between Christian terms and local experience remains. For instance, in cases of adultery, as in the affair that divided Rino and Anud, discussed in chapter 4, the various parties may feel ashamed (*mukai*) but not necessarily guilty in the Christian sense (Kipp 1990:129). The shame lies in getting caught and in having the affair come to light; it is less the consequence of ongoing temptation. Maneo lack the terms and corresponding concepts to relate the act (adultery) to the generalized condition (a state of sin) that supposedly motivated it. Nonetheless, through the language of Christian interlocutors such connections are being drawn. Words give shape to the innate and indeterminant (Keane 1997b:55; Comaroff and Comaroff 1991:255). The Word of God transports believers from darkness to light. Of course, delivery is never entirely assured (Rafael 1987:326). In addition to problems of translation, of connecting words to experiences, Christianity in Maneo is packaged in formal Indonesian that few understand very well, although their comprehension, I think, does exceed their verbal facility.[10] The *GPM* leadership seem unconcerned; their view, an Augustinian view, is that it is not necessary or even possible to see (or hear) the truth in its entirety (as expressed literally in the Word), but enough simply to turn one's gaze in the right direction (see Taylor 1989:140). For them, the key to realizing truth is practice. If the ability to glean the truth is sometimes exaggerated and the individual is held responsible for his or her salvation, the enormous obstacles to realizing it are not.

Of course, Maneo traditionalists understand words differently, just as they perceive the world differently. They hold that uttered sacred words connect recondite knowledge to the world, revealing what is in the world but otherwise hidden. In traditional ritual contexts, Maneo use such words to summon and transform. The most powerful words are also dangerous and must be hidden. They conjure a power not contingent upon faith—the very efficaciousness of Maneo sacred words being measured by the need to protect persons, especially young children and pregnant women, from it. Even "able" men (*manoa*) who possess it are believed to live shortened lives as a result. Fortunately or not, such knowledge is scarce; the conspicuous absence of power in Maneo confirms the elusiveness of the right words—the original words that must be recited (when they are revealed) only in their proper order. Knowledge is *sejarah* (history). Since history is connected as a series of events and as one ancestor succeeded by another, the implication is that what is not known must be missing. Either it was appropriated (or stolen) by Maneo who left and who have since forgotten their ancestry, or knowledge was somehow misplaced. Because of this connectedness, in theory the recovery of knowledge is possible, just as so many branches of a tree lead back to a single trunk (*peruna lai totuna*) (see Traube 1989). In this way, Maneo traditionalists can accept Christianity (as well as Islam) as divergent paths (*hala*) or branches in their history that others have misconstrued as the ultimate truth (Viswanathan 1998:30).[11]

Even more devout Christians, like Semas the church leader from Siahari, invoked and reworked history in ways that affirmed and inflected religious meanings. For instance, he claimed that in the recent past Maneo knew how to fly, as the *sowakapati* do (the spirits from the east who can assume the shape of bats and birds) and fell once they, his near ancestors, converted. Curiously, no one else, experts included, claimed Maneo could fly, though they did assert some recent deterioration of their hunting and fighting abilities. Traditionalists also noted that their ancestors were larger and had lighter skin, implying that the decline in their abilities had other physical correlates. Semas drew the connection to flying because of the fact that even people as adept as Maneo in climbing trees do occasionally fall in the course of trying to capture rare birds for the market or hunting for food high in the canopy, like cuscus, lizards, a species of python, bandicoot, betel nut, coconuts, canari nuts, and various immature fruits. Though perhaps they fall no more often than in the past, by linking such accidents to Christianity, and thus to an imagined past when no Maneo would ever have fallen from trees, Semas construes falls as a sacrifice, for which he could expect a substantial divine return.[12]

For Minggus, a religious skeptic and a leading traditionalist, the priority of Maneo history is confirmed by the loss Christianity's reappearance denotes—the fact the faith had to be reintroduced—and by his own deft resituating of biblical events, places, and characters. I cannot claim to know whether he knew he was fabricating a belief or apprehending it as inspired revelation. What was critical was his ability to graft, for instance, biblical genealogies onto Maneo ones (see also Kipp and Rogers 1987:4). On one occasion, he did this by tracing a Maneo clan connection to the biblical figure Aesop, through Aesop's father, Ismael, the son of Abraham through his second wife, Hajar. On another occasion, when a minister in Maneo Ratu on the coast referred to Eden as the "land of milk and honey," Minggus concluded Eden was Maneo since no other place had as much honey. He used knowledge the minister lacked to draw connections between biblical surroundings and nearby river valleys, cliffsides, and mountain summits.

When Maneo repeat knowledge, they literally evoke a hidden reality and the connectedness of things in it. It is unnecessary to believe uttering a particular word in a particular spot—a place where certain words become taboo (*makahala*)—will have any particular outcome or result; it simply does. And out of fear of the consequences they never deliberately test the proposition. After an accident or disaster, the search for an explanation can always lead to suspected violations. In contrast, Christian knowledge usually fails this test of efficacy. Minggus once laughed to me about a church song sung around the holidays praising God by invoking the name over and over "*O Tuhan, Tuhan, Tuhan....*" The existence of God was not in dispute, nor the belief that God can only be approached or summoned through words. What amused him was the repetition; Maneo deities and ancestors, he insisted, need only be called once, and one might easily die from invoking the name of the supreme deity. Repeating God's name, thus, could be seen as fantastically reckless.[13] Of course, the fact that nothing apparently happens when the song is sung indicates that either the Christian God is relatively powerless or too busy being summoned to respond every time. Minggus surmised, too, he might be angry. Whatever the reason, this repetition is evidence of a lesser word uttered merely as a simulacrum, with the power only to represent and not to conjure.

Yet the challenge Christianity poses is not so easily dismissed; nor is the difference with traditional beliefs so clearly drawn. Locating knowledge as something outside the self offers a way to access the power it contains, provided the right connections are made (see also Keane 1997c:687). For several months after we arrived, whenever the subject of *sejarah* came up people referred obliquely to the *buku tembaga* (the copper book). The idea of the book possibly originated from the Dutch books, actually embossed letters, which were given to local rulers or *rajas* to confer government legitimacy, though they would have also known the importance believers placed on the Bible and Koran as well. (*Kitapu*, Maneo for book, derives from the Indonesian, *kitab*.) At my first meeting with Minggus, he described the book as containing the prototypes of all mechanical things such as radios, Hondas, and airplanes—objects that enter into Maneo purview however distantly—as well as the names of all the ancestors and events that brought the first ancestors into being. These facts were the original versions, the Greek Ideas, as in Plato's theory, on which all copies were based (Plato 1974:596b–599b). Like the Platonic Idea, the presence of the book and the history it denoted allowed experts like Minggus to denigrate as ersatz and inferior the signs of superior wealth and power of others—the people who possessed airplanes and speedboats. As a further sign of the power it contained and as a warning to those like myself might be expected to pursue it, the *buku tembaga* was said to lie hidden in the mountains supposedly guarded by a giant python. For some months, Minggus intimated he had seen it. But gradually, as my interest grew in the subject of Maneo history and of what Minggus knew, he referred to it less and less. Finally in response to a question about the book, he said, pointing to his head, "the copper book is in here" (*buku tembaga ada di sini*).

The admission, though, was not the breakthrough it might have seemed. Minggus had simply begun to understand and shape my quest differently, as it became apparent that I was not launching a search for the book in the forest. He relocated the book, I think, to keep the focus on him since he knew that much of my work concerned the more prosaic aspects of social life that did not require his expertise. But tempting me with his knowledge was not simply self-interest on his part; my work followed on the heels of a university student from Ambon who had written a *skripsi* (an undergraduate college thesis) on Maneo history a decade or more before. From Minggus's perspective, even if *sejarah* was not what I was after in coming all the way to Maneo, it was the only quest that could have brought me, and it was what I should have pursued. It was a testament to just how lost I was to have stumbled back to the source while failing to realize the real reason that drew me. Eventually, by dangling bits of information that made me think we would reach an end (or a historical beginning), I began to take more of an interest in what he knew and paid him the respect that was his due as the authority on Maneo *sejarah*.

If conversations with Minggus left me more perplexed the more I learned—like a pointillistic painting, the image lost shape the closer I approached—others in the village who knew of our late conversations were more convinced of something tangible being exchanged. Just after I left Seram in 1993 for a brief visit back to the United States, work suddenly began on an enormous cement processing plant near the village of Laimu, between the Maneo villages of Maneo Ratu and Yamalatu. When I returned, some Maneo suspected I had been involved, specifically, that I had acquired wealth and knowledge to undertake the project, to turn a limestone mountain into cement, through my interviews with Minggus. For his part, Minggus had not seemed too worried. In fact, he was the one who told me of the rumors and may have fanned them in the first place since the story reinforced the connection between the knowledge he possessed and the enormous power visible in the project. Yet, though he may have felt he disclosed nothing of such value and power, he could only be convinced of this if he lacked faith in his representations of knowledge. My reappearance, two months later, thus may have reassured him as much as it did others. If Christianity along with all the other changes were revealing to him and others the extent of Maneo poverty and isolation, the supposition that knowledge had been appropriated was increasingly becoming an article of faith.

Values and the Religious Imagination

Maneo sought from Christianity some confirmation of their views of history and their status in the world, for without it conversion would have left them no different from others, just poorer and more isolated. They were not embracing or defending some essential identity by converting, nor were they abandoning a discrete Maneo identity by becoming Christian. The conversion process represented a struggle over ideas and ownership—reconciling what was clearly Maneo with what was less explicitly so (Ricoeur 1973). As well as seeing or being promised certain practical benefits from adopting the faith, better health or even salvation, they hoped to gain some evidence of their uniqueness and dignity, which the wider world of government officials, traders, travelers, and some church representatives refused to acknowledge. Maneo understood that by becoming Christian they could become cosmopolitan and modern as a means to obtain, encompass, and resist the claims and criticisms of outsiders. But each tentative step toward organized religion led them away from preconversion values. Perhaps more than beliefs, it was their manner of thinking about them that changed. Consider Maneo myths, the stories they tell of events in the distant past.

Myths establish ownership to territory and explain features in the world, from the differences between people—different, in part, from having different origins—to features on the physical landscape. They describe heroes and the powers Maneo once possessed. More interestingly, myths offer ways to think creatively about and maneuver through the incongruous circumstances of social life.[14] They do not contain explicit rules; instead, they make values emergent in the interactions of mythic figures, values that help guide contemporary Maneo by giving them the moral bearings to manage their own lives. By changing proportions—mythic dramas are played out on a big stage—the decisions of mythic

166   Chapter 6

figures at critical junctures enable the living to see the different consequences of actions and to reflect on the different conceptions of community.

Of particular interest to me was the myth recounting the demise of a race of giants that once lived on Seram. I heard it twice. The first time, Tomas told the story; it was early on in fieldwork after Jennie and I had gone on a long hunting trip to a place in the mountains where giants had once lived. At the time, the story did not strike me as being about anything current. The second time, recounted below, Minggus filled in some details of names and places. Its relevance became apparent only later.

> After the Maneo moved to the New World (*Nusa Holuwa*) from the old, there existed a race of giants (*atalai*), numbering roughly two hundred. (Minggus insisted they were as tall as trees, 40 to 50 meters high, so big, he said, that their shit made mountains.) The giants lived alone on a cliffside known as Shililia along the ridge of mountains to the south of the Maneo villages. During the rainy season when the mountains were shrouded in clouds, they would descend using a vine and search for humans to eat, particularly women and children. One day, during the monsoon, a Maneo ancestor, Shialaka Salakatota, went hunting. Before he left, he warned his wife, Aishilu, not to cook any pig when he was away since the scent attracts *atalai*. (Despite their great size the *atalai* typically waited for men to leave on hunting expeditions before hunting women and children themselves.) Just as Shialaka had warned, an *atalai* came and killed Aishilu and took the baby back to its cave. When Shialaka returned and discovered his wife and child missing, he followed the giant's trail. Meeting it at its cave the *atalai* offered Shialaka what resembled betel nut, but was instead tree bark ("*ia fakisala lumuae*"). Shialaka refused the offer. The giant then offered him some pork, but Shialaka saw from the skull nearby that the meat was not from a pig but from his wife. He declined this offer, too, saying literally "I don't know how to eat pork" ("*ya'a mana'aesi kai hahua*"), adding insultingly, "if the quantities are small like this." The giant ate anyway and afterwards Shialaka offered it tobacco that he had spiked with sleeping medicine. As the *atalai* slept, Shialaka killed it and chopped it into pieces, then took his baby, who had been crying in the back, and fled down the cliff, cutting the vine as he went so as to prevent other giants from following.
>
> When the other giants found out what had happened, they made their way to the village and challenged the people to a fight. In preparation, the people built their village into a fortress and equipped themselves with arrows and spears. The giants, having little to fear, armed themselves only with blunt sticks and sago palm branch shields. For the first six days the battle was a slaughter; the giants laughed when the arrows flew at them and they killed as many as a hundred men each day. Finally, a Maneo ancestor appeared, a *kapitan* (a war leader), who directed two men, Shiaola Tamala and Tatakikenae Boiratan, to go to Shililia, the *atalai*'s home, to where a giant eagle (*lusia potoa*) had made its nest (*manuakuwana*). The ancestor promised Shiaola that if he removed the nest he would become a *kapitan* too and would defeat the giants at Kokolaesi. This he did and the two men hacked the male giants to pieces, all but one, whose body along with a basket, turned to stone. All the female *atalai* became deer and scattered to the forest.

The story explains the appearance of deer (which are not indigenous to the island), human ascendancy in the world, and Maneo rule of central Seram. Minggus added some of the names to Tomas's telling to make clear that when the authority to rule was transferred (*"overed"*) it was to ancestors in his, the Tamala, clan specifically. At the time, I was mostly interested in getting the facts straight. Other Maneo listeners, I think, experienced the telling differently. They would have heard it many times over with different points and perhaps different names being recalled. They, particularly children, would have participated more imaginatively in its telling. They would have wondered who the giants were and about the differences between them and humans. Like the giants Homer and Lucretius write about in classical Greek and Roman literature, the *atalai* are quite human in certain respects. The death of the *atalai* who killed Aishilu, for example, fueled in them the desire for murderous revenge no different than the understandable human desire for retaliation. But the human resemblance utterly falls short in other areas. The *atalai* can only react to their situations; they lack intelligence, evinced by the fact they hunt their prey through scent, like other animals. As they strive and fail such tests of humanness as offering real betel to guests (they offer tree bark instead), they expose themselves as incompetent hosts. Crude imitation reveals the absence of a discriminating intelligence that constitutes human morality.

Of course, the giants possess a superhuman strength that comes from their alleged hardness (a masculine characteristic). *Atalai* are to humans as men are to women. Men purport to possess greater physical strength than women because of their hardness. Even the otherwise ungendered *atalai* take on these qualities after their defeat; when male giants died they turned to stone whereas their female counterparts became deer and scattered into the forest. The myth also demonstrates the limits of strength without wisdom and cooperation—feminine qualities manifest in human softness. As a complement to masculine hunting prowess and warrior skills, feminine softness also imbues people (as opposed to giants) with an acuity and foresight; the vulnerability that comes from being soft reminds Maneo that, unlike the *atalai*, they must cooperate and adapt. Significantly, this includes honoring their ancestors who in turn give them the strength to defeat the *atalai*. Thus, cooperating among themselves and, at the same time, reaching beyond the living community to remember and propitiate the ancestors is defined as a uniquely human quality. Yet it is not easy; cooperation is not always possible, and Maneo history is replete with conflicts that drove people apart and changed history. As the *atalai* remind Maneo, it is out of the necessity for cooperation and compromise that angry passions arise (see Nussbaum 1994:265–268).

Maneo did not simply replace the *atalai*, though they did vanquish them. *Atalai* were not buried and not forgotten; they are remembered precisely to shed light on the qualities that differentiate Maneo from them. The telling of a myth, thus, represents a starting point for thinking about the life of people in association. It affords insight into how to comport oneself. Since values are not codified, the stories in which they are embedded need to be recounted so that the values can be thought about and made available to inform social life. My sense, however, is that the myth is not often told nowadays. Children and younger adults know the story but rarely discussed it. Crowded out by more exciting entertainment alternatives, it has lost an audience and lost some of its cogency. Perhaps too, in not being told, the values which the myth illuminate have ossified to some extent and have become less relevant precisely for this reason. I suspect giants are simply taking their place alongside accounts of other phenomena like nuclear bombs, international capital, and Jakarta politics as things in the world, but distant. The story is no longer the mirror it once was for reflecting on the present conditions of Maneo life, even as those conditions remain very much the same.

The shift in focus is away from "ways of being in the world," modeled by heroes and perspicacious actors, to mere beings (or things) "in the world." Living is disconnected from being—one's understanding of one's entanglements; alternatives are defined differently. It is this new perspective that Christianity speaks to. It has helped usher in the new perspective by supplanting opportunities that might have been taken to tell myths and consider their import. In the new world, threats arise from partially understood, but visible, imbalances in power and wealth, rather than from failures to act in certain ways, for instance, by failing to honor the advice of ancestors, or failing to coordinate efforts against real but mostly invisible enemies. Maneo are not so much becoming secular as they are becoming more Christian, but in offering moral absolutes at this point in the engagement, Christianity asks less of moral imagination.

Conversion and Identity: A Tentative Conclusion

In the twilight of one early Saturday evening, residents of the village of Maneo Rendah divided as they did each week to convene on the north and south sides of the village for a prayer meeting. This week the meeting was at our host's house. "*James, seng usah pigi*" (you do not have to go), our host Homi said. Feeling even more intruded upon, Jennie and I retreated down the main path of the village and sat on a little bench across from a man, Rino, who was sitting by himself avoiding the prayer meeting on his side of the village. I waved, "*malas bersembahyang*" (tired of prayer), he said, searching for an excuse that could justify our refugee status. It was an eerie moment alone in the village while the two sets of prayer services were being conducted. The village seemed entirely elsewhere.

Rino's ambivalence, I believe, was more widespread than prayer service attendance would indicate. Maneo were never swept up in religious frenzy, at least not like more recent evangelical conversions. Protracted over much of the last century, conversion describes a complicated trajectory. As a result, they consider themselves indelibly Christian since most were born to Christian parents. Many have organized the tempo of their lives around their involvement in the church. But given that they were left without formal religious instruction for periods of time as long as a decade or more, their experience with doctrine has yielded variable and heterodox sets of beliefs about the particulars of Christianity. Conversion remains a fact; and Maneo did not resist it as a few groups did elsewhere on Seram. No doubt, at several historic junctures they were challenged to abandon certain practices; a few resisted, while most Maneo villagers did not. As I have described, by and large their attitude was one of pragmatism. The introduction of Christianity around or just after the 1918 influenza epidemic may have contributed to its acceptance, for if traditional healing and divination practices had not been so tested, and not been found wanting, they may have been loath to reject them. In other words, abandoning the *sanafa* and other pagan practices would have constituted a sacrifice only if people thought them effective, or more effective than Christian practices they were just discovering. Acceptance was piecemeal. My friends and informants, the sons and daughters (and grandsons and granddaughters) of the Maneo who first embraced the faith, did not simply acquiesce; they made choices that affirmed their beliefs even as they were just beginning to understand the meaning of having "entered" religion. Because it began with parents and grandparents, to resist at this late stage would have meant opposing them. To be "too lazy to pray" on occasion does not imply lack of faith. Conversion was and is inextricably linked to the reasoning that helped tip the decision years ago and kept Maneo returning to the fold week after week.

To be sure, the promises of the church do not trade exclusively on misery and marginality in this world in return for redemption in the next. Christianity promises progress and development to the *jemaat* as a return on conversion (see Duncan 1998). Becoming Christian was entangled in the yearning for modernity. Through it, for instance, Maneo hope to learn the true value of things (Keane 1997a:154), if only by making themselves less vulnerable to being taken advantage of, even as conversion may have increased their exposure to such deceit. Being "more discriminating," they are also increasingly aware of the extent of government indifference. The church was played off against the state, which was perceived as more capricious and dangerous. No government official from the *camat*'s office ever visited the mountain settlements the entire time we were there. Maneo likely did not care except that the church has been sending outside ministers to Maneo off and on for most of the last century. Conversion has given them membership into a larger collectivity and an answer to the pejorative term *alifuru* they had not had. Moreover, a decade or two into the process, conversion was facilitated by what little people knew of traditional beliefs; the less people knew, the freer or less encumbered they may have been to accept Christianity. Though I would not suggest that all who lacked a deep understanding of local history converted, not knowing *sejarah* simply made this easier. In this sense, they saw Christian conversion as something of an exploration, and partly an exploration of their own traditions, since access to the recondite knowledge of Maneo experts had been denied them. It also offered material for fashioning a more comprehensive world view, though perhaps less relevant and attuned to the particular ways of being in Maneo.

Notes

1. As Christianity has been embraced by Maneo and as Maneo are becoming more culturally Christian—that is, similar and more identifiable as Christian as opposed to other identities—their participation in a global movement also enhances Maneo prospects for flourishing by remaining where they are. This is not to imply that mountain life requires abandoning traditional *adat* beliefs or conversion to Christianity, though the Bati in the mountains of far eastern Seram who converted to Islam represent perhaps the one exception. My point instead is that once conversion began it came to be perceived that way but that the choice was never so simple as being Christian or not.

2. Maneo perceived that the church was separate from colonialism and colonial authorship of the doctrine and that their act of converting could be seen alternatively as a form of resistance or dissent (Viswanathan 1998:45). In a sense, the distance spanned in the initial encounter was considerable enough for various interpretations to emerge without eliding the others. Through this encounter, Christianity, like no other institution, has brought Maneo marginality into their view. But given the logic of Maneo historiography, the position of margins and peripheries is also reversible. The emptiness conversion creates is filled (Keane 1997a:157). In this way, conversion also deepened or enriched understanding of Maneo centrality.

3. The Ethical Policy was the name given to a particular attitude that took hold among a new cadre of Dutch rulers around 1900. Arising after reports of the declining welfare of local populations, especially in Java, it was intended to promote indigenous economic, social, and, to some extent, political reform. It was also grounded in thoroughly racist notions of European superiority.

4. Most village Maneo have been baptized (*permandian*) and go by biblical names (Luke, Yusup, Herod, and Batsebah). But recent names also include the more secular Clinton and Ronald (after two recent U.S. presidents). There is even a James, who is referred to as Mister, and nicknames for big talkers like Loudspeaker and Harmoko (after the former Minister of Communication).

5. Consider the way religious authorities collapsed distinct spirits such as *topoyea* and *sowakapati*, referring to them collectively as "*setan*" (devils) in Ambonese-Malay (see also Hoskins 1987:151). When in 1989 an American missionary in Ambon who had worked on Seram reported a great evil exists there, he had simply overestimated it, calling all spirits "devils," some of which were frightening but not evil per se.

6. Over the course of two years, there were several youth conferences. Whereas in the past, Maneo young men would have travelled to take heads, they travel now under the auspices of the church with the expectation of finding colleagues or even spouses.

7. A person's relationship with God is made manifest in his or her interactions with others. Persons live together or associate in some ways so that they may bear witness to one another. The church offers a forum for publicly assessing the religious merits of actions and for delineating what is properly religious from what is not. It also permits (some would say falsely) a determination of who is more righteous—which is critical if space in heaven is limited. In this competitive light, the escalation of church building represented a way to make manifest a community's superior devotion.

8. On the first Sunday after we moved from Siahari to Maneo Rendah, the *GPM* preacher, a man from the island of Damar in South Maluku, raised his concern regarding the planned move of five families to the Transmigration site. With just twenty-five resident families to begin with in Maneo Rendah, this relocation threatened an already precipitous population decline since it followed the recent move of two other families. The five families had signed up for Transmigration under a program allowing for the resettlement of local populations, and as part of this they were promised a house, a half a hectare of land, some tools, and a year's supply of rice and dried fish. While the immediate rewards were obvious, family heads (all men, though with the agreement of their wives) cited better schooling opportunities for their children. All claimed the moves would be temporary and that it would be possible to retain residence in both the village and the Transmigration unit—a distinct possibility—despite the unit authority's stipulation that they not move back and forth. Once the families moved, though, it turned out that with one exception they rarely returned to the village—this in contrast to the weekly return of residents to Siahari (described in the introduction). Of course distance may have been a factor; the journey from Siahari to the Trans could be covered in little more than an hour, whereas to walk to the mountain settlements required a full day when the weather cooperates. Yet the issue of why they do not return must be assessed in terms of why persons felt compelled or wanted to leave in the first place. In fact, in Siahari, one of the first families to enter the Transmigration site was the one of the local church leader, Semas.

9. Residents of Kabailu may have felt some urgency to defend themselves against accusation; in addition to the murder just described, another recent suspicious death, and the marriage irregularities, there was an alleged murder of a missionary from Ambon in the 1920s. According to Maneo elsewhere, this murder supposedly brought about the decline of much of Kabailu's population, as divine retribution for this sin.

10. Maneo laughed about one of the phrases never translated "*in excelsis Deo*." In general, the *GPM* was less concerned about the translation of religious texts into local languages than more evangelical Christians in the region were. The Christian SIL International (formerly the Summer Institute of Linguistics), which had a strong presence in the region during the 1980s and part of the '90s, applies linguistics to recover the proto- or ur-language that existed at the beginning, at least according to one linguist/missionary I met. In addition to Bible translation, he described the work as inspired, in part, by the promise of discovering the true word otherwise missing in the degenerated spoken languages of the world. He later confided his own belief that the original language before Babel had been English. As a native English-speaker, he felt confident he already possessed the truth or at least enjoyed a shortcut to it.

11. Maneo experts borrowed from other religious traditions. Recognizing Abraham as one of their own, experts recount the journey of seven Maneo brothers to Mecca and how one became Muslim and was responsible for spreading Islam. The seven brothers in this story parallel the story of the seven Wali who introduced Islam to Indonesia. To honor this connection, Maneo claim that Muslims from the village of Laimu on the coast once brought water from the ancestral site (*huni keramati*) in the mountains to Mecca then returned it to the ceramic jug buried at the site on the mountain. Of course, Maneo isolation in the forests of Seram and their lack of status and standing in the world serves as a way to explain their marginality as an undeserved consequence of outsider's misrecognition or loss of their own traditions. Their visible poverty hides and indexes an invisible wealth; as pieces of history are filled in, what is unknown comes into view.

12. Conversion meant entering into a debt relation with the Dutch and their God, although Christianity is now seen as much as a Maneo story. The idea of debt deflects the full force of hierarchy; it is a way of displacing demands from totalizing hierarchy (Rafael 1987:336).

13. Maneo understand the power of spoken words. Like the Hebrew God, their ancestral spirits can be heard but not seen, thus, speaking their names must be avoided (Arendt 1978:119). These truths are invisible and manifest only as a consequence of uttering them, usually by mistake. Through effects, knowledge is objectified, but made remote and hidden. Somewhat differently, the language of Christianity (its location in a book) presupposes communication for its dissemination (Keane 1997b). When recited, believed, and embraced, Christian words create a space for God. Faith is confessed publicly, as in Augustine's Confessions, so that others might recognize the same interior spaces and place for God in themselves.

14. Myths contain a pedagogical, religious purpose (Hicks 1987). They idealize the past, making the past replete with heroes, not idealizing the goodness of persons per se. After the descent into the New World, people acquired characteristics (*karunia*) unique to them and their descendants.

7

Community in the Visible Spectrum

> Small towns are not characterized by deeper friendships but by people finding ways to manage the irritation and contempt that are the results of proximity.
> Garrison Keillor, *New York Times*, Feb. 8, 1998

Discontent does not run especially deep in Maneo society, or at least it did not during the period of our fieldwork in the early 1990s. If this impression still applies, even in the present context of civil religious war in the Moluccas, one of the reasons is that Maneo can adjust proximity; they can disperse if tensions arise. But this leads to a contradiction: As bad as things get when people reside too closely for a time, inclining people to flee from one another to give tensions a chance to abate, relations can worsen and are likely to worsen when people reside apart too long. Living together has value insofar as it signals that doing so warrants the effort necessary to minimize discord, at least most of the time. Yet sociality is vulnerable. There is no certainty that people can surmount problems surrounding kinship identity and relational ambiguity where there are multiple and conflicting ways of charting relations (as discussed in chapters 2, 3, and 4). Or that they can manage predicaments engendered by exchange where even successful resolution exposes the underlying risks the practices pose to the relationships of the persons involved (see chapter 5). Or that they can successfully contain fears over adultery and their perception of their substitutability. Yet small towns and villages could easily fail if there were not some incentive to try to negotiate differences and ameliorate tensions. Relationships could give way and community could collapse with little trace, especially if contingent outside events exacerbate already high anxieties. It happens. By investigating processes whereby trust and mutuality are undermined we can illuminate the conditions not otherwise discernable that enable communities—especially voluntary, moral ones—to persist.[1]

The most perilous episode in recent Maneo history, where the possibility of disappearance was most acute, came just after the short-lived *Republik Maluku Selatan* (*RMS*) or Republic of South Maluku movement collapsed in 1950. When *RMS* leaders and loyalists fled to Seram they brought their desperate struggle to the interior, creating havoc. Maneo faced a situation reminiscent of the chaos confronting the Ilongot of the Philippines during World War II and the Huk Rebellion in the 1950s (Rosaldo 1980) and the turmoil experienced by the Meratus during the Banjar-led rebellion in South Kalimantan against the government of Indonesia in the 1950s (Tsing 1993). Like the Ilongot and Meratus, Maneo memories of the war remain vivid. Those memories and the complex circumstances surrounding the various stories of events forty years afterwards reveal the continuing enmities and, also, the strategies used to contain them. The outcome turned out to be relatively benign for Maneo (though not for the *RMS*). Few were hurt, none were killed. Although a number of families moved from the mountains to the coast after the conflict, and some remained in the forest, no one I talked to claimed to have left out of enmity. Whatever animosity motivated decisions, or followed from them, have been buried, albeit not too far from the surface to be periodically uncovered by accident or design.

The central argument of this chapter, and indeed of the book, is that without the effort put into fostering community the situation likely would have turned out differently and Maneo might have disappeared forever when residents were forced to scatter. "What if" arguments are speculative; for comparative purposes, less to prove the case than to illustrate the processes, I will describe the disappearance of a group of friends and colleagues of the literary giants Osip and Nadezhda Mandelstam in Moscow during Stalin's brutal purges in the 1930s. Though the circumstances of their community and the threats differ, I will argue that the Moscow group's demise, which was inevitable given their prominence, was hastened by inattentiveness to and denial of the dangers they faced. The Mandelstam's cadre of friends lacked the wherewithal to escape from one another when they had the chance and suffered worse because of it. Maneo, too, were unaware of the approaching danger, but their response was decisive and in a sense rehearsed.

The Maneo Flight

Shortly after Indonesia defeated the Dutch and gained independence in 1949, *RMS* politicians and military leaders began an unsuccessful struggle to fashion a separate nation covering central and south Maluku. However, by 1950, they had been routed by the Indonesian army from their central base of support in Ambon and the surrounding islands and had been forced to retreat to the relatively isolated interior of Seram.[2] The *RMS* had no natural constituency in the mountains of central Seram. Most of their supporters were landowners (*orang kaya*) and *raja*s from more densely populated coastal areas closer to Ambon who had benefited from 350 years of Dutch rule. For them, Indonesian independence did not promise freedom (Chauvel 1990:350–351). Maneo and others in the mountains were simply too isolated to have suffered or benefited much from the Dutch. Mountain residents would see an Indonesian government dominated by Javanese outsiders as similarly distant and foreign. In a desperate move to win over these mostly Christian mountain people, the *RMS* exploited religious differences. They distributed flyers describing what would happen under a Muslim-dominated government, warning of prohibitions on hunting pig and intimating menacingly of circumcision. When the *RMS* retreated into the mountains, they continued their fight by raiding arms caches and by enlisting and coercing the aid of local groups. Several Maneo men were conscripted as guides for the soldiers; everyone else was forced to transport food supplies from Seti to Manusela, an arduous two-day walk, which did nothing to engender support for the *RMS* cause. Elders described the *RMS* fighters as "harsh." In the months that followed, the *RMS* managed to repel one *TNI* (Indonesian Armed Forces) offensive that resulted in the burning of a Seti village to the northeast of Maneo. A second, more decisive invasion in 1951, launched unexpectedly out of the mountains to the west, succeeded in overrunning the *RMS* bases and Maneo settlements.

With no warning of the invasion, residents of the westernmost villages of Maneo Rendah and Kabailu fled in different directions with whomever they were with. Residents of Maneo Tinggi, five kilometers to the east, were able to flee together after being alerted to the direction of the invasion by those fleeing before them. Accounts of the experience from Maneo Tinggi residents contain relatively little drama, they simply moved their village to a safer area further east. However, for residents of Maneo Rendah and Kabailu the choice of direction and company turned out to be crucial. Some fled south over the mountain at the pass above Ulu Aeya, recalling the shouts and gunfire of *TNI* troops behind them. Many of these refugees settled in an area known as Wokana Potoa (Big Garden) on the south side base of the mountains, though no one remembers having much food there. Gradually, nearly everyone around Wokana Potoa came out on the south coast and reported to local officials, who asked them to surrender their hunting equipment for fear they might be used as weapons. Families then sent a single member back into the mountains to search for other kin and within several months nearly everyone on the south side descended. To the north, the situation remained perilous. For some time, possibly months, the army occupied the main village of Maneo Rendah, while *TNI* soldiers with local guides pursued *RMS* stragglers and their suspected Maneo supporters. Maneo did not know what to expect; because of this their fear grew the longer they remained apart. Specifically, they worried that those former neighbors, kin, and affines who had simply chosen a different direction in which to flee in those few crucial minutes had become spies who would reveal their whereabouts to the new government authorities. Elders described how no one could trust anyone other than the closest kin and those with whom they fled. In fact, long after the army left, having wiped out the last of the *RMS* resistance, some families remained in the forest for years, and a few never returned at all.

During the first several months of fieldwork, Jennie and I collected brief accounts of the travails of the time. Only after having lived there for about a year and having spent time in all six Maneo villages, did we set about acquiring specific stories to find out exactly who fled with whom. One August night, Homi described the journey of his immediate family to a cave, Lioloa, high in the mountains, about ten kilometers south of the village. After what may have been a month or more of hiding he and some family members were apprehended and forcibly returned to the village by an Indonesian Army patrol, which either spotted a faint trail to their camp or saw smoke from their fires. Much to their astonishment, instead of being punished for their support of the *RMS* they received food and clothing. This was part of a strategy by the military to return the Maneo to their villages and separate the dwindling numbers of *RMS* army regulars living in the forest from any local supporters. After the capture, Homi's uncle, Firiz, who had eluded the *TNI* patrol, ventured to the village one night to talk to his family and find out what happened. Discovering the gifts of food and clothing that awaited them, he set out to locate and bring back his sister who had fled with her husband and kin to a different area in the lowlands some twenty kilometers to the north. The trip proved nearly fatal. Homi, who was perhaps five years old at the time and too young to recall much of this personally, became very emotional as he described what happened next; his voice grew louder. He said his uncle had found his sister and was then threatened by his affines who did not believe his story and feared he would reveal their position to the army. When I interrupted to ask who had issued this threat, Homi gestured to a neighbor's house just twenty yards away. At that very instant, our house was struck and shaken under a barrage of rocks. We grabbed flashlights, spears, and bow and arrow and rushed outside. Several people were waiting in the darkness; other houses had been hit. "*Masiae*," someone whispered. Homi and the rest agreed *masiae* (evil people from the forest) had visited. After cautiously poking around the edge of the village, we returned to our houses and the evening and our interview came to an end.

The Stalinist Design for Civil Disengagement

Nadezhda Mandelstam's remarkable memoir, *Hope Against Hope* (1978), offers the second case I wish to consider, although it is politically and geographically far removed from Seram. In the book, she recounts her life with her husband, the poet Osip Mandelstam, and the collapse of their cohort of fellow artists and intellectuals in the Soviet Union in the 1930s. This group, the Mandelstams among them, had been early targets for surveillance by the state police and were under suspicion of harboring heterodox political views, fueled no doubt by their Jewish ancestry. The memoir begins after Osip recited to the couple's friends a poem critical of Stalin, information which one of them passed on to the authorities. Terror built gradually. The Mandelstams were not arrested immediately. Their prominence made officials reluctant to move against them, at least not without some provocation or confession. What they soon realized instead was that the police sought to harass them with interrogations and visits from barely camouflaged security agents. Protracted harassment served a broader aim of undermining trust among the Mandelstams and their friends. The strategy induced the collapse of their community from within, thus, avoiding the risk of mobilizing them or sending them into flight through more overt forms of persecution.

Arguably, destruction and imprisonment were inevitable no matter what the Mandelstams did. Under Stalin's direction, the police needed no pretext to justify purging those out of favor if none could be found (Applebaum 2003). But at least at the beginning, no one could foresee the extent and ultimate goal of the persecution. This uncertainty, even as the threat became clear, makes their story so compelling. Against their better judgment, the Mandelstams harbored hope of evading the trap. But the longer they held out, the more they and their colleagues stretched the net, unwittingly trapping persons who otherwise might have survived. In short, false hopes encouraged by the lack of real information allowed the threat to unfold slowly. Though there is no proof, I suspect that some in their circle might have delayed or avoided imprisonment had several of the key actors in Nadezhda Mandelstam's account responded more decisively, reduced their contact with one another, and disappeared.[3] By failing to do so, in the end they faced a choice that might have been avoided: to save themselves by sacrificing their friends and colleagues. If the Mandelstams denied the threat until it was too late, the Maneo did not: partly because of the swift and undeniable threat of annihilation from the *TNI*, and partly because they were better practiced in vigilance.

Virtue in Practice

Like the Mandelstams, Maneo faced a dilemma: Aware of what could happen if they were too trusting, they could also anticipate what they might become, and what would happen to their community, should they retreat too far from others. Asociality and ignoring the well-being of friends holds a certain horror. But unlike the Mandelstams, Maneo could strike a balance, and they were prepared; flight in this instance followed previous flights from perceived dangers. It would be misleading to see dispersal as unthought reaction impelled by self preservation, however. Significantly, in fleeing from friends and neighbors, they were not surrendering them to the army. Flight, like a poison pill, was a strategy to avoid the trap of having to betray each other.[4] Is this virtue? In an ideal world probably not, but extending the definition and returning to the Aristotelian view outlined in the introduction, it is insofar as virtue inheres in doing what is reasonable. In light of the consequences, the Maneo practice of retreating from each other in times of danger represents a pragmatic move. It is also virtuous because dispersal in a small but significant way makes it possible to "extend" collective effort and render responsiveness more overt (MacIntyre 1984:187). Groups of Maneo maintained their distance from one another in recognition of the predicament their sudden reappearance might cause. This awareness is reciprocated; though separated, between them empathy accumulates. When people are living alongside others, the signs of mutual concern inspire greater trust and add to a community's coefficient of civility—the overall quality that permits people to act magnanimously in the interest of the greater good. Looking at virtue as collectively enabled, as much a product of practice as an aim, is not intended to deny a place for such singular and heroic virtues as courage. But what the Mandelstam and Maneo cases make clear is the need to understand virtue with respect to its obstacles, the factors that inhibit trust and give people, especially people in close proximity, reason to mistrust.

Maneo were alert to the precariousness of their situation during the *RMS* period. They were accustomed to peril, I believe, because of the pervasiveness of sorcery (*mauna*), a threat which they feel most acutely in the close proximity of others whose actions are known to be capricious and out of the ordinary (cf. Wikan 1990). One young Maneo mother told us that her husband's uncle who lived next door was using sorcery to make her child ill. Such suspicions are widespread, though naming the sorcerer, as in this instance, was more unusual. The danger, discussed below, is that accusations may lead to counter-accusations or new attacks. Sorcery lies in the background of many interactions; fear of it accentuates Maneo awareness of the peril of living their lives through others and reminds them that their own lives, in some ways, are not completely their own. As sorcery follows certain relational pathways, threats reveal the intertwining and embeddedness of people's lives in others. Even if sorcery is not implicated—many illnesses do not offer clear etiologies—the potential for it alerts people to the need to adjust and compensate for the various twists and turns that complicate their interactions. It reminds Maneo to do what they can to prevent the threats leading to an attack from cresting in the first place.

Sorcery also informs their understanding of the world. In the narratives that weave people's relations together, sorcery is the plot device invoked when people become stuck. Helpless to move, accusations impute responsibility for problems to others; other people's actions (or inaction) are scrutinized for signs of deliberate intent to use sorcery. Nor is it even necessary for the accused to be entirely conscious of using sorcery. Sorcery is viewed as a projection of intent, even if the agent is not entirely aware of it. Attributing a malady or misfortune to black magic helps map, in the absence of other information, a chain of cause and effect. The fear it inspires compels people (even skeptics) to respond and, short of any open accusation, to do so tactically and preemptively. In general, sorcery encourages strategies to manage uncertainty in the interstices of what they know of others and their objectives, to reduce the probability of being targeted in attack. There is still a risk no matter what one does, but as the economist Frank Knight observed risk unlike uncertainty can be controlled to some extent and, hence, is better tolerated (Knight 1921).[5] To control risk, Maneo endeavor to balance obligations and commitments among their various relationships. Paradoxically, in a sense, sorcery beliefs and the imperative to avoid it contributes to sociality, even if it vitiates community life in other ways. Sorcery gives people the incentive and opportunity to develop alertness to how their actions may be perceived—and skill in shaping those perceptions. Maneo endeavor to deflect acrimony and reduce the possibility their own actions will be seen as duplicitous. They do this by shifting registers between public and private discourse, disclosing feelings and pursuing different designs only to select audiences.

Maneo are captive to their relationships; they can talk about leaving their villages, but many have no wish to do so even when the options are viable and the threats are real. Elsewhere, where physical proximity does not expose people to such a degree, friends and colleagues manage uncertainties by ducking out of sight. In the short term, this might have been an effective response by the Mandelstams, not to deny that arrest was probably inevitable given the extent of Stalin's murderous campaign against both critics and allies. They hesitated to avoid colleagues who were less familiar or who might betray them, because they sensed little need to be wary. (If they felt safer together, they still knew that the secret police—the *NKVD*—typically made their arrests at night). The Mandelstams also may have harbored the illusion that the state would protect them from the excesses and duplicity of others. Lulled into a false sense of security, they fatally neglected to consider that state agents might act outside the rule of law. Finally, the Mandelstams endangered themselves by being unwilling to voice suspicions and risk the consequences of alienating some of their colleagues to preserve the façade of normalcy. They continued to participate in the community life of Soviet intellectuals long after doing so ceased to be safe. Disastrously, being a poet, Osip may have seen his circle of colleagues as an audience and, thus, could not resist reciting the poem critical of Stalin that landed him and Nadezhda in so much trouble. Yet an audience resembles community in a very limited sense, imagined but largely untested. Being unwilling to query their friends and acquaintances initially, the Mandelstams had no assurance of their designs and no knowledge of any extra identities they may have harbored as spies. Thus they had no way of preventing the poem from being overheard by an unintended audience. In short, Osip might have been more discrete, unless his aim was to precipitate a challenge.

In contrast, the Maneo avoided one another when they felt threatened. By dispersing, as they have at times throughout the past, they preserve tolerance by not taxing it, by not forcing others to confront the choice between their own survival and community. Maneo are accustomed to being overheard and spied upon. For them, more than an audience, community describes a site for the social reverberations of practice. Though their ability to shape actions is limited, nonetheless, they seek to answer the vicissitudes of social life and foster community both as an answer to sorcery concerns, as well as to fulfill a condition for wholesale social renewal, that is, by reversing the fragmentation, residential instability, and poverty that charts much of the Maneo past since the beginning.[6] To foster sociality is to respond to the overwhelming imbalance of power, especially since Dutch pacification in the first decade of the twentieth-century. They understand that they are outnumbered and give that fact an explanation. One myth attributes European origins to maggots which are white, like Westerners, and multiply rapidly by feasting on the carcasses of others. Through the story, Maneo claim people of European descent as their own, as they claim all outsiders as originally Maneo. It is a strategy that gives them some control over more numerous, wealthy, and powerful people.[7] The risk of this cultural embrace of the outside is that it can introduce external conflicts that otherwise would have no presence in Maneo life. Disputants in local conflicts may harden their positions as they find justification in outside events. Given a reason to infer local connections to broader world events, people become willing participants and partisans in more global conflicts. During the *RMS* period and its aftermath, for example, supporters and dissenters found deeper cause for divisions between them. And, as I will discuss in chapter 8, tensions have been exacerbated as Christians and Muslims throughout Maluku and the neighboring province of Central Sulawesi project back onto ancestors divisions reimagined as more divisive and impermeable than they were.

Friendship and Commitment

Community endures; shifts in residence are not more frequent because Maneo recognize that participation in social life is voluntary and that they can move if relationships deteriorate. Yet community is precarious precisely because they have no real political or economic need to live together. Extensive forest in the mountains, where roughly half the population now lives, dispersed clan ownership of that land, and widely distributed sago groves and gardens enable Maneo to live apart. In stories of the past they are reminded that fleeing has been an effective response to outside threats, from the 1918 influenza epidemic and the Japanese occupation during World War II to the *RMS* movement from 1950–53.[8] Even in calmer times, the presence of the forest alternative to village life affords them a refuge to negotiate, by avoiding, disputes with neighbors and kin with whom they coreside.[9] Community is also voluntary inasmuch as the Maneo lack recourse to effective institutions for adjudicating disputes. They recognize that turning to outside authorities would compromise local relations. What holds community together are the myriad intertwined relations and mutual obligations.[10] Of course, the structured interactions and expectations among certain affinal relations, for example among affines, do impose considerable stability; however, ties among in-laws create distance, whereas consanguinal ties, especially among siblings, are relatively close and unstructured. The Maneo term for same-sex sibling, *efa*, the most undifferentiated of all their relations, is also the same one used to denote friend—there being no clear line between the two.

Friendships are voluntary relations. But more too is at stake in a sense than friendship in coordinating relations and fashioning a community that is voluntary. First, among multiple sets of friends it is imperative to strike a balance. As Aristotle notes, there are practical limits to the number of friends one may have (1984:NE 1156b25–30; 1171a1–5). A community of friends requires that friends of friends have to be friends too, which becomes more difficult moving out from core relations, since the resources devoted to sustaining associations can be scarce. Scarcity need not be a limiting factor, however. While it can apply to the sharing of material objects and, thus, necessitate choice and the exclusion of certain parties, material exchanges are not the only condition animating community. Goodwill and trust need not be scarce, even when suspicions of sorcery abound.

Aristotle's second caveat about the politics of friendship is more relevant. Because of the possibility of relationships atrophying, or even failing, friendships require actions to communicate good intentions that are themselves subject to failure and misinterpretation (Aristotle 1984:EE 1245b25; Derrida 1997:255–56).[11] Because of sorcery, Maneo know they cannot eliminate disturbances to their relations and cannot take friendships for granted. They can respond to threats of evil specters like *masiae* by dispersing or, short of that, by moderating actions. They can also respond to threats from within by continuing to live together in villages with all the obligations this entails, thus signaling some seriousness in intent to fulfill these obligations, even if they never do. Living side by side can foster trust, but the link is tenuous. In small communities, such as Siahari and Kabailu, with fewer than twenty houses, the strands of community can appear to come undone when people disperse to hunting grounds and clove orchards during the dry season. The abandoned houses serve as haunting reminders of the former occupants, both living and dead, for those residents left behind. Maneo believe that traces of others may become infused or reoccupied by certain spirits, *topoyea* (spirits of the dead), who become more dangerous within the shared physical space of the village. As a result, when the majority of residents scatter to the forest to hunt, garden, and process sago, members of other households who might have been expected to remain—the elderly or those with important resource sites nearby—also disperse. They feel too vulnerable to spirits when alone or nearly alone in the village. In contrast to Aristotle's first observation about friendship noted above, Maneo community presupposes a critical mass below which the physical space of the village can no longer sustain it, and its emptiness opens the way to occupation by invisible, malevolent nonhumans. Because security is an effect of coresidence and not an explicit aim of practice—no one would admit to using sorcery (and using it even defensively would likely invite suspicion)—staying would go unrequited; it would be unrecognizable as a gesture demanding a response. (The forbearance of remaining as others leave satisfies no higher calling in Maneo.) If the number of residents falls below the threshold, living in a half-abandoned village populated with ghosts would seem merely foolhardy.

The Mandelstams, in contrast, haunted by a more dangerous specter, refused to cut off contact with friends and fellow artists until it was too late. Toward the end, before Osip Mandelstam entered the prison system from which he never returned, awareness of being surrounded by informants gave rise to despair. If the fear of spirits reminds Maneo of the uncertainty of their world, it also helps instill and allow for the exercise of a moral sensibility with respect to it. Fear does not lead to despair.

I have already proposed that moral life is predicated on the capacity and willingness to see others from their perspectives and to act accordingly to ameliorate their concerns. The presence of others certainly facilitates this work of seeing. Maneo see each other daily on the verandas of their houses; they pass each other on their way to gardens and sago groves; and they visit while bathing at the river at the end of the day. In a sense, moral perspicuity accumulates through such casual and recurrent interaction. For this reason, people doubt the possibility of living morally in the forest away from others; living in the forest describes living for oneself. Maneo realize, too, that living in community and being moral exposes them to various requests and demands that invariably compromise relations and subject them to the opaque intentions of others. So they seek to deflect suspicions directed at them and mitigate the trepidation aroused by the suspected intentions of those around them—intentions that shift between good and ill depending on the slights suffered, and the otherwise anonymous or random misfortunes that befall them. Maneo believe those intent on doing them harm have the means for acting on those intentions, usually through sorcery and the use of poison (*mauna*). The most notorious sorcerer in Maneo, a man who was eventually killed in retaliation for his actions, reportedly had two hearts. He attended church regularly. Yet the presence of the second heart predisposed him to maliciousness over and against the more generous inclinations of a normal heart. The absence of any outward indications of two hearts tempers the pleasures of company and again reminds Maneo of the need for vigilance.

The Denouement

In a sense the Maneo flight in response to the sudden appearance of the Indonesian army in 1951 was rehearsed. Similarly, when Homi began to tell us what had happened to his family during this time of the story's dramatic interruption when *masiae* stoned our house just as names were being named had a certain familiarity. It raises the question: who are *masiae* and why would they deign to interrupt such a story? What does their presence signify? Jennie and I had been told early on *masiae* live in villages to the east—a fact which makes them resemble humans—and that they roam widely for the purpose of creating mischief like throwing stones, or, more seriously, causing illness, even death (see also Ellen 1993). Traveling mostly at night and so nearly invisibly, they hover on the margins of Maneo settlements; occasionally they slip into them. In a sense, *masiae* are perfect strangers and an equal opportunity threat. They pose a danger to everyone. No Maneo knows any of them. And they have no position in the web of kin relations. Yet they are immediately recognizable as a group. Rock throwing and other thumps in the night form part of their repertoire of practices (some of their more benign ones). Of course, it is assumed no one other than *masiae* would throw stones at houses. Belief in them is encouraged further by the church and the state. For the now deposed New Order regime, these nearly invisible figures on the margins of communities offered perhaps the only local correlates for the equally elusive communists portrayed in primary school texts or on radio. For the church, *masiae* represent minions of the devil, small proof of the biblical account of world history. The fact Seram seemed awash in evil spirits, according to one Western missionary, meant its inhabitants were in special need of religious instruction.

When Maneo identify others in kinship terms it constitutes a pragmatic move establishing a relation that carries with it certain assumptions about the type and quality of interaction, specifically about what is expected of one another. In contrast, because *masiae* stand apart, they lack the invitations, which kin terms provide, to participate in social life. When they participate, they do so surreptitiously and unresponsively except, it turns out, to the malevolent designs of other Maneo. Their very lack of morality reflects back an expected if unmarked morality in normal human interactions. When *masiae* enter a village to inflict real harm, they require a pretext that may be found in one of two ways. First, they can lure Maneo into making some offense. For instance, just after Jennie and I arrived we were warned not to utter any exclamation or accusation in the event any of our belongings disappeared, even if our garden appeared disturbed by wild pigs. If we accused anyone or damned the pigs, and if *masiae* were behind it, as they might be, the lost object would reappear and we would fall ill. We were warned, further, that there are no limits to the lengths they would go to cause harm, even setting up one of their own to trip the spear in an animal trap so as to acquire with the injury or death of a comrade a motive for revenge. Maneo hunters told us of their wariness whenever coming upon sprung but empty traps, fearful both of injured pigs and of *masiae* who might be waiting nearby armed with invisible poisonous arrows that they point at their victims and mimic firing. If an arrow finds a victim, he or she begins to feel the chill of the poison, falls ill, and usually dies.

The second and more unsettling method for attack is through contract. Maneo believe *masiae* can be hired by neighbors or kin to kill enemies or to settle some score within the community, usually in exchange for the porcelain also used as marriage gifts. In this way, *masiae* are transformed from a mere ghost-like presence and guardians of comportment on the margins of villages to active agents serving as the extensions of the intentions or desires of neighbors. In short, they afford anonymity behind which Maneo may seek reprisal, and for possibly the smallest of slights since there are no repercussions—though I should add that the slights often seem great to those who suffered them. Not being accountable, people have no reason to measure responses; there needs to be no proportionality between the provocation and the use of *masiae* for retaliation. Adding to the temptation to use sorcery is the fact that the scores to settle endure and descendents may harbor the animosities their ancestors bore, but which everyone else has forgotten, for generations. Avenging grievances is a way for Maneo to honor their ancestors. In sum, this possibility of familiars acting through *masiae*, hiding their malevolent designs behind them, raises the stakes and social value of expressions of goodwill. Like the doctrine of predestination among Calvinists, Maneo endeavor to make displays of conviviality without any certainty that those feelings will reciprocated or that other's expressions of it are genuine. And even if goodwill does prevail for a while the situation could change suddenly should some new grievance surface.

Returning to the story of the stone throwing, if the circumstances and timing of the *masiae* attack raised suspicions, I had more concrete reasons for skepticism. This encounter with them, in fact, had been my second. A *masiae* attacked the settlement of Siahari the year before. One evening, several neighbors reported having spotted a human figure, a *masiae*, they said, in the moonlight at the edge of the village. Our host there, Samos, approached me and motioned for me to accompany him outside. I followed, and following his lead I too picked up and heaved a couple of rocks that landed loudly on the roof of an empty house nearby. The village fell silent, Samos struggling hard to stifle laughter. Having acted on this occasion as *masiae* do and having some evidence that Maneo play the role too, I suspect that on the evening of our story a year later in Maneo Rendah, the *masiae* was not a stranger but a neighbor, specifically, our host Homi's younger brother who lived close by. My guess is that he had overheard our interview and, anticipating where it was going with the disclosure of the other neighbor's involvement in the *RMS* dispute, sought to bring it to an end. Who or what threw the rocks, however, is the less interesting and less important question. The real mystery is why the *masiae* explanation received such ready concurrence.

I am certain that what friends were prepared to concede that night in the dark outside Homi's house is not necessarily consistent with what they believed or knew or would be willing to discuss on other, more private occasions. This is not to imply they do not believe in *masiae* as a cause of human suffering. They do, and they have compelling reasons for believing so. But just as some incidents attributed to them are done at the bidding of Maneo themselves, sometimes, too, it appears, Maneo may disguise their own actions behind the *masiae* allegation. Any apparent confusion over the truth, which would be the effect only if Maneo were interested in full disclosure, as in kinship, disappears when the meaning of such statements are sought in intended effects. The intent was to channel conversation away from the event of forty years before and the identification of the issuers of the threat. Our host's younger brother could not simply have come over and reproached his older brother without provoking some disagreement. By adopting the *masiae* signature, rock throwing, he was able to end the story being told.

As I said, *masiae* are a hidden agency, and by being hidden, they reveal their presence in traces and by acts linked to them by ascription or assignation. Given that *masiae* appearances are not subject to independent confirmation, they appear following accusations that summon them (Beidelman [1986]1993). In a way, they do not portend trouble so much as represent a response to it. Because of their invisibility, people can identify them as acting subjects in the affairs of the village without knowing the real agency involved. People can agree about *masiae*, or about the *sense* of *masiae* to use Gottlob Frege's term (1966), without knowing precisely what they are agreeing about, that is, the reference denoted when *masiae* are identified. Naming *masiae*, in other words, elicits a public recognition that confirms their agency because they have been linked to such rock throwing incidents in the past. As Hannah Arendt observes, such recognition does not reveal a truth uncovered at the end of a story, however; it merely destroys a deception and ends inquiry (1978:39). *Masiae* are introduced in conversations to mark points where accusations or the pursuit of agency can go no further, at least publicly. On several occasions when *masiae* were alleged to have appeared or been responsible for some incident, listeners agreed and discussion ended.[12] The one exception was when someone from another village, after hearing the story of a *masiae* killing, claimed that the person who had supposedly discovered one in his trap had lied. As in other contexts, the commentator was in no position to independently assess the credibility of the other person's claim. But he called the alleged killing "bullshit" (*mukuhaha*) to convey his disrespect for the young man who claimed to have done so.

There are practical reasons for terminating conversation when *masiae* are suspected in some misfortune. For a precondition for *masiae* attack, such as accusing someone of hiring them, might easily become an animating condition that brings it about. That is, whether such suspicions are correct or not, an accused person might actually seek out *masiae* to exact revenge. Again, there is no way to be sure. While Maneo claim to have killed persons suspected of using sorcery, evidence is usually insufficient to help narrow the field of suspects, both because of *masiae* anonymity and the number of community members with probable cause. Sorcerers themselves are said to have two hearts, but that does not hold for the Maneo hiring them. When they are talking and they invoke *masiae* publicly, the reason is to channel potentially divisive discourse about accusations and responsibility in nonpublic ways. Of course, they are also caught. As *masiae* solve certain problems by publicly deflecting accusations that would prove socially disruptive, they contribute to others. Sorcerers become props in living dramas and a malign presence on the edge of the community that simply cannot be rationalized away as mere projections of something else. Even the seemingly innocuous fact of someone's relative well-being may arouse suspicion that the person is using magic to repel attack. And Maneo surmise if one is using sorcery defensively to protect himself from harm, there is no reason for that person not to use that knowledge to act preemptively and more offensively against perceived enemies. Thus public trust and with it a sense of community are balanced against the terror of people's private suspicions. Under these circumstances, keeping such fears private is not merely polite, civility is contingent upon it. Of course, keeping quiet may not be possible or even desirable. Memories have to be honored and slights cannot be ignored. The moral acuity that people bring to these situations lies in the skill with which they continue conversations, but in lower registers and out of earshot of those who would take offense.

At the same time, the presence of *masiae* which threaten all people also makes it possible to appear to be above their entreaties to inflict revenge. And this ability to appear to transcend evil and act selflessly is key to conveying sociality despite people's differences and disagreements.[13] To illustrate, when a man recently moved himself and his immediate family from the mountain settlement of Maneo Tinggi to the coastal Maneo village of Yamalatu, he did so, he told his former neighbors, because of fear that a *masiae* had been killed in one of his pig traps. He reasoned that the *masiae*'s companions would use the event to seek revenge against him, his kin, even his neighbors, as such collateral attacks are commonplace and as *masiae* are generally indifferent to the identity of the victim. Whether the man believed he had killed a *masiae*—perhaps he saw blood and some unusual signs nearby—the claim diverts attention from other sources of discontent, specifically his relationships with the people around him, who, I would venture to guess, may have been more directly responsible for his move. He needed a public pretext. Even if he harbored nothing against his kin, moving could still be criticized as selfish, as too blatant an expression of the desire to get ahead. By invoking sorcery, leaving could be construed more positively as a sacrifice to endure in order to save other family members remaining in the mountains, for *masiae* would soon learn of his departure and set traps for him elsewhere. The man's neighbors and kin appeared to accept the explanation or at least kept suspicions about ulterior motives to themselves.

There is a sense of theater to *masiae*. Like Javanese shadow puppet shows and the Japanese Bunraku theater, visible human performers displace onto nonhuman others what by convention cannot be seen as coming from them directly (Keeler 1987:242). Audiences participate by suspending disbelief to preserve the illusion, enough so as to see the plays of virtue and evil for what they are, as parables. The parables are repeated and truths emerge through collective witnessing. Living the stories, as it were, makes it possible to experience the virtue of sparing others by rising above the temptation, even the expectation of summoning these evil people to settle a score. This kind of dissimulation, as Georg Simmel notes, enlarges worlds (1950:330). Eschewing them, thus, becomes an act of magnanimity. Even more, *masiae* foster civility by encouraging discretion when people might otherwise trace connections between suspected sorcery and its human agents. Of course, Maneo do not always refrain; the urgency to identify a culprit may be too great and the danger of not doing so too acute lest a perpetrator attack again.

Betrayal

If Maneo believed in spirits that might not have existed, the same cannot be said for the spies among the Mandelstams' circle of friends in the Soviet Union in the 1930s. The Mandelstams did not want to believe. Eventually, without knowing who was behind it, a series of arrests and interrogations led them to the undeniable truth of the presence of spies among them. Then, discovery of the identity of the agents and informants became all consuming. Nadezhda Mandelstam described how any success, mere survival even, suggested to others some likely complicity in Stalin's campaign of terror. And complicity was achieved on an enormous scale. The Mandelstams and their friends were right to see their colleagues as turning on them. Survival for many meant spying themselves, even on friends, turning everyone into agents of state repression. The choice to do so appeared to be a choice between life and death. However, the choice was a false one, a matter of correlation not causation; insidiously, a person's betrayal of another to save him or herself was invariably answered by their own betrayal by someone else—a paradox few could see. The cumulative effect of this false bargain was to prevent people who otherwise might have acted en masse to derail the process by refusing to spy, from seeing such refusal as futile. With nobler alternatives blocked, to have acted courageously under the circumstances would have been merely foolhardy. In the end, it hardly mattered who had become an informant because former friends readily pointed to each other as responsible for their misfortune. Accusing others absolved them of responsibility for their own acts of informing. Unable to retreat from others around them and caught in this trap of mutual incrimination, friends and colleagues lost all perspective to see others as they would see themselves (Aristotle 1984:NE 1170a29–b6). What little good fortune anyone experienced at the time, says Mandelstam, was deemed to be the result of miracles not humanly authored (1978:94).

Maneo, as I have described, faced a similarly dire situation in 1951, enduring a harsh occupation by a largely unwelcome coterie of desperate *RMS* soldiers. For Maneo, however, the menace was clear. When the decisive Indonesian army attack did come, they were prepared to scatter. Some hid out for just a week or two; others remained on the run for a year or more. Of course, for those in the mountains, as time wore on, uncertainty grew in proportion to the distance they placed between each other. They had no assurance during the interval apart that others had not joined the Indonesian side. But separation fostered wariness rather than hopelessness, a subtle yet important distinction. Setting distance between them represented a strategic move, and a move that had precedence; it was calculated to avoid misunderstanding knowing that one's own sudden appearance might arouse suspicions of spying. Critically, too, not all contact ceased. Several men described how they had received sisters who had been sent to them as emissaries. That sisters were not perceived as threats reflects the close and idealized nature of the cross-sex sibling tie, particularly from the brother's perspective, and the concomitant belief that sisters could not be turned to spy on them. Of course, when Homi's uncle, Firiz, reversed this convention and ventured to find his sister he did not simply blunder. He perhaps knew he would find his in-laws (his sister's husband's kin) who would have no reason to view his sudden appearance as benign. Firiz may have calculated that risk was worth taking and that his mission would succeed in allaying suspicions once his in-laws' fears were not realized. Firiz happened to be one of my closest informants, yet he refused to disclose any details of the story to me and changed the subject whenever I brought it up as though embarrassed to have put his neighbors in the position of having to trust him with their lives.

In the stable years after the *RMS* period, until 1994 when I left, the risks have abated. Maneo have acquired more magnanimity in their assessment of the designs of others. Nonetheless, they remain wary, especially so, I suspect, in light of the civil conflict that engulfed the region in 1999. Reaching this point has taken some effort; trust has been banked and equanimity practiced. In the aftermath of the *RMS* turmoil, Maneo did not restore civility by airing and seeking to resolve the root causes of their differences (Just 2001:104). Though Christian, they do not try to expiate guilt through confessional practices.[14] Nor has the absence of what would pass for justice, redress, or score settling elsewhere merely been a consequence of the inability to assign culpability. In fact, as I have argued, there are probably few real secrets given the thin walls and the proximity of houses. What secrets there are, are allowed because of the restraint Maneo exercise in not exposing or responding publicly to what others suspect or reveal privately (Simmel 1950:330).[15] Again, *masiae* beliefs themselves encourage this restraint insofar as they enable people to act morally either anonymously by throwing stones and so redirecting inquiry or by reducing pressure on others to name names and voice complaints. There is a tacit recognition that social problems are too complex to be evaluated against absolute standards of right or wrong; people's lives are too intertwined. Instead, they do what they can, often surreptitiously through discrete sorts of gestures aimed at reducing uncertainty, mitigating possible misunderstanding, and containing sources of divisiveness. In some stories, they choose to mention only certain points and highlight select themes depending on the context in which they tell them. This perspicuity enables Maneo to move through the complex dilemmas and contradictory demands of social life with little more than good will and a supply of rocks.

Memory and Forgetting

Maneo stories of the *RMS* period and the aftermath differ. Versions differ because people witnessed events from their own vantage points. Homi and his family high on the mountainside after being flushed out by the Indonesian army would have seen their village occupied and heard the patrols hunting for them. They would have known what was coming. Homi's father's in-laws or affines (and Homi's as well), who fled north to the expanse of low lying sago groves, witnessed much less and may never have heard the patrols. They emerged from the forest long after the army left. Their experiences were similar but not overlapping, except when Firiz appeared, he was accused of betraying them to the military, and threatened. That shared encounter, too, was seen quite differently. Had Firiz wanted to avoid a chance meeting with his in-laws he clearly could have. Knowing it was no accident, his in-laws suspected the worst. The versions of events differ as histories as distinct from memories or recollections. Assembled as a synthetic narrative, the stories reflect different perspectives on various social tensions within and between different communities forty years later. They are told so that different audiences might imagine the social landscape and the moral propensities of the persons involved in particular ways (Ricoeur 1992:170).

In general, historic recitations help instill values such as honoring ancestors and elders, and the importance of fulfilling promises and pursuing otherwise lost causes. In this light, Nadezhda Mandelstam's story, written decades after the purge of the 1930s, stands as a cautionary, moral tale. She is not vindictive; significantly, she does not blame those friends and colleagues suspected of betraying her and her husband. Instead, she invites readers to imagine themselves as others caught in a tragic predicament where hope was self-delusional and honor easily betrayed. She reminds us of the fragility of goodness when goodness is taken for granted.

In a similar vein, many of the various narratives of the *RMS* history, and particularly the abbreviated account of the flight we heard when we first arrived, reminds audiences of the calamities and hardships visited upon them in the absence of trust. But Homi's longer version of the *RMS* disaster, which calls for continued vigilance, goes further by identifying the persons for whom such vigilance is warranted. It was partly a political move. The numerically dominant Ipapoto clan in Maneo Rendah (his in-laws) still suffer from the reputation of their ancestor Wara'a. None of them occupied important positions within the church or in village politics. Homi's story would serve to remind listeners of reasons to continue to be suspicious of them. However, I doubt he began our interview with the intention of having his story overheard. On another occasion, while drunk, he did openly accuse Ipapoto clan members of something like moral turpitude. This night however, quite sober, I think his enthusiasm got the better of him and the story carried him away, raising the volume of its own telling. In a way, the story of the *RMS* period enacts various possibilities for its recitation, warranting the inclusion of certain details or their exclusion and differences in volume. In the middle of the story, Homi fell temporarily under its spell to cast aspersion certainly but also to honor his kin. Again, his uncle, the story's protagonist, had no interest in telling the story. If I am correct in guessing that Homi's brother stoned our house, he did so out of respect for the state of relations with his neighbors who had been on the side issuing the threat to his uncle years before, less enthralled by the telling and overhearing only part of it. The brother was right to be concerned about the volume and audience. In my own case, though I have changed some details, I have not kept events of the time in confidence.

I was never asked not to record these and other interviews on tape or in notebooks, but some may have found it disconcerting that I might replay tapes of conversations for others. They were concerned that the information might affect people's reputations. More importantly, as noted in chapter 7, knowledge is transforming: Recall that some people suspected I had used knowledge I had acquired from interviews with Minggus to build a cement factory on Seram's coast. In the extreme, the Mandelstams, too, suffered for lack of control over the flow of information. Soviet security agents used copious records to help foment terror. Having no way to elide records, in effect, everyone became complicit in the observations of others. This surveillance, in turn, allowed persons to justify decisions to inform, even if they had nothing to reveal, because they could reasonably suppose the state already knew. The appearance of a complete record left no room for persons to try to act on behalf of others by withholding information. This "temptation of innocence," as Levinas calls it (1996:290), enabled surveillance from everywhere. At the height of the terror, a friend tells Nadezhda Mandelstam to be careful of her little dog because the secret police had taught it to write (1970:37).

Maneo do not keep written records of events and not simply because most cannot. Forgetting is not left up to chance. The copper book, for example, that Minggus described as the repository of all knowledge is supposedly hidden in the mountains and guarded by a giant python and lizard in case someone should stumble onto it. As I have noted, when Minggus intimated that the knowledge of the book was in his head, he was not denying its existence. After our interview with Homi, we talked to the neighbor who had supposedly been on the side issuing the threat during the *RMS* era. He gave us the briefest of accounts, as did Firiz, although both men had excellent memories and easily recalled details of other, more distant events. The neighbor similarly made no mention of the murder of another suspected government spy, a non-Maneo man, before Firiz arrived on the scene, a story others had confirmed. As suggested, these accounts were not entirely the author's own stories to tell. In the neighbor's case, his reluctance to talk about the incident, rather than present a competing narrative justifying the threat, represented an effort to silence the history altogether, to allow it to be buried by more generic recollections of the time (Ricoeur 1992). Others participate in the silence out of a sense of civility. In a generation, perhaps, the details of the story will be lost. Of course, complications arise from the fact that secrets cannot always be kept. Dogs may write, thoughts may be read, or, more commonly, persons may have other interests in disclosing them. Homi may have perpetuated a grievance as a way to honor the elder who had suffered it, though this man himself was unwilling to participate directly. He may also have sought to use the event as "dirty laundry" to undermine public confidence in the accused.

Conclusion

I have argued that the presence of rogue, invisible enemies on the margins of Maneo communities fosters a sense of vulnerability and a chronic unease regarding the hidden designs and undisclosed grievances of community members. I have also described how Maneo civility depends on the goodwill of others in the absence of more institutionalized mechanisms or procedures for instilling it. Community is sustained because of such efforts. It slips when ostensibly moral actions merely serve political ends, when, for example, Homi sought to impugn his neighbors and not just honor his kin. In the Maneo universe, *masiae* remind people of the need for vigilance. But along with the afflictions and suffering they cause, they allow evil to insinuate itself from without, calling attention to, without identifying the source of, animosities within. On one hand, *masiae* beliefs help Maneo move through entanglements by creating a sense of urgency and momentum lest the other party resort to them. On the other hand, the presence of these shadowy others implicates the shadowy intentions of familiars, thus, undermining efforts to create feelings of conviviality and community. With such fear in the air, one would suppose that Maneo would choose to live among those they trust, for instance, close kin. While this is, in fact, the case, as I have described, and kin do tend to coreside, close ties do not afford insurance against *masiae* attack. For even among kin there may be some undisclosed grudge that leads one to turn to *masiae* to seek redress; or, more likely, because of expectations of higher levels of cooperation, offense may be taken when these expectations go unfulfilled. Against the possibility of attack, Maneo create a "surplus of sociality" (Levinas 1996:165) to keep *masiae* at bay, which they do by managing appearances, and by elevating comity over probity. In effect, *masiae* encourage Maneo to act in ways that remove the appearance of having any reason to invoke their help in seeking revenge. This is done through the myriad of discrete gestures, like sharing harvests as Maneo women do, and sitting side by side during church services, which demonstrate a certain practical wisdom. It also reflects the successful negotiation of at least some of the dilemmas of social life—doing again, as Aristotle writes, the best they can (1984:NE 1163b15–18).

Notes

1. The preceding chapters have explored how kinship and marriage contribute to the composition of villages by inducing, as it were, empathies and enmities depending on how people are positioned. The present chapter shifts focus to the more general moral parameters and contours of practice, the telos or aim of which is movement through various relational entanglements. Movement requires signs, visible in choices, of people's flexibility and willingness to undertake actions out of concern for others, with at least the appearance of intending to assuage their concerns. Whether and how a community emerges is an open question (Taylor 1995:181). Valeri (2000) describes the role of the Huaulu taboo system in mediating relations and boundaries between them and the world (including the deceased and various fauna and flora). For them, taboo appears as a moral system. Absent it—again, Maneo being Christian have abandoned most taboos (if they ever had a similar system)—they improvise and seek other ways to foster moral awareness.

2. By the time the *RMS* abandoned Ambon, some political leaders, among them the Minister of Defense, Manusama, had fled to western New Guinea (now Irian Jaya), still controlled by the Dutch (until 1961), and from there to Holland. Others were caught before they could escape by the advancing Indonesian Army. The most important *RMS* figure, Soumokil, the movement's chief of foreign affairs, was executed in 1966 (Chauvel 1990). An *RMS* government remains in exile in The Netherlands, but fifty years after the defeat there is little of the original political will left to the movement despite claims by some Muslim propagandists of their behind-the-scenes machinations in the present civil-religious conflict.

3. The possibility of flight was entertained by others facing persecution at the time. Evgenia Ginsburg, for example, was advised by her mother to flee her home as her trial grew near. She spent nearly two decades in prison, labor camps, and exile.

4. Both the Maneo and Soviet cases refer to the experiences of persons in close proximity, with zero degrees of separation, vulnerable to the capriciousness of others and at the same time dependent on their goodwill. With this exposure, people are aware of the interactions of others, and aware of being observed, and they take measures to appeal to and appease others, to adjust immediate commitments in light of other ongoing interactions and relations (see Calhoun 1995:209).

5. Risk is measurable uncertainty, says Knight in his 1921 book *Risk, Uncertainty, and Profit*. Risk can be understood as probability, though not necessarily a very accurate assessment, and the aim of managing it is to reduce it. Uncertainty, in contrast, is doubt about the future that cannot be insured against. It is a condition of relative powerlessness. Both uncertainty and risk are endemic; a key social barometer is the extent to which the former becomes the latter.

6. Maneo took refuge in the forest during the worldwide influenza epidemic of 1918, where they fared much better than did residents of other villages who remained together. And they did so later, in 1945, at the close of World War II, to avoid detection from Allied and Japanese planes criss-crossing overhead. Nowadays, too, couples will flee to the forest for a few months in order to force marriages that their parents may be reluctant to accept. Retreat to the forest offers a way to manage some of the contingencies and animosities of social life by managing appearances through movement between and into different spaces. Often, returns occasion celebrations.

7. There is a certain inevitability that the conditions for reconstituting community will be met. Of course, Queen Elizabeth (a Maneo ancestor) will likely never return and courts will never recognize patents on such Maneo discoveries as the Palm Pilot and Pocket Fisherman, and yet it almost does not matter. The objects of kinship and ownership claims are sufficiently substitutable—again, who would know—that as long as no other identities are given, anyone returning might fill that role. Strangers might be recognized, like Atan Boiratan's alleged offspring, as kin. Nor is there any explicit millenarian expectation of a return; community instead is infused in the general hope for recognition that confirms the basic premise of Maneo antecedent origins.

8. The lack of effective authority is sometimes praised and at other times lamented (even by the same people). In one story, Tomasi, the public works coordinator, told of the effort of an ambitious *raja* to build a tower of rocks to the moon. The task required the assistance of members of the community. When their first efforts failed, the *raja* admonished them to work harder whereupon they abandoned him and his project altogether. While Tomasi could laugh at the hubris of building a tower to the moon, the new school he was in charge of building was no joke. Fortunately, construction was completed quickly and without any real problems.

9. Community can refer to both the subject and sites of dialogue—public spaces for conversation, for referencing and self-referencing, establishing identity and place. While much of the effort of community is directed toward transcending the particulars of experience, to make experience generalizable and comparable (see Keane 1997a:98), community also includes hidden spaces, places for competitiveness (where this is not openly tolerated) and asocial proclivities. Similarly, dialogues are not only joined they are overheard. Registers shift depending on the intended and unintended audiences.

10. Communication makes intent intelligible to others (Habermas 1990:23). Action is moral to the extent it communicates intent that is acceptable to others. In a sense, *masiae* are perfectly understood because their intents are transparent despite the elusiveness of the actual referent (the physical person). Curiously, no one seems particularly concerned about *masiae* while they are living in the forest, sleeping in sago groves or at garden or hunting sites. Susceptibility to attack happens to be greater in the village because of greater visibility there. Also, there, more instances of mischief are attributed to *masiae*.

11. Because disputes are never fully resolved, in a sense, the history of any dispute always begins in the middle (Carsten 1997:222). Like a typhoon caused by a butterfly flapping its wings an ocean away, finding a root cause of any dispute is only possible from a certain, necessarily biased reconstruction of events that invariably fails to account for resistance to it. Knowing this, as a practical matter, Maneo are usually discrete about vetting their complaints.

12. The Calvinists sought to display signs of being chosen, for to suffer doubt was to yield to the temptations of the devil. To allay it required intense worldly activity (Weber 1958:111–112). This raises the ethnographically interesting question about how and whether a perfect community can be imagined. In the Western Christian tradition, community may be a route to salvation. For example, Augustine observes that man's relation to God refers to a community's relationship among its members; through such relations, divinity is achieved. To share in goodness, he says, is to make it grow, and doing God's work of making goodness grow, requires bearing witness to each other and pointing out each other's errors (1958:329–330). But Augustine understood a community of people is necessarily fallible, and the notion of a perfect community a chimera. By contrast, Aristotle invokes gods differently to make a similar point about the imperfectability of human associations, with echoes in Maneo. He describes the Greek gods not suffering for other gods or mere mortals; when they do interact, they use each other for frivolous aims, as Maneo sorcerers use others. Aristotle tells us that a community of gods, like a community of sorcerers in Maneo, would make for poor company indeed—a point similar, too, to Socrates's when he urged hiding from the young the gods' reported indiscretions (Plato 1974: Book III 390a–391e [60–62]). Aristotle observes that for men to live like gods, unconcerned with others would constitute supreme arrogance. Even if one could act with impunity, appearances would have to suggest, at a minimum, that acts are not taken entirely out of malice or for purely selfish aims, and that deliberation reflects something more, even if guarantees of mutual cooperation or civility are absent.

13. Aristotle proposes that it is morally superior to know others than to be known (and to be recognized by others); it follows from the value ascribed to good deeds over any honors that might accrue from those deeds (1984:EE 1239a35–b2). The argument, however, can be turned on its head. Knowledge of a certain kind can pose considerable risk to civility, that is, when one discovers, or at least believes they have, some evil intent behind a gesture. The coefficient of civility is diminished when Maneo assign responsibility for some misfortune to *masiae* hired by someone in the community, especially if someone receives intimations of their own suspected involvement in something they know they had no part of. By knowing a lot, one does not necessarily know better about the intents of others. Precisely because of familiarity, then, people (Maneo included) seek confirmation of the sincerity of expressions of goodwill as a condition of their own commitment to the well-being of others.

14. Although Christian, Maneo place little stock in confession and forgiveness. Such expressions, for example, "*minta maaf*" (excuse me), are self-deprecating terms intended

to lower expectations and minimize one's responsibility for the possible consequences of actions. By avoiding the assignation of responsibility they foster some civility (a meaningful façade) in public discourse.

15. Secrecy can contribute to generalized goodwill. Beidelman observes that the creation of public silences makes it possible to remove the politically and socially inexpressible (Beidelman [1986]1993:8). And Simmel notes people can act anonymously to deflect remuneration for any good works they may have authored. In a sense, fostering civility requires some dissembling. However, he points out too that "although the secret has no immediate connection with evil, evil has an immediate connection with secrecy" (1950:330). In other words, secrets permit duplicity and betrayal.

8

In the Crucible of Violence

> The old disease, thought Rubashov. Revolutionaries should not think through other people's minds. Or perhaps they should? Or even ought to? How can one change the world if one identifies oneself with everybody? How else can one change it? He who understands and forgives—where would he find a motive to act? Where would he not? Arthur Koestler, *Darkness at Noon*

On January 19, 1999, as the month of Ramadan, the holiest time in the Muslim calendar, was coming to a close, a fight broke out in the Batu Merah neighborhood in Ambon City between a Christian minibus driver and one or more Bugis Muslim youths. The immediate circumstances of the fight remain unclear. One of the Muslim youths involved may have been the bus conductor, charged with collecting passengers and fares for a Bugis Muslim owner, or he may have been a petty thug, one of many from either religious group, extorting drivers for loose change. Regardless, it was not an extraordinary event. Scuffles had been common occurrences around the rough and tumble bus stations and busy markets in Ambon when I was there in the 1980s and 1990s. But by the late 1990s, the context in which they occurred, if not their frequency, was changing. Ethnic tensions freighted with religious overtones were running high, exacerbated by the lingering economic crisis that began two years earlier and by a half century of in-migration of mostly Muslim Butonese, Bugis, and Makassarese from Sulawesi that was upsetting, at least in the opinion of Christians, the relative demographic and political balance that once existed between them and native Ambonese Muslims.[1] As a result, in hindsight, disagreements over such trivial matters as bus fares had the potential to tap a deeper discontent and spread to the broader community. When the fighting began, one attack fed another, increasing in ferocity with the spread of more lethal weapons and loss of life. By 2003, with deaths numbering in the thousands and as many as 700,000 people displaced from their homes in the provinces of Maluku and North Maluku, the foundations of civil life had been destroyed.

How did the destruction, displacement, and loss of life reach such levels? Except for the anti-Communist pogrom in 1965—a bloodbath that cost over 500,000 lives—Indonesia has experienced nothing like it. Followed, as it was, by the violence that accompanied the East Timor independence referendum, ethnic and religious conflict in central Sulawesi, and renewed fighting in Aceh province, events in Maluku gave the disturbing impression of a nation coming apart. Scholars, reporters, and other observers have espoused a variety of theories and ideas to explain it.[2] Most agree that the implosion of civil society in Maluku did not result from the accumulation of local grievances as so much dry tinder and that the conflict represents more than simply an atavistic struggle over religious identities, acknowledging that religious rhetoric on both sides contributed to the intensity of the violence (Bubandt 2000). From the outset, intense media coverage helped magnify and distend the broader significance of rioting. Having been portrayed, after the fact, as a model for interreligious harmony, Maluku's descent into violence was quickly taken as proof of the incompatibility of Islam and Christianity, the line espoused by leading partisans. In tandem with some mainstream media, these partisan accounts—published before the smoke from the fires had cleared—portrayed attacks against their side as part of a concerted campaign of expulsion or forced conversion, conveniently ignoring their own acts of aggression (e.g., Kastor 1999; Putuhena 1999). Partisan authors rewrote historic religious divisions as deeper and more diverging than they were; their reporting made the violence appear inevitable so as to subvert possibilities for imagining a religiously and ethnically diverse future. For their part, Muslim propagandists disinterred the specter of the moribund Republic of South Maluku separatist movement of the 1950s (now based in the Netherlands), reconstituting it as exclusively Christian (which it was not), calling the *RMS* the *Republic Maluku Serani* (Christian) instead of *Selatan* (south) (Putuhena 1999:60–63). On the other side, for example, a Christian website reported unsubstantiated allegations of a chemical attack against a Christian village.[3]

More serious analyses of the conflict fall into two categories. The first, pursuing urgent questions of responsibility, deduces from the pattern of conflict, from its sudden start, lulls, and renewed outbreaks, the fingerprints (and deep pockets) of Suharto loyalists and so-called Green (Islamist) Generals. Suharto had been forced to resign from the presidency in May 1998. Once the successor governments of B. J. Habibie and later Abdurrahman Wahid assumed office they initially failed to grasp the dangerousness of the rioting, then overreacted to it, creating an opening for those seeking to capitalize on the chaos. Notably, their administrations failed to anticipate that some local soldiers and police would take sides as their family and friends became victims and that the practice of billeting undersupplied troops with local families ensured that many soldiers would identify with their plight and give, sell, or trade weapons and ammunition for food and cigarettes. Eventually, what the military brass described euphemistically as "contamination" did become a significant enough problem for the leadership to acknowledge publicly—noting that some 10 percent of the roughly 14,000 soldiers and police stationed in Maluku had deserted and were assumed to have joined the struggle. More egregiously, they failed to anticipate that even if they did not become "contaminated," security forces personnel simply could not avoid the perception of partisanship because of religious and ethnic affiliations, as when troops were sent from South Sulawesi, the ancestral home of many of the displaced victims.

Behind the bungling and miscalculation, scholars see more systematic efforts to inflame passions. In particular, they note that several high-ranking generals (among them former Armed Forces Chief Wiranto, Major Generals Kivlan Zein and Djaja Suparman) all had links to rival factions of Moluccan gangsters (*preman*) and had on previous occasions been involved in financing, training, and transporting mobs to sites of protest and rioting elsewhere in the country. High-level complicity can be adduced from weapons proliferation as well. Indonesia restricts private ownership of firearms, yet rifles and a steady stream of ammunition found their way to local militias. Some weapons distribution may have been opportunistic. However, security forces support also eased the way of an estimated 3,000 Laskar Jihad extremist fighters from training camps in Java past police guarding the port of Surabaya and onto ships to Ambon in April 2000, followed shortly by their weapons. This, despite President Wahid's orders that they not be allowed. Analysts speculate that raising the specter of religious violence and secession could help justify the military's political role in preserving stability after the fall of Suharto, just as civilian politicians began to press for curtailing it. Civil war in Maluku also diverted attention from abuse and corruption charges against these generals. And once fighting became endemic, security forces benefited from operating checkpoints and providing additional security to homes, businesses, and offices, even as their own interests in forestry and fisheries in the region continued to thrive without disruption.[4]

Another set of explanations focus on underlying social, political, and economic instabilities that permitted violence to gain a local foothold: from the collapse of the patronage system after Suharto's fall (van Klinken 2001) to the shrinking business opportunities in the wake of the Asian financial crisis, and to land shortages, exacerbated by waves of immigration (Bartels 2000; Aragon 2001). Rising poverty hit hard the region undergoing rapid demographic transformation. Around Ambon City where one quarter of residents were recent immigrants, there was a perception that the immigrants were better businessmen, particularly in areas of trade and transportation, than the Ambonese they were displacing (see Tomagola, *Tempo*, Feb. 1, 1999). The trouble was compounded by the fact these immigrants were not party to informal local agreements about ownership and access. Contributing to rising tensions, too, were state policies that appeared to favor one religious group, Muslims, over Christians, or that did not go far enough to redress perceived imbalance. Critically, once the rioting began, the descent into violence was hastened by a decades long process of political centralization that undermined the position of local authorities and robbed institutions for dispute mediation, such as the inter-religious "*pela*" alliances, of their effectiveness (Laksono 2002; Bartels 2000).[5] The New Order regime imposed order by suppressing dissent and local conflict. After the short-lived Habibie administration attempted to reverse this process and delegate greater autonomy to the provinces, the lid came off, and when the security forces could not or would not contain it, mob violence proliferated.[6]

Between these two approaches, one focused on prime movers, the other on underlying causes, the line of inquiry I pursue seeks to understand how social upheaval created opportunities for "instigators" as conflict enveloped the broader segments of the Moluccan public. Scholars note that random and indiscriminate crowd violence is profoundly disorienting (Tambiah 1996). Patsy Spyer writes about "atmospherics," a climate of heightened suspicion and paranoia. In Maluku, the suffering, loss of life, and displacement created enormous uncertainty, fanned by rumors and threats both real and imagined, and driven by collective fear and anger. In the maelstrom, actions became unpredictable; mob violence induced more of it as the uncertainty it created penetrated deeper into public consciousness, trapping and affecting more people. By the same token, had the conditions exacerbating uncertainty somehow been reduced, conflict may have been contained with less devastation. This is not to say that the violence could have been prevented considering the resources made available to combatants by those outsiders who sought to gain from it; nor am I interested in minimizing the culpability of prime instigators. Rather, my contention—focusing on uncertainty—is merely that violence gained momentum as it undermined the conditions under which persons would ordinarily deliberate based on the predictable consequences of actions, deliberation that otherwise fosters community sensibilities and preserves "balance."

The concept of "balance," described in the introduction, derives from a collective capacity and willingness to negotiate differences and entertain various solutions to social dilemmas and enmities. Balance pertains to the ground from which people respond to challenges to sustain those relations and enable people to move through situations. In the epigraph to the chapter, it is evinced in the back and forth ruminations of Arthur Koestler's fictional protagonist Rubachov, a leading Soviet thinker and Party member, just after his imprisonment by Stalin, in the very fact he perceived a choice between the headlong pursuit of ideals on the one hand and taking action to ensure the quality of relationships on the other. Losing balance, or acquiring "motion," comes from setting aside concerns about individuals or relations. As orientations converge around particular causes, for instance, to right wrongs or to defend against foes (real or imagined), concern for others assumes value with respect to this common purpose. In the extreme, in the crucible of violence, certain forms of communalism may emerge predicated only on motion, for example, exacting revenge, creating the appearance of community without the mutual orientation and sociality actual ones demand.

How has communalism taken hold? If Moluccans shared much before the violence, they possessed little sense of shared identity, being divided politically, ethnically, religiously, by language, and by a lot of salt water. The most far-flung province in Indonesia, Maluku could be considered a unified place only in the fanciful discourse of official texts on culture (e.g., Upacara Maluku [DepDikBud 1985]), or as imagined in the empty vessel of the Maluku House exhibit at the Taman Mini theme park in Jakarta, a Disney-inspired creation celebrating the former New Order regime's vision of the nation. The reality of a Moluccan society was more an amalgam of lived communities, villages, and neighborhoods, constituted on the basis of proximity, interaction, and kinship, knit together, if only barely, by thin transportation, communication, and kin networks. Moluccans, it could be said, experienced the region selectively in journeys and in stories chronicling the movement of different peoples to villages, towns, and markets; and literally, this traveling public spread nascent civil society with them. Awareness of Maluku was instilled in the movement and mingling of ordinary people, people like themselves yet different, at once strangers and familiars sharing part of their journeys across town or the province. Traveling yielded civility premised on interdependence, given that routes were often impassable, journeys could be delayed, and transportation was unreliable. The relative safety of most casual encounters in turn fostered trust, encouraged tolerance, and enabled goodwill to accumulate, albeit slowly, given the reality that most neighborhoods and villages were divided into Christian and Muslim quarters and that it was merely necessary for persons from different backgrounds to get along. That Moluccans did so most of the time and for centuries despite differences and disagreements reflects more than mere tolerance. It evinces some perspicuity to seek alternatives to violent confrontation by turning to traditional institutions or, even after those lost much of their efficacy, to devise more novel solutions, including scapegoating and separation.

The violence that began in January 1999 ended this unfettered interfaith mingling. The mingling had served as evidence of the possibility of diverse civic life; but being shallow—conferring goodwill by not undermining it—it required constant affirmation. Once people could no longer extend trust in simple interactions, not knowing, for instance, where or when attack would come, goodwill dissipated. Five years later, while pitched battles have ended, with Muslims occupying most of the northern Leihitu peninsula on Ambon island, Christians controlling most of the southern Leitmur peninsula, and the city of Ambon remaining divided, continued bombing and sniping attacks in the border zones ensures that life in Central Maluku remains divided, even as many refugees in southeast Maluku and the new province of North Maluku have returned home and begun to restore some semblance of normalcy to their lives. Terror persists now—the latest round which began in April 2004 has left forty-one dead, and over 10,000 residents of Ambon have been forced to flee their homes—despite the absence of any attainable territorial objectives, in part, because neither side possesses an overwhelming advantage in numbers (though the arrival of Laskar Jihad in 2000 did put Christian forces on the defensive). Early on, in the first year of fighting, relative parity encouraged leaders on both sides to seek strategic advantages where they could. Indeed, those keen to participate in reconciliation efforts (and seen as unwilling to press advantages) were themselves abandoned or even threatened by followers seeking to advance their own political positions (Tomagola pers. comm.), conditions which made it easy for nefarious outside agents to exploit. And the sheer density of populations on the borders keeps the threat of attack high, especially in Ambon city. The dilemma currently is that even as continuing terror necessitates separation, the respective populations may not be separated enough to allow enmities to settle; yet, as that separation wears on, it also raises the obstacles to reconciliation.

I have argued that terror whatever the cause, whether sorcery or religious enmities, constricts the space in which people form and exercise moral judgments in everyday interactions. Without this space, terror begins to feel ordinary and people become, in a sense, tools of violence, serving its ends. To be sure, this myopia, an obscuring of vision, represents no moral failing. Rather, it is a consequence of a subtle shift in the ground of moral practice that eliminates opportunities for honest brokers or intermediaries to reach out, interact, and exchange with ethnic and religious others. Once those traditional venues were eliminated, the fog of fear settled in, permeating and changing people's moral bearings—a change most apparent as a consequence of shifts around margins and midpoints. Not enough Moluccans tried to negotiate differences or find alternatives to violence. Moral sensibilities were compromised sufficiently so that the reasonable choice in difficult situations was to turn one's back on the violence, to avoid confrontation with kin, for instance, who may have participated in riots, or to overlook the humanity of the other. As violence cast its shadow, the reference group for moral practice, in normal times more indeterminate, defined by whom one knew and elastic enough to accommodate nearly anyone became explicit and exclusive. Lines of humanity became inscribed in check points and no-man zones that divided and constrained people's daily movements; and, after the fact, these boundaries were recast in diverging historical trajectories, as propagandists distilled or essentialized communal differences from the flow of Moluccan experience that had once been more entwined. Terror enveloped people, compressing time and restricting its victims' capacity to assess safety and culpability independently, turning everyone into potential combatants or victims. Moreover, violence foreshortened people's horizon of moral possibility; it limited the reach of moral imagination just as fear, paradoxically, gave a vertiginous sense to religious identity, bringing that stamp to the fore of being. As religious identification was inflated, morality hemmed in within these narrowed religious boundaries no longer permitted people to see the suffering of religious others as their own. Failing to see the consequences of actions and inactions, people become inured or indifferent to harm. As the uncertainty terror created compelled people to restrict moral choices, not being tested by reaching out, the latitude for moral action became compressed and distorted, unraveling the delicate fabric that had been Moluccan civil society.

A Brief Chronology

Although there had been a number of small skirmishes in and around Ambon prior to January 19, the first signs of trouble began far away in Jakarta on November 22, 1998, with rioting between rival gangs of Muslim and Christian Ambonese security guards at a Chinese-owned gambling hall.[7] Under suspicious circumstances, fighting there led to the destruction of a nearby mosque, and in retaliation, Muslim youths, allegedly trucked into the neighborhood, burned over

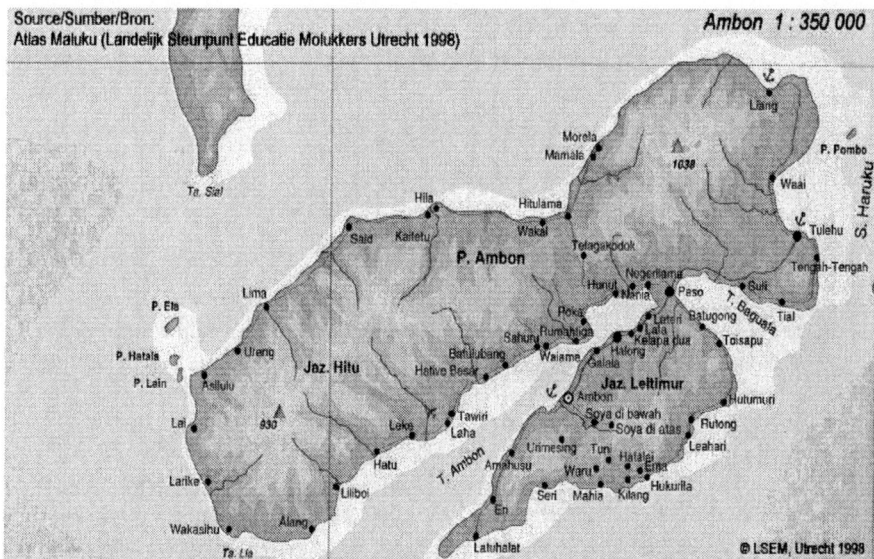

Figure 8.1 Ambon

twenty churches. Thirteen were killed in that attack. In the aftermath, many of the gang members, both Muslim and Christian, returned to Ambon. Eight days later and a thousand miles away, a Christian youth congress in Kupang, West Timor, concluded with an otherwise peaceful march to protest the church burnings in Jakarta. The march was hijacked when witnesses reported an unknown group of youths rampaged through an ethnically Bugis neighborhood in Kupang and destroyed a mosque. Violence then descended on Dobo, the central town in the Aru archipelago in southeast Maluku on January 14, leaving eight dead.

In Ambon, on January 19, hours after the altercation at the bus station described above, a large Muslim crowd led by outsiders, witnesses reported, descended on the Christian neighborhood of Batu Merah Dalam and burned it to the ground, egged on by shouts that the local mosque had been burned. Less than two hours later, a church and several homes were attacked in the Ambon City neighborhoods of Silale, Waihaong, and Jalan Baru. Nearby, Christian residents of Kudamati counterattacked, burning Butonese and Bugis-owned kiosks and pedicabs throughout the night, destroying Muslim homes in the center of the city, and spray-painting anti-Muslim and pro-*RMS* slogans where they went. The following day, Christian mobs destroyed over a hundred homes in the neighborhood of Batu Gantung, forcing some 240 Muslim families to flee to other Muslim kampungs. In retaliation, Muslim gangs destroyed the Christian villages of Benteng Karang and Telagakodok to the east of the city, killing as many as forty. Christians in the town of Passo, where the large Muslim mob had been confronted, then turned their ire on Muslims living nearby. Across Ambon Bay, a Bible camp retreat, on the grounds of Pattimura University, was attacked leaving six people dead. While not far from there, fighting between the Christian village of Hative Besar and the Muslim settlement of Kamari led to the demolition of 180 homes and a mosque in Kamari, forcing residents to flee to a nearby army base. By the end of the second day, all the major markets in Ambon city had been burned down and thousands were homeless.[8]

Fighting continued on January 22 when five Butonese were dragged out of a pickup truck, doused with gasoline, then set afire in Mangga Dua. After more violence in the village of Benteng, a Balinese elite strategic reserve soldier was killed, perhaps mistaken for an ethnic Bugis; soldiers then opened fire, killing one of the Christian youths. Two days later, on January 24, violence spread to the island of Manipa, and a week after that, between the third and fifth of February, fights broke out on Seram and on the island of Saparua. Up to this point, in all these battles, crowds faced off with *senjata rakitan* (homemade weapons)—including *parang* (machete), sticks, rocks, gasoline soaked rags, fish bombs, Molotov cocktails, and flaming arrows—while police and military largely stood by, unwilling or unable to intervene, claiming disingenuously that the post-Suharto emphasis on human rights prevented them from taking action for fear of future prosecution. In early February, however, in response to criticism, security forces did adopt shoot on sight orders to quell rioting. Thus began a steep escalation in death tolls. When fighting began on February 14, on Haruku Island, most of the two dozen victims were shot by members of the security forces, establishing a pattern of military and police excesses.

After a fitful calm, fighting returned to Ambon City on February 23, when several explosions and fire spread through Christian neighborhoods and residents responded by burning a mosque in Karang Panjang. Northeast in the Leihitu peninsula of Ambon island, police opened fire on a Muslim crowd attempting to respond to the burning of a Butonese settlement on the edge of the Christian village of Waai. The Muslim *raja* of neighboring Tulehu then pounded a mosque drum mobilizing a community "jihad" against any and all residents of Waai. By the end of the day, some twenty-eight people were dead. A week later, on March 1, 200 Christians from the village of Ahuru attacked a Muslim neighborhood in Batu Merah, killing several as they prayed—a theme repeated in accounts of similar attacks on both sides. (This violence was notable too for having involved a police officer whose house had been burned earlier in the day.) On March 6, police in civilian clothes reportedly opened fire on a group of Christians manning a barricade near the Silo church. And despite renewed peace efforts two days earlier, on March 10, the military killed five and wounded another thirty in the neighborhood of Benteng Atas. Soon after, crowds of up to a thousand on each side confronted one another in the vicinity of Airmata Cina, though marines managed to keep them separate.

So far, rioting had been limited to Ambon and the surrounding islands of Central Maluku. However, on March 31, fighting broke out in Tual, followed by Larat in the Regency of Southeast Maluku, fueled in part by the presence of refugees from Ambon and other affected areas. By the time peace was negotiated there (a peace that held) the death toll had reached 142, with some 13,000 forced out of their homes. Around Ambon, fighting abated for several months during the run up to the June 1999 national elections. But on July 27, rock throwing between rival camps led to renewed rioting. And violence erupted for the first time on August 18 in the newly established province of North Maluku between the migrant Makian and the indigenous populations in the sub-district of Kao on the island of Halmahera (Duncan forthcoming). While that fighting lasted only a few days, violence was reignited in October, this time leading to the expulsion of the entire Makian community and the destruction of their homes. In a familiar pattern, the Makian then fled to the neighboring islands of Ternate and Tidore, where violence in early November forced more than 12,000 (mostly Christians) to flee to Halmahera and North Sulawesi. Thousands more were displaced in Muslim-led attacks in southern and western Halmahera. In retaliation, Christians in Tobelo in northern Halmahera killed nearly 400 Muslims and destroyed their homes and mosques.

During this time, fighting intensified in Ambon. On September 10, troops opened fire, killing at least ten rioters near al-Fatah mosque. Thirty-seven people were killed in Ambon on November 26, one of the bloodiest days of the conflict in the city. On Seram, on December 3 and 4, near the district capital of Masohi, forty-two were killed. Then on December 12, riots spread to the island of Buru for the first time, and fighting escalated in Ambon, culminating in the destruction of the Silo Church.

The Tobelo massacre and continuing violence around Ambon fueled pro-Muslim demonstrations throughout the country. In Jakarta on January 7, more than 100,000 Muslims, including senior officials, marched to calls for a jihad. The fighting entered a new phase in May 2000 when some 3,000 Laskar Jihad militia arrived in Maluku, followed quickly by a succession of Muslim victories that effectively secured a corridor of Muslim hamlets into Ambon. On June 21, Muslim militia overran the police mobile brigade headquarters and armory on the outskirts of the city with apparent military support. In the aftermath of that attack, President Abdurrahman Wahid declared a state of civil emergency in the two devastated provinces, and in view of the bias of security forces, calls began for international peacekeepers. Throughout the month of July, the Laskar Jihad initiated attacks on the Christian villages of Waai, Poka, and Rumah Tiga and destroyed entirely the campus of Universitas Pattimura along with five other villages and neighborhoods around Ambon in the next several months. The pace of attacks slowed in August, coinciding with the introduction of the Joint Battalion (*Yon Gab*)—elite special forces troops from the army, navy, and air force—and by an apparent tactical shift by the Laskar Jihad to focus on consolidating areas under its control. Even after *Yon Gab* was withdrawn in November 2001, following accusations of bias against the Muslim militias, subsequent fighting was mostly limited to small skirmishes, raids from speed boats, bombings, and sniper incidents.

The Mailino II Peace Agreement was signed February 12, 2002, bringing a formal end to hostilities; and after some resistance, the Laskar Jihad movement was finally disbanded in October 2002, following the Bali nightclub terrorist bombing. In the last year, a few local leaders have been arrested, including two

Christian militia leaders, Alex Manuputty and Berty Loupatty, who were sentenced to three-year prison terms for their role in the violence. However, the radical cleric Jafar Umar Thalib, the leader of Laskar Jihad, who was arrested the previous May, was acquitted. Peace held throughout most of 2003 because Muslims and Christians largely occupied discrete territories. But the continuing problem of resettling tens of thousands of refugees, unremitting conflict in the Poso area in the nearby island of Sulawesi, and the latest round of violence in 2004 raises further uncertainty about the long-term future of civil society in the region.

Rumors and Uncertainty

I have argued that uncertainty exacerbated the duration, extent, and intensity of the conflict and contributed to the level of the destruction of Moluccan civil society. Uncertainty, manifest as an inability to assess and manage threats, was not simply a consequence of a failure of preparation. As Spyer observes (2002), setting up command posts and communication centers in the days leading up to the initial outbreak of violence may have actually hastened it, in a sense, by making it too easy to accede to calls for conflict. Preparations were a response to uncertainty; but individual efforts to reduce the odds of getting caught in the crossfire, in effect, raised uncertainty for everyone by doing little to quell the causes of conflict.

Uncertainty arose from not knowing. Within a short span of time of the onset of violence, ways of acquiring information had changed, as communications were interrupted and thousands were forced from their homes. The displaced and those receiving the displaced found themselves unable at times to distinguish real dangers from the noise or echoes of violence in stories of attacks and atrocities told. They had no way to ascertain, for instance, a stranger's propensity to exaggerate and, thus, had no way to put unconfirmed reports and accounts of violence in proper perspective. And displacement brought a surfeit of information, not a shortage. The retellings of events from different points of view gave vividness to violence to those who did not witness it; one family's loss became compounded by the losses of many. Moreover, because of the confusion around reports, single events or attacks became refracted and multiplied; the variations became accretions adding to the perceived scope and scale of violence. Threats appeared to come from everywhere at once, and exaggerated accounts became accepted truth. Like the practice of pounding rocks against metal poles to signal danger, the swirling stories and actual violence reinforced the sense of peril that compelled people to react as if all rumors were real. The specter of mob violence, figuratively and literally, changed conversations; it increased the furtive one-way dissemination of information, of details of where, when, who, and how attacks occurred, facilitated by "handie-talkies" (Aditjondro 2001). Given that it was more important to know and have unconfirmed insight than to be certain, people suspended standards of credulity that gave rumor (*kabar burung* or bird news) an ancillary status in ordinary times with respect to more reliable first-hand or authorized information sources.

As a consequence, close to the source, the information being trafficked tended to reinforce the need for caution by playing on uncertainty, amplifying it, and robbing threats of proportionality. However, down the chain of communication, the effect was different and less predictable. With sufficient volume and rapidity in the rate at which stories circulated, rumors could reach critical mass, encouraging persons not otherwise connected to events to act on them and incite violence (Tambiah 1996:290). They became disposed to violence. Spot fires thus ignited in distant places. The tragedy that beset Punky van den Broeke and his family in the Banda islands southeast of Ambon is illustrative of the confusion sown by misinformation. The story was reported by Iwan Setiawan in the August 13, 2000, edition of the Indonesian weekly magazine *Tempo* and relayed to me by a friend who had visited Banda shortly after the incident. On April 20, 1999, upon hearing rumors that a Christian soldier or police officer had beaten a Muslim man on a nearby island, a mob attacked and slaughtered most of the van den Broeke family. Up to this point, the small chain of the Banda Islands, which is predominantly Muslim, had experienced little of the mayhem plaguing Ambon and the surrounding islands. Not only was the response to the alleged assault massively disproportional to the purported cause, it was incongruous given that Punky and most of his family were Muslim. It must have come as some shock then when Punky learned of the mob's approach. Believing their anger was directed at him alone, he sent his family to hide in an empty house nearby while he hid on the beach. Unable to locate him, the mob found then killed his wife, mother, an aunt, and two daughters, sparing only a daughter and a son who was severely wounded in the attack. After Punky discovered the bodies of his family members, he confronted his attackers and asked that they kill him too; their frenzy spent, the mob dispersed instead. During the subsequent arrest and investigation of two dozen neighbors, it emerged that some had whispered doubts about the sincerity of Punky's religious convictions and that he was not Muslim enough. (Punky had converted to Islam, the religion of his wife's family two decades earlier.) This may have been a pretext, however. Punky's family owned a large nutmeg estate, perhaps the largest on the island of Banda Besar, and it is easily conceivable that ring leaders used the rumors and the alleged assault to mobilize support against the van den Broeke family to claim the estate for themselves.

Rumors' authors tend to be anonymous. Like the writers of the pamphlets that circulated in Ambon embellishing atrocities and exaggerating threats, that anonymity reduces incentives for discretion in the event deliberate fabrications are ever exposed. Rumors may originate as honest accounts of events, but the point is that they need not be. And there is no control for distortions. Without accountability, people need have little conviction of the truth of the stories they are reporting, and unless the deception comes to light no one is the wiser. In the ever-shifting terrain of communal violence, such deliberate distortions are Scud Missiles; cheap and indiscriminate, they clothe invective and give focus to more diffuse fears and enmity. Most significantly, everyone becomes implicated either for spreading them (or not stopping the spread) or for the repercussions.[9] Like whispering "fire" in a crowded room, among the accused the innocent have little opportunity for disavowing the deceit.

Willingness to believe was proportional to the need to know, for instance, what routes were safe, where food could be found, when and where attacks were occurring. Such information was gleaned from every source. Amidst the chaos, rumors more than filled the void left by the absence of other, more reliable information from newspapers, radio, or television. They created confusion about which versions were correct, and they spilled into mainstream sources, finding their way to reporters with no other way to catch fast-moving events (Aragon 2001:60). Some reporters representing partisan radio and newspapers, in turn, lent credibility to rumors of brutality committed by the other side. And these reports and rumors provided a narrative for the videos of violence that were widely circulated throughout the fighting (Spyer 2002). Some of the most pernicious of rumors (as against Punky) directed suspicions and accused co-believers of treachery, purporting to expose breaches in the borders that kept them safe from religious others. Such breaches were likely few and rarely led to identification of actual traitors, but merely to the people who, following the logic Koestler describes in his novel *Darkness at Noon*, might become traitors as a consequence of their inconsistent beliefs and opinions.[10] As the two sides separated, the danger from spies grew, fed by paranoia about the perviousness of boundaries and the impossibility of isolating threats. Suspected spies were executed for merely trading with the other side, implying the exchange of loyalties along with mere goods. They were executed summarily based on flimsy evidence of having friends or family in the other camp, having misplaced identity cards, or being unable or unwilling to account for movements, their bodies then publicly displayed as a warning to others. These periodic executions reminded others of the need to comport themselves in ways that would appear beyond suspicion. Yet sustained vigilance and conformity amidst all the accusations, rumors, and stories induced en masse moral fatigue, which inclined enough people, I believe, to accede to accusations of spies and traitors in their midst. Lacking support from others, protestations against excesses became too risky lest one become the target of those suspicions. In this way, fear robbed ordinary people of their ability to weigh for themselves the truth of suspicions and it made participation in calls to defend the faith and retaliation compulsory, the only sure route to survival. Finally, uncertainty created an environment in which the everyday tendentiousness of civil life, felt most acutely in the presence of religious others, could no longer be tolerated, not only because of the threat posed by the "other," but from one's own cobelievers. Religious identity, indexed by white (Muslim) and red (Christian) headbands, became a marker of safe and dangerous company, and the border zones between faiths became impossible.

Frenzy and Revenge

The various accounts of the fighting in Maluku convey the impression that every attack is connected to some previous one, that once triggered, violence begets more violence, forming a cycle of tit for tat until one side is vanquished, a ceasefire is imposed, or the fury behind it somehow dissipates. Scholars elsewhere remind us communal violence has a particular structure. Sustaining it are riot captains and local henchmen competing among themselves for the allegiance of followers, which they do by staying out in front of the arc of violence and depicting the restraint of others as cowardice. These captains draw from the energy of the crowd. Violence is not foisted on them, and followers are not simply reacting to the whims of leaders or, more blindly, to save themselves. Some participants, and it is not entirely predictable who, in the course of rioting engage in horrific actions, mutilating corpses or cannibalizing victims on their own initiative. In fact, some acts captured on film may have been intended for such public display. This frenzy, sufficient enough to overcome ordinary aversion and restraint, provides leaders leverage to respond to, elevate, and direct anger. But its source lies in the oscillation of crowd sentiment between fear and anger that collapses perspective and conflates local antipathies, grievances, and score settling with the broader aims of purging or extermination (Tambiah 1996:282–291). In the vortex of communal violence, moral perspective is distended. It is distended, too, by the fact that direct action offers a kind of cathartic release. Oddly, participating in a rampage does not presuppose individual indifference to suffering. Indeed, in communal contexts, collective rage displays righteous concern for those affected by it. And to the extent the response entails inflicting harm on another—a choice by no means inevitable—such retaliation may also be necessary to thwart further attack.

Out of the confusion of mob violence, motives emerge to focus, direct, and validate passions. Chief among these passions is revenge. Calling violence revenge (*membalas dendam*) serves to set the world right; it evens scores as it deflects attention from questions of personal responsibility for violence by assigning cause to the perfidies of others. Outrageous acts called revenge are thus rendered more ordinary, bearable, even mundane. And retaliation is detachable. By overshadowing the persons for whom the actions are taken, anyone can. There need be little proportionality between attack and retaliation, especially as many seek to exact it. Moreover, revenge offers a way to stake a claim to relationships with victims in the absence of other ties. Honoring them by avenging them, demonizing the other, and conducting armed attack, establishes membership; and such displays of fealty earns one a place among others. In this way, revenge narratives animate community of a sort, expressing a social proximity or affinity to victims. But unlike kin relations (real or fictive) and lived community membership, these implied ties are not generally reciprocal. When people make displays of belonging, they are projecting persona; interactions are only imagined and idealized, not lived. The cumulative effect of projecting and measuring identity may be mass movement, as distinct from community, particularly as those identities are forged in violence.

One of the consequences of mob violence is the threat anger poses to the angry. It hardens them, robbing participants of compassion. Seeing outsiders as deserving attack diminishes one's own humanity (Nussbaum 1994:423), leaving one vulnerable to the blandishments of would-be leaders whose political ambitions are served by hijacking and fanning popular rage for their own ends. The people suffering may be convinced that revenge is a solution and a way to attain justice whether it is or not, or that the targets are the right ones, but those ends are usually incidental to the sponsors of violence. In fact, more immediately, violence may have little to do with restoring well-being inasmuch as the experience of release from anger only requires the expression of anguish. It does not demand an equivalent or overwhelming response—a difference that makes forgiveness and, short of that, restraint possible. In ordinary times, but even around the edges of mob violence during periods of upheaval, somewhat unheroic restraint is evinced in the difference between mere rock throwing and fire bombing, between displays of unity and determination on one side and humiliation and extermination on the other. If heralds of revenge and their political sponsors were silenced, I am convinced, reasoning and deliberating would exercise a more cautionary influence.

Communalism and the Question of Calling

Muslim and Christian mobs have mobilized in violence; refugees of the same faith have united in the quest for safe havens. Yet such collectivities endure only as long as barriers to interreligious movement prevent alternatives and there remains nothing more to entangle people in the lives of others. They are communities by default, predicated on similarity. Ben Anderson refers to communities of identity (what I call communal movements) as "phantom communities" (1998:44) because convictions tend to ebb and flow. He notes that beliefs flow as people feel the need to compensate for being distant from perceived centers of faith (Anderson 1998:60)—or, I would add, as they feel under siege. Communal movements are not predicated on relationships; what relationships exist tend to be unfettered by obligations and negotiations. Being generic, undifferentiated, and predicated on shared identity, participants in communal movements are in a sense substitutable. People acting on the basis of shared faith alone have little on which to test and prove, as it were, the value of those relationships.

In other words, some sui generis expression of the value of relationships is missing from communalism. Such expressions can assume different forms. As described in this book, Maneo make community a value by disparaging it at times, making the act of living together appear as sacrifice. Though the sacrifice is in some ways contrived, nonetheless, individual contributions to community are thus made manifest. Contriving such value tests is certainly not unique to Maneo; it is central to all communities. For example, on a larger scale and with more at stake, the theme of sacrifice is central to the Athenian general Pericles's funeral oration, delivered at a critical phase in the Peloponnesian War. In his speech, as recounted by Thucydides, Pericles celebrates the valor in the soldier's decision to sacrifice his life (Thucydides 1951; Loraux 1986:101).[11] That decision, Pericles suggests, demonstrated the soldier's response to a higher calling to fight and die on behalf of his fellow Athenians. By portraying death as a sacrifice, he erases any doubt or wavering, even the possibility that a soldier's optimism about his chances of survival helped him take his first steps onto the battlefield. Consequently, the deaths of soldiers not only seem honorable but also intended by them: that they deliberately sacrificed themselves on behalf of fellow soldiers and citizens (the audience for the speech). This veneration is intended to instill, by example, the same motivation among the living, inculcating and habituating them and the broader citizenry to surrender their lives for each other if necessary. Channeling intention, however, poses enormous challenges, and strategies may never be entirely effective. Yet members or citizens at least can envision community through the heroism and commitment to them by others.

In contrast, in religious-based communal movements one can die for one's beliefs, and death can easily be represented as a measure of one's convictions, but it makes less sense to say one died for one's cobelievers. Partly this reflects the indiscriminate nature of the rioting and the fact most casualties of mob violence are bystanders not combatants. But it is also part of the logic that religious martyrdom does not presuppose a willingness to die for others.[12] What is emphasized in the context of communal violence is treachery, and even fallen combatants or soldiers tend to be perceived as victims of it. The difference is subtle; in communalism, only obliquely are orientations toward others asserted. Because attacks are opportunistic and justified as retaliation, actions become disconnected from the values of community. Persons may participate in mob violence as a way to assert membership; however, expressions of commitment on behalf of deceased others—the reason for revenge—does not occasion any real give and take. The absence of mutual orientations is evinced further in the ends of communal struggles. Zealots on both sides of the conflict in Maluku have expressed a desire to clear the region of nonbelievers, not only to make it safe, but to bring about a divine or perfect community in God's eyes. When Jafar Umar Thalib, the Laskar Jihad commander, for instance, ordered the execution of a Muslim rapist in Ambon, it was for violation of a covenant with God, not for any disruption the crime caused in relations among believers. Relations tend to be subordinate; members are asked to obey, not necessarily to forgive or accept each other. Tellingly, Islam and Christianity both mandate charity not empathy; empathy cannot be ordered. Yet certain social arrangements, not typical of communal movements, do foster the conditions for generating it—relations that differentiate members and make those characteristics meaningful, if not simply unavoidable. Such negotiations slow mobilization but animate civil life. If this distinction between communalism and community is overdrawn, and certainly communities can be deeply religious, the implication still holds: that there is nothing more to sacrifice for a movement that offers only a safe haven or represents a stage along the way towards spiritual perfection. Significantly, too, striving for conformity to realize these goals leads to a dilemma: When people cannot control the world, they shrink it and extend goodwill only to those meeting their criteria as deserving of it.

Finally, what does the emergence of "phantom" communities portend for the state and civil society? Fifty years since independence, Indonesia has emerged from under the yoke of dictatorship, only to be challenged by previously contained ethnic and religious antipathies, forces that were exacerbated by anti-democratic policies of forced integration and resource exploitation. The political vacuum now left at Indonesia's center, and the resulting competition among the retinue of former first-family members and hangers-on vying for a stake in the new regime, is permitting, even encouraging more bellicose reassertions of ethnic and religious identities. Citizens, in some ways legitimately, perceive that the political system is rigged against them and that such ritualized forms of popular participation as elections lack real import. By encouraging direct action, identity politics does represent an alternative. Yet direct participation also has allowed those struggling to keep their grip on power a tactical foothold, giving them opportunities to exploit local antipathies—a process made easier by Suharto's long suppression of conditions conducive to generating civil life. Looking back, it is apparent how little the New Order regime did to foster mutual regard in citizens' orientations: The state homogenized local traditions—sites where such community commitments could be enacted—and excised obligations from relationships. With less to challenge them, citizens of the New Order had less opportunity to test and thereby enhance the mutuality of relations around them. From this perspective, the post–New Order communal violence in Maluku represents, not the exception, but perhaps a scenario that will be played out differently throughout much of the archipelago, a payment for drawing down reserves of civility on a regional level and for stifling meaningful interfaith and interethnic participation in civil discourse. Feeling increasingly vulnerable to global market forces, many citizens seek to shield themselves behind utopian yearnings for forms of solidarity that fuel more virulent strains of sociality by projecting insecurities on social and religious others.[13] There is no denying that religiously homogenous communities may emerge from the rubble around Ambon and other sites of recurring violence. But diminishing diversity (measured against a more heterogeneous past) represents a concession to fear that impedes the ability of persons to see across lesser divides. In the end, hope lies in the public reaction to the violence, when the outrage provoked by thugs and extremists in Maluku inclines enough people to take chances to reach across social divides to test relations and expand the parameters of community.

Notes

1. The demographic balance between Muslims and Christians began to shift with state sponsored migration. Since the beginning of the Transmigration Program, between 75,000 and 100,000 migrants moved to Maluku, most to rural areas on the province's larger, less populated outlying islands (see Tandjung and Sutomo 1998; see also www.websitesrcg.com/ambon/Transmig.htm). Most migrants arrived from Java, the site of the most densely populated areas of the country. In addition, tens of thousands (mostly from the provinces of Sulawesi) migrated "spontaneously" to more densely populated areas of Maluku following kin and various business opportunities.

2. A sample of works on violence in Maluku in English include Aditjondro (2001), Bartels (2000), Burbandt (2000), Klinken (2001) Spyer (2002), Duncan (forthcoming), International Crisis Group Report No. 10 (2000), International Crisis Group Asia Report No. 31 (2002), and Human Rights Watch Report (1999). I have also relied on reports from Indonesian and non-Indonesian newspapers and magazines.

3. See Aditjondro (2001:115–116) for a discussion of the campaign to spread the misconception of *RMS* complicity. For reports of gassing Christian villages on July 24, 2000 (http://www.colorq.org/HumanRights/Maluku/weapons.htm).

4. With only one-third of the military's budget met by the state, the difference is made up in the aggressive pursuit of fisheries and forestry opportunities and, it is suspected, in selling bullets, leasing weapons, providing security for business. While state complicity is sometimes dismissed as "conspiracy," no observer of Indonesian politics can seriously discount the desperate criminal lengths Jakarta political elites would go to in order to secure their grip on power, even if their machinations did not dictate the precise course of events.

5. The policy (*Undang-Undang* No. 5), drafted in 1979, turned local village leaders into state servants and compromised their authority by making it contingent on the delivery of services and their place in the line of command (Bartels 2000:13).

6. One Christian resident of Ambon lamented, "Under Suharto, we went too long without a fire. If there had been even a little flame we could have put it out and learned from the experience. We don't know how to solve problems now" (Seth Mydans, *New York Times*, Feb. 9, 2000).

7. The chronology of events is well known, perhaps too much so, as partisans on both sides have sought to use it to advance the justness of their cause. The problem, too, is that events covered are selective, and lower-level conflicts are often ignored by sources (mostly press accounts). In addition, the way events are situated implies a line of causation that may be more apparent than real (Tambiah 1996). Despite the complications, establishing a bare outline serves to convey both the spread of violence and the growing sense of uncertainty it created.

8. Initially, in the first several weeks of the conflict, combatants made some distinction about targets. That is, Muslim migrants were attacked, not Ambonese Muslims; likewise, Catholics were spared fighting that targeted Protestant neighborhoods and churches. But this discrimination was short lived. As fires spread uncontrollably, so did the violence, as the smoke literally obscured visibility, especially around churches and mosques. Houses of worship had become rallying places and targets of attack, thus,

smoke near them were assumed by followers to be assaults and would bring supporters down from the hills to defend them, though on several occasions it was barrels outside that were burning.

9. A suspicious letter allegedly sent to the head of the Protestant Church in Halmahera in North Maluku urging followers to cleanse the region of all Muslims was one example of using falsehoods to provoke a violent response. As the story of the letter circulated, it helped spark new rounds of violence. Similarly, a Christian resident of the island of Haruku allegedly set fire to his own house in order to blame Muslims living nearby. And, according to new evidence, an attack in the Christian hamlet of Soya on April 28, 2002, killing twelve, was staged by Christian gangs and military supporters in a likely attempt to spark retaliation.

10. In Koestler's novel, Rubashov concedes to the logic of the accusations against him. "Without becoming aware of it, they [he and his interrogator Gletkin] had become accustomed to these rules for their game, and neither of them distinguished any longer between actions which Rubashov had committed in fact and those which he merely should have committed as a consequence of his opinions" (1963:222).

11. In her analysis of the funeral oration, Loraux (1986:101) writes: "What confers on the citizen's death its eminent valor does not belong to the order of actions or deeds.... Memory is to be attached more to the decision than to the act of the dead. Pericles shows that the essential thing lies not in the [act] but in the intention that motivates it. So the hierarchy of civic values must be assumed by each citizen, deciding in a lucid act of will that happiness lies in freedom, and freedom in courage." The eulogy, then, is addressed above all to a decision, which is a choice: and the dead have chosen between their lives and the city.

12. What is asserted is a cause, principle, or divine commandment that brought about the attack. A death, in turn, calls for a response, a retaliation, but it does not establish a calling. Even in the case of suicide bombings, the sacrifice is for the cause, less for one's coreligionist or fellow community member.

13. The faith-based communalism that appears to followers and many observers as a harder substratum of social life, below a more recent and ephemeral bureaucratic edifice of civil life, offers no substitute for the conditions that actually animate community interaction and mutuality. If presumed ties and similar experiences appear more real because they are so horrific, walking past check points, destroyed mosques or churches, crowds with red or white headbands, manifests merely the contours of community life, not the more enduring content.

Bibliography

Aditjondro, George J.
2001 "Guns, pamphlets and handie-talkies: how the military exploited local ethno-religious tensions in Maluku to preserve their political and economic privileges." In *Violence in Indonesia,* eds. Ingrid Wessel and Georgia Wimhöfer. Abera Verlag: Hamburg. Pp. 100–128.

Andaya, Leonard Y.
1993 *The World of Maluku: Eastern Indonesia in the Early Modern Period.* Honolulu: University of Hawaii Press.

Anderson, Benedict
1991 *Imagined Communities: Reflections on the Origin and Spread of Nationalism.* New York: Verso.
1998 *The Spectre of Comparisons: Nationalism, Southeast Asia and the World.* London: Verso.

Appadurai, Arjun
1986 "Introduction: commodities and the politics of value." In *The Social Life of Things: Commodities in Cultural Perspective*, ed. Arjun Appadurai. Cambridge: Cambridge University Press. Pp. 3–63.

Applebaum, Anne
2003 *Gulag: A History*. New York: Doubleday.

Aragon, Lorraine V.
1996 "Twisting the gift: translating precolonial into colonial exchanges in central Sulawesi, Indonesia." *American Ethnologist* (23):43–60.
2000 *Fields of the Lord: Animism, Christian Minorities, and State Development in Indonesia*. Honolulu: University of Hawaii Press.
2001 "Communal violence in Poso, Central Sulawesi: where people eat fish and fish eat people." *Indonesia* 72:45–79.

Arendt, Hannah
1959 *The Human Condition.* New York: Anchor.
1978 *The Life of the Mind.* San Diego: Harcourt Brace & Co.

Aristotle
1984 *The Complete Works of Aristotle*, ed. J. Barnes. Princeton: Princeton University Press.

Atkinson, Jane M.
1987 "The construction of an Indonesian minority religion." In *Indonesian Religions in Transition*, eds. Rita S. Kipp and Susan Rodgers. Tucson: University of Arizona Press. Pp. 171–186
1989 *The Art and Politics of Wana Shamanship*. Berkeley: University of California Press.
1990 "How gender makes a difference in Wana society." In *Power and Difference: Gender in Island Southeast Asia*, eds. Jane M. Atkinson and S. Errington. Stanford: Stanford University Press. Pp. 59–93.

Augustine
　1958 *City of God.* (An abridged version from the Translation by Gerald G. Walsh, Demetrius B. Zema, Grace Monahan, and Daniel J. Honan.) New York: Image Books.
　1963 *The Confessions of St. Augustine.* Trans. Rex Warner. New York: Mentor.
Baker, James N.
　1988 *Descent and Community in Tidore.* Doctoral dissertation. University of Michigan.
　1994 "Ancestral traditions and state categories in Tidorese village society." In *Halmahera and Beyond,* ed. Leontine E. Visser. Leiden: KITLV Press. Pp. 35–57.
Baran, Paul. A., and Paul M. Sweezy
　1966 *Monopoly Capital: An Essay On the American Economic and Social Order.* New York: Monthly Review Press. P. 14.
Barnard, Alan, and Anthony Good
　1984 *Research Practices in the Study of Kinship.* London: Academic Press.
Barnes, John A.
　1967 "Genealogies." In *The Craft of Social Anthropology,* ed. A. L. Epstein. London: Tavistock. Pp.101–127.
Barnes, R. H.
　1980 "Marriage, exchange and the meaning of corporations in eastern Indonesia." In *The Meaning of Marriage Payments,* ed. John Comaroff. New York: Academic Press. Pp. 93–124.
Bartels, Dieter
　1986 "Can the train ever be stopped again? Developments in the Moluccan community in the Netherlands before and after the hijackings." *Indonesia* 41:23–45.
　2000 "Your God is no longer mine." <http://www.geocities.com/ambon67.>
Battaglia, Debbora
　1990 *On the Bones of the Serpent: Person, Memory, and Mortality in Sabarl Island Society.* Chicago: University of Chicago Press.
　1992 "The body of the gift: memory and forgetting in Sabarl mortuary exchange." *American Ethnologist* 19(1):3–18.
　1993 "At play in the fields (and borders) of the imaginary: Melanesian transformations of forgetting." *Cultural Anthropology* 8(4):430–442.
Beidelman, Thomas O.
　1993 [1986] *Moral Imagination in Kaguru Modes of Thought.* Washington D.C.: Smithsonian Institution Press.
Bellah, Robert N.
　1973 "Introduction." In *Emile Durkheim on Morality and Society: Selected Writings,* ed. Robert N. Bellah. Chicago: University of Chicago Press. Pp. ix–lv.
Bercovitch, Eytan
　1994 "The agent in the gift: hidden exchange in inner New Guinea." *Cultural Anthropology* 9(4):498–536.
Bloch, Maurice
　1989 *Ritual, History and Power: Selected Papers in Anthropology.* London School of Economics Monographs on Social Anthropology No.58. London: Athlone.
Bloch, Maurice, and Jonathan Parry
　1989 "Introduction: money and the morality of exchange." In *Money and the Morality of Exchange,* eds. Jonathan Parry and M. Bloch. Cambridge: Cambridge University Press. Pp. 1–33.

Blum, Lawrence
  1987 "Particularity and responsiveness." In *The Emergence of Morality in Young Children*, eds. Jerome Kagan and Sharon Lamb. Chicago: University of Chicago Press. Pp. 306–337.
Boon, James A.
  1977 *The Anthropological Romance of Bali, 1597–1972: Dynamic Perspectives in Marriage and Caste, Politics and Religion*. Cambridge: Cambridge University Press.
  1990 "Balinese twins times two: gender, birth order, and "household" in Indonesia/Indo–Europe." In *Power and Difference: Gender in Island Southeast Asia*, eds. J. M. Atkinson and S. Errington. Stanford: Stanford University Press. Pp. 209–233.
Borgatti, Stephen P., and Martin G. Everett
  1992 "Notions of position in network analysis." In *Sociological Methodology*, ed. P. Marsden. London: Basil Blackwell. Pp. 1–35.
Borneman, John
  1996 "Until death do us part: marriage/death in anthropological discourse." *American Ethnologist* 23(2):215–235.
Boswell, James
  1993 *The Life of Samuel Johnson LL.D*. Chicago: Encyclopedia Britannica Inc. Great Books of the Western World, No. 41. Pp. 172, 182, 194.
Bourdieu, Pierre
  1977 *Outline of a Theory of Practice*. Trans. R. Nice. Cambridge: Cambridge University Press.
  1990 *The Logic of Practice*. Stanford: Stanford University Press.
  1997 "Marginalia: some additional notes on the gift." In *The Logic of the Gift: Toward an Ethic of Generosity*, ed. A. D. Schrift. New York: Routledge. Pp. 231–241.
Bowlin, John R., and Peter G. Stromberg
  1997 "Representation and reality in the study of culture." *American Anthropologist* 99(1):123–134.
Brenner, Suzanne
  1998 *The Domestication of Desire: Wealth, Women, and Modernity in Java*. Princeton: Princeton University Press.
Bubandt, Nils
  2000 "Conspiracy theories, apocalyptic narratives and the discursive construction of the 'violence in Indonesia'." *Antropologi Indonesia* 24(63):15–32.
Calhoun, Craig
  1995 *Critical Social Theory: Culture, History, and the Challenge of Difference*. Cambridge: Blackwell.
Carsten, Janet
  1995a "The substance of kinship and the heat of the hearth: feeding, personhood, and relatedness among Malays in Pulau Langkawi." *American Ethnologist* 22(2):223–241.
  1995b "The politics of forgetting: migration, kinship and memory on the periphery of the Southeast Asian state." *Journal of the Royal Anthropological Institute* (n.s.) 1:317–335.
  1997 *The Heat of the Hearth: The Process of Kinship in a Malay Fishing Community*. Oxford: Clarendon Press.

Carrier, James G.
 1995 *Gifts and Commodities: Exchange and Western Capitalism since 1700.* London: Routledge.
Chagnon, Napoleon A.
 1968 *Yanomamö: The Fierce People.* New York: Holt, Rinehart, and Winston.
Chatterjee, Partha
 1993 *The Nation and Its Fragments: Colonial and Postcolonial Histories.* Princeton: Princeton University Press.
Chauvel, Richard
 1990 *Nationalists, Soldiers and Separatists.* Leiden: KITLV Press.
Clamagirand, Brigitte
 1980 "Social organization of the Ema." In *The Flow of Life: Essays on Eastern Indonesia*, ed. James J. Fox. Cambridge: Harvard University Press. Pp.134–151.
Collier, Jane F.
 1988 *Marriage and Inequality in Classless Societies.* Stanford: Stanford University Press.
Collier, Jane F., and Michelle Z. Rosaldo
 1981 "Politics and gender in simple societies." In *Sexual Meanings: The Cultural Construction of Gender and Sexuality*, eds. Sherry B. Ortner and Harriet Whitehead. Cambridge: Cambridge University Press. Pp. 275–329.
Comaroff, Jean, and John Comaroff
 1991 *Of Revelation and Revolution: Christianity, Colonialism, and Consciousness in South Africa, Volume One.* Chicago: University of Chicago Press.
Comaroff, John
 1980 "Introduction." In *The Meaning of Marriage Payments*, ed. John Comaroff. New York: Academic Press. Pp. 1–47.
 1982 "Dialectical systems, history and anthropology: units of study and questions of theory." *Journal of Southern African Studies* 8(2):143–172.
Cook, John W.
 1999 *Morality and Cultural Difference.* New York: Oxford University Press.
Cooley, Frank L.
 1966 "Altar and throne in central Moluccan societies." *Indonesia* 11:135–156.
Das, Veena
 1995 *Critical Events: An Anthropological Perspective on Contemporary India.* Delhi: Oxford.
Davis, Natalie Z.
 1983 *The Return of Martin Guerre.* Cambridge: Harvard University Press.
de Certeau, Michel
 1984 *The Practice of Everyday Life.* Trans. S. Rendell. Berkeley: University of California Press.
DepDikBud (Departemen Pendidikan dan Kebudayaan)
 1985 *Upacara Tradisional yang Berkaitan dengan Peristiwa Alam dan Kepercayaan Daerah Maluku.* Departemen Pendidikan dan Kebudayaan Proyek Inventarisasi dan Dokumentasi Kebudayaan Daerah. Jakarta.
Derrida, Jacques
 1997 *Politics of Friendship.* Trans. by G. Collins. London: Verso.
Dewey, John
 1994 *The Moral Writings of John Dewey*, ed. James Gouinlock. Amherst, NY: Prometheus Books.

Dijk, Toos van, and Nico de Jonge
　1987 "The house on the hill: moieties and double descent in Babar." *Bijdragen tot de Tall-, Land-, en Volkenkunde* 143:54–104.
Dumont, Louis
　1983 *Affinity as a Value: Marriage Alliance in South India, with Comparative Essays on Australia*. Chicago: University of Chicago Press.
Duncan, Christopher R.
　1998 *Ethnic Identity, Christian Conversion and Resettlement among the Forest Tobelo of Northeastern Halmahera, Indonesia*. Doctoral Dissertation. Yale University.
　2003 "Untangling conversion: religious change and identity among the Forest Tobelo of Halmahera, Indonesia." *Ethnology* 42:307–322.
　Forthcoming "The other Maluku." *Indonesia*.
Duranti, Alessandro
　1993 "Intentions, self, and responsibility: an essay in Somoan ethnopragmatics." In *Responsibility and Evidence in Oral Discourse*, eds. Jane H. Hill and Judith T. Irving. New York: Cambridge University Press. Pp. 24–47.
Durkheim, Emile
　1953 "Individual and collective representations." In *Sociology and Philosophy*. Trans. D. F. Pocock. London: Cohen and West LTD. Pp. 1–34.
　1965 *The Elementary Forms of Religious Life*. [1915] New York: Free Press.
　1973 *Emile Durkheim on Morality and Society: Selected Writings*, ed. R. N. Bellah. Chicago: University of Chicago Press.
Edwards, Ian D., John Proctor, and Soedarsono Riswan
　1992 "Rain forest types in the Manusela National Park." In *Natural History of Seram*, eds. Ian D. Edwards, Alastair A. MacDonald and John Proctor. Andover, Hampshire: Intercept Ltd. Pp. 63–74.
Ellen, Roy
　1978 *Nuaulu Settlement and Ecology: An Approach to the Environmental Relations of an Eastern Indonesian Community*. Verhandelingen van het Koninklijk Instituut voor Taal-, Land- en Vokenkune 83. The Hague: Martinus Nijhoff.
　1988a "Foraging, starch extraction and the sedentary lifestyle in the lowland rainforest in central Seram." In *Hunters and Gatherers*, eds. T. Ingold, D. Riches, and J. Woodburn. Oxford: Berg. Pp. 117–134.
　1988b "Ritual, identity, and the management of interethnic relations on Seram." In *Time Past, Time Present, Time Future: Essays in Honor of P. E. de Josselin de Jong*, eds. David S. Moyer and Henri J. M. Claessen. Dordrecht, The Netherlands: Poris Publications. Pp. 117–135.
　1993 "Anger, anxiety, and sorcery: an analysis of some Nuaulu case material from Seram, Eastern Indonesia." In *Witchcraft and Sorcery in Southeast Asia*, eds. C. W. Watson and Roy Ellen. Honolulu: University of Hawaii Press. Pp. 81–97.
Errington, Shelly
　1989 *Meaning and Power in a Southeast Asian Realm*. Princeton: Princeton University Press.
Euripides
　1959 *The Phoenician Women*, eds. David Grene and Richard Lattimore. Translated with an introduction by Elizabeth Wyckoff. Chicago: University of Chicago Press. P. 84.
Evans-Pritchard, E. E.
　1951 *Kinship and Marriage Among the Nuer*. Oxford: Clarendon Press.

Ferguson, James
  1988 "Cultural exchange: new developments in the anthropology of commodities." *Cultural Anthropology* (3):488–513.
Firth, Raymond
  1951 *Elements of Social Organization*. London: Watts & Co.
  1964 *Essays on Social Organization and Values*. London: Athlone Press.
Flanagan, Owen
  1991 *Varieties of Moral Personality*. Cambridge: Harvard University Press.
Fortes, Meyer
  1949 *The Web of Kinship among the Tallensi*. London: Oxford University Press.
  1962 "Introduction." In *Marriage in Tribal Societies*, ed. Meyer Fortes. Cambridge: Cambridge University Press. Pp. 1–13.
  1969 *Kinship and the Social Order: The Legacy of Lewis Henry Morgan*. Chicago: Aldine.
  1983[1959] *Oedipus and Job in West African Religion*. Cambridge: Cambridge University Press.
Fox, James J.
  1980 "Introduction." In *The Flow of Life: Essays on Eastern Indonesia*, ed. James J. Fox. Cambridge: Harvard University Press. Pp.1–18.
Fox, Robin
  1967 *Kinship and Marriage: An Anthropological Perspective*. Harmondsworth: Penguin.
Freeman, John D.
  1961 "On the concept of the kindred." *Journal of the Royal Anthropological Institute* 91(2):192–220.
  1962 "The family system of the Iban in Borneo." In *The Developmental Cycle in Domestic Groups*, ed. J. Goody. Cambridge: Cambridge University Press. Pp. 15–52.
Frege, Gottlob
  1966[1892] *Translations from the Philosophical Writings of Gottlob Frege*. Oxford: Blackwell.
Freud, Sigmund
  1950 *Totem and Taboo: Some Points of Agreement Between the Mental Lives of Savages and Neurotics*. Trans. James Strachey. London: Routledge and Kegan Paul Ltd.
Fricke, Tom
  1990 "Elementary structures in the Nepal Himalaya: reciprocity and the politics of hierarchy in Ghale–Tamang marriage." *Ethnology* 29(2):135–58.
  1995 "Marriage change as moral change: culture, virtue, and demographic transition." Paper prepared for the 1995 seminar in honor of John Caldwell: The Continuing Demographic Transition. Session title: "Anthropology and demography: is the marriage working?" August 14–16, Canberra, Australia.
Fricke, Tom, W.G. Axinn, and A. Thornton
  1993 "Marriage, social inequality, and women's contact with their natal families in alliance societies: two Tamang examples." *American Anthropologist* 95(2):395–419.
Geertz, Clifford
  1973 *The Interpretation of Cultures*. New York: Basic Books.

Geertz, Hildred, and Clifford Geertz
    1964 "Teknonymy in Bali: parenthood, age-grading and genealogical amnesia." *Journal of the Royal Anthropological Institute* 94(2):94–106.
Gellner, Ernest
    1987 *The Concept of Kinship: And Other Essays on Anthropological Method and Explanation*. Oxford: Basil Blackwell.
George, Kenneth M.
    1996 *Showing Signs of Violence: The Cultural Politics of a Twentieth-Century Headhunting Ritual*. Berkeley: University of California Press.
Gibson, Thomas
    1988 "Meat sharing as a political ritual: forms of transaction versus mode of subsistence." In *Hunters and Gatherers*, eds. T. Ingold, D. Riches, and J. Woodburn. Oxford: Berg. Pp. 165–179.
Giddens, Anthony
    1986 *The Constitution of Society: Outline of the Theory of Structuration*. Berkeley: University of California Press.
Gilligan, Carol
    1984 "The conquistador and the dark continent: reflections in the psychology of love." *Daedalus* 113(3):75–95.
Goodenough, Ward H.
    1951 *Property, Kin, and Community on Truk*. Yale University Publications in Anthropology No. 46. New Haven: Department of Anthropology, Yale University.
    1956 "Componential analysis and the study of meaning." *Language* 32:195–216.
Goody, Jack
    1990 *The Oriental, the Ancient, and the Primitive*. Cambridge: Cambridge University Press.
Graeber, David
    1995 "Dancing with corpses reconsidered: an interpretation of Famadihana (in Arivonimamo, Madagascar)." *American Ethnologist* 22(2):258–278.
Gregory, Christopher A.
    1982 *Gifts and Commodities*. London: Academic Press.
Grzimek, Benno R. O.
    1991 *Social Change on Seram: A Study of Ideologies of Development in Eastern Indonesia*. Doctoral Dissertation. University of London.
Gudeman, Stephan
    1992 "Markets, models and morality." In *Contesting Markets: Analyses of Ideology, Discourse and Practice*, ed. Roy Dilley. Edinburgh: Edinburgh University Press. Pp. 279–293.
Habermas, Jurgen
    1990 *Moral Consciousness and Communicative Action*. Trans. C. Lenhardt and S. W. Nicholsen. Cambridge: MIT Press.
    1991 *The Structural Transformation of the Public Sphere*. Trans. Thomas Burger Cambridge: MIT Press.
Hagen, James M.
    1995 "Lost but not forgotten." Paper presented at the 94th Annual Meeting of the American Anthropological Association, Washington, D.C.
    1997 "'Read all about it': the press and the rise of national consciousness in early twentieth-century Dutch East Indies society." *Anthropological Quarterly* 70(3):107–136.

Hayes, Adrian C., Deny Hidaati, Herry Yogaswara, Andy Zaelany
   1999 *Population and Environment Issues in Maluku: The Case of Western and Northern Seram*. PPT-LIPPI and the Demography Program, Research School of Social Sciences, Australian National University.
Hefner, Robert W.
   1993 "Introduction: world building and the rationality of conversion." In *Conversion to Christianity: Historical and Anthropological Perspectives on a Great Transformation*, ed. Robert W. Hefner. Berkeley: University of California Press. Pp. 3–44.
   2000 *Civil Islam: Moslems and Democratization in Indonesia*. Princeton: Princeton University Press.
Held, G. J.
   1957 *The Papuas of Waropen*. Koninklijk Instituut voor Taal-, Land-, en Volkenkunde 2. The Hague: Martinus Nijhoff.
Herzfeld, Michael
   1995 "It takes one to know one: collective resentment and mutual recognition among Greeks in local and global contexts." In *Counterworks: Managing the Diversity of Knowledge*, ed. Richard Fardon. London: Routledge. Pp. 124–142.
Hicks, David
   1987 "Space, motion, and symbol in Tetum religion." In *Indonesian Religions in Transition*, eds. Rita S. Kipp and Susan Rodgers. Tucson: University of Arizona Press. Pp. 71–97.
Hirshfeld, Lawrence A.
   1986 "Kinship and cognition: genealogy and the meaning of kinship terms." *Current Anthropology* 27(3):217–229.
Homans, George C., and David M. Schneider
   1955 *Marriage, Authority, and Final Causes: A Study of Unilateral Cross-Cousin Marriage*. New York: Free Press.
Hoskins, Janet
   1987 "The headhunter as hero: local traditions and their reinterpretation in national history." *American Ethnologist* 14(4):605–622.
   1993 *The Play of Time: Kodi Perspectives on Calendars, History, and Exchange*. Berkeley: University of California Press.
Howell, Signe
   1989 "Of persons and things: exchange and valuables among the Lio of eastern Indonesia." *Man* (n.s.) 24:419–438.
Human Rights Watch
   1999 "Report on violence in Ambon." March 1999, Vol. 11, No.1.
Huntington, Richard, and Peter Metcalf
   1979 *Celebrations of Death: The Anthropology of Mortuary Ritual*. Cambridge: Cambridge University Press.
International Crisis Group
   2000 "Indonesia: overcoming murder and chaos in Maluku." Report No. 10, Jakarta/Brussels, December 19, 2000.
   2002 "Indonesia: the search for peace in Maluku." Asia Report No. 31, Jakarta/Brussels, February 2002.
Jameson, Fredric
   1981 *The Political Unconscious: Narrative as a Socially Symbolic Act*. Ithaca: Cornell University Press.

Johnson, Mark
    1993 *Moral Imagination: Implications of Cognitive Science for Ethics*. Chicago: University of Chicago Press.

de Josselin de Jonge, P. E.
    1980 "The concept of the field of ethnological study." In *The Flow of Life: Essays on Eastern Indonesia*, ed. J. J. Fox. Cambridge: Harvard University Press. Pp. 317–326.

Just, Peter
    2001 *Dou Donggo Justice: Conflict and Morality in an Indonesian Society*. Lanham, ML: Rowman & Littlefield.

Kahin, George M.
    1961 *Nationalism and Revolution in Indonesia*. Ithaca: Cornell University Press.

Kastor, Rustam
    2000 *Fakta, data dan analisa konspirasi politik RMS dan Kristen menghancurkan umat Islam di Ambon-Maluku*. Yogyakarta: Wihdah Press.

Keane, John
    1998 *Civil Society: Old Images, New Visions*. Stanford: Stanford University Press.

Keane, Webb
    1994 "The value of words and the meaning of things in eastern Indonesian exchange." *Man* 29(3):605–629.
    1997a *Signs of Recognition: Power and Hazards of Representation in an Indonesian Society*. Berkeley: University of California Press.
    1997b "Knowing one's place: national language and the idea of the local in Eastern Indonesia." *Cultural Anthropology* 12(1):37–63.
    1997c "From fetishism to sincerity: on agency, the speaking subject, and their historicity." *Comparative Study of Society and History* 39(4):674–693.
    1998 "Money is no object: materiality, desire, and modernity in an Indonesian society." In *Regime of Value: Materiality and Modernity*, ed. F. R. Meyers. Santa Fe, NM: School of American Research Press.
    1999 "The materiality and locality of everyday lives: a review essay." *Indonesia* 68:178–186.

Keeler, Ward
    1987 *Javanese Shadow Plays, Javanese Selves*. Princeton: Princeton University Press.

Kelly, Raymond C.
    1977 *Etoro Social Structure: A Study in Structural Contradiction*. Ann Arbor: University of Michigan Press.
    1993 *Constructing Inequality: The Fabrication of a Hierarchy of Virtue Among the Etoro*. Ann Arbor: University of Michigan Press.

Kipp, Rita S.
    1984 "Terms for kith and kin." *American Anthropologist* 86:905–26.
    1990 *The Early Years of a Dutch Colonial Mission: The Karo Field*. Ann Arbor: University of Michigan Press.
    1993 *Dissociated Identities: Ethnicity, Religion, and Class in an Indonesian Society*. Ann Arbor: University of Michigan Press.

Kipp, Rita S., and Susan Rogers
    1987 "Introduction: Indonesian religions in society." In *Indonesian Religions in Transition*, eds. Rita S. Kipp and Susan Rodgers. Tucson: University of Arizona Press. Pp. 1–31.

van Klinken, Gerry
　2001 "The Maluku wars: bringing society back in." *Indonesia* 71:1–26.
Knight, Frank H.
　1921 *Risk, Uncertainty, and Profit*. Houghton Mifflin Company. Library of Economics and Liberty. 26 May 2005. <http://www.econlib.org/library/Knight/knRUP1.html.>
Koestler, Arthur
　1963 *Darkness at Noon*. Trans. Daphne Hardy. New York: Macmillan.
Kopytoff, Igor
　1986 "The cultural biography of things: commoditization as process." In *The Social Life of Things: Commodities in Cultural Perspective*, ed. A. Appadurai. Cambridge: Cambridge University Press. Pp. 64–91.
Laksono, P. M.
　2002 "We are all one: how custom overcame religious rivalry in Southeast Maluku." *Inside Indonesia*, 70 (April–June).
Lambek, Michael
　1993 *Knowledge and Practice in Mayotte: Local Discourses of Islam, Sorcery, and Spirit Possession*. Toronto: University of Toronto Press.
Latinis, Kyle
　2000 "The development of subsistence system models for island Southeast Asia and Near Oceania." *World Archeology* 32(1):41–67.
Leach, Edmund R.
　1965 *Political Systems of Highland Burma: A Study of Kachin Social Structure*. Boston: Beacon Press.
　1971 *Rethinking Anthropology*. London: Athlone Press.
Lévi-Strauss, Claude
　1960 "On manipulated sociological models." *Bijdragen tot de Taal-, Land-, en Volkenkunde* 116:45–54.
　1963 *Totemism*. Trans. Rodney Needham. Boston: Beacon Press.
　1969 *The Elementary Structures of Kinship*. Trans. J. H. Bell and J. R. von Sturmer. Boston: Beacon Press.
　1973 *Tristes Tropiques*. Trans. J. Weightman and D. Weightman. New York: Simon and Schuster.
Levinas, Emmanuel
　1996 *Basic Philosophical Writings*, eds. Adriaan T. Peperzak, Simon Critchley, and Robert Bernasconi. Bloomington: University of Indiana Press.
Levine, Donald N.
　1995 *Visions of the Sociological Tradition*. Chicago: University of Chicago Press.
Li, Tania M.
　1999 "Marginality, power, and production: analyzing upland transformations." In *Transforming the Indonesian Uplands*, ed. Tania M. Li. Amsterdam: Harwood. Pp. 1–44.
Loraux, Nicole
　1986 *The Invention of Athens: The Funeral Oration in the Classical City*. Trans. Alan Sheridan. Cambridge, MA: Harvard University Press.
Lounsbury, Frank G.
　1962 "Review of 'Structure and sentiment: a test case in social anthropology,' by Rodney Needham." *American Anthropologist* 64:1302–1310.

Lucretius
    1946 *On the Nature of Things*. Trans. Charles E. Bennett. New York: Walter J. Black Inc.
Martodirdjo, H. S.
    1994 "Organisasi sosial orang Tugutil di Halmahera." In *Halmahera and Beyond*, ed. Leontine E. Visser. Leiden: KITLV Press. Pp. 115–137.
Marx, Karl
    1977 *Karl Marx: Selected Writings*, ed. D. McLellan. Oxford: Oxford University Press.
MacIntyre, Alisdair
    1984 *After Virtue: A Study in Moral Theory*. Notre Dame: University of Notre Dame Press.
Mandelstam, Nadezhda
    1978 *Hope Against Hope: A Memoir*. Trans. Max Hayward. New York: Atheneum.
Mauss, Marcel
    1967 *The Gift: Forms and Functions of Exchange in Archaic Societies*. Trans. I. Cunnison. New York: W.W. Norton.
McKinnon, Susan
    1991 *From a Shattered Sun: Hierarchy, Gender, and Alliance in the Tanimbar Islands*. Madison: University of Wisconsin Press.
McVey, Ruth T.
    1965 *The Rise of Indonesia Communism*. Ithaca: Cornell.
Meillasoux, Claude
    1984 *Maidens, Meal, and Money: Capitalism and the Domestic Community*. Cambridge: Cambridge University Press.
Miller, Daniel
    1995 "Consumption and commodities." *Annual Review of Anthropology*. (24):141–61.
Milne, A. A.
    1928 *The House at Pooh Corner*. Methuen. P. 39.
Munn, Nancy
    1977 "The spatiotemporal transformation of Gawa canoes." *Journal de la Société des Océanistes* 33(54–55):39–53.
    1992[1986] *The Fame of Gawa: A Symbolic Study of Value Transformation in a Massim (Papua New Guinea) Society*. Durham: Duke University Press.
Murdock, George P.
    1960 *Social Structure in Southeast Asia*. Chicago: Quadrangle.
Needham, Rodney
    1962 *Structure and Sentiment: A Test Case in Social Anthropology*. Chicago: University of Chicago Press.
    1971 "Remarks on the analysis of kinship and marriage." In *Rethinking Kinship and Marriage*, ed. R. Needham. London: Tavistock. Pp. 1–34.
Nettle, Daniel, and Robin I. M. Dunbar
    1997 "Social markers and the evolution of reciprocal exchange." *Current Anthropology* (38):93–99.
Nietzsche
    1966 *Thus Spoke Zarathustra*. Trans. Walter Kaufmann. New York: Penguin Books
Noricks, Jay
    1989 "The ethnographer as detective: solving the puzzle of Niutao land tenure

rules." In *Culture, Kin, and Cognition in Oceania: Essays in Honor of Ward H. Goodenough*, eds. Mac Marshall and John Caughey. Washington, D.C.: Special Publication of the American Anthropological Association, No. 25. Pp. 43–54.

Nussbaum, Martha C.
1986 *The Fragility of Goodness: Luck and Ethics in Greek Tragedy and Philosophy*. Cambridge: Cambridge University Press.
1990 *Love's Knowledge: Essays on Philosophy and Literature*. Oxford: Oxford University Press.
1994 *The Therapy of Desire: Theory and Practice in Hellenistic Ethics*. Princeton: Princeton University Press.

Opler, Morris E.
1979[1936] "An interpretation of ambivalence of two American Indian tribes." In *Reader in Comparative Religion: An Anthropological Approach*, eds. William A. Lessa and Evon Z. Vogt. New York: Harper & Row. Pp.382–392.

Ortner, Sherry B.
1997 "Fieldwork in the postcommunity." *Anthropology and Humanism* 22(1):61–80.

Ortner, Sherry B., and H. Whitehead
1981 "Introduction: an accounting for sexual meanings." In *Sexual Meanings: The Cultural Construction of Gender and Sexuality*, eds. S. Ortner and H. Whitehead. Cambridge: Cambridge University Press. Pp. 1–27.

Padgett, John F., and Christopher K. Ansell
1993 "Robust action and the rise of the Medici, 1400–1434." *American Journal of Sociology* 98(6):1259–1319.

Pannell, Sandra
1990 "'Now we follow our father': Christianity, colonialism, and cultural transformation on the island of Damer, Maluku Tengarra." *Cakalele, Maluku Research Journal* 1:27–46.

Parmentier, Richard
1987 *The Sacred Remains: Myth, History and Polity in Belau*. Chicago: University of Chicago Press.

Parry, Jonathan
1989 "On the moral perils of exchange." In *Money and the Morality of Exchange*, eds. Jonathan Parry and Maurice Bloch. Cambridge: Cambridge University Press.

Pauwels, Simonne
1994 "Sibling relations and (in)temporality: toward a definition of the House (Eastern Indonesia)." In *Halmahera and Beyond: Social Science Research in the Moluccas*, ed. Leontine E. Visser. Leiden: KITLV Press. Pp. 79–96.

Peletz, Michael G.
1988 *A Share of the Harvest: Kinship, Property, and Social History Among the Malays of Rembau*. Berkeley: University of California Press.
1995 "Kinship studies in late twentieth-century anthropology." In *Annual Review of Anthropology* 24:343–372.

Peterson, Jean T.
1984 "Cash, consumerism, and savings: economic change among the Agta foragers of Luzon, Philippines." In *Research in Economic Anthropology, Vol. 6*, ed. B. Isaac. Greenwich, CT: JAI Press.

Plato
1974 *The Republic*. Trans. G. M. A. Grube. Indianapolis: Hackett Publishing Co.

Putuhena, Husni M.
  1999 *Tragedi Kemanusiaan dalam Kerusuhan di Maluku: Sebuah Prosesi Ulang Sejarah Masa Lalu*. Ambon: np.
Radcliffe–Brown, A. R.
  1965 *Structure and Function in Primitive Society*. New York: The Free Press.
Rafael, Vincente L.
  1987 "Confession, conversion, and reciprocity in early Tagolog colonial society." *Comparative Studies in Society and History* (29):320–339.
Rawls, John
  1971 *A Theory of Justice*. Cambridge: Harvard University Press.
Rappaport, Roy A.
  1979 *Ecology, Meaning, and Religion*. Berkeley: North Atlantic Books.
Ricoeur, Paul
  1970 *Freud and Philosophy: An Essay on Interpretation*. Trans. Denis Savage. New Haven: Yale University Press.
  1973 "The critique of religion." *Union Seminary Quarterly Review* (28)205–212.
  1992 *Oneself as Another*. Trans. Kathleen Blamey. Chicago: University of Chicago Press.
Robbins, Joel
  1994 "Equality as a value: ideology in Dumont, Melanesia and the West." *Social Analysis* 36:21–70.
  1998 "Becoming sinners: Christianity and desire among the Urapmin of Papua New Guinea." *Ethnology* 37(4):299–316.
  2001 "Secrecy and the sense of an ending: narrative, time, and everyday millenarianism in Papua New Guinea and in Christian fundamentalism." *Comparative Study of Society and History* (43):525–551.
Robbins, Joel, and David Akin
  1998 "An introduction to Melanesian currencies: agency, identity, and social reproduction." In *Money and Modernity: State and Local Currencies in Melanesia*, eds. David Akin and Joel Robbins. Pittsburgh: University of Pittsburgh Press. Pp. 1–40.
Rorty, Richard
  1979 *Philosophy and the Mirror of Nature*. Princeton: Princeton University Press.
  1989 *Contingency, Irony, and Solidarity*. Cambridge: Cambridge University Press.
  1991 *Objectivity, Relativism, and Truth*. Cambridge: Cambridge University Press.
Rosaldo, Renato
  1980 *Ilongot Headhunting, 1883–1974: A Study in Society and History*. Stanford: Stanford University Press.
  1989 *Culture and Truth: The Remaking of Social Analysis*. Boston: Beacon Press.
Rubin, Gayle
  1975 "The traffic in women: notes on the 'political economy of sex'." In *Toward an Anthropology of Women*, ed. Rayna R. Reiter. New York: Monthly Review Press. Pp. 157–210.
Sachse, F. J. P.
  1922 *Seran*. Mededeelingen, Encyclopædisch Bureau, Aflevering XXIX. Weltevreden: G. Kolff & Co.
Sacks, Oliver
  1970 *The Man Who Mistook His Wife for a Hat*. New York: Summit Books.

Sahlins, Marshall
   1965 "On the ideology and composition of descent groups." *Man* 65:104–107.
   1972 *Stone Age Economics*. Chicago: Aldine-Atherton.

Scheffler, Harold W., and Floyd G. Lounsbury
   1971 *A Study in Structural Semantics: The Siriono Kinship System*. New Jersey: Prentice Hall.

Schieffelin, Bambi B.
   1990 *The Give and Take of Everyday Life: Language Socialization of Kaluli Children*. Cambridge: Cambridge University Press.

Schneider, David
   1965 "Some muddles in the models: or, how the system really works." In *The Relevance of Models for Social Anthropology*, ed. M. Banton. A.S.A. Monographs 1. London: Tavistock. Pp. 25–85.
   1980 *American Kinship: A Cultural Account*. Chicago: University of Chicago Press.
   1984 *A Critique of the Study of Kinship*. Ann Arbor: University of Michigan Press.

Scott, James C.
   1976 *The Moral Economy of the Peasant*. New Haven: Yale University Press.
   1998 *Seeing Like a State*. New Haven: Yale University Press.

Setiawan, Iwan
   2000 "Punky dan kebun pala pembawa maut." *Tempo* August 13.

Sewell, William
   1992 "A theory of structure: duality, agency, and transformation." *American Journal of Sociology* 98(1):1–29.

Sherman, George D.
   1990 *Rice, Rupees, and Ritual: Economy and Society among the Samosir Batak of Sumatra*. Stanford: Stanford University Press.

Shweder, Richard A., Manamohan Mahapatra, and Joan G. Miller
   1987 "Culture and moral development." In *The Emergence of Morality in Young Children*, eds. Jerome Kagan and Sharon Lamb. Chicago: University of Chicago Press. Pp. 1–83.

Simmel, Georg
   1950 *Sociology of Georg Simmel*. Trans. and ed. K. H. Wolff. Glencoe: Free Press.

Smith, DeVerne R.
   1981 "Palauan siblingship: a study in structural complementarity." In *Siblingship and Oceania: Studies in the Meaning of Kin Relations*, ed. Mac Marshall. Association for Social Anthropology in Oceania Monograph no. 8. Lanham, Md.: University Press of America. Pp. 225–273.

Smith, R. C.
   1995 "The gift that wounds: charity, the gift economy and social solidarity in indigenous Amazonia." Paper delivered at Forest Ecosystems in the Americas: Community Management and Sustainability. Univ. of Wisconsin, Feb. 3–4, 1995.

Sophocles
   1996–2000 *Oedipus the King*. Trans. by F. Storr. The Internet Classics Archive. http://classics.mit.edu//Sophocles/oedipus.html.

Spyer, Patricia
   2000 *The Memory of Trade: Modernity's Entanglements on an Eastern Indonesian Island*. Durham: Duke University Press.
   2002 "Fire without smoke and other phantoms of Ambon's violence: media effects, agency and the work of imagination." *Indonesia* 74:21–36.

Stokhof, W. A. L.
  1981 "Holle lists: vocabularies in languages of Indonesia, vol. 3/1. Southern Moluccas; Central Moluccas: Seram (I)." *Pacific Linguistics*. Series D, no. 35.
Strathern, Marilyn
  1984 "Subject or object? women and the circulation of valuables in Highlands New Guinea." In *Women and Property, Women as Property*, ed. Renee Hirschon, London: Croom Helm. Pp. 159–78.
  1987 "Introduction." In *Dealing with Inequality: Analyzing Gender Relations in Melanesia and Beyond*, ed. Marilyn Strathern. Cambridge: Cambridge University Press. Pp. 1–32.
  1988 *The Gender of the Gift: Problems with Women and Problems with Society in Melanesia*. Berkeley: University of California Press.
Strauss, Leo
  1964 *The City and Man*. Chicago: Rand McNally.
Tambiah, Stanley
  1996 *Leveling Crowds: Ethnonationalist Conflicts and Collective Violence in South Asia*. Berkeley: University of California Press.
Tandjung, Ichwan R., and Haryoto Sutomo
  1998 *Updated Tables for People, Land, and Sea: Development Challenges in Eastern Indonesia*. PPT-LIPPI and Demography Program, Research School of Social Sciences, Australian National University.
Taylor, Charles
  1989 *Sources of the Self: The Making of the Modern Identity*. Cambridge: Harvard University Press.
  1995 *Philosophical Arguments*. Cambridge, MA: Harvard University Press.
Thomas, Nicholas
  1991 *Entangled Objects: Exchange, Material Culture, and Colonialism in the Pacific*. Cambridge, MA: Harvard University Press.
Thucydides
  1951 *The Complete Writings of Thucydides: The Peloponnesian War*. New York: Random House.
Timofeyev, Lev
  2001 "Deep in the woods: Solzhenitsyn, a new book, and the new Russia" (interview with David Remnick). *The New Yorker* August 6, 2001
Toulmin, Stephan
  1990 *Cosmopolis: The Hidden Agenda of Modernity*. Chicago: University of Chicago Press.
Traube, Elizabeth G.
  1986 *Cosmology and Social Life: Ritual Exchange Among the Mambai of East Timor*. Chicago: University of Chicago Press.
  1989 "Obligations to the source: complementarity and hierarchy in an eastern Indonesian society." In *The Attraction of Opposites: Thought and Society in the Dualistic Mode*, ed. D. Maybury-Lewis and U. Almagor. Ann Arbor: University of Michigan Press. Pp. 117–141.
Trawick, Margaret
  1990 *Notes on Love in a Tamil Family*. Berkeley: University of California Press.
Tsing, Anna L.
  1993 *In the Realm of the Diamond Queen: Marginality in an Out-of-the-way Place*. Princeton: Princeton University Press.

Turnbull, Colin M.
   1972 *The Mountain People*. New York: Simon and Schuster.
Turner, Terrence
   1979 "The Gê and Bororo societies as dialectical systems." In *Dialectical Societies: The Gê and Bororo of Central Brazil*, ed. D. Maybury-Lewis. Cambridge, MA: Harvard University Press. Pp. 147–178.
Turner, Victor
   1969 *The Ritual Process: Structure and Anti-Structure*. Ithaca: Cornell University Press.
Tuzin, Donald
   1997 *The Cassowary's Revenge: The Life and Death of Masculinity in a New Guinea Cult*. Chicago: University of Chicago Press.
Valeri, Valerio
   1975–76 "Alliances et échanges matrimoniaux à Seram Central (Moluques)." *L'Homme* 15(3-4):83–107; 16(1):125–149.
   1980 "Notes on the meaning of marriage prestations among the Huaulu of Seram." In *The Flow of Life: Essays on Eastern Indonesia*, ed. J. Fox. Cambridge, MA: Harvard University Press. Pp. 178–192.
   1989 "Reciprocal centers: the Siwa/Lima system in the central Moluccas." In *The Attraction of Opposites: Thought and Society in the Dualistic Mode*, eds. D. Maybury-Lewis and U. Almagor. Ann Arbor: University of Michigan Press. Pp. 117–141.
   1990a "Autonomy and heteronomy in the Kahua ritual: a short meditation on Huaulu society." In *Rituals and Socio-cosmic Order in Eastern Indonesian Societies*, eds. C. Barraud and J. D. M. Platenkamp. *Bijdragen tot de Taal-, Land-, en Volkenhunde* 146:56–73.
   1990b "Both nature and culture: reflections on menstrual and parturitional taboos in Huaulu (Seram)." In *Power and Difference: Gender in Island Southeast Asia*, eds. J. Atkinson and S. Errington. Stanford: Stanford University Press. Pp. 235–272.
   1990c "Constitutive history: genealogy and narrative in the legitimation of Hawaiian Kingship." In *Culture Through Time: Anthropological Approaches*, ed. Emiko Ohnuki-Tierney. Stanford: Stanford University Press. Pp.154–192.
   1994a "'Our ancestors spoke little:' knowledge and social forms in Huaulu." In *Halmahera and Beyond: Social Science Research in the Moluccas*, ed. L. Visser. Leiden: KITLV Press. Pp. 195–212.
   1994b "Buying women but not selling them: gift and commodity exchange in Huaulu alliance." *Man* 29(1):1–26.
   2000 *The Forest of Taboos: Morality, Hunting, and Identity among the Huaulu of the Moluccas*. Madison: University of Wisconsin Press.
Visser, Leontine E.
   1989 *My Rice Field is My Child: Social and Territorial Aspects of Swidden Cultivation in Sahu, Eastern Indonesia*. Trans. Rita DeCoursey. Providence: Foris Publication.
Viswanathan, Gauri
   1998 *Outside the Fold: Conversion, Modernity, and Belief*. Princeton: Princeton University Press.
Wagner, Roy
   1977 "Analogic kinship: a Daribi example." *American Ethnologist* 4(4):623–642.

Weber, Max
   1947 *The Theory of Social and Economic Organization*, ed. Talcott Parsons. New York: Free Press.
   1958 *From Max Weber: Essays in Sociology*. Trans. Hans H. Gerth and C. Wright Mills. New York: Oxford University Press.
Weiner, Annette B.
   1992 *Inalienable Possessions: The Paradox of Keeping While Giving*. Berkeley: University of California Press.
Weinstock, Joseph A
   1987 "Kaharingan in Southern Borneo." In *Indonesian Religions in Transition*, eds. Rita S. Kipp and Susan Rodgers. Tucson: University of Arizona Press. Pp. 71–97.
Wikan, Unni
   1990 *Managing Turbulent Hearts: A Balinese Formula for Living*. Chicago: University of Chicago Press.
Williams, Raymond
   1960 *Culture and Society, 1780–1950*. Garden City, NY: Doubleday & Company, Inc.
Wouden, F. A. E. van
   1968 *Types of Social Structure in Eastern Indonesia*. Trans. R. Needhan. Koninklijk Instituut voor Taal-, Land-, en Volkenkunde Translation Series, vol. 11. The Hague: Martinus Nijhoff.
Yanagisako, Silvia, and Collier, Jane F.
   1987 "Toward a unified analysis of gender and kinship." In *Gender and Kinship: Essays Toward a Unified Analysis*, eds. Jane F. Collier and Silvia Yanagisako. Stanford: Stanford University Press. Pp. 14–50.
Zeitlyn, David
   1993 "Reconstructing kinship or the pragmatics of kin talk." *Man* (n.s.) 28(2):199–224.

Newspapers and magazines: the *New York Times*, *Kompas*, *Jakarta Post*, *Jawa Post*, *Republika*, and *Tempo*.

Index

Concepts

Adoption: 68, 70, 112–113, 120, 126 n.10
Agency: concept of, 15, 128n. 19, 132; moral, 7; ascribing to others, 55, 149; with respect to *masiae*, 184–186; in kinship narrative, 77; and desire, 92; self determination, 153; Christian, 157; and (men's) social standing, 117, 122; two hearts, 160–161
Alliance (affinity): changes in, 93, 95, 142, 145; determination of, 57–59, 78, 133, 137; exchanges, 44–45, 133; meaning of, 81–86, 94, 96–97, 99n. 7–8, 100n. 12, 124, 126n. 7, 138, 143; obligations towards, 14, 86, 136, 141, 180
Ancestors: agency of, 55–56, 160; in mythic history, 12–13 29, 59, 83, 162–163; the status of, 52, 56–57, 69; knowing, 55–56, 60–61, 67, 69–71, 74n. 3, 180; rights conferred through, 66; honoring, 183
Arata (*see also* marriage payments)

Betrayal: 113, 177, 179, 186–187, 189, 194n. 15, 206, 209
Blood: 7, 24n. 8, 58, 67, 69–70, 94, 146n. 6

Civility: xi–xiv, 13, 16, 177, 185–186, 188, 190, 193n. 13, 194n. 14–15, 210; civil life xi–xiii, 5, 26n. 16, 206, 210, 212n. 13; civil society (disintegration of), xi–xiv 195–196, 200; creating civil society 199, 204; civil tolerance 5
Community: at rest and in motion, 4–5, 8, 11, 16, 22, 23 n.4, 195, 198, 207–210; Christian, 30, 151, 153, 155, 157; collapse of, 16, 173, 176–177; communalism, x, 5–6, 16, 207–210; concept of, ix, x, xii–xiii, 2–14, 16–18, 20–21, 22n. 1, 23n. 5, 26n. 16, 26n. 20, 27n. 22–23, 76n. 18, 99n. 8, 179–182, 192n. 7, 192n. 9, 193n. 12, 207–210; contingency of, 2–3, 11–13, 15–17, 22; contributions to 113, 122, 174, 180, 207; fostering (a sense of) 4, 11–12, 16–17, 21–22, 107, 114, 151, 179, 185; imagined 6, 23n 6, 179; normative (as rules or order), xiii, 13–14, 24n. 9; representations of, xiii, 6–7, 9, 11, 23n. 6, 24n. 7, 99n. 4; threats to, 178, 181–182

Deception: 57, 62, 64–65, 75 n.11–12, 81, 179, 185–186
Desire: 62–63, 77–82, 87, 89–92, 94, 97–98, 102n. 21–23, 112, 138; love, 79–80, 90, 95

Economy: cash earning, 1, 30, 43–45, 127n. 12, 137; gardening, 36–37, 113–114, 127n. 13; hunting, 15, 33, 48n. 9, 117–118, 163; sago production, 34–35, 48n. 10, 49n. 11; subsistence, 1, 32, 156–157
Equality and hierarchy: state integration, 10, 47–48n. 3; equality, 13, 25n. 11, 30, 81, 117, 122–123, 128–129n. 22; hierarchy (inequality), 79, 85, 99n. 8, 135, 159–160
Exchange (*see also* marriage payments): 14, 131–132, 137–144,

231

232   Index

Exchange (*continued*) 173, 183; of
    women (in marriage), 99n. 5, 108;
    sharing, 27n. 22, 33, 37, 113–114,
    117–118, 127n. 13–14, 139–143,
    180–181
Experience: in conflict, x; shared xii,
    27n. 21, 77, 198–200; with respect
    to community, 2–4, 7, 11–12, 21,
    26n. 16, 159, 192n. 9; the social
    terrain of, 22n. 1, 26n. 16, 26n. 19,
    95, 192n. 4; with respect to
    kinship, 53–55, 59, 61–62, 65–66,
    68–70, 73n. 1

Friendship: 14, 20–21, 180–181, 186–
    187

Gender: cosmology of, 47 n.1, 48 n.8,
    72, 83, 167; division of labor 32–
    37, 113; identity, 91; kinship, 60,
    69, 86, 89, 94, 99n. 5, 103n. 26,
    107–115, 117–118, 122–124,
    125n. 4, 127n. 14, 167; residence,
    46, 107–115, 117–118
Genealogy: 51, 53, 56, 65, 67, 70, 73,
    75n. 13, 85, 100n. 11, 163
Good (goodness and goodwill):
    fostering, 14–15; conception of,
    15, 132; 145n. 2, 172n. 14, 178;
    fragility of, 189; preserving, 183,
    194n. 15; extending, 17, 161, 181,
    188, 193n. 12, 210; manifesting,
    13, 143, 145, 183, 193n. 13

History (*see also RMS* and myth):
    conversion, 150–155, 161–164,
    169, 170n. 2–3; *KNIL*, 52, 57;
    Maneo 38–46, 89–90, 92, 180,
    192n. 6; Maneo theory of, 71, 95,
    162–164, 170n. 2, 179, 193n. 11;
    RMS period, 173–176, 187–189;
    Soviet Union, 176–177, 179, 181,
    186–187, 189; subsistence 35–37
Household: 34–37, 39, 41, 46– 47,
    105–112, 119–121, 124, 126n. 11,
    128n. 21

Identity: collective or shared, 2, 5–7,
    16–17, 74n. 2, 151, 153, 155, 198,
    208; emergent, 30, 71, 87–88, 95,
    169n. 1, 207–208; kinship (see
    also recognition), 51–57, 64–68,
    75n. 12, 90; religious, x, 9, 153,
    155, 159, 165, 169n. 1, 200, 206,
    210; redundancy and substitution,
    6, 58, 64– 66, 69, 106, 112, 117–
    124, 192n. 7, 208; relational, 26
    n.20, 53–54, 74n. 2, 90; sameness
    and difference, 5–8, 16, 54–55, 58,
    61–62, 65, 72, 74n. 2, 82–83, 106,
    122–124, 159
Incest: 18, 62–63, 72, 74, 75 n.8, 87–
    89, 119–120
Intent (motivation): 14–15, 131–132,
    145n. 1, 181–182, 184, 193n. 10,
    209; in kinship designation, 59–
    61, 76n. 17; in marriage, 79, 80–
    81, 85, 93–94, 137–138;
    interpreting 14, 17, 19–21, 92,
    132, 170 n.7, 178, 209; self
    interest, 18, 22, 122–124, 131,
    140–141, 193n. 12

Kinship (*see also* alliance, siblingship,
    marriage, and relationships): clan
    (*soa*), 29, 46, 57–59, 68–70, 74n.
    2, 84–85, 89–90, 123, 132;
    classification, 51–55, 63, 66–69,
    72–73, 74n. 2, 83, 88–89, 112–
    113, 159; descent 59, 69, 71, 74n.
    5, 76n. 18, 133; encompassing
    outsiders, 18, 67, 71; experience,
    ix–x, 2, 5, 46–47, 53–54, 60–61,
    66–73, 74n. 1, 93, 106–107, 122,
    124, 173; narratives of 54–55, 65,
    68, 92–93; recruitment (see also
    marriage), 59–60, 69–70, 112–
    113, 128n. 21, 132–133, 137, 139;
    structure, 24n. 7, 71, 74 n.5, 78–
    79, 106, 112, 117–118, 124, 125n.
    2, 127n. 15, 180; system of, 57–
    61, 69, 72–73, 82–83, 106;
    theories, 24n. 7, 26n. 16, 53, 73,
    76n. 18, 80, 83, 91, 102n. 22, 112
Knowledge: 31–32, 51–68, 70–73, 75n.
    13–14, 82, 85, 88, 100n. 11, 107,
    125n. 4, 139, 190; accuracy of,
    53–54, 66, 72–73, 73n. 1, 204–
    206; acquisition and transmission,
    65, 76n. 13, 125n. 4, 169; danger

of, 56, 67; disclosure (*see also* secrets), 66–68, 70, 72–73; use of, 51, 53, 60–61, 66, 73, 185, 189

Laskar Jihad, 7, 197, 199, 203–204, 209

Marriage (*see also* alliance and incest): adultery, 120–122, 124, 141, 158, 161–162; arranged, 78–79, 92–93, 101–102n. 19; choice in, 77–82, 84–85, 87, 89–91, 93–94, 96–97, 102n. 20, 119–120, 124, 127–128n. 17–18; conflict over, 78–80; 93–97; consequences, 77–79, 81–82, 86–88, 92, 96–97, 99n. 8, 100n. 12, 105; meaning of, xi, 58, 77, 107–108, 110; patterns of, 83–86, 93–95, 101n. 14–15, 108–111, 125–126n. 6, 140; prohibitions 40, 78, 81, 87–90, 97; rules and violations, 58, 78–79, 81–83, 86–87, 95–96, 100–101n. 13, 133

Marriage Payments (*see also* exchange): 58–60, 83–84, 86–89, 93, 96–97, 107–112, 124, 125n. 5, 126n. 7, 131–144, 147n. 12; changes, 44–45, 135, 137–139, 142–145; sale or purchase with non-Maneo, 18, 133, 135, 183; *arata*, 133–135, 138, 142, 146n. 8, 147n. 18; to resolve disputes, 120; scarcity of, 131, 137, 140–144, 146n. 9, 146n. 11

Morality (*see also* Aristotle): deliberation, 14–16, 19, 21–22, 26n. 16, 131–132, 140, 144; dilemmas, 17, 140–141; generosity, 3, 15–16, 114, 138–140, 142–144, 186–188; imagination, 9, 24–25n. 10, 167–168, 200; norms, 13–14, 26n. 17, 26n. 19, 131, 138–139, 147n. 14–15,158–159; responsiveness, xiii, 16, 19, 132, 138, 177; understanding and sensibility, xii–xiii, 4–5, 16–17, 23n. 3, 138, 181–182, 185, 188, 191n. 1, 198, 200, 207

Memory (and forgetting): ancestors, 52, 55–56, 58–61, 63–65, 70–72, 74n. 7, 83, 94, 107–108, 113; community, 212n. 11; in Durkheim, 8; exchange, 144; mythic origins, 31–32; *RMS* period, 188–190; transgressions, 97

Myth: 12, 15, 21, 26n. 16, 29, 31, 48n. 4, 48n. 6, 56, 67; Old World, 71–72, 83, 91, 165–168, 172n. 14, 179–180

Ownership: 31–33, 35–36, 49n. 11, 118, 152, 165; belonging, 2–3, 6, 12, 18, 58, 207; of knowledge, 75n. 13

Politics: 189–190, 192n. 8; communalism, 196–197, 199, 207–208; through church offices, 159–160; through kinship designations 61; titles and offices, 10–11, 25n. 12, 30–31, 47n. 2, 47–48n. 3

Power: 5, 162, 165; disparities, 12, 18, 31, 149, 168, 179–180; *kapitan*, 19; women, 48n. 8, 94, 112

Property children (*see also* adoption): 60, 68, 100n. 11, 112–113, 120, 126n. 10, 142

Recognition: of community division, 22; of places, 31; in kinship, 54–58, 60–67, 69–73, 108, 137, 144; in non-Maneo relations 151, 184–185, 192n. 7; misrecognition, 57, 60–65, 71, 73, 88

Relationships: 54, 74n. 2, 118, 138, 159; entanglements, x, 3–4, 9, 12, 16–17, 19, 24, 24n. 10, 115, 136, 178, 188, 191; maneuvering within, 5, 12, 26n. 16, 109–111, 149–150, 153, 165–166, 178, 188–191, 191n. 1, 198; orientations, 2, 9, 13, 27n. 21, 54, 67–68, 106–107, 111, 118, 132, 198, 209; perspectives from within, 18, 51, 106, 139, 191n. 1; quality of, 6–7, 20–21, 22n. 1, 26n. 20, 45, 54, 71,

Relationships, quality of (*continued*) 117–118, 122, 128n. 21, 138, 183, 186; tensions, 19, 106, 113–115, 117, 136, 141–142, 145, 173

Religion: Christianity (the church), 1, 10, 30, 40–42, 82, 87–88, 150–153, 155–163, 165, 168–169, 182, 188, 193n. 12; civil religious conflict (Muslim and Christians), ix–xi, 5, 41, 43, 195–197, 199–206, 208–209, 212n. 9; conversion, 151–156, 159, 165, 168–169, 196, 205; *GPM*, 9, 12, 39–41, 137, 151–152, 155–157, 162; Islam, 31, 33, 152, 17n. 11, 174–175

Representation: collective, x, xiii, 6–9; of ancestors, 55–56; social relations, 54 58, 61, 67–68, 72, 83, 143, 145

Residence: dispersal 3–4, 17, 49n. 13, 109, 157, 177, 179, 181, 185–186, 192n. 6; dispersal in history, 39–41, 46–47, 48n. 4, 89, 119, 127n. 16, 174–176, 187; *kapia*, 105, 120, 125n. 5, 141; mobility, 146n. 5, 149–150; the Trans, 42–43, 171n. 8; newlyweds, 96, 119; patterns of, 1–3, 11, 19, 21–22, 33, 35, 46–47, 128n. 20; proximity, xii, 2–3, 108, 113–114, 119, 127n. 17, 173, 179, 181–182, 191, 192n. 4; upon marriage, 107–115, 121, 125n. 5

Revenge: 5, 116, 167, 183, 185, 198, 207–209

Risk: xi, 16–17, 21, 136–137, 142, 178–179, 187, 192n. 5

Ritual: 8–9, 24n. 9–10, 56, 125n. 1, 137, 144, 156, 161

Republik Maluku Selatan (*RMS*) (*see also* history): xi, 35, 41, 46, 152, 159, 173–176, 178, 180, 184, 187–190, 191n. 2, 196

Secrecy: discretion, 5, 14–16, 19–20, 114, 144, 178–179, 184–186, 188–191, 192n. 9, 200, 205; of intentions, 19–20, 149, 161, 178, 182–184, 190, 194n. 15; hiding, 35, 41, 49n. 13, 175–177, 183, 187; of social ties, 66–68; in courtship, 80, 95; knowledge, 25n. 14, 151, 162–164, 171, 172n. 13, 190, 193; in exchange, 117, 137, 139, 141–145, 145n. 1, 146n. 11

Sentiment: anger, 63, 87, 96–97, 109–110, 167, 198, 205–208; compassion, 16, 208; in kinship and marriage, 99n. 3, 118, 126n. 10, 159; empathy, xii–xiii, 16, 21, 25n. 15, 177, 191n. 1, 209; enmity, xi, 3, 13, 15, 20, 22, 40, 112, 114, 159, 191n. 1, 206–208; jealousy, 15, 39, 92; private and public, 8, 15, 70, 114, 121, 178–179, 185; shame, 76n. 16, 80, 87, 101n. 18, 114, 119, 121–122, 126n. 7, 146n. 7, 161–162, 187; suspicion, 3–4, 12, 27n. 21, 111–112, 118, 122, 124, 185, 187–189, 193n. 13, 198, 206

Sex (see also desire): 63, 72, 83, 89, 91, 101n. 17–18, 122

Siblingship: xii, 46–47, 59, 72, 74n. 6, 75n. 18–19, 83, 106, 112, 117, 122–124, 125n. 3, 128n. 21, 143, 180, 187

Social solidarity: x–xi, xiii, 2, 5, 8–9, 13, 18, 24n. 9, 26n. 19, 131, 145, 210

Sorcery: beliefs, 14–16, 161, 178, 181–186, 190–191, 193n. 13; allegations, 42, 56, 100n. 9, 101n. 18, 117, 178, 184–185; *masiae* 19, 56, 176, 181–186, 193n. 10, 193n. 13; *mauna*, 19, 178, 182; *sowakapati*, 170n. 5; two hearts, 160–161, 182, 185; *topoyea*, 170n. 5, 181

The State (*see also* Transmigration and history): agents, 10, 25n. 12, 30–31, 47–48n. 3, 157, 164, 169; beyond, xii, 10–11, 21, 27n. 23, 30, 149–150, 154, 169, 174–176; practices, 5, 9–10, 34, 40–43, 45, 73, 87–88, 105, 120, 137, 147n. 14, 149–152, 157, 182, 187, 196–198, 202–203, 210, 211n. 4, 211n. 5; resistance, 25n. 14, 30–31, 49n.

Index 235

13, 149–151, 165; Soviet Union, 176–177, 179, 181, 186, 189–190, 198
Taboo: 14–15, 31, 118, 160, 163
Transmigration: 1, 10, 21, 33, 42–43, 109, 157, 171n. 8, 211n. 1
Trust: fostering, xii, 3, 15, 18, 145–146n. 4, 177, 181, 199; limits to, 161, 175, 177–178, 185; loss of, xi, xiii, 5, 12, 145–146n. 4, 175–176, 199; sociology of, 8, 12, 16, 18–20, 22, 27n. 21, 112, 173, 181, 185, 187, 189, 191
Truth: 53, 60–61, 63, 66–67, 82, 162, 172n. 13, 184, 186, 204–206

Uncertainty: 3, 18–19, 22, 66, 90, 173, 177–179, 181, 185, 187–188, 192n. 5, 198, 200, 204–206, 211n. 7
Value: 8, 24n. 10, 77, 79, 90–91, 94, 102n. 22, 114, 127n. 14, 131, 145n. 2, 146n. 11, 165–168, 173, 188, 208
Violence: ix–xi, xii, 3–5, 7, 195–210, 211n. 7–8
Virtue: 19–20, 22, 145, 175, 177–178, 186
Volition: 3–4, 20–22, 29, 77–78, 140, 152–153, 177, 186–187, 212n. 11

Personal Names

Anderson, Benedict: 23n. 6, 208
Arendt, Hannah: 3, 184
Aristotle: xiii, 3, 13, 20–21, 25n. 16, 114, 131–132, 177, 180–181, 191, 193n. 12–13
Augustine: 161–162, 172n. 13, 193n. 12

Barnard, Alan, and Anthony Good: 53
Beidelman, Thomas: 9, 194n. 15
Bercovitch, Eytan: 142, 145n. 1
Blum, Lawrence: 16
Borgotti, Stephen, and Martin Everett: 106
Bourdieu, Pierre: 80–81, 99n. 6, 145n. 4

Carsten, Janet: 71, 76n. 18

Davis, Natalie: 65, 75n. 11–12
de Certeau, Michel: 101n. 16
Dewey, John: 14–15
Durkheim, Emile: xiii, 8, 23n. 5, 24n. 8

Ellen, Roy: 35, 48n. 7, 127n. 3

Flanagan, Owen: 14
Fortes, Meyer: 26n. 16, 75n. 10, 99n. 5
Frege, Gottlob: 184
Freud, Sigmund: 55, 62–63, 75n. 9, 91, 102n. 21

Geertz, Clifford, and Hildred: 71
Giddens, Anthony: 15
Goody, Jack: 126n. 8
Guerre, Martin: 64–65, 75n. 11–12

Howell, Signe: 145n. 3

James, William: 9

Knight, Frank: 178, 192n. 5
Koestler, Arthur: 195, 198, 206, 212n. 10

Lambek, Michael: 53
Levinas, Emmanuel: 190
Lévi-Strauss, Claude: 63, 83, 89, 98n. 1
MacIntyre, Alisdair: xiii, 145n. 2
Mandelstam, Nadezhde, and Osip: 176–179, 181, 186–187, 189
Mauss, Marcel: 131, 138, 147n. 14, 147n. 15

Needham, Rodney: 78, 99n. 3, 100n. 12, 102n. 20
Nussbaum, Martha: xiii, 14, 145n. 2

Oedipus: 63–63, 75n. 10

Pericles: 209, 212n. 11
Plato: xiii, 164

Queen Elizabeth: 31, 67

Ricoeur, Paul: 54, 61
Robbins, Joel: 123
Romeo and Juliet: 80, 92, 98
Rorty, Richard: 69

Sacks, Oliver: 62
Sahlins, Marshall: 147n. 13
Scott, James: 26n. 17
Simmel, Georg: 186, 194n. 15
Socrates: 18, 193n. 12
Spyer, Patsy: 198

Strauss, Leo: 4, 23n. 4
Suharto: 5, 152, 196–197

Trawick, Margaret: 91, 102n. 22, 112
Tsing, Anna: 10–11
Turnbull, Colin: 17–18

Valeri, Valerio: 24n. 7, 56, 59, 99n. 77, 100n. 12, 147n. 15, 191n. 1

Weber, Max: 55, 131
Weiner, Annette: 145n. 1, 145n. 3